Christianity with an Asian Face

Christianity with an Asian Face

Asian American Theology in the Making

Peter C. Phan

ORBIS BOOKS

Maryknoll, New York 10545

Founded in 1970, Orbis Books endeavors to publish works that enlighten the mind, nourish the spirit, and challenge the conscience. The publishing arm of the Maryknoll Fathers and Brothers, Orbis seeks to explore the global dimensions of the Christian faith and mission, to invite dialogue with diverse cultures and religious traditions, and to serve the cause of reconciliation and peace. The books published reflect the opinions of their authors and are not meant to represent the official position of the Maryknoll Society. To obtain more information about Maryknoll and Orbis Books, please visit our website at www.maryknoll.org.

Manufactured in the United States of America.
Manuscript editing and typesetting by Joan Weber Laflamme.

Library of Congress Cataloging in Publication Data

Phan, Peter C., 1943–
    Christianity with an Asian face : Asian American theology in the
making / Peter C. Phan.
        p. cm.
Includes index.
    ISBN 1–57075–466–7
    1. Asian Americans—Religious life. 2. Theology, Doctrinal. I.
Title.
    BR563.A82 P43 2003
    230'.089'95073—dc21

                                        2002014159

Dedicated to
Doctor Linda L. Stinson
for her invaluable assistance
in helping me navigate
the shoals between
East and West

Contents

PART ONE

LIBERATION AND THEOLOGY
Methodological Issues

PART TWO

INCULTURATION
Toward an Asian American Theology

Preface

By any measure Asian American Christian theology, as distinct from studies in Asian religions, is still in its infancy, compared with Black and Hispanic (Latino/a) theologies, for instance. Currently the number of Asian American theologians and Asian doctoral students in theology, as distinct from seminarians, is minuscule, and their scholarly output small. There have been so far, to the best of my knowledge, neither professional associations of Asian American theologians nor scholarly journals devoted to Asian American theology.

Yet the need for a robust Asian American theology is more urgent than ever as the ranks of Asians in the United States have swelled dramatically in recent decades. Such a theology will have to retain its distinctly Asian features while reflecting its social location in the United States, the world's only surviving superpower. In other words, what is needed is a truly intercultural theology that digs deep into the Asian cultural and religious humus as well as into the stories of daily struggle by Asian immigrants and refugees to rebuild their lives in their adopted country. The result of this endeavor will be a hybrid theology, neither fully Asian nor fully American, yet authentically American and authentically Asian.

This book represents a very modest attempt at furnishing some building blocks for constructing an Asian American theology whose contours still remain vague. It is my fervent hope that others will join in this challenging project, indispensable for the life of the American church.

I would like to take this opportunity to thank the Louisville Institute for a generous grant to support this research on Asian American theology and the Catholic University of America for a sabbatical. My thanks are also extended to Dr. Jonathan Tan for his proficient help in preparing the manuscript. I also owe a heavy debt of gratitude to Dr. William Burrows, managing editor of Orbis Books, for his constant encouragement and support. Without him, this and other books of mine would not have seen the light of day. Lastly, my sincere thanks are extended to Catherine Costello and Joan Laflamme for their careful work on the manuscript.

A word on why I have omitted diacritical marks on Vietnamese words is necessary for those who note they are missing. The reason for adding them is that the same Vietnamese word written in the Latin alphabet, when marked with one of five different diacritical marks and the unaccented tone, can have entirely different meanings. Those who know Vietnamese, however, can easily supply them. For those who do not, they add nothing and immensely complicate the typesetter's work.

Finally, many of the chapters in this book first appeared as papers delivered at conferences and in journals. I am grateful to the publishers of the journals in which they appeared and to the people who have attended my lectures. Their questions, comments, and criticisms have helped me clarify what I meant to say and given me an occasion to revise my opinions when I realized I needed to give some ideas further consideration. Below are original titles and places where the original versions of these chapters can be found.

Thanks to the editors and publishers of these books and journals for permission to rework and republish these materials. "A Common Journey, Different Paths, the Same Destination: Methods in Liberation Theologies" first appeared in *A Dream Unfinished*, edited by Eleazar Fernandez and Fernando Segovia (Maryknoll, N.Y.: Orbis Books, 2001, 129-51); "Kingdom of God: A Theological Symbol for Asians?" appeared first in *Gregorianum* 79/2 (1998): 295-322; "Jesus the Christ with an Asian Face" was published in *Theological Studies* 57 (1996): 399-430; "Jesus as the Eldest Son and Ancestor" appeared first in *Studia Missionalia* 45 (1996): 25-55; "*Ecclesia in Asia*: Challenges for Asian Christianity" appeared first in *East Asian Pastoral Review* 37/3 (2000): 215-32; "Human Development and Evangelization: The First to the Sixth Plenary Assembly of the Federation of Asian Bishops' Conferences" was printed in *Studia Missionalia* 47 (1998): 205-27; and "The Dragon and the Eagle: Toward a Vietnamese-American Theology" was first published in *Theology Digest* 49/3 (2001): 203-18.

—Peter C. Phan
Octave of Easter, 2002

Introduction

The presence of Asians and Pacific Islanders—defined by the U.S. Census Bureau as "any of the original peoples of the Far East, Southeast Asia, the Indian Subcontinent, or the Pacific Islands"—in the United States of America has been growing by leaps and bounds. Census 2000 counted 11,898,828 Asians in racial categories that include East, South, and Southeast Asians, and mixed-raced Asians, a whopping 50 percent increase since the previous decade.[1] A good number of these Asian and Pacific newcomers are Christian, both Protestant (mostly Presbyterian and Baptist) and Catholic (Roman as well as Eastern). The importance of the latter's presence has recently been recognized by the United States Conference of Catholic Bishops with its pastoral statement *Asian and Pacific Presence*.[2]

Needless to say, these new immigrants and refugees, with their distinctive cultural, religious, and, more specifically, Catholic traditions, pose serious challenges to the U.S. church. Perhaps the most difficult of these challenges is to develop an appropriate theology to undergird the church's ministry to these new arrivals.[3] Whereas black and Hispanic (Latino/a) theologies have made significant strides and have been recognized as "adults" in the theological world, Asian American theology is still in its infancy.[4]

Asian American theology, as implied by its dual character, is neither purely Asian nor purely American. An offspring of the marriage of two widely divergent cultural and religious heritages, it bears all the marks of a *mestizo*, a mixture of the two traditions. On the one hand, with the United States as its home, it faces questions and challenges proper to its social location and has at its dis-

---

[1] For helpful histories of Asian Americans, see Ronald Takaki, *Strangers from a Different Shore: A History of Asian Americans* (New York: Penguin Books, 1989); Stanley Karnow and Nancy Yoshihara, *Asian Americans in Transition* (New York: The Asia Society, 1992); and David Palumbo-Liu, *Asian/American: Historical Crossings of a Racial Frontier* (Stanford, Calif.: Stanford University Press, 1999).

[2] USCCB, *Asian and Pacific Presence: Harmony in Faith* (Washington, D.C.: USCCB, 2001), 6, 9. Currently, 2.6 percent of American Catholics are Asian and Pacific. In 1999, 9 percent of priests ordained in the United States were of Asian and Pacific descent.

[3] For helpful proposals to respond to these challenges, see USCCB, *Asian and Pacific Presence*, 29-30.

[4] For a discussion of these three ethnic theologies, see Peter C. Phan, "Contemporary Theology and Inculturation in the United States," in *The Multicultural Church: A New Landscape in U.S. Theologies*, ed. William Cenkner (New York: Paulist Press, 1996), 109-30, 176-92.

posal theological resources different from those of its countries of origin. On the other hand, it cannot but dig deep into its Asian religious and cultural traditions to find resources to answer these questions and meet these challenges. Paradoxically, while neither fully Asian nor fully American, an Asian American theology is *both* Asian and American, embodying the resources, methodologies, and characteristics of both theologies, and in this sense, will be richer than either theology by itself. An Asian American theology is by nature an *intercultural* theology, forged in the cauldron of the encounter between two vastly different cultures.

As *Asian*, this emerging Asian American theology owes a great debt to the theologies that have been developed in Asia throughout the last two millennia to inculturate the Christian faith. The Saint Thomas Christians of the Syro-Malabar and Syro-Malankara churches with their Syriac theological heritage; Persian Christians of the Nestorian tradition who came to China during the T'ang dynasty in the seventh and eighth centuries; members of various religious orders, in particular the Jesuits, who evangelized the greater part of Asia in the seventeenth century; legions of missionaries, both Catholic and Protestant, who revived the church's evangelizing enterprise in Asia in the nineteenth century; Asian bishops and theologians of our own times—all of these people have made permanent contributions to the elaboration of Asian theologies.

Among these contributors pride of place must be given to the Federation of the Asian Bishops' Conferences (FABC), founded in 1970, and its various offices and institutes. The sheer quantity, thematic comprehensiveness, and theological depth of the documents it has produced in the last thirty years dwarf all the previous theological achievements of the Asian churches and allow Asian theologians to stand tall in the company of their Western colleagues. In addition to its teachings on various substantive issues, the FABC has advocated a new way of being church and of doing theology in Asia. This new way consists in a triple dialogue, namely, dialogue with Asian cultures (inculturation), with Asian religions (interreligious dialogue), and with Asian peoples, especially the poor (liberation). Asian American theology will have to undertake this triple task of liberation, interreligious dialogue, and inculturation, and in this way will contribute significantly to contemporary theological method and ecclesiology.

As *American*, this aborning American-Asian theology must be done with a full and vivid awareness that its social location is one of power and domination. For good or for ill, Asian Americans are citizens of a country that will remain for the foreseeable future the world's only military and economic superpower. Rich or poor, they all benefit from the wealth and power of their adopted country. The passport they hold carries much weight around the world and entitles them to the basic human rights denied to citizens of other countries. They participate in an economic system of free markets that has been successful, by and large, in producing financial gains for those able and willing to embrace it.

These political and economic advantages do not, however, accrue to Americans without heavy costs to others. As a group, Americans consume a disproportionate amount of the earth's resources, with deleterious effects on the ecology, in order to enjoy and maintain their sacrosanct "American way of life."

Their political and military leaders do not hesitate to use their country's massive military arsenals to crush those who are perceived to threaten America's "vital interests" and its citizens' "life, liberty, and the pursuit of happiness." Through globalization, the United States extends its political and economic hegemony throughout the world, exercising new forms of imperialism and colonialism. As a result, the gap separating America from other countries grows larger and the very few rich get richer, while the teeming masses of the poor (among them, women and children in particular) get poorer.

Asian Americans, willy-nilly, are part of this system of racial, gender, economic, and political exploitation and domination. None of them now has clean hands, even though they may have come to the United States from poor and oppressed countries. But precisely because of their backgrounds and histories, Asian Americans cannot forget or ignore the cries and tears of their fellow citizens in their adopted country and of the people in their former homelands, when they attempt to do their own theologies. Of necessity, Asian American theology must be guided by the concern for the liberation of those who are deprived of the minimal conditions for a decent human life. Its beacon must be God's kingdom of peace and justice and love.

The essays here collected, written on various occasions, have been informed by this twin focus on liberation and inculturation. They are intended as building blocks for an Asian American theology. Part 1, composed of three chapters, explores the new method of Asian American theology. The first chapter examines how the experience of being an immigrant and a refugee can serve as a resource for theology. An immigrant is marked by displacement and suffering as well as by "in-betweenness." This existential condition facilitates the construction of an intercultural theology, a collaborative enterprise among black, Latino/a, and Asian theologies, with its multiple sources and distinct methodology. The second chapter elaborates in detail the method employed by the different types of liberation theologies, of which Asian American theology is a subcategory. It is shown to consist of three steps: social-analytic mediation, hermeneutical mediation, and practical mediation. By adopting this triple mediation Asian American theology will be able to make a unique contribution. The third chapter evaluates the usefulness as well as the limitations of philosophy as a tool for the inculturation of the Christian faith in Asia, using Pope John Paul II's encyclical *Fides et Ratio* as a launching pad and foil for the discussion.

Part 2 develops some substantive issues of Asian American theology. The central issue of any liberation theology is the symbol of the reign of God. The fourth chapter highlights six challenges that Asia poses to the use of this symbol and argues that the image of the kingdom of God still retains its evocative power for Asians, especially those living in the Confucian culture, provided that its subversive as well as transcendent dimensions, present in Jesus' preaching, are retrieved and vigorously affirmed.

The next three chapters attempt to elaborate an Asian Christology. The fifth chapter presents three influential Asian Christologies as represented by Aloysius Pieris, Jung Young Lee, and Chung Hyun Kyung, who deployed Asian monastic traditions, *yin* and *yang* philosophy, and feminist thought respectively to paint a portrait of Jesus meaningful to Asians. Chapter 6 attempts to limn Jesus as the Eldest Son and the Ancestor par excellence on the basis of the widespread Asian practice of ancestor veneration. Chapter 7 presents and evaluates the story-based Christology of C. S. Song, one of the most prolific and influential Chinese theologians living outside of Taiwan and China.

The last four chapters deal with practical issues facing the church in Asia and Asian American Christians. Chapter 8, on the basis of Pope John Paul II's apostolic exhortation *Ecclesia in Asia*, discusses Christian mission in Asia in terms of a new way of being church: church as a communion of communities; as a participatory community of discipleship of equals; as a community engaged in the triple dialogue with Asian cultures, religions, and peoples, especially the poor; and as a prophetic witness to the reign of God. Chapter 9 examines in detail one of the fundamental tasks of the Asian churches, namely, human development and liberation, as embodied in the final statements of the plenary assemblies of the FABC. Chapter 10 focuses on catechesis, one essential aspect of the church's evangelizing mission, by examining how the inculturation of catechesis is understood in the new *General Directory for Catechesis* and how it was practiced by Alexandre de Rhodes, a seventeenth-century Jesuit missionary to Vietnam, in his celebrated *Cathechismus* and by the *Catechism for Filipino Catholics* of the Catholic Bishops' Conferences of the Philippines. The last chapter, a sort of recapitulation of the whole book, offers a programmatic outline of an Asian, more specifically, Vietnamese American theology. It is hoped that the dragon and the eagle, symbols of the two countries brought together by a tragic war, will learn to dwell together in harmony and peace.

I am deeply aware that these essays are little more than the first steps toward constructing an Asian American theology. Missing in this volume is a discussion of the task of interreligious dialogue incumbent upon Asian American theology, a lacuna I hope to remedy in my next book. At any rate, to construct an Asian American theology requires the collaboration of experts in many different fields. Unfortunately, the number of Asian American theologians (as distinct from scholars of religious studies) is still very small, and Asian American students who embark upon theological studies as an academic career (as distinct from pastoral ministry) are at present few and far between. I offer these reflections as an invitation to other Asian American theologians to join in the challenging and exciting task of building bridges between the cultural and religious worlds of Asia and the United States in service to the Christian faith.

Abbreviations

ASIPA	Asian Integral Pastoral Approach
ATESA	Association of Theological Education in Southeast Asia
CCC	*Catechism of the Catholic Church*
CT	*Catechesi Tradendae*
DP	*Dialogue and Proclamation*
EA	*Ecclesia in Asia*
EAPR	*East Asian Pastoral Review*
EN	*Evangelii Nuntiandi*
FABC	Federation of Asian Bishops' Conferences
FR	*Fides et Ratio*
GCD	*General Catechetical Directory*
GDC	*General Directory for Catechesis*
PTCAB	*Programme for Theology and Cultures in Asia Bulletin*
RM	*Redemptoris Missio*
SEAJT	*South East Asia Journal of Theology*
SEDOS	*Servizio di Documentazione e Studi*
USCCB	United States Conference of Catholic Bishops
VJTR	*Vidyajyoti Journal of Theological Reflection*

PART ONE

Liberation and Theology

Methodological Issues

1

The Experience of Migration as Source of Intercultural Theology in the United States

Migration has been an ever-present worldwide fact of life, but currently demographers are talking of it as a new global phenomenon, given the increasingly large number of people who leave their homeland, by force or by choice, because of economic poverty, violence, war, and political and/or religious persecution, in search of better living conditions and freedom elsewhere, legally or illegally.[1] Migration is a highly complex phenomenon, with significant economic, socio-political, cultural, and religious repercussions for the migrants, their native countries, and the host societies.[2] It has been the subject of research

---

[1] For a recent study of world migration, see Robin Cohen, ed., *The Cambridge Survey of World Immigration* (Cambridge: Cambridge University Press, 1995). Douglas S. Massey distinguishes four periods of international migration: the mercantile period (1500-1800), the industrial period (1800-1925), the period of limited migration (1925-1960), and the postindustrial period (1960-). This last period constitutes a sharp break with the past in that migration now is a truly global phenomenon: "Rather than being dominated by outflows from Europe to a handful of former colonies, immigration became a truly global phenomenon as the number and variety of both sending and receiving countries increased and the global supply of immigrants shifted from Europe to the developing world." See Douglas S. Massey, "Why Does Immigration Occur? A Theoretical Analysis," in *The Handbook of International Migration: The American Experience*, ed. Charles Hirschman, Philip Kasinitz, and Josh DeWind (New York: Russell Sage Foundation, 1999), 34.

[2] For a discussion of the feasibility of a "grand theory" of immigration, especially to the United States of America, see Alejandro Portes, "Immigration Theory for a New Century: Some Problems and Opportunities," in Hirschman, Kasinitz, and DeWind, *The Handbook of International Migration*, 21-33. Portes argues that a unifying theory purporting to explain the origins, processes, and outcomes of international migration would be so abstract as to be futile and vacuous. Rather, he suggests that mid-level theories explaining the origins, flows, employment, and socio-cultural adaptations of immigrants in specified areas are preferable to all-encompassing theories. For further theoretical studies on migration, see David Guillet and Douglas Uzzell, eds., *New Approaches to the Study of Migration*, Rice University Studies 62/3 (Houston, Tex.: William Marsh Rice University, 1976), especially the essay by Sylvia Helen Forman, "Migration: A Problem in Conceptualization," 25-35; and Caroline B. Brettell and James F. Hollifield, eds., *Migration Theory: Talking across Disciplines* (New York and London: Routledge, 2000), especially chapter 5 by Caroline Brettell, "Theorizing Migration in Anthropology: The Social Construction of Networks, Identities, Communities, and Globalscapes," 97-123.

in different disciplines, primarily sociology, anthropology, politics, and economics. Recently it has also engaged the attention of social ethicists[3] and systematic theologians.[4]

It is a common practice to distinguish between internal and external (or transnational) migrants, the former seeking safety and shelter within their own countries, and the latter in foreign lands. It is also common to single out among the latter the special category of refugees. Refugees are those whose emigration from their homeland is not motivated by economic reasons but caused by war or political and/or religious repression; as a consequence they are limited in their ability to set up transnational networks in their homeland until there is a change in the political situation there.

In this chapter the focus is more on transnational migrants, including refugees, because, generally speaking, their existential condition provides a greater source for theological reflection than that of internal migrants, though what is said of the former also applies to the latter, albeit perhaps not to the same extent. Furthermore, special attention is given to recent transnational migrants in the United States of America, not only because the United States is quintessentially a country of immigrants, but also, as will be shown shortly, immigrants into the United States in the last quarter of the twentieth century bring with them challenges and problems as well as resources and traditions quite different from those brought by the earlier immigrants from Europe.[5] The first part of the chapter explores the existential condition of recent non-European immigrants in the United States as the new context for doing theology. The second part examines how this existential condition of the immigrant determines the interculturality of theology in terms of its epistemology, hermeneutics, and methodology. The third part attempts to survey the resources made available by these non-European immigrants for a U.S. intercultural theology.

------

[3] For the challenges of migration to ethics, see Dietmar Mieth and Lisa Sowle Cahill, *Migrants and Refugees*, Concilium 1993/4 (Maryknoll, N.Y.: Orbis Books). The editorial at the beginning of this volume of the series summarizes well these challenges: "Taken as a whole, and seen in its varied aspects, this topic [migration] represents a challenge to social ethics. The moral grounding of rights and duties, the working out of a conception between autonomy and integration, the balancing out of the various claims and the consequences of structural help on the basis of the analysis of structural 'sins,' the conceptualization of prejudices and aggressions, the anthropological and ethical significance of foreignness and a native land, all these are key themes for ethics" (vii). In this chapter I prescind from the ethical aspects of migration.

[4] Even though an explicit focus on migration is still scarce in systematic theology, related themes such as exile and the land as theological symbols have been extensively studied.

[5] For a helpful work on refugees and immigrants in the United States, see Francesco Cordasco, ed., *Dictionary of American Immigration History* (Metuchen, N.J.: The Scarecrow Press, 1990). A collection of older essays is still useful: George E. Pozzetta, ed., *American Immigration and Ethnicity* (New York: Garland Publishing, 1991). From the Catholic standpoint, a useful collection of primary sources on Asian American Catholics is in Joseph M. Burns, Ellen Skerret and Joseph M. White, eds., *Keeping Faith: European and Asian Catholic Immigrants* (Maryknoll, N.Y.: Orbis Books, 2000), 229-307.

A NEW WAVE OF IMMIGRANTS AND THEIR EXISTENTIAL CONDITION

Contrary to the prediction of most demographers that the flow of immigrants into the United States would decrease after the restrictive laws of the 1920s, the country now receives near record numbers of legal immigrants each year, and the second generation—those born in the United States with one or both parents born abroad—is larger than ever before. This dramatic increase of immigration is due to the Hart-Celler Act of 1965 and recent amendments to it, especially the Immigration Reform and Control Act of 1986 and the Immigration Act of 1990. Between 1920 and 1965 legal immigration to the United States averaged about 206,000 per year, most of it from northern and western Europe. Between the mid-1960s to the mid-1990s, the number of immigrants averaged over 500,000 per year, not counting illegal immigrants.[6]

Non-European Immigrants in the United States and Contextual Theologies

What is of great significance in this unexpected phenomenon is that these new immigrants hail from parts of the world other than Europe and therefore bring with them challenges as well as resources vastly different from those of the still dominant white, Euro-Americans, whether Catholic or Protestant.[7] The 2000 census documented the dramatic growth of the minority groups and their impact on American society. Already in 1989, Allan Figueroa Deck referred to the influx of Hispanics (Latinos/as) into the United States as "the second wave."[8] According to the 2000 census the Hispanic population had increased by more than 50 percent since 1990.[9] Native Mexicans aside, Hispanic immigrants came

---

[6] Under the 1986 Immigration Reform and Control Act any illegal resident who could demonstrate that he or she had lived in the United States before 1982 was eligible to apply for citizenship. Three million undocumented aliens took advantage of this opportunity. At the end of the amnesty program in October 1988, it was estimated that 2.7 million illegal residents remained in the country who would provide the social networks for the coming of more illegal immigrants. During the decade of 1990-2000, according to the Immigration and Naturalization Service (INS), another 2.4 million immigrants entered the United States illegally. The INS estimates that as of October 1996 there were 5 million illegal aliens living in the United States.

[7] Before 1925, 85 percent of all international migrants originated in Europe, but since 1960 there has been a dramatic increase in emigration from Africa, Asia, and Latin America.

[8] Allan Figueroa Deck, *The Second Wave: Hispanic Ministry and the Evangelization of Cultures* (New York: Paulist Press, 1989).

[9] Mexicans constitute 58.5 percent, Puerto Ricans 9.6 percent, Cubans 3.5 percent, Central Americans 4.8 percent, South Americans 3.8 percent, Dominicans 2.2 percent, Spaniards 0.3 percent, and all other Hispanics 17.3 percent. These figures are taken from the U.S. Census Bureau, compiled by Betsy Guzmán in an essay entitled "The Hispanic Population" (May 2001). In the census, "people of Hispanic origin" meant those whose origin was Mexican, Puerto Rican, Cuban, Central or South American, or some other Hispanic origin. The terms *Hispanic* or *Latino* were also used interchangeably.

mainly from Mexico, Cuba, Puerto Rico, and the countries of Central America (in particular El Salvador).

Asians too have experienced an enormous increase in the past decades. Prior to 1965, immigration from Asia, especially from the so-called Asian Pacific Triangle, had been prohibited on the basis of prejudices about the racial and ethnic inferiority and cultural unassimilability of Asians.[10] But things have changed drastically since then. During the 1990s the Asian American population grew nearly 50 percent to reach a little over 10 million in 2000. The five largest Asian American groups reported by the 2000 census are Chinese (2.4 million), Filipino (1.8 million), Indian (1.6 million), Vietnamese (1.1 million), and Korean (1.0 million). In addition to Hispanics and Asians, mention also should be made of a significant number of immigrants from the Caribbean and the Pacific Islands.

The changes in the origin, size, and composition of these newer immigrant groups have contributed to what has been called the "browning of America." As the authors of a recent study put it:

> These so-called new immigrants—those arriving in the post 1965 period—are phenotypically and culturally distinct from the old immigrants, who more closely resembled Anglo-Americans in terms of their physical characteristics and cultural patterns. . . . Moreover, research shows that the new immigrants are less inclined than the old immigrants to blend fully into American society. Most prefer, instead, to preserve and maintain their own cultural heritages and identities.[11]

This shift is evidenced by the fact that instead of speaking of "assimilation," research on recent immigrants now refers to their "adaptation" to and "incorporation" into American society, which no longer possesses a single core culture but many mode-diverse cultural matrixes.[12]

It goes without saying that this recent immigration has had a profound impact on all sectors of American society, not only in terms of what the United

---

[10] Anti-Asian immigration legislation culminated in the Tydings-McDuffe Act of 1934, which can be traced back as far as the 1882 Chinese Exclusion Act, the Gentlemen's Agreement of 1908, and the 1917 and 1924 Immigration Acts. For an exposition of the American anxiety about the "Yellow Peril," see David Palumbo-Liu, *Asian/American: Historical Crossings of a Racial Frontier* (Stanford, Calif.: Stanford University Press, 1999), 31-42.

[11] James H. Johnson Jr., Walter C. Farrell, and Chandra Guinn, "Immigration Reform and the Browning of America: Tensions, Conflicts, and Community Instability in Metropolitan Los Angeles," in Hirschman, Kasinitz, and DeWind, *The Handbook of International Migration*, 391.

[12] See the following chapters in Hirschman, Kasinitz, and DeWind, *The Handbook of International Migration*: Richars Alba and Victor Nee, "Rethinking Assimilation Theory for a New Era of Immigration," 137-60; Herbert J. Gans, "Toward a Reconciliation of 'Assimilation' and 'Pluralism': The Interplay of Acculturation and Ethnic Retention," 161-71; Rubén G. Rumbaut, "Assimilation and Its Discontents: Ironies and Paradoxes," 172-95; and Min Zhou, "Segmented Assimilation: Issues, Controversies, and Recent Research on the New Second Generation," 196-211.

States as the receiving country has to do for these migrants, whether short-term, cyclical, or permanent,[13] but also in terms of the multiple benefits they indisputably bring to American society. For good or for ill, the shape of the U.S. political, social, economic, cultural, and religious landscape has changed as the result of the massive presence of these non-European immigrants.

With regard to the religious arena in particular, it is well known that a great majority of Latinos/as are Roman Catholic, though the Protestant, especially Pentecostal, presence is growing. Among Asian Americans, Roman Catholicism, though a tiny minority in Asia except in the Philippines (some 3 percent of the total Asian population), has a significant membership; it is estimated that in the United States 19 percent of Chinese (393 thousand), 65 percent of Filipinos (1.4 million), 30 percent of Vietnamese (329 thousand), and 8 percent of Koreans (91 thousand) are Catholic. There is little doubt that the American churches, the Roman Catholic Church in particular, have been significantly affected in different ways by these new arrivals.

In terms of theology as an academic discipline, at least as it is practiced in the United States, the presence of non-European immigrants has begun to have a significant impact on how theology is done, because theology, as is widely acknowledged today, must be contextual, and in this case, intercultural.[14] The issue here is not simply the unfamiliar sources and resources, which are very different from those hitherto used by Western theologians, and from which intercultural theology will have to draw its materials, as will be examined in the next part of the chapter, but more fundamentally, the very existential condition of the immigrant itself. In other words, the theologically important question concerns first and foremost the very nature of being an immigrant and refugee. This existential ontology of the immigrant entails a distinct epistemology and hermeneutics, a particular way of perceiving and interpreting reality, that is, oneself, others (in particular, the dominant others and fellow groups of immigrants), the cosmos, and ultimately, God. Consequently, if the experience of immigration is to constitute the context for theology, then it is vitally important for the theologian to ascertain the contours of the existential predicament of the immigrant and its attendant epistemology. This existential predicament provides, as it were, a perspective—the *objectum formale quo*, to use a Scholastic

---

[13] A study published by the Rand Corporation in November 1985 entitled *Current and Future Effects of Mexican Immigration in California* suggests that there are three types of Mexican immigrants: short-term (usually tied with agricultural, seasonal jobs), cyclical (with regular returns to the same employers), and permanent (usually with families settled in the United States). See Deck, *The Second Wave*, 12-15.

[14] On the multicultural and intercultural character of contemporary theology, see the following works: Robert Schreiter, *Constructing Local Theologies* (Maryknoll, N.Y.: Orbis Books, 1985); idem, *The New Catholicity: Theology between the Global and the Local* (Maryknoll, N.Y.: Orbis Books, 1997); and Stephen Bevans, *Models of Contextual Theology* (Maryknoll, N.Y.: Orbis Books, 2002). Hispanic/Latino theology, with its own professional association and journal, has emerged as a voice to be reckoned with. To a lesser extent, Asian American theology has begun to contribute to the theological enterprise in the United States.

expression—for the elaboration of a theology not merely about but *out of* the migration experience.

The Experience of Immigration: Displacement and Suffering

What is the existential condition of a transnational immigrant and refugee? From the findings of various social-scientific research, it is clear that its most obvious features include violent uprootedness; economic poverty; anxiety about the future; and the loss of national identity, political freedom, and personal dignity. What Teresa Okure writes of African refugees applies as well to those of other countries, though not necessarily to the same degree of severity:

> Refugees basically seek safety in their lives, survival, food, and shelter. They nourish a strong hope of returning one day to their homes or homeland. In refugee camps, they encounter hunger and disease, poor sanitary conditions, cultural alienation heightened by ignorance of the language of the host country, the loss of a sense of identity, rejection of the host country or confinement to camps, and exploitation in terms of hard labor for low pay. Children are separated from parents, husbands from wives; women are exploited and violated, often by the very persons who are expected to be their saviors. Children grow up without a sense of identity, roots, culture. They have poor educational facilities, if any. Confined to camps, if they are lucky to be in one, like animals in a cage they grow up in an artificial context. This leaves a negative psychological impact on them, sometimes for life. Refugees experience uprootedness, the lack of a sense of belonging, abuse, ignominy and general dehumanization.[15]

A theology out of the context of migration must begin with personal solidarity with the victims of this abject condition of human, often innocent, suffering. Theologians speaking out of the migration experience must "see" for themselves this "underside of history" (Gustavo Gutiérrez), "listen" to the "stories" of these victims (C. S. Song), preserve their "dangerous memory" (Johann Baptist Metz), and to the extent possible, "accompany" them in their struggle for liberation and human dignity (Roberto Goizueta).[16]

The Experience of Immigration: Being Betwixt-and-Between

In addition to this dehumanizing condition, transnational migrants also exist, from a cultural perspective, in a betwixt-and-between situation that is the hallmark of marginalization. They live and move and have their being between two

---

[15] Teresa Okure, "Africa: A Refugee Camp Experience," in Mieth and Cahill, *Migrants and Refugees*, 13.

[16] On the first step of liberation theology, that is, concrete solidarity with the poor and the marginalized, see Leonardo Boff and Clodovis Boff, *Introducing Liberation Theology*, trans. Paul Burns (Maryknoll, N.Y.: Orbis Books, 1987), 1-6, 22-24; my discussion in chapter 2 herein. On the theology of accompaniment, see Roberto Goizueta, *Caminemos con Jesús: Toward a Hispanic/Latino Theology of Accompaniment* (Maryknoll, N.Y.: Orbis Books, 1995), esp. 1-46.

cultures, their own and that of the host country. In this "in-between" predicament they belong to neither culture fully yet participate in both. As I have pointed out elsewhere, to be betwixt and between is to be neither here nor there, to be neither this thing nor that. Spatially, it is to dwell at the periphery or at the boundaries, without a permanent and stable residence. Politically, it means not residing at the centers of power of the two intersecting worlds but occupying the precarious and narrow margins where the two dominant groups—those of the homeland and the host country—meet, and consequently being deprived of the opportunities to wield power in matters of public interest. Socially, to be betwixt and between is to be part of a minority, a member of a marginalized group. Culturally, it means not being fully integrated into and accepted by either cultural system. Linguistically, the betwixt-and-between person is bilingual but usually does not achieve mastery of both languages and often speaks with a distinct accent. Psychologically and spiritually, the immigrant does not possess a well-defined and established self-identity but is constantly challenged to forge a new sense of self out of the resources of the two often conflicting cultural and spiritual traditions.[17]

This betwixt-and-between predicament, while a source of much soul-searching and suffering, can be an incentive and resource for a creative rethinking of both cultural traditions, the native and the foreign. Being in-between is, paradoxically, being *neither* this *nor* that but also being *both* this *and* that. Immigrants belong fully to neither their native culture nor to the host culture. By the same token, however, they belong to both, though not fully. And because they dwell in the interstices between the two cultures, they are in a position to see more clearly and to appreciate more objectively, both as insiders and outsiders (emically and etically), the strengths as well as the weaknesses of both cultures; as a result, they are better equipped to contribute to the emergence of a new, enriched culture. Hence, to be in-between as an immigrant is to be *neither*-this-*nor*-that, to be *both*-this-*and*-that, and to be *beyond*-this-and-that.[18]

---

[17] See Peter C. Phan and Jung Young Lee, eds., *Journeys at the Margins: Toward an Autobiographical Theology in American-Asian Perspective* (Collegeville, Minn.: Liturgical Press, 1999), 113. For this understanding of marginality, see Jung Young Lee, *Marginality: The Key to Multicultural Theology* (Minneapolis: Fortress Press, 1995), 29-76. See also Eugene Brody, ed., *Behaviors in New Environments: Adaptation of Migrant Populations* (Beverly Hills, Calif.: Sage Publications, 1979), especially Eugene Brody, "Migration and Adaptation," 13-21, and Henry P. David, "Involuntary International Migration," 73-95.

[18] This predicament is not dissimilar to what Fernando Segovia describes in his evocatively titled essay "Two Places and No Where on Which to Stand: Mixture and Otherness in Hispanic American Theology," in *Mestizo Christianity: Theology from the Latino Experience*, ed. Arturo L. Bañuelas (Maryknoll, N.Y.: Orbis Books, 1995), 29-43. From an anthropological point of view, this "in-betweenness" is equivalent to a liminal situation as described by Victor Turner. As such, "in-betweenness" intimates anomaly, insofar as people in liminality are no longer what they were ("neither this") nor are they yet what they will be ("nor that"); however, they are not stuck in the present but project themselves toward the future ("beyond this-and-that"). They live between memory and imagination. On memory and imagination as two inseparable modes of doing theology, see my essay "Betwixt and Between: Doing Theology with Memory and Imagination," in Phan and Lee, *Journeys at the Margins*, 113-33.

Such an existential predicament lends itself well to an articulation of an intercultural theology that responds to the needs of our times determined by the all-encompassing process of globalization. Contemporary immigrants in the United States more often than not have come from an underdeveloped country and now have to find their way in a technologically advanced country. Economically, in many cases, they were supported by the socialist or state economy of their native countries, whereas now they have to earn their livelihood in a neo-capitalist system and a market economy. Politically, they were deprived of the most basic human rights, and now they live in a society whose constitution guarantees all sorts of freedoms. Culturally, they were victims of Western colonization, and now they have to retrieve their cultural heritage, which more often than not is premodern, in a modern and postmodern age. Spiritually and morally, they were guided by a vision of life and ethics that privileged the family and the community, and now they are part of a society permeated by a highly individualistic ethos. The inevitable and at times tragic collision among these contradictory forces and systems *within* the persons of the immigrants themselves and often among the different generations of the immigrants' families makes the immigrants the privileged sites of intercultural encounters. They embody the *tiempos mixtos*—premodernity, modernity, and postmodernity—that form the matrix of an emergent multicultural, intercultural theology.[19]

AN INTERCULTURAL THEOLOGY FROM THE IMMIGRANTS' EXPERIENCE OF CULTURES AS A GROUND OF CONTEST IN RELATIONS

In light of the in-between predicament of the immigrant, a theology out of the experience of migration cannot but be intercultural. More important, in the United States, given the many culturally diverse ethnic groups that increasingly make up its population, theology must be *inter-multicultural*. That is to say, a North American intercultural theology is not only a theology shaped by the encounter between *two* cultures, the dominant (Anglo/European/white) culture and a minority culture (for example, Latino), but by the much more complex and challenging encounter of *several* cultures at the same time (white and Latino and black and Asian and Native American and so on).[20] To express this point with prepositions, the encounter is not *between* but *among* cultures. The complexity of this theology will appear all the more daunting when one calls to

---

[19] On the notion of *"tiempos mixtos,"* see Fernando Calderon, "America Latina, identidad y tiempos mixtos, o cómo ser boliviano," *Imagenes desconoscidas* (Buenos Aires: CLASCO, 1988), 225-29.

[20] This point has been made by María Pilar Aquino in "Theological Method in U.S. Latino/a Theology: Toward an Intercultural Theology for the Third Millennium," in *From the Heart of Our People: Latino/a Explorations in Catholic Systematic Theology*, ed. Orlando Espín and Miguel H. Díaz (Maryknoll, N.Y.: Orbis Books, 1999), 24-25: "U.S. Latino/a theology may not renounce its intercultural cradle. This is a theology born within a reality where a number of religious traditions and several theological formulations converge. European, Latin American, European-American, Afro-Latin and African American, Native American, and feminist traditions and elaborations have been welcomed and critically embraced."

mind that each culture contains within itself several significant varieties and is itself an ever-changing and dynamic reality. Throw into this ethnic and cultural mix the gender component, and the shape of this intercultural theology becomes even more unwieldy.

The Inter-Multicultural Character of Theology

Despite its complexity, this inter-multicultural character must be accepted as the epistemological, hermeneutical, and methodological vantage point for the yet-to-emerge intercultural theology in the United States. In this respect a North American intercultural theology promises to be far more interesting, and by the same token, exceedingly more difficult to construct, than a monocultural or even duocultural theology. To delineate the contours of this emerging intercultural theology, in this section I reflect further on the epistemological, hermeneutical, and methodological implications of the existential ontology of the immigrants for intercultural theology and on the resources it brings to such a theology.

The multicultural dialogue that shapes a theology out of the experience of migration is fortunately not foreign to many groups of immigrants in the United States but is an intrinsic part of their collective history. As Virgilio Elizondo has argued, the reality of *mestizaje* (the mixing of the Spanish and the Amerindian) and *mulataje* (the mixing of the Spanish and the African) is the fundamental characteristic of many Hispanics and thus makes interculturality a necessary matrix for Hispanic theology and church life.[21] This is no less true of African Americans, that is, Americans of African descent whose ancestry dates back to the period of slavery in the United States and whose cultural lineage is traced, through the history of the slave trade, back to Africa (in particular West Africa), as well as of black Americans, including recent immigrants from Africa, Central and South America, and the Caribbean. Their cultural and religious identity has been shaped by a long and painful encounter with the dominant white culture and religion.[22] Asian Americans, too, bear within their history

---

[21] See Virgilio Elizondo, *The Galilean Journey: The Mexican-American Promise* (Maryknoll, N.Y.: Orbis Books, 1983); idem, *The Future Is Mestizo: Life Where Cultures Meet* (Oak Park, Ill.: Meyer-Stone Books, 1988). See also his earlier two-volume work, *Mestizaje: The Dialectic of Cultural Birth and the Gospel* (San Antonio, Tex.: Mexican American Cultural Center, 1978). It is interesting to note that the mixed race *(mestizaje)*—the *raza cósmica*—had been proposed by José Vasconcelos as a new era of humanity occurring in the Aesthetic Age. Such a *raza cósmica*, according to Vasconcelos, is already present in the peoples of Latin America insofar as they incorporate in themselves the Indian, European, and African "races." See his *The Cosmic Race/La raza cósmica*, trans. with intro. D. T. Jean (Baltimore and London: The Johns Hopkins University Press, 1979).

[22] See in particular Gayraud S. Wilmore, *Black Religion and Black Radicalism: An Interpretation of the Religious History of African Americans,* 3d ed. (Maryknoll, N.Y.: Orbis Books, 1998); and James H. Cone and Gayraud S. Wilmore, eds., *Black Theology: A Documentary History, Volume I, 1966-79* and *Black Theology: A Documentary History, Volume 2, 1980-1992* (Maryknoll, N.Y.: Orbis Books, 1993).

the mixture of cultures, in particular the Japanese, Koreans, and Vietnamese, who have absorbed, often by force, the Chinese/Confucian culture. Of course, this in-between cultural standing of these new non-European immigrants is exacerbated as they try to make their home in the United States, since they have to contend not only with the dominant culture but also with the cultures of fellow immigrant groups.

A North American intercultural theology from the perspective of migration will take this preexisting multicultural experience of these new arrivals as the vantage point from which to perceive and know reality (epistemology), to interpret it (hermeneutics), and to guide the articulation of a Christian understanding appropriate for and relevant to the betwixt-and-between predicament of immigrants facing multiple cultures (methodology). The resulting theology would then be truly inter-multicultural.[23]

Epistemology of Inter-Multicultural Theology: Seeing from the Margins

Epistemologically, intercultural theology must be multi-perspectival. It must look to several cultures for insights and validation. It is understandable that theologians at first turn to the cultures of their own ethnic groups as the context in which to construct a theology in dialogue and even in confrontation with the dominant theology. Thus black theology, Latino/a theology, and Asian American theology have emerged in the United States in this chronological order. Recently, there have been auspicious attempts at crossing ethnic as well as denominational boundaries to construct an inter-multicultural theology and to articulate a common theological method.[24]

In this effort, however, intercultural theology must be aware that for the immigrant, who embodies the *tiempos mixtos* and often feels torn among competing cultures, culture is experienced not as an integrated and integrating whole (as in premodernity and modernity) but primarily as a ground of contest in relations (as in postmodernity). In recent years the modern concept of culture as an

---

[23] Because the neologism *inter-multicultural* is cumbersome, in this chapter the term *intercultural* is sometimes used, but only in the sense intended by "inter-multicultural" as explained above.

[24] Works that attempt to carry out this multi-partnered theological dialogue include Eleazar S. Fernandez and Fernando F. Segovia, eds., *A Dream Unfinished: Theological Reflections on America from the Margins* (Maryknoll, N.Y.: Orbis Books, 2001), which brings together African American, Asian American, and Hispanic-Latino/a theological voices; and Anthony B. Pinn and Benjamin Valentin, eds., *The Ties that Bind: African American and Hispanic American/Latino/a Theologies in Dialogue* (New York: Continuum, 2001), which includes articles by African American theologians with responses from Latino/a theologians and vice versa. For reflections on ethnic theologies in the United States and a common methodology, see my essays "Contemporary Theology and Inculturation in the United States," in *The Multicultural Church: A New Landscape in U.S. Theologies*, ed. William Cenkner (New York: Paulist Press, 1996), 109-30, 176-92, and "A Common Journey, Different Paths, the Same Destination: Method in Liberation Theologies," in Fernandez and Segovia, *A Dream Unfinished*, 129-51.

integrated and integrating whole into which members of the society are socialized has been subjected to a searching critique. The view of culture as a self-contained and clearly bounded whole, as an internally consistent and integrated system of beliefs, values, and behavioral norms that functions as the ordering principle of a social group and into which its members are socialized, has been shown to be based on unjustified assumptions.[25] Against this conception of culture it has been argued that (1) it focuses exclusively on culture as a finished product and therefore pays insufficient attention to culture as a historical process; (2) that its view of culture as a consistent whole is dictated more by the anthropologist's aesthetic need and the demand for synthesis than by the lived reality of culture itself; (3) that its emphasis on consensus as the process of cultural formation obfuscates the reality of culture as a site of struggle and contention; (4) that its view of culture as a principle of social order belittles the role of the members of a social group as cultural agents; (5) that this view privileges the stable elements of culture and does not take into adequate account its innate tendency to change and to innovation; and (6) that its insistence on clear boundaries for cultural identity is no longer necessary, since it is widely acknowledged today that change, conflict, and contradiction are resident *within* culture itself and are not simply caused by outside disruption and dissension.[26]

Rather than as a sharply demarcated, self-contained, homogeneous, integrated, and integrating whole, culture today is seen as a ground of contest in relations and as a historically evolving, fragmented, inconsistent, conflicted, constructed, ever-shifting, and porous social reality. In this contest in relations the role of power in the shaping of cultural identity is of paramount importance, a factor that the modern concept of culture largely ignores. In the past, anthropologists tended to regard culture as an innocent set of conventions rather than a reality of conflict in which the colonizers, the powerful, the wealthy, the victors, the dominant, the host can obliterate the beliefs and values of the colonized, the weak, the poor, the vanquished, the subjugated, the immigrant, so that there has been, in Serge Gruzinski's expression, "la colonisation de l'imaginaire."[27] This role of power is, as Michel Foucault and other masters of suspicion have argued,

---

[25] See Pierre Bourdieu, *Outline of a Theory of Practice* (Cambridge: Cambridge University Press, 1977); James Clifford, *The Predicament of Culture* (Cambridge, Mass.: Harvard University Press, 1988); George Marcus and Michael Fischer, *Anthropology as Cultural Critique* (Chicago: University of Chicago Press, 1986); Ulrich Beck, *Risk Society: Toward a New Modernity* (London: Sage, 1992); Homi K. Bhabha, *The Location of Culture* (London: Routledge, 1994); Jonathan Friedman, *Cultural Identity and Global Process* (London: Sage, 1994); Mike Featherstone, *Undoing Modernity: Globalization, Postmodernism and Identity* (London: Sage, 1995); Kathryn Tanner, *Theories of Culture: A New Agenda for Theology* (Minneapolis: Fortress Press, 1997).

[26] For a detailed articulation of these six objections to the anthropological concept of culture, see Tanner, *Theories of Culture*, 40-56.

[27] Serge Gruzinski, *La Colonisation de l'imaginaire: Sociétés indigènes et occidentalisation dans le Mexique espagnol XVIe-XVIIIe siècle* (Paris: Gallimard, 1987). English translation, *The Conquest of Mexico* (Cambridge: Polity, 1993).

central in the formation of knowledge in general.[28] In the formation of cultural identity the role of power is even more extensive, since it is constituted by groups of people with conflicting interests, and the winners can dictate their cultural terms to the losers.

This predicament of culture is exacerbated by the process of globalization, in which the ideals of modernity and technological reason are extended throughout the world (globalization as extension), aided and abetted by a single economic system (neoliberal capitalism) and new communication technologies.[29] In globalization geographical boundaries, which at one time helped define cultural identity, have collapsed, especially for immigrants. Even our sense of time is largely compressed, with the present predominating and the dividing line between past and future becoming ever more blurred (globalization as compression). In this process of globalization, a homogenized culture is created, consolidated by a "hyperculture" based on consumption, especially of goods exported from the United States, such as clothing, food, and entertainment. U.S. immigrants, especially the young ones, are daily enticed, even assaulted, by this hyperculture.

Such a globalized culture is not, however, accepted by local cultures hook, line, and sinker. Between the global and the local cultures there takes place a continuous struggle, the former for political and economic dominance, the latter for survival and integrity. Because of the powerful attraction of the global culture, especially for the young, local cultures often feel threatened by it, but they are far from powerless. To counteract its influence, they have devised several strategies of resistance, subversion, compromise, and appropriation. In this effort religion more often than not has played a key role in alliance with culture.

---

[28] See Michel Foucault, *The Archaeology of Knowledge*, trans. A. M. Sheridan Smith (New York: Pantheon Books, 1972); idem, *Discipline and Punish: The Birth of Prison*, trans. Alan Sheridan (New York: Vintage Press, 1975); Michael Kelly, ed., *Critique and Power: Recasting the Foucault/Habermas Debate* (Cambridge, Mass.: MIT Press, 1994); Michel Foucault, *Madness and Civilization: A History of Insanity in the Age of Reason*, trans. Richard Howard (New York: Vintage Books, 1988); idem, *Language, Counter-Memory, Practice: Selected Essays and Interviews*, ed. Donald Bouchard, trans. Donald Bouchard and Sherry Simon (Ithaca, N.Y.: Cornell University Press, 1977); idem, *Power/Knowledge*, trans. Colin Gordon (New York: Pantheon Books, 1987); idem, *Politics, Philosophy, Culture: Interviews and Other Writings*, ed. Lawrence D. Kritzman, trans. Alan Sheridan (New York: Routledge, 1988).

[29] For a discussion of the historical development of globalization, see the works of Immanuel Wallerstein, *The Modern World-System I: Capitalist Agriculture and the Origins of the European World-Economy in the Sixteenth Century* (New York: Academic, 1974) and *The Modern World-System II: Mercantilism and the Consolidation of the European World-Economy, 1600-1750* (New York: Academic, 1980); Anthony Giddens, *Modernity and Self-Identity: Self and Society in the Late Modern Age* (Stanford, Calif.: Stanford University Press, 1991); and Roland Robertson, *Globalization: Social Theory and Global Culture* (London: Sage, 1992). In general, Wallerstein attributes an exclusively economic origin to globalization; Giddens sees it rooted in four factors, namely, the nation-state system, the world military order, the world capitalist economy, and the international division of labor; and Robertson highlights the cultural factors in globalization.

Moreover, globalization affects not only non-Western countries but also, like a boomerang, returns to hit the thrower. This is seen, for example, in France, Britain, and Portugal, where people of their former colonies come to live and thereby create a multicultural and multi-ethnic situation unknown hitherto. The same situation occurs also in the United States, where because of economic and political pressures, people from South America and Asia have come in recent decades to settle in large numbers, as legal or illegal immigrants, thus diversifying the racial, ethnic, and cultural composition of the population.[30]

Like the anthropological concept of culture as a unified whole, the globalized concept of culture as a ground of contest in relations has its own strengths and weaknesses. On the positive side it takes into account features of culture that are left in the shadow by its predecessor. While recognizing that harmony and wholeness remain ideals, it views culture in its lived reality of fragmentation, conflict, and ephemerality. Cultural meanings are not simply discovered ready-made but are constructed and produced in the violent cauldron of asymmetrical power relations. The globalized concept of culture recognizes the important role of power in the formation of cultural identity. Furthermore, it sees culture as a historical process, intrinsically mutable, but without an a priori, clearly defined *telos* and a controllable and predictable synthesis. On the debit side, this postmodern concept of culture runs the risk of fomenting fundamentalistic tendencies, cultural and social ghettoization, and romantic retreat to an idealized past.[31]

Hermeneutics of Inter-Multicultural Theology: Suspicion, Retrieval, and Reconstruction

In light of this postmodern understanding of culture as a ground of contest in relations fortified and spread by globalization, an inter-multicultural theology will no longer be able to start from a universalized concept of culture or culture in general, inevitably shaped by the dominant culture, and then proceed to an application of it to ethnic cultures. Rather, hermeneutically and methodologically, it must begin with what Fernando Segovia has aptly termed "minority studies."[32] Taking a cue from Gilles Deleuze's and Félix Guattari's proposals

---

[30] For a brief discussion of globalization, see Schreiter, *The New Catholicity*, 4-14. Social scientist Arjun Appadurai lists five factors that have contributed to the "deterritorialization" of contemporary culture: ethnoscape (the constant flow of persons such as immigrants, refugees, tourists, guest workers, exiles), technoscape (mechanical and informational technologies), financescape (flow of money through currency markets, national stock exchanges, commodity speculation), mediascape (newspapers, magazines, TV, films), and ideoscape (key ideas such as freedom, welfare, human rights, independence, democracy). See his "Disjuncture and Difference in the Global Economy," *Public Culture* 2/2 (1990): 1-24.

[31] On these three tendencies or cultural logics dubbed as antiglobalism, ethnification, and primitivism, see Schreiter, *The New Catholicity*, 21-25.

[32] See his insightful and challenging essay, "Introduction: Minority Studies and Christian Studies," in Fernandez and Segovia, *A Dream Unfinished*, 1-33.

for a "minor literature" as a deterritorialized, political, and collective discourse embedded within every literature and critically appropriating the insights of Abdul JanMohamed and David Lloyd on "minority discourse" (as opposed to "ethnic discourse"),[33] Segovia proposes, as I understand him, an intercultural theology as a "minor literature" and "a Christian minority discourse."[34]

Such a Christian minority discourse will obviously start with a "hermeneutics of suspicion," unmasking the asymmetrical relation between the dominant and minority cultures and the forces of power at work in such a relation.[35] With regard to the immigrants in the United States, this hermeneutics will seek to show that the American ideal of the melting pot is far from being "a highly successful model of a multiethnic, multicultural, multireligious, and polyglot society."[36] As Benjamin Schwarz has argued, in its past history America successively engaged in swallowing up peoples and cleansing ethnics, subscribed to a project of imperial expansion, was involved in a nationalist-separatist conflict between its North and South, and adopted a policy of racial exclusion and maltreatment toward a sizeable segment of its population.[37] Furthermore, Segovia has shown that even the recent and more enlightened views of Arthur M. Schlesinger Jr., David Kennedy, and Samuel P. Huntington still take the assimilation of the new immigrants into the American society as the goal—which is, in fact, turning them into "born-again Anglo-Americans."[38] A hermeneutics of

---

[33] "Ethnic culture" is sharply contrasted with "minority culture" insofar as the former "faces inward—toward its own internal concerns and problems, its own traditions and histories, its own projects and dreams," whereas the latter "faces outward—toward a dominant state formation, capable of bringing destruction upon it either by violence or by assimilation. . . . Out of this confrontation emerges a minority discourse—an appositional discourse marking the actual or potential destruction in question at the hands of the dominant culture, but also offering the grounds for a critique of this culture in terms of its own internal logic and projects" (ibid., 23).

[34] Segovia calls this field of study "multipolar and multilingual, cacophonous and conflicted" (ibid., 30). It is similar to what I have called "inter-multicultural theology" in a culture as a ground of contest in relations.

[35] This hermeneutics of suspicion—inspired by the three great "masters of suspicion," Nietzsche, Marx, and Freud—is a familiar feature of Latin American liberation theology and feminist theology. For the use of this hermeneutics in black Catholic theology, see M. Shawn Copeland, "Method in Emerging Black Catholic Theology," in *Taking Down Our Harps: Black Catholics in the United States*, ed. Diana L. Hayes and Cyprian Davis (Maryknoll, N.Y.: Orbis Books, 1998), 128-29; in Latino/a theology, see Aquino, "Theological Method in U.S. Latino/a Theology," 11-14.

[36] Benjamin Schwarz, "The Diversity Myth: America's Leading Export," *The Atlantic Monthly* 275/5 (May 1995), 60, quoted in Fernando Segovia, "Melting and Dreaming in America: Visions and Re-visions," in Fernandez and Segovia, *A Dream Unfinished*, 242.

[37] See the summary of Schwarz's essay in Segovia, "Melting and Dreaming in America," 242-43.

[38] See ibid., 245-61. The works he examines are Arthur M. Schlesinger Jr., *The Disuniting of America: Reflections on a Multicultural Society*, rev. and enl. ed. (New York and London: W. W. Norton, 1998); David Kennedy, "Can We Still Afford to Be a Nation of Immigrants," *The Atlantic Monthly* 278/5 (November 1996): 42-68; and Samuel P. Huntington, "The Erosion of American National Interests," *Foreign Affairs* 76/5 (September-October 1997): 28-49.

suspicion will provide an intercultural theology with a more complete and complex history of immigration, one that involves, as Segovia puts it, "intertwined accommodation and conflict, ever-present and ever-expanding hybridity, and a mangled project of exalted principles and despicable behavior."[39] Thus, in this story the immigrants' success stories must be placed in the context of their suffering from opposition, prejudice, discrimination, exploitation, and marginalization at the hands of the dominant society. These two inseparable sides of the immigrants' experience must be allowed to complement and illumine each other.

The next step is to retrieve this "underside of history" as lived by the immigrants, their stories of hard struggle for physical survival and for human dignity, especially stories of women who are triply discriminated against (because they are poor and minority and female); stories of how their faith in the God who vindicated Jesus and gave him a new and transcendent life over death inspired and sustained them to overcome bouts of self-doubt and despair; stories of hope; stories of effective solidarity of immigrants with one another in a community of love and mutual acceptance, of shared spiritual and material resources, of common work to build a more just and equitable society across gender, racial, ethnic, economic, and political differences; and, yes, even stories of immigrants' mutual suspicion and jealousy, of self-reliant "model immigrants" over against public-welfare-dependent ones, of earlier immigrants scapegoating and discriminating against more recent ones, for fear that the American pie would be cut into too many slices.

Furthermore, the hermeneutics of retrieval must also pursue archival "archeology" into the immigrants' cultural, moral, religious, and ritualistic traditions and customs, their language and myths, often marginalized by the dominant society, or forgotten, or even ridiculed by the immigrants themselves for their quaint, premodern appearance in a modern and postmodern society. But this archeology must not be undertaken out of a romantic nostalgia for the "good old days" or out of a purely historical interest to serve the academy; rather, its goal is to rediscover the abiding truths and values inherent in the immigrants' cultures capable of sustaining them in their struggle for full humanity. Consequently, these cultures should be subjected to critical scrutiny and evaluation as stringent and rigorous as those applied to the dominant culture.

Lastly, the hermeneutics of reconstruction aims at shaping, out of the resources of the immigrants' cultures and those of the dominant one, a new culture, a *tertium quid*. This step is necessary because, as pointed out above, the immigrants are not only betwixt-and-between cultures but also *beyond* them. Of course, the contours of this emerging culture still remain blurred and hazy. Nevertheless, however indistinct the shape of such a culture still is, it is clear that, because of the morally mixed history of the United States, made of both lights and shadows, a U.S. intercultural theology is forbidden, as Segovia has correctly pointed out, to make the three claims of "American exceptionalism"

---

[39] Segovia, "Melting and Dreaming in America," 267.

that have been made by an earlier theology inspired by the Manifest Destiny myth. That is, it must renounce "any and all claims to national election (a 'chosen people'), a national promise (a 'promised land'), and national mission (a 'light to the nations')."[40]

Inter-Multicultural Theology: Method

Socio-Analytic Mediation

As is clear from what has been done so far, an intercultural theology out of the experience of migration must first of all make use of the social sciences, in particular of sociology, political science, and economics, as well as of the history of American immigration in order to obtain as accurate a portrait as possible of the immigrants in the United States and to trace the various factors that contribute to their oppressive plight. This first methodological step has been called by Clodovis Boff the "socio-analytic mediation" of theology.[41] This mediation has also been called for by Latino/a and black theologians.[42]

In addition to socio-political analysis, intercultural theology must, as has been argued above, dig deep into the humus of the immigrants' lives to find resources for reflection. This is what Latino/a theology refers to as *lo cotidiano*.[43]

---

[40] Ibid., 267.

[41] See Clodovis Boff, *Theology and Praxis: Epistemological Foundations*, trans. Robert Barr (Maryknoll, N.Y.: Orbis Books, 1987) and *Teoria do Método Teológico* (Petropolis, Brazil: Vozes, 1998). For an analysis of the three mediations of liberation theologies, of which intercultural theology is a subset, see *Teoria do Método Teológico*, chapter 2. Among liberation theologians the one most insistent upon the need for theology to dialogue with the social sciences is Juan Luis Segundo, whose theological project is to dialogue with the social sciences in order to "deideologize" the customary interpretation of the Christian faith and its language that hide and legitimate oppression or social injustice. For a helpful collection of Segundo's writings, see Juan Luis Segundo, *Signs of the Times: Theological Reflections*, ed. Alfred Hennelly and trans. Robert Barr (Maryknoll, N.Y.: Orbis Books, 1993), especially his two essays "Theology and the Social Sciences" (7-17) and "The Shift within Latin American Theology" (67-80). It is important to note that in the last-mentioned essay Segundo was critical of his colleagues for having made the poor rather than the deideologizing of Christian tradition the primary locus or source of theology.

[42] See Orlando Espín, *The Faith of the People: Theological Reflections on Popular Catholicism* (Maryknoll, N.Y.: Orbis Books, 1997), 3: "Historical and cultural studies had to be engaged, that the social sciences had to become partners in dialogue." See also Shawn Copeland, "Method in Emerging Black Catholic Theology," 129-30. For further reflections on the relationships between theology and the social sciences, see my essay "Social Science and Ecclesiology: Cybernetics in Patrick Granfield's Theology of the Church," in *Theology and the Social Sciences*, ed. Michael H. Barnes (Maryknoll, N.Y.: Orbis Books, 2001), 59-87. Clearly, then, intercultural theology is by necessity a multidisciplinary enterprise. Furthermore, this dialogue of intercultural theology with the humanities must include philosophy as a partner, a point well argued by Alejandro García-Rivera, "The Whole and the Love of Difference: Latino Metaphysics as Cosmology," in Espín and Díaz, *From the Heart of Our People*, 54-83.

[43] On *lo cotidiano* as a source for intercultural theology, see Aquino, "Theological Method in U.S. Latino/a Theology," 38-39.

The stories of these lives are often not recorded in history books written by victors but must be retrieved from the forgotten and oppressed past to form the "dangerous memory" (Johann Baptist Metz) by which the stimulus for social transformation may be nourished and sustained. The telling, of course, often takes verbal form, in prose or poetry, but is not limited to it. It can also be done in songs, drama, dance, ritual, symbolization, visual art, and folklore.[44]

One of the results of storytelling as a theological method is contextualization. Storytelling makes intercultural theology concrete, rooted in real life experiences, and historical. Through stories the narrator acknowledges her or his inescapable social, political, and economic location and implicitly affirms the validity of his or her experience. By the same token, in recognizing the contextuality of their own theologies, intercultural theologians also carry out, at least indirectly, an ideology critique insofar as they reject the claims to universality of the dominant or official theology and show that it too is inescapably located in a particular social, political, and economic context. On the other hand, storytelling helps bridge the gap inhibiting communication among people of diverse cultures because stories create a communal fund of wisdom from which intercultural theologians can draw inspiration for their reflection. In this way storytelling contributes to building up a kind of concrete universality, out of particular stories and histories, from below as it were, rather than the kind of abstract universality and normativity that the dominant theology attempts to impose on others from above.[45]

Hermeneutical Mediation

The socio-analytic mediation is followed by the "hermeneutical mediation," by which the sociological and historical data and their theoretical constructions are given a properly theological interpretation by using appropriate biblical symbols and doctrinal traditions. It is important to note that this interpretation does not seek a one-to-one equivalence between the biblical symbols and their doctrinal interpretations (for example, the Hebrew exiles and the theological interpretations of their deportation) on the one hand and present-day data and their sociological theories (for example, the U.S. immigrants and the various theories about migration) on the other. Nor does it seek to establish a direct correspondence between the ratio between the biblical events and their historical contexts (for example, the Hebrew exiles and their Babylonian context) and the ratio between our political events and their historical contexts (e.g., the immigrants and their U.S. context). Such attempts would be prone to biblicism, fundamentalism,

---

[44] Miguel H. Díaz highlights this narrative quality of Latino/a theology in his essay "*Dime con quién andas y te diré quién eres* (Tell me with whom you walk, and I will tell you who you are): We Walk-with Our Lady of Charity," in Espín and Díaz, *From the Heart of Our People*, 153-71.

[45] Orlando Espín argues for this sort of "universality," which he terms "universal relevance" in contrast to "universal validity." See his "An Exploration into the Theology of Grace and Sin," in Espín and Díaz, *From the Heart of Our People*, 143 n. 6.

and eisegesis, which would lead to applying to present-day immigrants what happened to and what was said of the Hebrew exiles without due regard to their vastly different contexts. Clearly, the exiled Hebrews are not identical to the U.S. immigrants, nor is the former's deportation in the sixth century B.C.E. identical to the latter's migration in the twenty-first century C.E. Furthermore, how the Hebrew exiles were related to their Babylonian context is not identical with how the U.S. immigrants are related to their U.S. context.

Rather, the goal of the hermeneutical mediation is to discover the possible *relationship* between the relationship obtaining between one set of terms (for example, the Hebrew exiles and their context) and the relationship obtaining between another set of terms (for example, the U.S. immigrants and their context). In other words, the hermeneutical mediation seeks the relationship between/among relationships obtaining between two or more sets of terms rather than an identity or correspondence between these sets of terms. In this mode of hermeneutical mediation intercultural theology is not on the one hand bound by a deadening conformity to past interpretations but rather enjoys a creative freedom to risk novel interpretations, and on the other hand is not buffeted by fanciful, context-free, and text-free lucubrations of postmodern deconstruction.[46]

There is, however, a new aspect in the hermeneutical mediation of a U.S. intercultural theology that has so far not been given adequate attention, and that is the increasing presence of Asians among U.S. immigrants. Christians in Asia form but a tiny minority of the Asian population (approximately 4 percent). They live among followers of other religions that, contrary to past missionaries' predictions, have not been vanquished by Christianity but rather have lately experienced a remarkable renaissance. Interreligious dialogue for them is not a luxury but an absolute necessity.[47] This multi-religious context, which is unique to Asian Christian immigrants, is not shared by black and Latino/a immigrants but is increasingly becoming a permanent fixture of the U.S. religious

---

[46] For a more detailed explanation of the hermeneutical mediation, see chapter 2 herein. On Latino/a biblical interpretation, see Jean-Pierre Ruiz, "The Bible and U.S. Hispanic American Theological Discourse: Lessons from a Non-Innocent History," in Espín and Díaz, *From the Heart of Our People*, 100-120. Fernando Segovia, in his helpful survey of Hispanic ways of reading the Bible, distinguishes five approaches to the Bible as represented by Virgil Elizondo, Ada María Isasi-Díaz, Harold Recinos, Justo González, and himself. See his "Reading the Bible as Hispanic Americans," in *The New Interpreters' Bible* (Nashville, Tenn.: Abingdon, 1994), 1:167-73. See also Justo González, "Scripture, Tradition, Experience, and Imagination: A Redefinition," in Pinn and Valentin, *The Ties that Bind*, 61-73.

[47] This point has been repeatedly emphasized by Asian theologians and the Federation of Asian Bishops' Conferences. See Gaudencio Rosales and C. G. Arévalo, eds., *For All the Peoples of Asia: Federation of Asian Bishops' Conferences. Documents from 1970 to 1991* (Maryknoll, N.Y.: Orbis Books, 1992; Quezon City, Philippines: Claretian Publications, 1992); and Franz-Josef Eilers, ed., *For All the Peoples of Asia: Federation of Asian Bishops' Conferences. Documents from 1992 to 1996* (Quezon City, Philippines: Claretian Publications, 1997).

landscape.[48] Just as feminism has thrown a monkey wrench into intercultural theology, so interreligious (and not merely ecumenical, intra-Christian) dialogue has made life exceedingly complicated for U.S. intercultural theologians who have hardly embarked upon this task.

With respect to hermeneutics, intercultural theology must practice what has been called *multi-faith hermeneutics*. In this hermeneutics, which takes into account the fact that the sacred scriptures of other religions are also revered and read as revelatory of the divine, the Christian Bible is not a priori granted a universal validity and normativity, "fulfilling" and abolishing in a kind of *Aufhebung* the other scriptures. Nor is it read simply side by side with other scriptures as if they do not complement, correct, and enrich each other. Rather, in multi-faith hermeneutics, each of the sacred books of all religions is first allowed to be unique and to speak on its own terms, without pretension to superiority and universal validity, and then all of them are brought to bear on one another to correct, validate, prolong, and complement the religious insights of each.[49] In this way, retrieving a universal wisdom from and out of particular wisdom traditions, a U.S. intercultural theology is not only multi-ethnic (or better, multi-minority) but also multi-religious.

Practical Mediation

The third and last mediation of a U.S. inter-multicultural theology is the "practical mediation." By this is meant not only the socio-political commitment of individual theologians in terms of the "option for the poor,"[50] but also as, in Clodovis Boff's terminology, "pistic criteriology." Praxis (orthopraxis), he rightly points out, cannot be used as a criterion for the truth of a *theological* doctrine (orthodoxy); the "theological criteriology" is only constituted by both internal consistency and coherence with what the community believes (faith). On the other hand, "pistic criteriology" refers to the inherent capacity of faith for socio-political transformation.[51] This transformation is not something explicitly sought out by the praxis of faith as its goal; in other words, faith is not subordinated to and instrumentalized for socio-political transformation. Rather, faith itself is performed for its own sake, "aesthetically," as, in Roberto Goizueta's words,

---

[48] It may be argued that the American religious context has always included the presence of Judaism and, lately, Islam. However, while there are many historical and doctrinal commonalities among these three "religions of the Book," such a thing cannot be said of the relationship between Christianity and other Asian religions such as Buddhism, Confucianism, Taoism, and so on.

[49] See R. S. Sugirtharajah, ed., *Voices from the Margin: Interpreting the Bible in the Third World* (Maryknoll, N.Y.: Orbis Books, 1991).

[50] On this practical mediation in Latino/a theology, see Aquino, "Theological Method in U.S. Latino/a Theology," 28-32. Aquino speaks of the three principles of this mediation: beginning with the "faith of the people," adoption of the "option for the poor and oppressed," and practicing a "liberating praxis."

[51] See Clodovis Boff, *Theology and Praxis*, 198.

"receptivity" and "response" to God's gift of life. In this way, praxis is distinct from poiesis.[52] But praxis as aesthetics is not authentic if it is not productive of socio-political transformation, and then it forces us to call into question the alleged truth of the doctrines upon which such a praxis is based. Thus, there is a dialectical tension between praxis and theory: Praxis exerts pressure on theory to examine itself critically; theory, in turn, reacting, modifies praxis; then theory and praxis are transcended; and the spiraling never-ending circular movement goes on and on.

PULLING THE RESOURCES TOGETHER
FOR AN INTERCULTURAL THEOLOGY

In this final part of the chapter I would like to draw up a list, by no means exhaustive, of the resources that Latino/a and Asian (and to a lesser extent, black) theologies can and should use *together* to construct a U.S. inter-multicultural theology from the perspective of migration.[53] Such a theology is by necessity a *teología de conjunto*, one done not only collaboratively by theologians with and in the midst of the community but also across racial and ethnic communities in a culture as a ground of contested relations. Most of these resources are well known and have already been used in various ethnic theologies.[54] My point in listing them is to cross-reference them so that their parallels and similarities may be brought to the fore.

1. With respect to the past, since missionary activities have played an essential role in shaping Christianity in Latin America and Asia, a careful study of the work of Christian mission in both continents since the sixteenth century is necessary for a better understanding of the late-Medieval, Iberian Catholicism that Hispanic and Asian immigrants in the United States have inherited. This

---

[52] On praxis as aesthetics, see Roberto Goizueta, "Fiesta: Life in the Subjunctive," in Espín and Díaz, *From the Heart of Our People*, 84-99. Goizueta has developed this idea in his earlier work, *Caminemos con Jesús*, 89-131.

[53] See Sixto J. Garcia, "Sources and Loci of Hispanic Theology," in Bañuelas, *Mestizo Christianity*, 105-23.

[54] Two brief but helpful overviews of the developments of black and Latino/a theologies with bibliographies are available in Anthony Pinn, "Black Theology in Historical Perspective: Articulating the Quest for Subjectivity," and Benjamin Valentin, "Strangers No More: An Introduction to, and an Interpretation of, U.S. Hispanic/Latino/a Theology," and their mutual responses, in Pinn and Valentin, *The Ties that Bind*, 23-57. Besides several anthologies on Latino/a theology, two analyses of Latino/a theology deserve mention: Eduardo C. Fernández, *La Cosecha: Harvesting Contemporary United States Hispanic Theology (1972-1998)* (Collegeville, Minn.: Liturgical Press, 2000) and Miguel H. Díaz, *On Being Home: U.S. Hispanic and Rahnerian Perspectives* (Maryknoll, N.Y.: Orbis Books, 2001). For Asian American theologies, see Phan and Lee, *Journeys at the Margins* (with a selected bibliography); Andrew Sung Park, *Racial Conflict and Healing: An Asian-American Theological Perspective* (Maryknoll, N.Y.: Orbis Books, 1966); and see also my discussion "The Dragon and the Eagle: Toward a Vietnamese American Theology," in Park, *Racial Conflict and Healing*, chap. 12.

common historical root will provide interesting parallels between these two U.S. groups of immigrants.[55]

2. With respect to the present, another source that binds Hispanic and Asian immigrants together is *lo cotidiano*. An inexhaustible source for intercultural theology, *lo cotidiano* includes the daily lives of immigrants as cultural hybrids *(mestizo/a* and *mulatto/a)*, their shared histories of economic and political marginalization, their experiences of living betwixt-and-between with nowhere to stand, and their struggles to live the Christian faith in everyday situations.[56] Incidentally, it must be noted that these "stories," at least in the United States (and increasingly, everywhere else, given the spread of the media culture) are not told only by the *abuelitas* (grandmothers) but massively by songs, popular novels, and especially the electronic media, at least for youth.

3. In rooting itself in *lo cotidiano,* intercultural theology must pay special attention to the role of women in both Latino/a and Asian communities. On the one hand, women have been frequent victims of the *machismo* prevalent in Latin cultures and of the patriarchalism in societies influenced by Confucianism. A woman in a Confucian society is taught to be bound by "three submissions" *(tam tung)*: When a child, she must submit to her father; in marriage, to her husband; in widowhood, to her eldest son. Her behavior is to be guided by "four virtues" *(tu duc)* that are designed to restrict women's role to the sphere of domesticity: assiduous housewifery *(cong),* pleasing appearance *(dung),* appropriate speech *(ngon),* and proper conduct *(hanh)*.[57]

This subordination of women is most often aggravated for women immigrants. While in their native countries their work, though heavy, is mostly confined to the home, in the United States, for economic survival, they have to work at a full-time job outside the home *and* take care of household chores that their men consider beneath them.

On the other hand, women play a key role in the transmission of cultural and religious values. Orlando Espín concludes his study of Latino/a anthropology with the following statement: "If we were to seek out and identify the more

---

[55] See, for instance, Moises Santoval, *On the Move: A History of the Hispanic Church in the United States* (Marknoll, N.Y.: Orbis Books, 1990); and Jay Dolan and Allan Figueroa Deck, eds., *The Notre Dame History of Hispanic Catholics in the U.S.: Issues and Concerns* (Notre Dame, Ind.: University of Notre Dame Press, 1994). On the Iberian roots of Vietnamese Christianity, see my book *Mission and Catechesis: Alexandre de Rhodes and Inculturation in Seventeenth-Century Vietnam* (Maryknoll, N.Y.: Orbis Books, 1998).

[56] On *lo cotidiano* as source of intercultural theology, see Aquino, "Theological Method in U.S. Latino/a Theology," 38-39. For an example of the theology of grace and sin, see Espín, "An Exploration into the Theology of Grace and Sin," 121-52. *Lo cotidiano* also plays a key role in *mujerista* theology.

[57] See Hue-Tam Ho Tai, *Radicalism and the Origins of the Vietnamese Revolution* (Cambridge, Mass.: Harvard University Press, 1992), 52-53 and David G. Marr, *Vietnamese Tradition on Trial 1920-1945* (Berkeley and Los Angeles: University of California Press, 1981), 190-99.

crucial daily relationships (and indeed the key protagonists in Latino/a popular Catholicism), mature women would easily appear as *the* leaders and interpreters of that religion and, most importantly, as *the ones with whom Latinos/as sustain the most meaningful and deepest of daily relationships.*"[58] Similarly, despite patriarchal and androcentric Confucianism, Asian women have held the highest political offices in their countries. A U.S. intercultural theology must therefore make its own the reflections of womanist, *mujerista*, and Asian American feminist theologies.[59]

4. Within *lo cotidiano* is what has been called *popular Catholicism,* that is, Catholicism as lived by the people and as distinct from (not opposed to) the Catholicism of religious specialists and of the official, hierarchical members of the church.[60] Even though popular Catholicism should not be identified with the sum of devotional practices, there is no doubt that Marian piety plays a large part in it, especially the devotion to our Lady of Guadalupe. Devotion to Mary also looms large in Asian popular Catholicism.[61] *Religiosidad popular* may very well be one of the strongest bonds that tie Latino/a and Asian American Catholics together.[62]

5. Popular devotion brings up a distinctive source for a U.S. intercultural theology, namely, the religious practices of Asian religions with which Asian American Catholics are familiar. These include, beside the reading of the sacred books of Asian religions, widespread practices such as meditation, monastic

---

[58] Espín, "An Exploration into the Theology of Grace and Sin," 141.

[59] For a dialogue between womanist and *mujerista* theologies, see Ada María Isasi-Díaz, "Preoccupations, Themes, and Proposals of *Mujerista* Theology," and Chandra Taylor Smith, "Womanist Theology: An Expression of Multi-Dimensionality for Multi-Dimensional Beings," in Pinn and Valentin, *The Ties that Bind*, 135-66.

[60] The writings of Orlando Espín on popular Catholicism are widely known. For a dialogue between black and Hispanic theology on popular religion, see Dwight N. Hopkins, "Black Theology on God: The Divine in Black Popular Religion" and Harold J. Recinos, "Popular Religion, Political identity, and Life-Story Testimony in an Hispanic Community," and their mutual responses, in Pinn and Valentin, *The Ties that Bind*, 99-132. For an excellent overview of Hispanic theology of popular Catholicism and critique, especially with regard to liturgical inculturation, see the following articles in *Liturgical Ministry* 7 (Summer 1998): James L. Empereur, "Popular Religion and the Liturgy: The State of the Question," 107-20; Mark Francis, "The Hispanic Liturgical Year: The People's Calendar," 129-35; Keith F. Pecklers, "Issues of Power and Access in Popular Religion," 136-40; Robert E. Wright, "Popular Religiosity: Review of Literature," 141-46. See also Arturo Pérez-Rodríguez, *Popular Catholicism: A Hispanic Perspective* (Washington, D.C.: The Pastoral Press, 1988); and Arturo Pérez-Rodríguez, *Primero Dios: Hispanic Liturgical Resource* (Chicago: Liturgy Training Publications, 1997).

[61] See my essay "Mary in Vietnamese Piety and Theology: A Contemporary Perspective," *Ephemerides Mariologicae* 51/4 (2001): 457-71.

[62] In privileging popular Catholicism as a source for a U.S. intercultural theology, attention should be paid to Justo Gonzalez's well-taken warnings about how it (especially in its Marian manifestations) is still rejected by many Protestants as rank superstition. See his "Reinventing Dogmatics: A Footnote from a Reinvented Protestant," in Espín and Díaz, *From the Heart of Our People*, 217-29.

traditions, prayers, fasting, and sacred dance. Of great significance among these devotional practices is the cult of ancestors, which had a three-centuries-long controversy in the history of Christian mission in Southeast Asia known as the Chinese Rites Controversy. An Asian American theology cannot afford ignoring these religious practices and the cult of ancestors in particular.[63]

6. Finally, it is necessary to point out that a U.S. inter-multicultural theology must foster a dialogue not only among various minority theologies but also with the dominant Euro-American theology. Without this dialogue there is the danger that the latter and the academic and ecclesiastical powers that support it will regard ethnic or minority theologies at best as an interesting but harmless exercise to be tolerated within a pluralistic context but without posing any challenge to itself, and at worst as a theological aberration to be suppressed. More positively, without this open dialogue between the dominant Anglo-European theology and minority theologies, in which none is granted a superior and normative status and a rigorous critique is directed to all, a U.S. theology will not be a full and faithful articulation of the "joy and hope" *(gaudium et spes)* of all Americans.

---

[63] For further discussion on the question of ancestor worship, see chapters 5 and 6 of this book, as well as my essays "Jesus as the Eldest Brother and Ancestor? A Vietnamese Portrait," *The Living Light* 33/1 (1996): 35-44; and "Culture and Liturgy: Ancestor Veneration as a Test Case," *Worship* 76/5 (2002): 403-30.

2

A Common Journey, Different Paths, the Same Destination

METHOD IN LIBERATION THEOLOGIES

Future historians of Christian theology will no doubt judge liberation theology to be the most influential movement of the twentieth century, possibly even since the Reformation.[1] They certainly will painstakingly document its emergence as independent theological movements in the late 1960s and will marvel at its spectacular expansion throughout the entire ecumene in a matter of just a couple of decades.[2] The profound influence of liberation theology will be evident not only from the way it has penetrated far-flung countries and continents and permeated all the branches of Christian theology, from biblical studies through systematics to ethics,[3] but also from the vigorous attacks orchestrated against its proponents by the ecclesiastical establishment as well as political authorities who have regarded it as the most pernicious threat to orthodoxy, democracy, and the capitalistic system.[4]

---

[1] For helpful general introductions to liberation theology, which are legion, see Ignacio Ellacuría and Jon Sobrino, eds., *Mysterium Liberationis: Fundamental Concepts of Liberation Theology* (Maryknoll, N.Y.: Orbis Books, 1993); Marc H. Ellis and Otto Maduro, eds., *The Future of Liberation Theology* (Maryknoll, N.Y.: Orbis Books 1989); Curt Cadorette et al., eds., *Liberation Theology* (Maryknoll, N.Y.: Orbis Books, 1992); and Peter C. Phan, "The Future of Liberation Theology," *The Living Light* 28/3 (1992): 259-71.

[2] For an excellent documentation of liberation theology, see Alfred T. Hennelly, ed., *Liberation Theology: A Documentary History* (Maryknoll, N.Y.: Orbis Books, 1990).

[3] The Orbis Books Theology and Liberation series attempts to reformulate basic theological themes in light of the theology of liberation.

[4] For the critique by the Vatican, see the documents by the Congregation for the Doctrine of the Faith, "Instruction on Certain Aspects of the 'Theology of Liberation,'" *Origins* 14/13 (1984): 193-204; "Instruction on Christian Freedom and Liberation," *Origins* 15/44 (1986): 713-28. For an evaluation of the Vatican's documents, see Juan Luis Segundo, *Theology and the Church: A Response to Cardinal Ratzinger and a Warning to the Whole Church*, trans. John W. Diercksmeier (Minneapolis: Winston Press, 1985); and Anselm Kyongsuk Min, *Dialectic of Salvation: Issues in Theology of Liberation* (Albany, NY: State University of New York Press, 1989). For a balanced

26

Even though it is customary to refer to liberation theology in the singular, it is obvious, even from a cursory study of its history, that it is by no means a homogeneous and uniform system. It has been practiced in different contexts and continents—North America, Central and South America, Africa, and Asia, just to mention areas where it has attracted a sizable number of adherents.[5] It has targeted various arenas of oppression—gender (white feminist, womanist, and *mujerista* theology), sexual orientation (gay and lesbian theology), race (black theology), class (Latin American theology), culture (African theology), and religion (Asian theology), again, just to cite a representative few. Of course, these forms of oppression are not restricted to a particular region; rather they are *each* widespread in *all* parts of the globe and are often intimately interlocked with one another and mutually reinforcing, so that any genuine liberation theology *anywhere* must fight against *all* forms of oppression, whether sexism, heterosexism, homophobia, racism, classism, or cultural and religious discrimination, siding in effective solidarity with victims of all forms of oppression. In this sense, it is appropriate to refer to liberation theology in the plural: liberation theologies. It is important to take account of this diversity of liberation theologies, since it is a common mistake to lump all liberation theologies together as an undifferentiated theological movement. This diversity has been well expressed by Susan Brooks Thistlethwaite and Mary Potter Engel:

> There are distinctive emphases in liberation theologies; they are not clones. None of them—North American feminist liberation theologies, womanist, *mujerista*, gay and lesbian liberation theologies, African American liberation theologies, Native American liberation theologies, Latin American liberation theologies, *minjung* theologies, or others, including those who as yet have not found a way to name their theological situation for themselves—is interchangeable with any of the others. Each has its own peculiar interests, emphases, viewpoints, analyses, and aims, dependent upon the requirements of its own particular social context.[6]

---

assessment of the critique of liberation theology, see Arthur F. McGovern, *Liberation and Its Critics: Toward an Assessment* (Maryknoll, N.Y.: Orbis Books, 1989). Opposition to liberation theology did not limit itself to silencing some of its more vocal exponents (e.g., Leonardo Boff) but used extreme measures to eliminate it, such as even the murder of six Jesuits and two women in El Salvador in 1989 and many other Christians engaged in the struggle for justice. Their deaths illustrate the nature of liberation theology, as Jon Sobrino has pointed out: "The corpses of the Jesuits show that this theology is not elitist but of the people, because it has risen in defense of the people and shared the people's destiny" (Jon Sobrino, Ignacio Ellacuría, and others, *Companions of Jesus: The Jesuit Martyrs of El Salvador* [Maryknoll, N.Y.: Orbis Books, 1990], 51).

[5] For presentations of liberation from the global perspective, see Alfred T. Hennelly, *Liberation Theologies: The Global Pursuit of Justice* (Mystic, Conn.: Twenty-Third Publications, 1995); Susan Brooks Thistlethwaite and Mary Potter Engel, eds., *Lift Every Voice: Constructing Christian Theologies from the Underside*, rev. and exp. ed. (Maryknoll, N.Y.: Orbis Books, 1998); and Priscilla Pope-Levison and John R. Levison, *Jesus in Global Contexts* (Louisville, Ky.: Westminster/John Knox Press, 1992).

[6] Thistlethwaite and Engel, *Lift Every Voice*, 5.

While acknowledging these important diversities, this chapter focuses on what binds liberation theologies together, namely, the essential elements of their method. It examines the resources liberation theologians make use of, their hermeneutical approaches, and their criteria of truth. In other words, it studies the three elements of the epistemology of liberation theology: the analytical, hermeneutical, and practical mediations.[7] It illustrates these methodological considerations with a wide-ranging appeal to the writings of a variety of liberation theologians themselves. It intends to show that liberation theologians, whatever their national and cultural provenance, are fellow travelers on a common journey, albeit by different routes, to the same destination.

A VARIETY OF GRIST TO THE THEOLOGICAL MILL: THE SOCIO-ANALYTIC MEDIATION

It has been asserted that liberation theology is not simply a theology of genitives in which liberation is no more than one subject among many, a conventional theology about some hitherto undiscovered reality or a way of dealing with a new theme. Rather, the claim is that liberation theology is a new way of doing theology in which liberation is a kind of horizon against which the whole Christian faith is interpreted.[8] In other words, it is essentially a theology with a new method.

Part of the methodological novelty lies in the partners-in-dialogue with which liberation theology converses, or to put it differently, in the kinds of grist it brings to its theological mill. Gustavo Gutiérrez has argued that in contrast to theology as wisdom and theology as rational knowledge, which dialogue almost exclusively with Neoplatonic and Aristotelean philosophies respectively, liberation

---

[7] See Clodovis Boff, *Theology and Praxis: Epistemological Foundations*, trans. Robert Barr (Maryknoll, N.Y.: Orbis Books, 1987), xxv. These three components correspond to the three acts of see-judge-act of the method of Catholic Action founded by Joseph Cardijn. On the connection between the method of liberation theology and that of Catholic Action, see Agenor Brighenti, "Raízes da epistemologia e do método da Teologia da Libertação. O método ver-julgar-agir da Ação Católica e as mediações da teologia latino-americana," diss., Catholic University of Louvain, 1993. See also Clodovis Boff, "Epistemology and Method of Liberation Theology," in Ellacuría and Sobrino, *Mysterium Liberationis*, 57-85; and Leonardo Boff and Clodovis Boff, *Introducing Liberation Theology*, trans. Paul Burns (Maryknoll, N.Y.: Orbis Books, 1987), 22-42.

[8] See Gustavo Gutiérrez, *A Theology of Liberation*, rev. ed., trans. Sister Caridad and John Eagleson (Maryknoll, N.Y.: Orbis Books, 1988), 12: "The theology of liberation offers us not so much a new theme for reflection as a *new way* to do theology. Theology as critical reflection on historical praxis is a liberating theology, a theology of the liberating transformation of the history of humankind—gathered into *ecclesia*—which openly confesses Christ." In *Lift Every Voice*, Susan Brooks Thistlethwaite and Mary Potter Engel use the building metaphor to express the radical challenge of liberation theology: "Liberation theologies are not about rearranging the furniture in the house of theology, or even about redecorating or remodeling the house. Rather, they are about rebuilding the foundation (method) and redesigning the floor plan (categories)" (14). Juan Luis Segundo explains this new way of doing theology in detail in *The Liberation of Theology*, trans. John Drury (Maryknoll, N.Y.: Orbis Books), 1976.

theology is a "critical reflection on praxis."[9] As reflection on historical praxis, liberation theology highlights certain Christian themes that might have been obscured in the past, such as charity as the center of Christian life, the intrinsic connection between spirituality and activism, the anthropological aspects of revelation, the very life of the church as a *locus theologicus*, the task of reflecting on the signs of the times, action as the starting point for theological reflection, the (Marxist) emphasis on the necessity of transforming the world, and the necessity of orthopraxis in addition to orthodoxy.[10]

Conversation with the Social Sciences

To carry out this critical reflection on historical praxis effectively, as part of its methodology liberation theology must enter into dialogue with the social sciences.[11] To help transform the structures that oppress the poor, liberation theologians must have an accurate knowledge of the concrete socio-political and economic conditions of the people to whom they convey the Christian message. The expression *preferential option for the poor* describes well the fundamental commitment or the "first act," to use Gutiérrez's memorable phrase, out of which liberation theologians are supposed to do their "second step" of reflection.[12] However, to know who are the poor in our society and the causes of their poverty requires more than expertise in the Bible and philosophy; what is needed is what Clodovis Boff calls the "socio-analytic mediation."

With regard to the relationship between theology and the social sciences, Clodovis Boff rejects five ways in which that relationship has been conceived

---

[9] Gutiérrez, *A Theology of Liberation*, 5. In an earlier lecture (July 1968) given at Chimbote, Peru, Gutiérrez gave a definition of theology in relation to praxis: "Theology is a reflection—that is, it is a second act, a turning back, a re-flecting, that come after action. Theology is not first; the commitment is first. Theology is the understanding of the commitment, and the commitment is action. The central element is charity, which involves commitment, while theology arrives later on" (in Hennelly, *Liberation Theology*, 63).

[10] See Gutiérrez, *A Theology of Liberation*, 5-11.

[11] Among liberation theologians the one most insistent upon the need for theology to dialogue with the social sciences is Juan Luis Segundo. For a helpful collection of Segundo's writings, see Juan Luis Segundo, *Signs of the Times: Theological Reflections*, ed. Alfred Hennelly, trans. Robert Barr (Maryknoll, N.Y.: Orbis Books, 1993).

[12] See Gutiérrez, *A Theology of Liberation*, 9: "The Christian community professes a 'faith which works through charity.' It is—at least ought to be—real charity, action, and commitment to the service of others. Theology is reflection, a critical attitude. Theology *follows*; it is the second step." For a critical evaluation of Gutiérrez's understanding of the preferential option for the poor in the light of Thomas Aquinas's notion of charity, see Stephen Pope, "Christian Love for the Poor: Almsgiving and the 'Preferential Option,'" *Horizons* 21/2 (1994): 288-312. See also Patrick H. Byrne, "*Ressentiment* and the Preferential Option for the Poor," *Theological Studies* 54 (1993): 213-41; and Stephen Pope, "Proper and Improper Partiality and the Preferential Option for the Poor," *Theological Studies* 54 (1993): 242-71. For a critical examination of the relationship between orthopraxis and doing theology, especially as proposed by Juan Luis Segundo, see Bernard J. Verkamp, "On Doing the Truth: Orthopraxis and the Theologian," *Theological Studies* 49 (1988): 3-24.

and practiced in the past. These he terms "empiricism" (absence of socio-analytic mediation), "methodological purism" (exclusion of socio-analytic mediation), "theologism" (substitution for socio-analytic mediation), "semantic mix"
(faulty articulation of socio-analytic mediation), and "bilingualism" (unarticu-
lated socio-analytic mediation).[13] Instead of these inadequate ways Boff recommends that we understand the relationship between the sciences of the social
and the theology of the political as "constitutive" insofar as the social theories
become the data for theology: "The sciences of the social enter into the theology of the political as a *constitutive part*. But they do so precisely at the level of
the raw material of this theology, at the level of its *material object*—not at that
of its proper pertinency, or formal object."[14]

Many Latin American theologians, at least in their early writings, adopted
the theory of dependence to explain the economic underdevelopment and exploitation in Latin America as the historical byproduct of the development of
other, mostly capitalist countries and hence called for the abandonment of the
developmental model in favor of liberation or "social revolution."[15] In his more
recent writings Gutiérrez has shown himself much more aware of the limitations of the theory of dependence.[16] Nevertheless, the tendency to seek the root
causes of all forms of oppression and to consider them in their historical development remains influential on the methodology of all types of liberation theology. For example, Black theology has traced the roots of African Americans'
socio-political and economic oppression back to racism and the ideology of
white supremacy.[17] Similarly, Asian feminist theologians have highlighted how

---

[13] See Clodovis Boff, *Theology and Praxis*, 20-29.

[14] Ibid., 31. Using Louis Althusser's epistemology, Boff suggests that the "third generality" of the social sciences—their theories—become the "first generality" of liberation theology—its raw data. This point will be elaborated in greater detail in the second
part of this chapter on the hermeneutical mediation.

[15] See Gutiérrez, *A Theology of Liberation*, 49-57. Gutiérrez cites the works of sociologists such as Fernando Henrique Cardoso, Theotonio Dos Santos, and André Gunder
Frank, among many others.

[16] See Gustavo Gutiérrez, "Theology and the Social Sciences," in *The Truth Shall Make
You Free: Confrontations*, trans. Matthew O'Connell (Maryknoll, N.Y.: Orbis Books,
1990), 53-84. Here Gutiérrez insists on the necessity of a critical use of social theories in
general: "We need discernment, then, in dealing with the social sciences, not only because
of their inchoative character . . . but also because to say that these disciplines are scientific
does not mean that their findings are apodictic and beyond discussion" (58).

[17] See in particular Gayraud S. Wilmore, *Black Religion and Black Radicalism: An
Interpretation of the Religious History of African Americans,* 3d ed. (Maryknoll, N.Y.:
Orbis Books, 1998); and James H. Cone and Gayraud S. Wilmore, eds., *Black Theol-
ogy: A Documentary History, Volume I, 1966-79* (Maryknoll, N.Y.: Orbis Books, 1993);
James H. Cone and Gayraud S. Wilmore, eds., *Black Theology: A Documentary His-
tory, Volume 2, 1980-1992* (Maryknoll, N.Y.: Orbis Books, 1993). George C. L.
Cummings has argued that black theology is rooted in six factors: the African slave
trade and American slavery, segregation in post-emancipation America, Martin Luther
King Jr. and the civil rights movement, Malcolm X and the Black Muslim movement,
Black Power and the black rebellions in the 1960s, and the struggle of black Christians to
define their identity and mission. See his *A Common Journey: Black Theology (USA) and
Latin American Liberation Theology* (Maryknoll, N.Y.: Orbis Books, 1993), 2. For black

"capitalism, patriarchy, militarism, and religio-cultural ideologies work together to escalate the degree of women's oppression."[18] Some U.S. Hispanic theologians perceive the origin of the marginalization of Hispanic Americans in the inability of Anglos to accept the reality of *mestizaje* and *mulataje*.[19]

The use of the social sciences, especially the theory of dependence and the concept of class struggle, has brought accusations of Marxist ideology against liberation theology. Liberation theologians have defended themselves successfully against such a charge, from Gutiérrez to his younger colleagues. They distinguish between Marxism as an atheistic and totalitarian ideology (which they vigorously reject) and as a tool of social analysis; they also point out the difference between class struggle as a fact (the existence of which cannot be denied in Latin America) and the Marxist interpretation of class struggle as a law of history.[20]

The Psychological Tools of Introspection and Interreligious Dialogue

Whatever success liberation theologians may have had in their self-defense against accusations of Marxism and however fruitful the dialogue between theology and the social sciences, Aloysius Pieris, a Sri Lankan liberation theologian, while recognizing the indebtedness of Asian theologians to their Latin American colleagues, has pointed out that "'liberation-theopraxis' in Asia that uses only the Marxist tools of social analysis will remain un-Asian and ineffective. It must integrate the psychological tools of introspection that our sages

---

Catholic theology, see Diana L. Hayes and Cyprian Davis, *Taking Down Our Harps: Black Catholics in the United States* (Maryknoll, N.Y.: Orbis Books, 1998), in particular M. Shawn Copeland's essay "Method in Emerging Catholic Theology," 120-44.

[18] Chung Hyun Kyung, *Struggle to Be the Sun Again: Introducing Asian Women's Theology* (Maryknoll, N.Y.: Orbis Books, 1990), 106. See also Virginia Fabella and Sun Ai Lee Park, eds., *We Dare to Dream: Doing Theology as Asian Women* (Hong Kong: Asian Women's Resource Centre for Culture and Theology, 1989).

[19] See Virgilio Elizondo, *The Galilean Journey: The Mexican-American Promise* (Maryknoll, N.Y.: Orbis Books, 1983). See especially his earlier two-volume work, *Mestizaje: The Dialectic of Cultural Birth and the Gospel* (San Antonio, Tex.: Mexican American Cultural Center, 1978) and *The Future Is Mestizo: Life Where Cultures Meet* (Oak Park, Ill.: Meyer-Stone, 1988). See also Roberto Goizueta, *Caminemos con Jesús: Toward a Hispanic/Latino Theology of Accompaniment* (Maryknoll, N.Y.: Orbis Books, 1995).

[20] See Gutiérrez, *The Truth Shall Make You Free*, 61-63, 69-75; Enrique D. Dussel, "Theology of Liberation and Marxism," in Ellacuría and Sobrino, *Mysterium Liberationis*, 85-102; and Arthur McGovern, "Dependency Theory, Marxist Analysis, and Liberation Theology," in Ellis and Maduro, *The Future of Liberation Theology*, 272-86. With regard to socialism in liberation theology, Peter Burns has carefully evaluated the critique of opponents of liberation theology, in particular Michael Novak, and has convincingly showed that such a critique is not well grounded. Burns also points out the danger that liberation theology may lose its distinctive thrust if it mutes its option for socialism as the result of the collapse of Communism. See Peter Burns, "The Problem of Socialism in Liberation Theology," *Theological Studies* 53 (1992): 493-516.

have discovered."[21] The reason for the necessity of this additional tool is the fact that, in Asia, besides "imposed poverty" there is also "voluntary poverty," which has been freely assumed, mainly by monks, to liberate others from imposed poverty and about which Marxist social analysis has nothing to say. This "introspection" not only serves as a bracing corrective to Karl Marx's thesis that religion is the opium of the people but also highlights the potential that religions have for social transformation.

Furthermore, this methodology has forged a new link between struggle for liberation and interreligious dialogue. Since Latin America is predominantly Christian, interreligious dialogue has not been an urgent issue for most of its theologians; nor has interreligious dialogue served as a method for theological reflection.[22] This is also true of black, Hispanic, and feminist theology in the United States. This is not, however, the case with Asia, which is the birthplace of most world religions and where Christians are but a tiny minority and therefore must collaborate with adherents of other religions in order to achieve their agenda for social transformation. By interreligious dialogue as a theological method is meant not only theological discussions among church representatives and academics, but also "dialogue of life," "dialogue of action," and "dialogue of religious experience."[23] It is from these four forms of interreligious dialogue that a theology of liberation must be constructed whose genuine wellspring is spirituality and not secular ideologies. Hence, it is of great significance that liberation theologians have increasingly turned to Christian spirituality as the quarry for their reflections.[24]

---

[21] Aloysius Pieris, *An Asian Theology of Liberation* (Maryknoll, N.Y.: Orbis Books, 1988), 80-81.

[22] Instead of interreligious dialogue, Latin American liberation theologians have recently paid attention to *religiosidad popular* as a source for liberation. See Cristián Parker, *Popular Religion and Modernization in Latin America*, trans. Robert Barr (Maryknoll, N.Y.: Orbis Books, 1996), which has a copious bibliography, 265-84; and Michael R. Candelaria, *Popular Religion and Liberation: The Dilemma of Liberation Theology* (Albany, N.Y.: State University of New York Press, 1990). Among theologians Pablo Richard, Diego Irarrázaval, Juan Luis Segundo, and Juan Carlos Scannone have produced significant works on this theme.

[23] See Pontifical Council for Interreligious Dialogue and Congregation for the Evangelization of Peoples, *Dialogue and Proclamation*, June 20, 1991 (Rome: Vatican Polyglot Press, 1991), no. 42.

[24] See, for instance, Gustavo Gutiérrez, *We Drink from Our Own Wells*, trans. Matthew O'Connell (Maryknoll, N.Y.: Orbis Books, 1984); Jon Sobrino, *A Spirituality of Liberation: Toward a Political Holiness*, trans. Robert Barr (Maryknoll, N.Y.: Orbis Books, 1988); Leonardo Boff, *Passion of Christ, Passion of the World,* trans. Robert Barr (Maryknoll, N.Y.: Orbis Books, 1987); Segundo Galilea, *Following Jesus* (Maryknoll, N.Y.: Orbis Books, 1981); Nestor Jaén, *Toward a Liberation Spirituality*, trans. Philip Berryman (Chicago: Loyola University Press, 1991); Virginia Fabella, Peter K. H. Lee, and David Kwang-sun Suh, eds., *Asian Christian Spirituality: Reclaiming Tradition* (Maryknoll, N.Y.: Orbis Books, 1992). On the spirituality of liberation theology, see Peter C. Phan, "Peacemaking in Latin American Liberation Theology," *Église et Théologie* 24 (1993): 25-41.

On the other hand, thanks to its new link with liberation, the very nature of interreligious dialogue has been transformed. It can no longer be carried out as a leisurely form of inculturation in which various elements are borrowed from other religions and grafted onto one's own—a kind of "theological vandalism," to use Pieris's expression.[25] Rather it should be practiced as part of the task of liberation, since inculturation, as Pieris puts it, is nothing but announcing "the good news *in our own tongues* to our people (that is, the content of inculturation)—namely, that Jesus is the new covenant or the defense pact that God and the poor have made against mammon, their common enemy (that is, the content of liberation). For liberation and inculturation are not two things anymore in Asia."[26]

Interreligious dialogue as part of the method of liberation theology also valorizes sacred texts and practices of Asian religions that have nourished the spiritual life of Asian people for thousands of years before the coming of Christianity into their lands and since then.[27] Intimately connected with these religious classics is what is commonly referred to as Asian philosophies.[28] Lastly, interreligious dialogue also highlights the importance of Asian monastic traditions with their rituals, ascetic practices, and social commitment for constructing a liberation theology.[29]

Stories from the Underside of History

Besides social analysis and psychological introspection accompanied by interreligious dialogue as part of their methodology, liberation theologians delve into people's lives to find resources for their reflection. Their stories provide the stimulus by which social transformation may be nourished and sustained. Among Asian liberation theologians, C. S. Song stands out as the preeminent "story theologian." Again and again he urges his fellow Asian theologians to make use of the stories not only of the Bible but also of poor and oppressed people, the "underside of history" (Gustavo Gutiérrez), and their folktales, old and new, as food for theological thought. Song believes that the most important skill for Asian theologians is the ability to listen theologically to the whispers, cries, groanings, and shouts from the depths of Asian suffering humanity. What is

---

[25] Pieris, *An Asian Theology of Liberation*, 53, 85.

[26] Ibid., 58.

[27] In this respect, see Aloysius Pieris, *Love Meets Wisdom: A Christian Experience of Buddhism* (Maryknoll, N.Y.: Orbis Books, 1988); and *Fire and Water: Basic Issues in Asian Buddhism and Christianity* (Maryknoll, N.Y.: Orbis Books, 1996).

[28] Highly significant in this regard are the prolific writings of Jung Young Lee, especially *Embracing Change: Postmodern Interpretations of the* I Ching *from a Christian Perspective* (Scranton, Pa.: University of Scranton Press, 1994) and *The Trinity in Asian Perspective* (Nashville, Tenn.: Abingdon, 1996).

[29] Even though the following authors cannot be regarded as liberation theologians, Thomas Merton, Bede Griffith, and Raimondo Panikkar have made important contributions to the dialogue on Western and Eastern monasticism.

needed, says Song, is the imagination, the "third-eye"—the power of perception and insight *(satori)*—that enables theologians to grasp the meaning beneath the surface of things. It is precisely this listening to and reflecting upon the stories of suffering people that make theology a liberation theology.[30]

Telling stories of the underside of history is also practiced by Korean *minjung* theology as its fundamental method.[31] As Young-Chan Ro has argued, the reality of *han*, which is "the cumulative unresolved feeling that arises out of people's experience of injustice," and which is the source of *minjung* theology, "reveals itself in the *telling* of tragic stories."[32] This storytelling method is also widely adopted by various black, Native American, and feminist theologies.

One of the results of storytelling as a theological method is contextualization. Storytelling makes liberation theologies concrete, rooted in real life experiences, and historical. Through stories, narrators acknowledge their inescapable social, political, and economic location and implicitly affirm the validity of their experience. By the same token, in recognizing the contextuality of their own theologies, liberation theologians also carry out, at least indirectly, an ideology critique insofar as they reject the claims to universality of the dominant or official theology and show that it too is inescapably located in a particular social, political, and economic context. On the other hand, storytelling helps liberation theologians bridge the gap inhibiting communication among people of diverse cultures because stories create a communal fund from which liberation theologians can draw inspiration for their reflection. In this way storytelling contributes to building up a kind of concrete universality out of particular stories and histories from below, as it were, rather than the kind of abstract universality and normativity that the dominant theology attempts to impose on others from above.

---

[30] Song himself is a highly skillful practitioner of story theology. For his reflections on stories as part of the theological method, see his ten theses in *Tell Us Our Names: Story Theology from an Asian Perspective* (Maryknoll, N.Y.: Orbis Books, 1984), 3-24, and "Five Stages toward Christian Theology in the Multicultural World," in *Journeys at the Margin: Toward an Autobiographical Theology in American-Asian Perspective*, ed. Peter C. Phan and Jung Young Lee (Collegeville, Minn.: Liturgical Press, 1999), 1-21. For Song's own theological works, see, in particular, *Third-Eye Theology: Theology in Formation in Asian Settings* (Maryknoll, N.Y.: Orbis Books, 1979; rev. ed. 1990); *The Compassionate God* (Maryknoll, N.Y.: Orbis Books, 1982); *Theology from the Womb of Asia* (Maryknoll, N.Y.: Orbis Books, 1986); his christological trilogy entitled *The Cross in the Lotus World,* which comprises *Jesus, the Crucified People* (New York: Crossroad, 1990); *Jesus and the Reign of God* (Minneapolis: Fortress Press, 1994); and *Jesus in the Power of the Holy Spirit* (Minneapolis: Fortress Press, 1994).

[31] On *minjung* theology, see Jung Young Lee, *An Emerging Theology in World Perspective: Commentary on Korean Minjung Theology* (Mystic, Conn.: Twenty-Third Publications, 1988); Andrew Sung Park, *The Wounded Heart of God* (Nashville, Tenn.: Abingdon, 1993); and Young-Chan Ro, "Revisioning *Minjung* Theology: The Method of the *Minjung*," in Thistlethwaite and Engel, *Lift Every Voice*, 40-52.

[32] Ro, "Revisioning *Minjung*," 49. According to Ro, *minjung* theology is "*mythos-* not *logos*-oriented theology. . . . [The] narrative element is understood to be essential to *minjung* theology, because *han* must be told, heard, touched, felt, and resolved. *A tragedy is not a tragedy until it is told*" (50).

"DO YOU UNDERSTAND WHAT YOU ARE READING?" (ACTS 8:30):
THE HERMENEUTICAL MEDIATION

Out of this abundance and variety of grist, how can one bake a single loaf of bread? Or to vary the metaphor, out of so many notes, how can liberation theologies avoid being a cacophony and instead produce a harmonious chorus? More fundamentally, how should these sources be used to construct a *Christian* theology of liberation? Like the eunuch who was asked by Philip, "Do you understand what you are reading?" readers of these sources may be forced to reply: "How can I, unless someone guides me?" (Acts 8:31). In other words, the next issue to be considered is the hermeneutical mediation of liberation theology: How should one interpret these various sources in such a way that they acquire what Clodovis Boff calls "theological pertinency"?[33] More specifically, how should liberation theologians correlate them with the Christian sources, namely, the Bible and tradition? After all, liberation theology is, as Gutiérrez has said, "a critical reflection on Christian praxis *in the light of the Word.*"[34]

The Hermeneutical Circle and Ideology Critique

One of the key elements of liberation theologians' interpretation of the Bible and tradition is the "hermeneutical circle." Juan Luis Segundo, an Uruguayan Jesuit who has written extensively on hermeneutics, describes it as "the continuing change in our interpretation of the Bible which is dictated by the continuing changes in our present-day reality, both individual and societal. . . . Each new reality obliges us to interpret the word of God afresh, to change reality accordingly, and then to go back and reinterpret the word of God again, and so on."[35] Segundo specifies further that the hermeneutical circle contains four steps:

> *Firstly* there is our way of experiencing reality, which leads us to ideological suspicion. *Secondly* there is application of our ideological suspicion to the whole ideological superstructure in general and to theology in particular. *Thirdly* there comes a new way of experiencing theological reality that leads us to exegetical suspicion, that is, to the suspicion that the prevailing interpretation of the Bible has not taken important pieces of data into account. *Fourthly* we have our new hermeneutic, that is, our new way of interpreting the fountainhead of our faith (i.e., Scripture) with the new elements at our disposal.[36]

---

[33] Clodovis Boff, *Theology and Praxis*, 67.
[34] Gutiérrez, *A Theology of Liberation*, 11, emphasis added.
[35] Segundo, *The Liberation of Theology*, 8.
[36] Ibid., 9.

Most liberation theologians adopt the hermeneutical circle, especially its ideology critique, in their interpretation of the Bible.[37] Thus, feminist theologians have unmasked the patriarchy and androcentrism hidden in Christianity;[38] Asian liberation theologians insist on reading the Bible in the postcolonialist context;[39] and black theology reveals racial motifs in the Bible.[40] Furthermore, liberation theologians often promote the interpretation of the Bible by the poor themselves, who learn how to question the teachings of the Bible from the perspective of their oppression.[41]

There is, however, another question that still needs clarification; namely, how to bring the various sources we have enumerated above into dialogue with the Bible so that what results from this correlation of the two sources—social theories, the teachings and practices of non-Christian religions, and stories of the underside of history on the one hand, and the Christian scriptures on the other—becomes Christian liberation *theology* and not just religious discourse, philosophy of religion, or the human sciences of religion.

The Hermeneutical Mediation

In answering this question Clodovis Boff's reflections on the second mediation of liberation theology—the hermeneutic mediation—are helpful. Drawing

---

[37] For general expositions of biblical exegesis in liberation theology, see Norman K. Gottwald, *The Tribes of Yahweh: A Sociology of the Religion of Liberated Israel, 1250-1050 B.C.E* (Maryknoll, N.Y.: Orbis Books, 1979); Norman K. Gottwald, *The Bible and Liberation: Political and Social Hermeneutics* (Maryknoll, N.Y.: Orbis Books, 1983); Fernando Belo, *A Materialist Reading of the Gospel of Mark*, trans. Matthew O'Connell (Maryknoll, N.Y.: Orbis Books, 1981); Michel Clévenot, *Materialist Approaches to the Bible*, trans. William J. Nottingham (Maryknoll, N.Y.: Orbis Books, 1985); J. Severino Croatto, *Biblical Hermeneutics: Toward a Theory of Reading as the Production of Meaning*, trans. Robert Barr (Maryknoll, N.Y.: Orbis Books, 1987); R. S. Sugirtharajah, *Voices from the Margin: Interpreting the Bible in the Third World* (Maryknoll, N.Y.: Orbis Books, 1991).

[38] For white feminists, see the works of Elisabeth Schüssler Fiorenza, Rosemary Radford Ruether, and Elizabeth Johnson. For Latina feminists, see the works of Elsa Tamez, Ada María Isasi-Díaz, and María Pilar Aquino. For Asian feminists, see the works of Chung Hyun Kyung and Kwok Pui-lan. For womanists, see the works of Diana L. Hayes, M. Shawn Copeland, Toinette M. Eugene, and Jamie Phelps. For a general evaluation of feminist hermeneutics in relation to liberation theology, see Sharon H. Ringe, "Reading from Context to Context: Contributions of a Feminist Hermeneutic to Theologies of Liberation," in Thistlethwaite and Engel, *Lift Every Voice*, 289-97.

[39] See R. S. Sugirtharajah, *Asian Biblical Hermeneutics and Postcolonialism: Contesting the Interpretations* (Maryknoll, N.Y.: Orbis Books, 1998).

[40] See Cain Hope Felder, *Troubling Biblical Waters: Race, Class, and Family* (Maryknoll, N.Y.: Orbis Books, 1980). Susan Brooks Thistlethwaite and Mary Potter Engel summarize ideology critique by liberation theologians: "All liberation theologians agree on one basic principle for the use of any source: suspicion. All sources, whether Marxist analyses, ancient Christian texts, the scriptures, or 'classic' literature, must be used critically and approached with the suspicion that they further the dominant mode of oppression" (*Lift Every Voice*, 11).

[41] The most famous collection of these interpretations is Ernesto Cardenal, *The Gospel in Solentiname*, 4 vols. (Maryknoll, N.Y.: Orbis Books, 1982).

on Louis Althusser's explanation of the process of theoretical practice, Boff suggests that the production of knowledge is composed of three moments.[42] First, a science as a production of knowledge begins not with real or concrete things but with general, abstract, and ideological notions that it encounters in a given culture and that it uses as its raw material (its "first generality"). The second moment of the theoretical practice, the "second generality," is the "working" on these data to produce a body or determinate system of concepts that determines a specific type of science. Out of this "working" on the first generality emerges a thought-product, a specific, concrete, scientific theory, the "third generality." To put it concisely, *"Theoretical practice produces third generalities by the operation of a second generality upon a first generality."*[43]

Theology, insofar as it is a "science" or theoretical practice, follows this three-step production: "Theological practice comprises a first generality—its 'subject,' or material object—a second generality, which is the body of its asymptotic or analogical concepts, and finally a third generality, the theological theory produced."[44] Anything whatsoever can be theology's first generality; there is nothing, including every source that has been mentioned in the first part of this chapter, that cannot be the raw material or subject matter of theology. But it becomes theology only if it is "worked on" in the second generality "in the light of revelation," what St. Thomas calls the "formal object" (the *objectum quo*, the *ratio secundum quam*, the *ratio qua*) of theology, that is, faith, to produce a body of theological knowledge or science.

As far as liberation theology is concerned, according to Clodovis Boff, its first generality is constituted by social theories (the third generality of the social sciences) as well as, it may be added, by other religious and cultural data such as those mentioned above. In its second generality liberation theology "works" on this first generality by means of theological concepts derived from the Bible and tradition through an adequate hermeneutics (the third generality of classical theologies, which Boff calls "first theology"). What results from this operation on the first generality constitutes liberation theology.

To give an example: In order to arrive at an understanding of what *liberation* means, liberation theologians must start not from the Bible or tradition but from the data of oppression and liberation as the social sciences understand them. These sociological concepts form the first generality of their theological science. The theologian does not work *with* but *upon* the concept of "liberation" derived from sociological studies. In this way the social sciences as well as other human sciences form an intrinsic and constitutive and not an adventitious

---

[42] Louis Althusser's works available in English include *Essays in Self-Criticism* (Atlantic Highlands, N.J.: Humanities Press, 1976); *Lenin and Philosophy and Other Essays* (New York and London: Monthly Review Press, 1971); *Politics and History: Montesquieu, Rousseau, Hegel, Marx* (New York: Schocken, 1978); *Reading Capital* (New York: Schocken, 1979); and *For Marx* (New York: Schocken, 1979). For Althusser's presentation of the process of theoretical practice, see, in particular, *For Marx*, chap. 4, no. 3; *Reading Capital*, 40-43; and *Lenin and Philosophy*, 60-63.

[43] Clodovis Boff, *Theology and Praxis*, 72.

[44] Ibid., 73.

part of theology. The theologian's task is to transform, with the help of the properly theological concept of "salvation" (the third generality of "first theology" now functioning as the second generality of liberation theology), the sociological concept of "liberation" (the third generality of sociology now functioning as the first generality of liberation theology) in such a way as to produce a theological theory that "liberation is salvation" (the third generality of liberation theology).[45]

Central to this theological practice to produce a liberation theology is clearly the second generality, that is, the "working" on the first generality of liberation theology that is constituted by the third generality of the social and other human sciences. In other words, it is the hermeneutical mediation between the social sciences and other sciences and the Bible and the Christian tradition, between our present social location and the past Christian writings. Here we come back to the hermeneutical circle spoken of above. Clodovis Boff draws our attention to the dialectical circularity between scripture as written text and word of God as scripture read in the church, between the creation of meaning and the acceptance of meaning, between structure as vehicle of communication and meaning as needing structure for support, and between hermeneutics as employment of technical apparatus of interpretation and hermeneutics as a creative reading.[46]

As to the process of correlating the scripture to our social location, Clodovis Boff warns us against two unacceptable common practices: the "gospel/politics model" and the "correspondence of terms model." The former sees the gospel as a code of norms to be applied to the present situation. Such application is carried out in a mechanical, automatic, and nondialectical manner; it completely ignores the differences in the historical contexts of each of the two terms of the relationship.

The latter sets up two ratios that it regards as mutually equivalent and transfers the sense of the first ratio to the second by a sort of hermeneutical switch. For instance, an attempt is made to establish an equivalency between the ratio of the first pair of terms and that of the second pair of terms:

scripture/its political context = theology of the political/our political context
exodus/enslavement of the Hebrews = liberation/oppression of the poor
Babylon/Israel = captivity/people of Latin America
Jesus/his political context = Christian community/current political context

Although better than the gospel/politics model insofar as it takes into account the historical context of each situation, the correspondence of terms model is still unacceptable because it assumes a perfect parallel between the first ratio and the second.

[45] Ibid., 87-88.
[46] Ibid., 135-39.

The Correspondence of Relationships Model

In contrast to these two models, Clodovis Boff proposes a "correspondence of relationships model," which he claims is in conformity with the practice of the early church and the Christian communities in general. In schematic form this model looks as follows:

$$\frac{\text{Jesus of Nazareth}}{\text{his context}} = \frac{\text{Christ + the church}}{\text{context of church}} = \frac{\text{church tradition}}{\text{historical context}} = \frac{\text{ourselves}}{\text{our context}}$$

reduced schema: $$\frac{\text{scripture}}{\text{its context}} = \frac{\text{ourselves}}{\text{our context}}$$

In this model the Christian communities (represented by the church, church tradition, and ourselves) seek to apply the gospel to their particular situations. But contrary to the other two models, this model takes both the Bible and the situation to which the Bible is applied in their respective autonomy. It does not identify Jesus with the church, church tradition, and ourselves on the one hand, nor does it identify Jesus' context with the context of the church, the historical context of church tradition, and our context on the other. The equal sign does not refer to the equivalency among the terms of the hermeneutical equation but to the equality among the respective relationships between pairs of terms. As Boff puts it:

> The equal sign refers neither to the oral, nor the textual, nor to the trans-
> mitted words of the message, nor even to the situations that correspond to
> them. It refers to the relationship between them. We are dealing with a
> *relationship of relationships.* An identity of senses, then, is not to be sought
> on the level of context, nor, consequently, on the level of the message as
> such—but rather on the level of the *relationship* between context and
> message on each side [scripture and ourselves in the reduced schema]
> respectively.[47]

This focus on the relationship between the terms of each pair and the equiva-lency among these relationships rather than on a particular text of the scripture to be applied allows both creative freedom in biblical interpretation (not "herme-neutic positivism") and basic continuity with the meaning of the Bible (not "improvisation *ad libitum*"): "The Christian writings offer us not a *what*, but a *how*—a manner, a style, a spirit."[48]

---

[47] Ibid., 149. This by no means implies that liberation theologians will not appeal to specific texts or books of the Bible. On the contrary, as the Boff brothers have pointed out, certain biblical books are favored by liberation theologians, such as Exodus, the Prophets, the Gospels, the Acts of the Apostles, and Revelation. See Boff and Boff, *Introducing Liberation Theology*, 34-35.

[48] Clodovis Boff, *Theology and Praxis*, 149.

One of the merits of Clodovis Boff's correspondence of relationships model of the hermeneutical mediation is that it safeguards the exegesis of liberation theologians from the dangers of biblicism, fundamentalism, and eisegesis to which some of their early works were prone. In this respect his hermeneutics would command wholehearted agreement from most liberation theologians. On the other hand, some recent liberation theologians would contest his granting primacy to the scripture as the norm according to which later interpretations are to be measured. Though he maintains that any genuine hermeneutical relationship ("dialectical hermeneutic") involves circularity, Boff believes that "this circularity functions within an *articulation with a dominant term*. The thrust of the dialectic-hermeneutic movement comes from *scripture* and is measured, in the last instance, upon scripture as *norma normans*."[49] In contrast to Boff, liberation theologians from a multi-religious context in which classics of other religions are widely read tend to deny the normativity of the Christian scriptures. For example, Kwok Pui-lan explicitly rejects the sacrality of the Bible, its status as canonical writing, and its normativity; she proposes a "dialogical model of interpretation" in which the Bible is seen as a "talking book" inviting dialogue and conversation.[50] R. S. Sugirtharajah calls for a "multi-faith hermeneutics" in which the sacred books of all religions are allowed to be unique and speak on their own terms; in which Christians do not claim that their story is superior to and more valid than other stories; and in which the universal Wisdom tradition is retrieved.[51] Furthermore, whereas Juan Luis Segundo and Clodovis Boff do not turn the hermeneutics of suspicion on to the Bible itself, many liberation theologians, especially feminists, have exposed the patriarchal and androcentric bias of the Hebrew-Christian sacred text.

Despite these important differences in their hermeneutical practice, all liberation theologians concur that the task of the interpreter is not only to uncover the objective meaning of the text and to solve the riddles of scholarship. Rather, the main goal of hermeneutics is to transform the unjust world, to take an "advocacy stance" (Elisabeth Schüssler Fiorenza) in favor of the poor and the oppressed, to enact the word of God in their context. In other words, essential to their theological method is *praxis*, which is the third mediation of the method of liberation theology.

"DOING THE TRUTH" (JOHN 3:21): THE PRACTICAL MEDIATION

All liberation theologians insist that prior to doing liberation theology one must "do" liberation: "The first step for liberation theology is pre-theological. It is a matter of trying to live the commitment of faith: in our case, to participate in some way in the process of liberation, to be committed to the oppressed. . . .

---

[49] Ibid., 149-50.

[50] See Kwok Pui-lan, *Discovering the Bible in the Non-Biblical World* (Maryknoll, N.Y.: Orbis Books, 1995).

[51] See R. S. Sugirtharajah, "Inter-Faith Hermeneutics: An Example and Some Implications," in Sugirtharajah, *Voices from the Margins*, 352-63.

The essential point is this: links with specific practice are *at the root* of liberation theology. It operates within the great dialectic of theory (faith) and practice (love)."[52]

The Theologian's Social Commitment

The Boff brothers suggest that there are three levels in which theologians can commit themselves to the poor and oppressed. The first, rather restricted, is sporadic or more or less regular participation in base communities and their activities; the second is alternating periods of scholarly work with periods of practical work; and the third is living and working permanently in solidarity with and among the people.[53] Which of these forms of social commitment is proper for an individual liberation theologian cannot be determined in advance. A choice of one or the other at a particular historical moment depends, as Clodovis Boff has shown, on the dialectical interplay among three factors or circles, namely, the relation between the social situation (society) and the personal position of the theologian (individual), the relation between analysis (sociology) and ethics (gospel), and the relation between the theologian as theoretician and the theologian as social agent.[54]

Of course, such a practical commitment does not of itself guarantee the truth of the liberation theologian's theoretical practice, because there is a difference between the epistemic locus and the social locus: in the former, the theologian acts as the epistemic agent and is related internally to the theological discipline through objective cognition, whereas in the latter, the theologian acts as the social agent and is related externally to the society through power. Nevertheless, through his or her social commitment the theologian acquires a "sensibility" or a heightened capacity to discern the relevance of the imperatives of the historical situation and is enabled to decide which thematic problem is of objective relevance or significance with respect to a given socio-historical conjuncture. In addition to this sensibility the capacity for critical analysis to examine and establish in a rigorous manner the relevance of the theological problematic to a particular historical situation is required.

Objections have been raised to the liberation theologian's social commitment in the name of the disinterested nature of science and knowledge ("knowledge for knowledge's sake"). It is argued that science *qua* science is no more revolutionary or reactionary than it is religious or atheistic. To obviate these objections, liberation theologians have pointed out that, insofar as it is a science,

---

[52] Boff and Boff, *Introducing Liberation Theology*, 22. For a balanced reflection on the relationship between orthopraxis and theological work, see Verkamp, "On Doing the Truth," 3-24.

[53] See Boff and Boff, *Introducing Liberation Theology*, 23. These three models of the liberation theologian's social commitment whereby a synthesis of theology and politics, theoretical practice and political practice, science and justice is achieved, are termed by Clodovis Boff as the "specific contribution," "alternating moments," and "incarnation" models respectively. See Clodovis Boff, *Theology and Praxis*, 168-71.

[54] See Clodovis Boff, *Theology and Praxis*, 171-73.

that is, from an epistemological point of view, theology is a disinterested cognition. However, insofar as it is a social positivity, that is, in virtue of its factual insertion into the fabric of social interests, theology is not an innocent, neutral, apolitical function but is a partisan and interested social instrument. As with any science, theology has to pass judgment on how it is to be employed, who is to employ it and for what purposes, who are to be its addressees, and so on, questions that cannot be answered in the epistemological order but only in the practical order. As Clodovis Boff puts it:

> All knowledge, including theological knowledge, is interested. It objectively intends precise finalities. It is finalized, mediately or immediately, by something external to itself. The true problem, consequently, does not reside in the alternative: interested or disinterested theology. The true problem lies in questions of this kind: What are the objective interests of a given theology? For what concrete causes is it being developed? In a word, *where* are its interests?[55]

Finally, there is no straight, logical path from theory to praxis or from praxis to theory. Since theory is constituted through a breach with praxis and since praxis is performed through a breach with theory, the passage from one pole to the other is not a necessary consequence but is always a human decision. It follows then, as Clodovis Boff argues, "that no theory, be it ever so rigorous or profound, will ever of itself engender praxis. The same holds for the inverse calculation: no praxis, be it as radical as you please, will ever, just on that account, issue in a theory. . . . Thus theory and praxis represent irreducible orders."[56]

Praxis as Criterion of Truth

In addition to the requirement of social commitment or praxis as part of their theological method, liberation theologians also maintain that there is an indissoluble link between orthodoxy and orthopraxis. Priority is given to orthopraxis. Sometimes this primacy of praxis over theory is expressed by saying that praxis is the criterion of truth.

Many liberation theologians are aware of the ambiguity of this statement. Gustavo Gutiérrez explicitly distances himself from the position.[57] For him, theology being "critical reflection on praxis in the light of the Word," the ultimate criteria of truth "come from revealed truth which we accept in faith and not from praxis itself."[58]

To prevent misunderstandings of this principle, Clodovis Boff makes a careful distinction between "theological criteriology" and "pistic criteriology." By

---

[55] Ibid., 191.
[56] Ibid., 193.
[57] Gutiérrez, *The Truth Shall Make You Free*, 181 n. 45.
[58] Ibid., 101.

the former he means criteria of truth for theology as a theoretical practice ("truth of theory"), and by the latter he means those of faith and love ("truth of praxis"). The former criteria are of an epistemological order and concern the theoretical practice of the theologian, whereas the latter are of an existential order and concern the concrete practice of the believer. In light of this distinction Clodovis Boff argues that "from the viewpoint of theological practice, (political) praxis neither is nor can be the criterion of (theological) truth. . . . The thesis that praxis is the criterion of truth is theologically nonpertinent. It seeks to compare the incomparable."[59] For theology as a theoretical practice there are only two criteria of truth, one of the logical order and the other of the positive order. The former controls the internal coherence of the theological production, and the latter its external agreement with the positivity of faith (what the Christian community believes). With regard to pistic criteriology, Boff notes that liberation theology often refers to the capacity of faith for social transformation. While acknowledging such a capacity, Boff warns against the acritical criterion of pragmatism with the primacy given to practical effectiveness and stresses the necessity of critically evaluating the ethical quality of a course of political action through the socio-analytic and hermeneutical mediations: "We may not embrace the ideology of orthopraxy, or praxiology, dispensing ourselves from a thorough reflection on the ethical content of a given practice and from a critique of the idea of efficacity and the 'theoretical short-circuit' that it tends to provoke."[60]

While maintaining the difference between theological criteriology and pistic criteriology, Boff reminds us that theology is dependent upon the practice of justice and love, as demonstrated by the social position of theology, its thematic relevance, and its political interests, which we have discussed above. Accordingly, says Boff, "pistic truth—a truth of praxis—and theological truth—a truth of theory—call for each other, and interact upon each other. And they do so in a rhythm that is not purely linear, but is ultimately measured by the basic 'scansion' or yardstick of the reality of faith. For the dialectical balance always leans toward the practical dimension."[61]

The Dialectic between Theory and Praxis

The final issue in the practical mediation of the method of liberation theology is the nature of the relationship between theory and praxis and its implications for the character of liberation theology itself. This relationship has been described as dialectical. By this is meant that the relationship is not a static but a dynamic one, so that theory and praxis are related to each other in perpetual motion. Because theory and praxis are bound up with each other in mutual inclusion

---

[59] Clodovis Boff, *Theology and Praxis*, 198.
[60] Ibid., 203. Boff further reminds us that the final and definitive verification of the truth of faith and the practice of justice does not occur until the eschaton and is the exclusive prerogative of God.
[61] Ibid., 205.

(perichoresis), and because they are distinguished from each other in difference *(chorismos)* at the same time, there is between them a ceaseless oscillation, a "dialectical movement," so that a total theological synthesis based on this kind of relationship between theory and praxis is never possible but always *in via*, under construction.[62] Consequently, liberation theologies are by necessity anti-dogmatic and "open and continually renewing."[63]

With respect to liberation theologies in particular, this dialectical drive in perpetual motion occurs first of all, as we have seen, between the two mediations—socio-analytic and hermeneutical—in the theoretical practice of theology in such a way that the pendulum of cognition never comes to a dead stop. But it occurs also at the more general level of the history in which theory and praxis are practiced. At this second level praxis holds an analytical primacy over theory, even though theory holds the key to the identity of praxis. This relationship, notes Clodovis Boff, "must be represented as a current receiving its first thrust from the side of praxis, ricocheting off theory, and returning to praxis and dislocating it—and so on, over and over again."[64] In other words, praxis exerts pressure on theory to examine itself critically; theory, in turn, reacting, modifies praxis; then theory and praxis are transcended; and the spiraling never-ending circular movement goes on and on.

"NEW WINE INTO FRESH WINESKINS" (MATTHEW 9:17):
A NEW THEOLOGY IN A NEW METHOD?

The theology of liberation, as has been said at the beginning of this chapter, seeks to be a "new way of doing theology." Of course, the contents of liberation theologies are new, at least if one goes by some of the names under which they are advocated: womanist, *mujerista, minjung,* and queer (gay and lesbian) theologies. A couple of decades ago these appellations were not even mentioned in theological encyclopedias. But what makes liberation theologies new and for some a threat is ultimately their method. As Juan Luis Segundo stated in 1974 in his lectures at Harvard: "It is the fact that the one and only thing that can maintain the liberative character of any theology is not its content but its methodology. It is the latter that guarantees the continuing bite of theology."[65]

Of course, it is not possible to describe with historical precision what came first in liberation theology, method or content. The question resembles the proverbial query about the chicken and the egg. Most likely, content and method occur simultaneously, though it often happens that reflections on method are undertaken only after a long practice at the craft or when the discipline is undergoing a

---

[62] For a description of *perichoresis* and *chorismos* between theory and praxis, see ibid., 210-213.

[63] Susan Brooks Thistlethwaite and Mary Potter Engel, "Making the Connections among Liberation Theologies around the World," in Thistlethwaite and Engel, *Lift Every Voice*, 11: "Theologies that are contextual, *praxis*-based, communal, and prophetic are theologies that are bound to remain open to change and ongoing revision."

[64] Clodovis Boff, *Theology and Praxis*, 216.

[65] Segundo, *The Liberation of Theology*, 39-40.

crisis or a paradigmatic shift. At any rate, the mutual dependence between content and method is picturesquely affirmed by Jesus when he says "neither is new wine put into old wineskins; otherwise, the skins burst, and the wine is spilled, and the skins are destroyed; but new wine is put into fresh wineskins, and so both are preserved" (Mt 9:17).

This is not the place to offer an extensive evaluation of the method of the theology of liberation with its three mediations—socio-analytic, hermeneutical, and practical. This chapter's principal intent has been to discern in the rich and even bewildering tapestry of liberation theologies the common thread that binds them together. That unifying thread is methodological. It is useful to enumerate in thesis form the ways in which the method as it has been described above can obviate some of the oft-repeated charges against liberation theology.

1. It is not accurate to say that various kinds of liberation theology that have been formulated after the emergence of Latin American liberation theology in the early 1970s are nothing but clones of it. Methodologically, for example, Asian liberation theology, though indebted to its Latin American older sibling, has introduced new methods of theologizing (for example, psychological tools of introspection, interreligious dialogue, inculturation, and storytelling) that make it quite distinctive. Furthermore, more recent liberation theologies have brought to the theological mill a variety of materials from their own specific social, cultural, and religious backgrounds.

2. It is not accurate to say that liberation theologies are fundamentally inspired by Marxism or are simply theological versions of the Marxist theory of class struggle. It is true that liberation theologies have made use of the sociological theory of dependence and Marxist tools of social analysis, but these concepts and theories (the "third generality" of the social sciences) are adopted as the "first generality" of liberation theology and are "worked" on in its "second generality"in the hermeneutical mediation by means of the theological concepts of "first theology" to produce a body of genuinely theological science (the "third generality" of liberation theology) .

3. It is not accurate to say that liberation theologies are biblically naive or are susceptible to biblical fundamentalism. The correspondence of relationships model is far more sophisticated than the gospel/politics and correspondence of terms models that are often thought to be the hermeneutical approaches of liberation theologies. This model avoids the Scylla of hermeneutic positivism of biblical fundamentalism and the Charybdis of *ad libitum* improvisation of postmodernism. On the contrary, it enables both creative freedom in biblical interpretation and basic fidelity to the meanings of the scripture and tradition.

4. It is not accurate to say that liberation theologians, with their requisite social commitment, abandon or at least jeopardize the objectivity and disinterestedness of theology as a pursuit of knowledge. Liberation theologians do recognize that theology, insofar as it is a theoretical practice, is a disinterested cognition and is no more revolutionary or reactionary than any other science. On the other hand, because theology is a social fact and because the theologian is not only a theoretician but also a social agent, theology is never neutral; the theologian is never socially uncommitted. The question is not whether theology

is neutral or the theologian is uncommitted but to *which* cause theology is partisan and the theologian engaged. Such a social commitment gives the theologian a "sensibility"whereby he or she can determine which theological problematic is required by a particular historical situation to which theology must be "relevant."

5. Finally, it is not accurate to say that liberation theologies lapse into epistemological empiricism and ethical pragmatism when they grant priority to orthopraxis over orthodoxy and make praxis into the criterion of truth. With a careful distinction between theological criteriology and pistic criteriology, liberation theologies recognize the difference between criteria of truth for theology as a theoretical practice (logical consistency and conformity to the contents of the faith) and the criterion of truth for faith as a political practice (the capacity of faith for social transformation). On the other hand, while maintaining this necessary distinction, liberation theologies are able to affirm the dialectical relationship between theory and praxis, both in the theoretical practice of theology (between the socio-analytic and hermeneutical mediations) and in their actual unfolding in history, so that the character of liberation theologies as a fundamentally open, ever-developing science can also be affirmed.

While the foregoing five remarks, and of course the entire chapter, may be construed as an apologia for liberation theology and its method, the main intention is to show that liberation theologians, despite their diversity of gender and economic background, national and ethnic origin, cultural and religious membership, are, by virtue of their shared method and tasks, fellow travelers in a common journey to the same destination. The temptation to dismiss liberation theology as passé must be resisted, especially in view of the moribund condition of socialism and the near-universal domination of the free-market system. On the contrary, thanks to the virtualities of its own method, liberation theology will be able to contribute to the emergence of a new kind of catholicity that is not a pretension to a false universalism but appreciates and promotes the particularity of each voice, especially the voices of those who have not been allowed to speak, and in and through these particular voices constructs a new harmony for the coming reign of God.

3

Inculturation of the Christian Faith in Asia through Philosophy

A DIALOGUE WITH JOHN PAUL II'S *FIDES ET RATIO*

Before his election to the see of Rome, Karol Wojtyla was already a celebrated philosopher in his own right, especially in the field of ethics, with widely recognized expertise in Thomism and phenomenology.[1] As pope, John Paul II has continued to demonstrate a deep concern, already pronounced in his philosophical writings, for the unity of human knowledge that is born out of the harmonious marriage between faith and reason. This concern is especially evident in the pope's encyclicals on Christian ethics, in which he insists both on the autonomy of human reason and on the necessity of divine revelation and urges a close collaboration between these two epistemological orders for a full knowledge of ethical truths.[2] However, the encyclical in which the unity of faith and reason constitutes the central focus of John Paul II's reflections is *Fides et*

---

[1] Wojtyla's best-known philosophical work, though generally regarded as highly abstract and abstruse, is *Osoba i Czyn* (Kraków: Polskie Towarzystwo Teologiczne, 1969). Its English translation by Anna-Teresa Tymieniecka, which bears the title *The Acting Person* (Dordrecht: Reidel, 1979), has been judged unreliable and criticized for having excessively phenomenologized Wojtyla's language and thought. A collection of Wojtyla's philosophical essays is available as *Person and Community: Selected Essays*, trans. Theresa Sandok (New York: Peter Lang, 1993).

For helpful comprehensive introductions in English to John Paul II's thought, see George H. Williams, *The Mind of John Paul II: Origins of His Thought and Action* (New York: Seabury, 1981); Ronald Lawler, *The Christian Personalism of Pope John Paul II* (Chicago: Franciscan Herald Press, 1982); Andrew Woznicki, *A Christian Humanism: Karol Wojtyla's Existential Personalism* (New Britain, Conn.: Mariel, 1980); Rocco Buttiglione, *Karol Wojtyla: The Thought of the Man Who Became Pope John Paul II*, trans. Paolo Guietti and Francesca Murphy (Grand Rapids, Mich.: Eerdmans, 1997); and Kenneth Schmitz, *At the Center of the Human Drama: The Philosophical Anthropology of Karol Wojtyla/Pope John Paul II* (Washington, D.C.: The Catholic University Press, 1993).

[2] See his encyclicals *Veritatis Splendor* (6 August 1993) and *Evangelium Vitae* (25 March 1995). English translations of these encyclicals are available in Pope John Paul II, *The Encyclicals of John Paul II*, ed. Michael Miller (Huntington, Ind.: Our Sunday Visitor, 1996), 674-771, 792-894.

Ratio, whose title itself, with the *et* (and) rather than the *aut* (or), is emblematic of the pope's fundamental stance in this matter.[3]

This chapter carries out a critical dialogue with John Paul II's teaching on the relationship between faith and reason as expressed in *FR*, especially with respect to the use of philosophy as a tool for the inculturation of the Christian faith in Asia.[4] The first part expounds the pope's view of the relation between faith and reason; the second part evaluates his proposal to use philosophy as an instrument for inculturating the Christian faith in Asia. The concluding part assesses the usefulness of this proposal with regard to some aspects of Confucianism.

FAITH AND REASON ACCORDING TO *FIDES ET RATIO*

The basic theme of *FR* is beautifully expressed in its opening lines with a metaphor depicting faith and reason as "two wings on which the human spirit rises to the contemplation of truth," by which, says John Paul II, the human heart fulfills its God-given "desire to know the truth." Before examining how *FR* understands the relation between faith and reason, it is helpful to delineate the context in which this relation is broached.[5]

Overview of the Encyclical

The encyclical begins with a preamble (nos. 1-6), titled with the Socratic injunction "Know Yourself," on the role of philosophy in asking about and

---

[3] For the English translation of *Fides et Ratio*, which was promulgated on 14 September 1998, see *Origins* 28/19 (22 October 1998): 318-47. The encyclical is cited hereafter as *FR*, followed by the article number in parentheses.

[4] I have already examined *FR* in relation to Asian philosophies in "*Fides et Ratio* and Asian Philosophies: Sharing the Banquet of Truth," *Science et Esprit* 51/3 (1999): 333-49.

[5] For studies on *FR*, see Louis-Marie Billé et al., *Foi et raison: Lectures de l'encyclique* Fides et Ratio (Paris: Cerf, 1998); Mauro Mantovani, Scaria Thuruthiyil, and Mario Toso, eds., *Fede e ragione: Opposizione, composizione?* (Rome: Libreria Ateneo Salesiano, 1998); Tomás Melendo, *Para leer la* Fides et Ratio (Madrid: Rialp, 2000); Timothy Smith, ed., *Faith and Reason: The Notre Dame Symposium*, (South Bend, Ind.: St. Augustine's Press, 2000); *Per una lettura dell'enciclica* Fides et Ratio (Vatican City: L'Osservatore Romano, 1999); Peter Henrici, "La Chiesa et la filosofia: In ascolto della 'Fides et Ratio,'" *Gregorianum* 80/4 (1999): 635-44; idem, "The One Who Went Unnamed: Maurice Blondel in the Encyclical *Fides et Ratio*," *Communio* (US) 26 (1999): 609-21; Joseph Kallarangatt, "*Fides et Ratio*: Its Timeliness and Contribution," *Christian Orient* 20 (1999): 22-39; Albert Keller, "Vernunft und Glaube," *Stimmen der Zeit* 217 (1999): 1-12; Job Kozhamthadam, "*Fides et Ratio* and Inculturation," *Vidyajyoti* 63 (1999): 848-59; Salvador Pié-Ninot, "La Encíclica *Fides et Ratio* y la Teología Fundamental: Hacia una propuesta," *Gregorianum* 80/4 (1999): 645-76; Kenneth Schmitz, "Faith and Reason: Then and Now," *Communio* (US) 26 (1999): 595-608; Angelo Scola, "Human Freedom and Truth according to the Encyclical *Fides et Ratio*," *Communio* (US) 26 (1999): 486-509; Tissa Balasuriya, "On the Papal Encyclical Faith and Reason," *Cross Currents* 49 (1999): 294-96; Avery Dulles, "Faith and Reason: A Note on the New Encyclical," *America* 179 (31 October 1998): 7-8; and Anthony Kenny, "The Pope as Philosopher," *The Tablet* 253 (26 June 1999): 874-76.

answering questions concerning the meaning of human life. It states that the church regards philosophy as "the way to come to know fundamental truths about human life" and at the same time as "an indispensable help for a deep understanding of faith and for communicating the truth of the Gospel to those who do not yet know it" (no. 5). Unfortunately, according to *FR*, contemporary philosophy "has lost the capacity to lift its gaze to the heights, not daring to rise to the truth of being," and as the result, is wallowing in agnosticism and relativism (no. 5). This lamentable situation prompts the pope to write with a twofold purpose: first, "to restore to our contemporaries a genuine trust in their capacity to know and challenge philosophy to recover and develop its own full dignity," and second, to concentrate "on the theme of truth itself and on its foundation in relation to faith" (no. 6).

The body of *FR* is composed of seven chapters, entitled successively as "The Revelation of God's Wisdom" (nos. 7-15), "*Credo ut intellegam*" (nos. 16-23), "*Intellego ut credam*" (nos. 24-35), "Relationship between Faith and Reason" (nos. 36-48), "Magisterium's Interventions in Philosophical Matters" (nos. 49-63), "Interaction between Philosophy and Theology" (nos. 64-79), and "Current Requirements and Tasks" (nos. 80-99). *FR* concludes (nos. 100-108) with appeals to philosophers, theologians, seminary professors, and scientists to "look more deeply at man, whom Christ has saved in the mystery of his love, and at the human being's unceasing search for truth and meaning" (no. 107). Just from the titles of the chapters, especially chapters 2, 3, 4, and 6, it is obvious that the central theme of the encyclical is the relationship between faith and reason, or correlatively, between theology and philosophy.

Faith and Reason: Basic Issues

The issue of the relationship between faith and reason is as old as Christianity and, arguably, as old as revelation itself.[6] Against biblical fundamentalism and fideism, it must be maintained that reason is unavoidably and inexplicably intertwined with revelation, at least in the sense that revelation, however a supernatural and gratuitous gift it may be, cannot but be received within the horizon of some particular human, even philosophical, understanding.[7] In addition to this direct implication of reason within revelation, there is a further task that believers must perform, namely, to decide reflectively, on philosophical and theological grounds, which philosophical horizon—for example, Platonic, or Aristotelian, or existential—is the most appropriate and valid (and not merely historically accepted) philosophy for an elaboration of the contents of the Christian

---

[6] Pierre d'Ornellas, auxiliary bishop of Paris, offers helpful reflections on *FR*'s concern with the unity of human knowledge in "Une préoccupation déjà ancienne pour l'unité de la connaissance," in Billé et al., *Foi et Raison*, 15-29.

[7] Awareness of this fact has profound implications for theology today, especially the discipline of historical theology, since it is the task of theology to bring about a contemporary understanding, which is itself historically conditioned, of another past understanding, which is also historically conditioned. Hence, the complex yet inevitable task of hermeneutics in theology.

faith. Finally, there are three other tasks that are incumbent upon believers in God's self-revelation in history as they address the issue of the relation between faith and reason: first, to justify *philosophically* the possibility of such a self-revelation; second, to vindicate *historically* the credibility of such a divine self-revelation if it has occurred at all; and third, and more fundamentally, to demonstrate whether this philosophical and historical foundationalism is compatible with the nature of the Christian faith, that is, whether the Christian faith would not be emptied of its specific character were it to be subjected to the tribunal of secular reason, whether historical or philosophical.[8]

In his encyclical John Paul II does not treat in any detail the above-mentioned issues, which are much debated in contemporary theology, though, of course, his answers to any of them can be inferred from his teaching on the relation between faith and reason. The pope begins on the one hand by affirming the fact of God's utterly gratuitous and supernatural self-revelation in history and

_____

[8] For recent studies of these issues, see Emerich Coreth et al., eds., *Christliche Philosophie im katholischen Denken des 19. und 20. Jahrhunderts*, 3 vols. (Graz: Styria, 1987-1990); Wolfhart Pannenberg, *Theology and the Philosophy of Science* (Philadelphia: Westminster, 1976); Helmut Peukert, *Wissenschaftstheorie, Handlungstheorie, fundamentale Theologie* (Frankfurt: Suhrkamp, 1978); Johann Baptist Metz, *Faith in History and Society: Toward a Foundational Political Theology* (New York: Seabury, 1979); Francis Schüssler Fiorenza, *Foundational Theology: Jesus and the Church* (New York: Crossroad, 1984); René Latourelle, *Finding Jesus through the Gospels* (New York: Alba House, 1979); idem, *Man and His Problem in the Light of Jesus Christ* (New York: Paulist Press, 1983); René Latourelle and Gerald O'Collins, eds., *Problems and Perspectives of Fundamental Theology* (New York: Paulist Press, 1982); David Tracy, *The Analogical Imagination: Christian Theology and the Culture of Pluralism* (New York: Crossroad, 1981); Franz-Josef Niemann, *Jesus als Glaubensgrund in der Fundamentaltheologie der Neuzeit: Zur Genealogie eines Traktats* (Innsbruck: Tyrolia-Verlag, 1983); George Lindbeck, *The Nature of Doctrine: Religion and Theology in a Postliberal Age* (Philadelphia: Westminster, 1984); Martin Cook, *The Open Circle: Confessional Method in Theology* (Minneapolis: Fortress, 1991); Avery Dulles, *The Craft of Theology: From Symbol to System* (New York: Crossroad, 1992); Thomas Guarino, *Revelation and Truth: Unity and Plurality in Contemporary Theology* (Scranton, Pa.: University of Scranton Press, 1993).

In particular on the issue of foundationalism in theology, see the helpful introduction by John E. Thiel, *Nonfoundationalism* (Minneapolis: Fortress Press, 1994) with discussions on philosophers such as Ludwig Wittgenstein, Wilfrid Sellars, Willard Van Orman Quine, and Richard Rorty, and on theologians such as Karl Barth, George Lindbeck, Ronald Thiemann, Kathryn Tanner, Hans Frei, and Stanley Hauerwas. See also a good survey by Thomas Guarino, "Postmodernity and Five Fundamental Theological Issues," *Theological Studies* 57 (1996): 654-89. For a helpful collection of essays on postmodern theology, see John Webster and George P. Schner, eds., *Theology after Liberalism* (Oxford: Blackwell, 2000). Among Roman Catholic theologians who argue for a non-foundationalist approach, besides Francis Schüssler Fiorenza, mentioned above, see Frans Josef van Beeck, *God Encountered: A Contemporary Systematic Theology*, vol. 1, *Understanding the Christian Faith* (San Francisco: Harper & Row, 1989); Nicholas Lash, *Easter in Ordinary: Reflections on Human Experience and the Knowledge of God* (Notre Dame, Ind.: University of Notre Dame Press, 1990): and James J. Buckley, *Seeking the Humanity of God: Practices, Doctrines, and Catholic Theology* (Collegeville, Minn.: Liturgical Press, 1992).

consequently rejects the rationalist critique of the possibility of such a divine self-revelation. On the other hand, he also affirms the capacity of human reason to know God. As to the relation between the knowledge of God through divine revelation and the knowledge of God through reason, John Paul II contents himself with repeating Vatican I's teaching that "the truth attained by philosophy and the truth of revelation are neither identical nor mutually exclusive" (no. 9).[9] These two "orders of knowledge," are, according to Vatican I's *Dei Filius*, distinct from each other both in their "source" and in their "object."

This double distinctness does not mean, however, that reason, though autonomous (because of its distinct source and object), can and should function apart from, much less in ignorance of, Christian faith:

> Revelation has set within history a point of reference which cannot be ignored if the mystery of human life is to be known. Yet this knowledge refers back constantly to the mystery of God, which the human mind cannot exhaust but can only receive and embrace in faith. Between these two poles, reason has its own specific field in which it can inquire and understand, restricted only by its finiteness before the infinite mystery of God (no. 14).

The basic issue to be elucidated, then, is the interplay between faith and reason. *FR* explicates this relationship in four parts. The first two (chapters 2 and 3) invoke the Augustinian-Anselmian formulas of "intellego ut credam" and "credo ut intellegam." The third (chapter 4), the heart of the encyclical, deals with the relationship between faith and reason; and the fourth (chapter 6) narrows this relation down to the "interaction between philosophy and theology."[10]

Faith in Search of Understanding: *Credo ut intellegam*

It is significant that in explicating the relationship between faith and reason *FR* begins with the "credo" rather than the "intellego." While deeply convinced that "there is a profound and indissoluble unity between the knowledge of reason and the knowledge of faith" (no. 16), John Paul II clearly and repeatedly privileges the role of faith over reason as the path to the truth: "Reason is valued without being overvalued. The results of reasoning may in fact be true, but

---

[9] On the relationship between Vatican I's *Dei Filius* and *FR*, see Mauro Mantovani, "Là dove osa la ragione. Dalla '*Dei Filius*' alla '*Fides et Ratio*,'" in Mantovani, Thuruthiyil, and Toso, *Fede e ragione*, 59-84. Mantovani points out that there is a basic continuity between the two documents in their stance on the relationship between faith and reason, though there are of course novelties in *FR*, such as its rejection of contemporary philosophical errors, its recognition of certain valuable aspects of contemporary thought, and its appreciation of Asian cultures.

[10] André-Mutien Léonard, bishop of Namur and former professor of philosophy at the University of Louvain, provides a helpful overview of *FR* in "Un guide de lecture pour l'encyclique *Fides et Ratio*," in Billé et al., *Foi et Raison*, 31-73.

these results acquire their true meaning only if they are set within the larger horizon of faith. . . . Faith liberates reason insofar as it allows reason to attain correctly what it seeks to know and to place it within the ultimate order of things in which everything acquires true meaning" (no. 20). This need of faith is, of course, caused by human sin, whereby "the eyes of the mind were no longer able to see clearly: Reason became more and more a prisoner to itself" (no. 22). This is why, says the pope, "the Christian relationship to philosophy requires thoroughgoing discernment" (no. 23). Here he invokes the Pauline opposition between "the wisdom of this world" and "the foolishness of the cross," not in order to suppress the indispensable role of reason but to affirm the necessity of faith for the discovery of truth: "The preaching of Christ crucified and risen is the reef upon which the link between faith and philosophy can break up, but it is also the reef beyond which the two can set forth upon the boundless ocean of truth. Here we see not only the border between reason and faith, but also the space where the two may meet" (no. 23).[11]

Reason in Search of Faith: *Intellego ut credam*

"Credo," however, is not to be separated from "intellego." Human life is a "journeying in search of truth." The quest for truth and understanding, says John Paul II, echoing Augustine's memorable phrase, is native to humans: "In the far reaches of the human heart there is a seed of desire and nostalgia for God" (no. 24). This quest for truth has been carried out by humans "through literature, music, painting, sculpture, architecture, and every other work of their creative intelligence," but "in a special way philosophy has made this search its own and, with its specific tools and scholarly methods, has articulated this universal human desire" (no. 24). This quest, however, is performed not only in theoretical reflection, but also in ethical decisions. Hence, the object of this quest is both truth and value.

This quest, the pope points out, often begins with questions about the meaning and direction of one's life. But the decisive moment of the search, he maintains, comes when we determine "whether or not we think it possible to attain universal and absolute truth." The pope goes on to affirm categorically: "Every truth—if it really is truth—presents itself as universal, even if it is not the whole truth. If something is true, then it must be true for all people and at all times" (no. 27). Ultimately, the pope claims, the search for truth is nothing but the search for God: "People seek an absolute which might give to all their searching a meaning and an answer—something ultimate which might serve as the ground of all things. In other words, they seek a final explanation, a supreme value, which refers to nothing beyond itself and which puts an end to all questioning" (no. 27).

---

[11] Obviously John Paul II's appeal to the Pauline contrast between the "foolishness of God" demonstrated on the cross and "human wisdom" elaborated in philosophy is no endorsement of fideism and fundamentalism.

Two further points made by *FR* concerning the "intellego ut credam" need to be mentioned. The encyclical notes that there are "different faces of human truth" or "modes of truth," or more simply, there are three ways of arriving at truth (no. 30): first, through immediate evidence or experimentation ("the mode of truth proper to everyday life and to scientific research"); second, through philosophical reflection ("philosophical truth"); and third, by means of religious traditions ("religious truths"). In addition, *FR* emphasizes the social character of the quest for truth. Though recognizing the necessity of critical inquiry, the encyclical points out that "there are in the life of a human being many more truths which are simply believed than truths which are acquired by way of personal verification" (no. 31). Hence, the necessity of entrusting oneself to the knowledge acquired by others and of bearing personal witness, even by way of martyrdom, to the truth (no. 32).

Relationship between Faith and Reason

Having affirmed the necessity of both faith and reason in the search for truth and value, *FR* moves on to discuss the ways in which their relationship has been enacted throughout Christian history (chapter 4). The purpose is not to present an exhaustive overview of how faith and reason interacted with each other in the past but to derive instructive lessons for a proper understanding of their relationship.[12] The first encounter between Christianity and philosophy took place of course in the first centuries of the Christian era. Of this phase *FR* summarizes the main features as follows: (1) The earliest Christians preferred to dialogue with philosophy rather than with the prevalent religions of their times because the latter were judged to be infected with myths and superstition, whereas the former made a serious attempt to provide a rational foundation for a belief in the divinity. (2) The first and most urgent task for the early Christians was not an intellectual engagement with philosophy for its own sake but "the proclamation of the risen Christ by way of a personal encounter which would bring the listener to conversion of heart and the request for baptism." Indeed, the gospel offered them such a satisfying answer to the hitherto unresolved question concerning the meaning of life that "delving into the philosophers seemed to them something remote and in some ways outmoded" (no. 38). (3) The early Christians were quite cautious in approaching the surrounding cultures. While deeply appreciative of their true insights, the early Christian thinkers were critical in adopting the philosophies of their times. *FR* highlights "the critical consciousness

---

[12] For studies of *FR*'s view of the relationship between faith and reason, see the following in Mantovani, Thuruthiyil, and Toso, *Fede e ragione*: Carlo Chenis, "'*Quid est veritas?*' Valore della '*ratio*' nei processi veritativi secondo la '*mens*' della Chiesa," 85-105; Aniceto Molinaro, "La metafisica e la fede," 107-18; Mario Toso, "La fede se non è pensata è nulla," 119-30; Armando Rigobello, "Il ruolo della ragione, la filosofia dell'essere, la comunicazione della verità: Luoghi speculativi per un confronto tra '*Fides et Ratio*' e pensiero contemporaneo," 131-37; Francesco Franco, "La filosofia compito della fede: La circolarità di fede e ragione," 155-75; and Rino Fisichella, "Rapporti tra teologia e filosofia alla luce di '*Fides et Ratio*,' 177-85.

with which Christian thinkers from the first confronted the problem of the relationship between faith and philosophy, viewing it comprehensively with both its positive aspects and its limitations" (no. 41). (4) The early Christian thinkers did more than perform "a meeting of cultures"; rather their originality consists in the fact that "they infused it [reason] with the richness drawn from revelation" (no. 41). *FR* summarizes its survey from the patristic era to Anselm: "The fundamental harmony between the knowledge of faith and the knowledge of philosophy is once again confirmed. Faith asks that its object be understood with the help of reason; and at the summit of its searching, reason acknowledges that it cannot do without what faith presents" (no. 42).

This harmony that exists between faith and reason was well established by Thomas Aquinas, for whom "just as grace builds on nature and brings it to fulfillment, so faith builds upon and perfects reason" (no. 43). For this reason *FR* calls Thomas "a master of thought and a model of the right way to do theology" (no. 43). Thomas is also praised for his emphasis on the role of the Holy Spirit in the process by which knowledge matures into wisdom. This gift of wisdom "comes to know by way of connaturality; it presupposes faith and eventually formulates its right judgment on the basis of the truth of faith itself" (no. 44). Thomas's granting of primacy to the gift of wisdom, however, did not make him belittle the complementary roles of two other forms of wisdom, that is, philosophical wisdom and theological wisdom.

Unfortunately, the delicate balance between faith and reason that Thomas established and maintained, according to *FR*, fell apart toward the end of the Middle Ages: "From the late medieval period onward, however, the legitimate distinction between the two forms of learning became more and more a fateful separation. As a result of the exaggerated rationalism of certain thinkers, positions grew more radical and there emerged eventually a philosophy which was separate from and absolutely independent of the contents of faith" (no. 45).

This "fateful separation" between faith and reason brought in its wake disastrous consequences, not least for reason itself. *FR* enumerates some of these: a general mistrust of reason and fideism, idealism, atheistic humanism, positivism, nihilism, the instrumentalization of reason, and pragmatic utilitarianism (nos. 46-47, 86-90). Nevertheless, John Paul II discerns even in these errors "precious and seminal insights which, if pursued and developed with mind and heart rightly tuned, can lead to the discovery of truth's way" (no. 48). These insights include "penetrating analyses of perception and experience, of the imaginary and the unconscious, of personhood and intersubjectivity, of freedom and values, of time and history" (no. 48).

Interaction between Philosophy and Theology

After its overview of the history of the relationship between faith and reason, *FR* addresses the narrower question of how philosophy (as representative of reason) should interact with theology (as representative of faith). The pope states that his purpose is not to impose a particular theological method but to reflect on some specific tasks of theology that by their nature demand a recourse to philosophy. Following the time-honored tradition, John Paul II distinguishes two functions of theology, namely, the *auditus fidei,* and the *intellectus fidei* and shows how philosophy contributes to the performance of each. With regard to the *auditus fidei*, philosophy helps theology with "its study of the structure of knowledge and personal communication, especially the various forms and functions of language" as well as its "contribution to a more coherent understanding of church tradition, the pronouncements of the magisterium and the teaching of the great masters of theology" (no. 65).

With regard to the *intellectus fidei, FR* explains the indispensable contribution of philosophy to dogmatic theology, fundamental theology, moral theology, and the study of cultures. I will postpone the discussion of the study of cultures to the next section of the chapter; here I will mention only how *FR* understands the role of philosophy in two theological disciplines. First, with regard to dogmatic theology, *FR* argues that "without philosophy's contribution, it would in fact be impossible to discuss theological issues such as, for example, the use of language to speak about God, the personal relations within the Trinity, God's creative activity in the world, the relationship between God and man, or Christ's identity as true God and true man" (no. 66). Second, with regard to fundamental theology, John Paul II argues that its task is to demonstrate the truths knowable by philosophical reason that "an acceptance of God's revelation necessarily presupposes" and to show how "revelation endows these truths with their fullest meaning, directing them toward the richness of the revealed mystery in which they find their ultimate purpose" (no. 67). These truths include, for example, "the natural knowledge of God, the possibility of distinguishing divine revelation from other phenomena or the recognition of its credibility, the capacity of human language to speak in a true and meaningful way even of things which transcend all human experience" (no. 67)

To conclude his exposition on the relationship between theology and philosophy, John Paul II uses the image of a circle with two poles.[13] On the one hand is the word of God, which is the "source and starting point" of theology; on the other is "a better understanding of it." Moving between these two poles is reason which "is offered guidance and is warned against paths which would lead it to stray from revealed truth and to stray in the end from the truth pure and simple. . . . This circular relationship with the word of God leaves philosophy enriched, because reason discovers new and unsuspected horizons" (no. 73).

PHILOSOPHY AND INCULTURATION OF THE CHRISTIAN FAITH IN ASIA

For those familiar with the Roman Catholic traditional understanding of the relationship between faith and reason, especially as mediated by Thomas Aquinas and the two Vatican councils, John Paul II's teaching offers no new or surprising insights, and rightly so, since his primary task is not to innovate but to stand

---

[13] However evocative the image, speaking of a circle with two poles is geometrically infelicitous. Perhaps it would be better to speak of an ellipse.

in continuity with the tradition.[14] Thus he continues to affirm the autonomy of reason and philosophy vis-à-vis faith and theology, as well as their necessary harmony and mutual collaboration, while at the same time categorically emphasizing the primacy of Christian revelation over philosophy as its guide and norm. Not surprisingly, to non-Catholic philosophers John Paul II seems to want to have his cake and eat it too. Whether this charge is valid or not is an open question, but the blame should not be laid at the pope's feet, since he does nothing more than restate the traditional Catholic position on the relationship between faith and reason.

This does not mean that *FR* does not contain novel accents and perspectives. For one thing, in spite of his severe critique of contemporary Western philosophy, John Paul II, as we have seen above, recognizes several of its positive achievements.[15] Moreover, his recommendation of Thomas Aquinas as the master and model for theologians is a far cry from Leo XIII's elevation of Thomas to the status of official philosopher of the Catholic church and Pius X's imposition of twenty-four theses of Thomistic philosophy to be taught in all Catholic institutions. In addition, while reiterating the importance of philosophical inquiry, John Paul has not forgotten the power of personal witness, in particular martyrdom, in convincing others of the truth of one's faith. But there is no doubt that one of the most interesting and challenging elements of John Paul II's teaching on faith and reason is his proposal to use philosophy as a tool for the inculturation of the Christian faith, especially in Asia. And to this we now turn.

John Paul II and Asian Philosophies

The relationship between the Christian faith and cultures, or to use a neologism, *inculturation,* has been a constant and deep preoccupation of John Paul II's pontificate.[16] In this section we focus on the pope's proposal of philosophy

---

[14] For a study of *FR*'s continuity with the tradition and its relative originality, see Kenneth Schmitz, "Faith and Reason: Then and Now," *Communio* (US) 26 (1999): 595-608.

[15] Of course, John Paul II is neither the first nor the only one to denounce the various errors of modern philosophy. As Anthony Kenny has pointed out, in criticizing modern philosophy he stands in the company of philosophers such as Gottlob Frege and Lugwig Wittgenstein, and it may be added, Martin Heidegger. See Anthony Kenny, "The Pope as Philosopher," *The Tablet* 253 (26 June 1999): 875. On the other hand, feminists will argue that other no less pernicious errors of modern philosophy, such as its patriarchal and androcentric bias, have not received the pope's attention.

[16] This concern is demonstrated in John Paul II's founding of the Pontifical Council for Culture in 1982 with its quarterly *Cultures and Faith*. John Paul II's writings on the theology of culture are voluminous. For a study of this aspect of John Paul II's theology, see Fernando Miguens, *Fe y Cultura en la Enseñanza de Juan Pablo II* (Madrid: Ediciones Palabra, 1994).

For helpful overviews of inculturation as a theological problem, see Marcello de C. Azevedo, "Inculturation," in *Dictionary of Fundamental Theology*, ed. René Latourelle and Rino Fisichella (New York: Crossroad, 1995), 500-510; and Hervé Carrier,

as a tool for inculturation of the Christian faith in Asia.[17] It is useful to preface
our discussion with a few remarks. First, it is important to recall that *FR*'s immediate objective is not to conduct a dialogue between the Christian faith and
Asian philosophies and religions as such but to defend the necessity of philosophy, particularly metaphysics, for theology and to heal the rift between the two
disciplines: "Metaphysics thus plays an essential role of mediation for theological research. A theology without a metaphysical horizon could not move beyond an analysis of religious experience nor would it allow the *intellectus fidei*
to give a coherent account of the universal and transcendent value of revealed
truth" (no. 83). It is within this context that John Paul II speaks of the encounter
between faith and culture. For a more complete presentation of the pope's view
on inculturation, recourse must be made to his other writings.[18]

Second, in his discussion of inculturation of the Christian faith in Asia in *FR*,
John Paul remains at a very general level. It is no disrespect to him to point out
that he is no expert in Asian philosophies and religions. Among recent thinkers
whom he mentions as exemplifying a "courageous research" into the "fruitful
relationship between philosophy and the word of God," no Asians or non-Asian
thinkers who have worked in Asia, and of course no Asian religious founders,
are named.[19] Even though *FR* mentions the Veda and the Avesta, Confucius and
Lao Tzu, Tirthankara and Buddha (no. 2), and Indian, Chinese, and Japanese
philosophies (no. 72), it is clear that John Paul II's knowledge of these is rudimentary.[20]

"Inculturation of the Gospel," ibid., 510-14. The number of general works on inculturation
has recently grown by leaps and bounds. Among the most helpful, from the Catholic
perspective, are Aylward Shorter, *Toward a Theology of Inculturation* (Maryknoll, N.Y.:
Orbis Books, 1988); Robert Schreiter, *Constructing Local Theologies* (Maryknoll, N.Y.:
Orbis Books, 1985); idem, *The New Catholicity: Theology between the Global and the
Local* (Maryknoll, N.Y.: Orbis Books, 1997); Stephen Bevans, *Models of Contextual
Theology* (Maryknoll, N.Y.: Orbis Books, 1992); Gerald Arbuckle, *Earthing the Gos-
pel: An Inculturation Handbook for the Pastoral Worker* (Maryknoll, N.Y.: Orbis Books,
1990); Michael Gallagher, *Clashing Symbols: An Introduction to Faith and Culture*
(New York: Paulist Press, 1998); Peter C. Phan, "Contemporary Theology and
Inculturation in the United States," in *The Multicultural Church: A New Landscape in
U.S. Theologies*, ed. William Cenkner (New York: Paulist Press, 1996), 109-30; 176-
92; idem, "Cultural Diversity: A Blessing or a Curse for Theology and Spirituality?"
Louvain Studies 19 (1994): 195-211.

[17] Some of the material that follows is taken from Phan, "*Fides et Ratio* and Asian
Philosophies," 333-49.

[18] Among the most important are *Catechesi Tradendae* (1979), nos. 52-54; *Slavorum
Apostolorum* (1985); *Redemptoris Missio* (1990), nos. 55-56, and *Ecclesia in Asia* (1999),
nos. 21-22.

[19] The thinkers mentioned are John Henry Newman, Antonio Rosmini, Jacques
Maritain, Etienne Gilson, and Edith Stein "in a Western context," and Vladimir S.
Soloviev, Pavel A. Florensky, Petr Chaadev, and Vladimir N. Lossky "in an Eastern
context" (no. 74). Apparently, the "Eastern context" does not include Asia in general (at
least insofar as recent thinkers with whom the pope is familiar are concerned). The list
underlines John Paul II's European cultural formation.

[20] For John Paul II's comments on Buddhism, which have provoked a storm of protest
from Asian Buddhists because of his reference to its "atheistic" system, see his *Crossing*

I find six significant, direct or indirect, references in *FR* to Asian philosophies. The first reference occurs when *FR* claims that people in different parts of the world with diverse cultures have dealt with the same fundamental issues such as Who am I? (anthropology), Where have I come from and where am I going? (cosmology), Why is there evil? (theodicy), and What is there after this life? (eschatology). As evidence, *FR* invokes the sacred texts of Hinduism (the Veda) and of Zoroastrianism (the Avesta), the writings of Confucius and Lao Tzu, and the preaching of Tirkhankara and the Buddha (no. 1).

The second reference is found in *FR*'s remark that philosophy has exerted a powerful influence not only in the formation and development of the cultures of the West but also on "the ways of understanding existence in the East" (no. 3).

The third reference takes place in the context of *FR*'s discussion of agnosticism and relativism. Lamenting the fact that a legitimate pluralism of philosophical positions has led to an undifferentiated pluralism that assumes that all positions are equally valid and therefore betrays "lack of confidence in truth," *FR* goes on to say that "even certain conceptions of life coming from the East betray this lack of confidence, denying truth its exclusive character and assuming that truth reveals itself equally in different doctrines even if they contradict one another" (no. 5).

The fourth reference occurs when *FR* explains the three stances of philosophy vis-à-vis Christian revelation, that is, a philosophy completely independent of the gospel, Christian philosophy, and philosophy as *ancilla theologiae* (no. 75).[21] Asian philosophies are said to belong to the first category because they were elaborated in "regions as yet untouched by the Gospel" and because they aspire to be "an autonomous enterprise, obeying its own rules and employing the powers of reason alone." This does not mean that they are cut off from grace, since "as a search for truth within the natural order, the enterprise of philosophy is always open—at least implicitly—to the supernatural" (no. 75).

---

the Threshold of Hope, ed. Vittorio Messori and trans. Jenny McPhee and Martha McPhee (New York: Alfred A. Knopf, 1994), 84-90. There is also a factual inaccuracy. *FR* mentions Tirkhankara as if he were an individual, like Gautama the Buddha, with whom he is paired. In fact, Tirkhankara (literally, "making a passage, crossing, ford") is an honorific title in Jainism for a person who, by example and teaching, enables others to attain liberation. It designates twenty-four ascetic teachers in a line reaching back into prehistory, the most recent of whom was Mahavira (traditionally 599-27 B.C.E.).

[21] According to *FR* the first stance is adopted by philosophy before the birth of Jesus and later in regions as yet untouched by the gospel. By "Christian philosophy" *FR* understands "a Christian way of philosophizing, a philosophical speculation conceived in dynamic union with faith." It includes "those important developments of philosophical thinking which would not have happened without the direct or indirect contribution of Christian faith" (no. 76). By viewing philosophy as *ancilla theologiae*, *FR* does not intend to affirm "philosophy's servile submission or purely functional role with regard to theology" but to indicate "the necessity of the link between the two sciences and the impossibility of their separation" (no. 77). *FR* does admit that the expression *ancilla theologiae* can no longer be used today but asserts that in this stance philosophy "comes more directly under the authority of the magisterium and its discernment" (no. 77).

The fifth reference is made in *FR*'s recommendation that Christian philosophers develop "a reflection which will be both comprehensible and appealing to those who do not yet grasp the full truth which divine revelation declares" (no. 104). This philosophy is all the more necessary today since "the most pressing issues facing humanity—ecology, peace, and the coexistence of different races and cultures, for instance—may possibly find a solution if there is a clear and honest collaboration between Christians and the followers of other religions" (no. 104).

The last and by far the most important reference to Asian philosophies is given in the context of *FR*'s discussion of the encounter between the gospel and cultures, or inculturation. Since the text touches the core of our theme, it is appropriate to cite it in full:

In preaching the Gospel, Christianity first encountered Greek philosophy; but this does not mean at all that other approaches are precluded. Today, as the Gospel gradually comes into contact with cultural worlds which once lay beyond Christian influence, there are new tasks of inculturation, which means that our generation faces problems not unlike those faced by the church in the first centuries.

My first thoughts turn immediately to the lands of the East, so rich in religious and philosophical traditions of great antiquity. Among these lands, India has a special place. A great spiritual impulse leads Indian thought to seek an experience which would liberate the spirit from the shackles of time and space and would therefore acquire absolute value. The dynamic of this quest for liberation provides the context for great metaphysical systems.

In India particularly, it is the duty of Christians to draw from this rich heritage the elements compatible with their faith in order to enrich Christian thought. In this work of discernment, which finds its inspiration from the council's declaration *Nostra Aetate*, certain criteria will have to be kept in mind. The first of these is the universality of the human spirit, whose basic needs are the same in the most disparate cultures.

The second, which derives from the first, is this: In engaging great cultures for the first time, the church cannot abandon what she has gained from her inculturation in the world of Greco-Latin thought. To reject this heritage would be to deny the providential plan of God, who guides the church down the paths of time and history. This criterion is valid for the church of every age, even for the church of the future, who will judge herself enriched by all that comes from today's engagement with Eastern cultures and will find in this inheritance fresh cues for fruitful dialogue with the cultures which will emerge as humanity moves into the future.

Third, care will need to be taken lest, contrary to the very nature of the human spirit, the legitimate defense of the uniqueness and originality of Indian thought be confused with the idea that a particular cultural tradition should remain closed in its difference and affirm itself by opposing other traditions.

What has been said here of India is no less true for the heritage of the great cultures of China, Japan and the other countries of Asia, as also for the riches of the traditional cultures of Africa, which are for the most part orally transmitted (no. 72).

Philosophy as a Tool for Inculturation of the Christian Faith in Asia

It would be useful to highlight and comment briefly upon some of the more important points *FR* makes with regard to philosophy as a tool for inculturation in this lengthy excerpt. First of all, the interaction between philosophy and theology is here seen in the context of the inculturation of Christianity into the local cultures. The necessity for Asian Christians to develop a philosophy by which their cultures may "open themselves to the newness of the Gospel's truth and to be stirred by this truth to develop in new ways" (no. 71) is recognized.

Second, of the cultures of Asia "so rich in religious and philosophical traditions of great antiquity," *FR* singles out that of India, which is said to be endowed with "a great spiritual impulse" and whose quest for the liberation of "the spirit from the shackles of time and space" provides the context for "great metaphysical systems."

Third, it is incumbent upon Indian Christians to draw from their rich cultural resources elements compatible with the Christian faith in order to enrich the Christian thought. It is interesting to note that *FR* sees inculturation as a reciprocal process, with Christian faith and theology not unilaterally enriching local cultures but being enriched by them as well.

Fourth, in order for inculturation to reach this goal, certain criteria and norms must be observed, and *FR* enumerates three:

1. The first criterion is "the universality of the human spirit, whose basic needs are the same in the most disparate cultures." By "universality of the human spirit" *FR* presumably means not only that certain fundamental philosophical and theological themes—such as the nature of the self, the origin of the world, the problem of evil, and the eternal destiny of the individual (no. 1)—have been addressed by all cultures, but also that humans, despite their cultural diversities, can and should communicate with one another. In other words, *FR* indirectly rejects the theory of incommensurability proposed by some pluralists according to which humans are so socially situated that genuine mutual understanding and judgment of another person's culture and values are logically impossible. As to the "basic needs" of the human spirit, *FR* does not elaborate on them, but in light of what *FR* has said elsewhere, these needs include the "need to reflect upon truth" (no. 6), and more specifically, the "truth of being" (no. 5).[22] In

---

[22] *FR* repeatedly asserts the duty of philosophy to search for ultimate and universal truth. Indeed, it laments the fact that contemporary philosophy "has lost the capacity to lift its gaze to the heights, not daring to rise to the truth of being" (no. 5). Instead of focusing on metaphysics, contemporary philosophers have concentrated their research on hermeneutics and epistemology, abandoning the investigation of being. John Paul II wants "to state that reality and truth do transcend the factual and the empirical and to vindicate the human being's capacity to know this transcendental and metaphysical

addition, there is the need to formulate the certitudes arrived at in a rigorous and coherent way into a "systematic body of knowledge" (no. 4) and to proclaim them to others.

2. The second criterion is that the church cannot "abandon what she has gained from her inculturation in the world of Greco-Latin thought." To reject this heritage, according to *FR*, is to "deny the providential plan of God, who guides the church down the paths of time and history." *FR* does not explain what it means when it says that Asian Christians cannot abandon what the church has gained from its encounter with the Greco-Latin heritage.[23] Furthermore, since it is also part of the plan of divine providence that the gospel be inculturated into the Asian soil, *FR* explicitly says that the fruits of this encounter will become in their turn "fresh cues for fruitful dialogue with the cultures which will emerge as humanity moves into the future" (no. 72).[24]

3. The third criterion is a corollary of the first. *FR* cautions that, given the universality of the human spirit, one culture cannot close itself off from other cultures in the name of its "uniqueness" and "originality." There is, however, an ironic twist to this warning. Whereas Western culture has long regarded itself as so unique and original that it has considered itself superior to and normative for all other cultures, now the cultures of Asia are seen more liable to fall to this chauvinistic temptation.

Critical Questions

No doubt there is much that is valuable in John Paul II's proposal to use philosophy as a tool for the inculturation of the Christian faith into Asia.[25] His admiration for the riches of Asian philosophies and religions is genuine. His insistence on the possibility and necessity of dialogue across cultures and religions is well taken. His reminder that inculturation has been a practice of the church from its very beginning and that there are lessons to be learned from the past is helpful. His warning against the danger of cultural chauvinism and xenophobia is also salutary.

---

dimension in a way that is true and certain, albeit imperfect and analogical" (no. 83). Against postmodern agnosticism and nihilism (see no. 91), *FR* affirms that "every truth—if it really is truth—presents itself as universal, even if it is not the whole truth. If something is true, then it must be true for all people and at all times. . . . Hypotheses may fascinate, but they do not satisfy. Whether we admit it or not, there comes for everyone the moment when personal existence must be anchored to a truth recognized as final which confers a certitude no longer open to doubt" (no. 27).

[23] I examine this criterion in detail in the last part of the chapter.

[24] I draw out the implications of this statement for theological methodology today in the last part of the chapter.

[25] For an evaluation of *FR* in terms of inculturation, see Job Kozhamthadam, "*Fides et Ratio* and Inculturation," *Vidyajyoti* 63 (1999): 848-59; Scaria Thuruthiyil, "L'inculturazione della fede alla luce dell'Enciclica *Fides et Ratio*," in Mantovani, Thuruthiyil, and Toso, *Fede e ragione*, 249-55; and Mario Midali, "Evangelizzazione nuova: Rilevanti indicazioni del *Fides et Ratio*," in Mantovani, Thuruthiyil, and Toso, *Fede e ragione*, 257-76.

There are, however, certain affirmations in *FR* that are open to challenge or even seriously misleading. A word should be said first of all about *FR*'s charge that "certain conceptions of life coming from the East" betray "a lack of confidence in truth, denying its exclusive character and assuming that truth reveals itself equally in different doctrines even if they contradict one another" (no. 5). Since the encyclical does not specify which "conceptions of life coming from the East" it refers to, it may be presumed that it has in mind the celebrated capacity of Asian religions to absorb various and apparently conflicting philosophies and practices and the Asian inclusive worldview that is embodied in Śaivism, the Middle Way of Nāgārjuna, and the concepts of *yin* and *yang*. Admittedly, this Weltanschauung tends to see complementarity in different and even *opposite* (not *contradictory*) views and practices, but it is a caricature to say that it lacks "confidence in truth," since it is precisely in order to reach the truth that such opposites are held together. Needless to say, no Asian "conception of life" can be accused of holding "different doctrines, even if they contradict one another," if by contradiction is meant logical self-contradictory negation and not simply *opposites*.[26] Perhaps, this charge is not simply a misunderstanding of a minor point in Asian philosophies but symptomatic of the fundamental difference between two ways of seeing reality.

In addition, it is significant that *FR* emphasizes the "exclusive character" of truth, which certain Asian "conceptions of life" are alleged to deny. The encyclical consistently speaks of "truth" in the singular and in the abstract, especially when it affirms the universal and absolute character of truth. This is particularly evident in the already cited text: "Every truth—if it really is truth—presents itself as universal, even if it is not the whole truth" (no. 27). Asian philosophies will have no problem with the first part of the pope's statement, namely, that every truth presents itself as universal. In terms of Bernard Lonergan's cognitional theory with its four transcendental precepts ("be attentive, be intelligent, be reasonable, and be responsible"), truth-claims are well founded and so can be true when they are made as the result of due attention to relevant evidence (attention), careful consideration of a range of hypotheses (intelligence), reasoned affirmation of a particular hypothesis as best corroborated by the available evidence (judgment), and choice of the values implied in the affirmation (responsibility).[27]

---

[26] For the Nyaya-Vaisheshika epistemology, which analyzes human knowledge in terms of the knowing subject, the object to be known, the known object, and the means to know the object, see Satischandra Chatterjee, ed., *The Nyaya Theory of Knowledge*, 2d ed. (Calcutta: University of Calcutta Press, 1950); and Karl H. Potter, ed., *Indian Metaphysics and Epistemology: The Tradition of Nyaya-Vaisheshika up to Gangesa* (Princeton, N.J.: Princeton University Press, 1977).

[27] See Bernard Lonergan, *Insight: A Study of Human Understanding* (London: Longman Greens, 1958); and idem, *Method in Theology* (New York: Herder, 1971). For studies on how *FR* understands the universality of truth, see Gaspare Mura, "L'universalismo della verità," in Mantovani, Thuruthiyil, and Toso, *Fede e ragione*, 139-43.

Asian philosophies, however, would make three significant qualifications.[28] First, truths are not the same as apprehension, understanding, and formulation of what is true. Truth, or better still, what is true (ontological truth) is by its very nature universal, and the judgment in which this truth is affirmed is true (truth as *adaequatio mentis ad rem*), but a particular apprehension, understanding, and formulation of the truth need not and indeed cannot be universal, given the intrinsically finite, incomplete, and historical character of human knowledge. Furthermore, truths do not and cannot exist independently from particular apprehensions, understandings, judgments, and formulations, floating as it were above time and space like a Platonic form. Truths always manifest themselves and are grasped in these particular epistemological acts (truth as *aletheia* or manifestation); their universality is always mediated in and through these limited and historically evolving acts of apprehending, understanding, judging, and formulating.

Second, Asian philosophies maintain that reality itself or what is ontologically true is not or at least does not manifest itself as one but as multiple. This view of reality itself as plural, or of the necessarily plural manifestation of reality, is found, for example, in Indian philosophies, even though they privilege the concept of the unity of all things in the universal Self *(Brahman, Ātman)* over the particularity of individual realities.[29] It is espoused especially by the Chinese philosophy of *yin* and *yang* and of the Five Elements *(wu-hsing)*, according to which the movement of reality—humanity and nature—is governed by an alternating multiplicity of contrary but unifying forces.[30] It follows then that no act of apprehending, understanding, judging, and expressing reality at any given time can fully and totally express reality. The best that can be achieved is relative adequacy between the mind's affirmation and reality.

---

[28] For an informative contrast between the Western and Chinese ways of conceiving truth, see David L. Hall and Roger T. Ames, *Thinking from the Han* (Albany, N.Y.: State University of New York Press, 1998), 103-46. Broadly speaking, Westerners ask, What is the Truth? (truth-seekers), whereas the Chinese ask, Where is the Way? (way-seekers). Western philosophy makes two assumptions, namely, that there is a single-ordered world and that there is a distinction between reality and appearance. The first assumption takes truth as coherence, and the second takes truth as correspondence between mind and reality. These two assumptions are absent in classical Chinese philosophy. Instead of the single-ordered world, the Chinese hold that the world is but the "ten thousand things" *(wanwu or wanyou)* and, instead of the distinction between reality and appearance, the Chinese hold that reality is essentially polar *(yin/yang)*. See also other works by the same two authors, *Thinking through Confucius* (Albany, N.Y.: State University Press of New York, 1987) and *Anticipating China: Thinking through the Narratives of Chinese and Western Culture* (Albany, N.Y.: State University of New York, 1995).

[29] For an illuminating account of this characteristic of Indian philosophies, see Hajime Nakamura, *Ways of Thinking of Eastern Peoples* (Honolulu: The University Press of Hawaii, 1964), 93-129.

[30] For a brief and helpful explanation of this theory, see *A Source Book in Chinese Philosophy*, trans. and comp. Wing-Tsit Chan (Princeton, N.J.: Princeton University Press, 1963), 244-88; and Fung Yu-lan, *A Short History of Chinese Philosophy* (New York: The Free Press, 1948), 129-42.

Third, Asian philosophies will draw out the implications of the second part of John Paul II's statement—"even if it is not the whole truth"—with regard to the use of philosophy as a tool for the inculturation of the Christian faith in Asia. Asian philosophies would affirm that *all* apprehensions, understandings, judgments, and formulations of any truth, revealed or otherwise, cannot be anything but partial. Partiality in knowledge, which is not the same as falseness, is not just an occasional mishap that can in principle be overcome by dint of mental efforts, as might be implied by the pope's qualification ("even if it is not the whole truth"), as though most of the time the "whole truth" is readily available, in philosophy as well as in revelation. Rather it is our inescapable lot to possess knowledge always in fragments, that is, partial and relatively adequate apprehensions, understandings, judgments, and formulations of reality. This fact does not of itself invalidate the claim that Jesus is the perfect and full revelation of God (which Christians may, of course, legitimately make), since the church's apprehensions, understandings, judgments, and formulations of this claim about Jesus and of the truths revealed by him will always remain partial and only relatively adequate, even in the case of infallible definitions.

It follows that in the inculturation of the Christian faith, it is not simply a matter of adaption (much less translation) of the Christian truths (most, if not all, of which have been formulated in Jewish-Greek-Latin-European categories) to an alien tongue and mode of thought. Rather, inculturation is a two-way process in which the Christian faith is given a better and more adequate apprehension, understanding, judgment, and formulation of itself, almost always at the cost of abandoning its own categories, and in which other faiths are in turn enriched by a better and more adequate apprehension, understanding, judgment, and formulation of themselves. Genuine intercultural encounter between the Christian faith and cultures always involves mutual challenge, critique, correction, and enrichment so that a new *tertium quid* will emerge.

FIDES ET RATIO AND THE INCULTURATION
OF THE CHRISTIAN FAITH IN CONFUCIANIST ASIA

The concluding part of this chapter assesses John Paul II's teaching on philosophy, and more specifically metaphysics, as a tool for inculturating the Christian faith in Asia by exploring its applicability to some aspects of Confucianism. The theme is vast, and limited space permits consideration of only two issues, the one methodological and the other substantive. The point here is neither to prescribe a method for the project of inculturating the Christian faith into cultures that are shaped by Confucianism, nor critically to review past efforts, both in theological reflection and church practices, to carry out this task.[31] Rather, attention will be drawn to some of the challenges and difficulties that the

---

[31] The works of seventeenth-century Jesuits in China and Vietnam, such as Matteo Ricci and Alexandre de Rhodes, are well known. See Peter C. Phan, *Mission and Catechesis: Alexandre de Rhodes and Inculturation in Seventeenth-Century Vietnam* (Maryknoll, N.Y.: Orbis Books, 1998).

inculturation of the Christian faith in Confucianist Asia will encounter if the method recommended by *FR* is implemented in a simplistic manner.

Metaphysics and Ontological Categories in Inculturation

FR argues vigorously for the use of philosophy in general and metaphysics in particular not only in theology but also in the inculturation of the Christian faith. To cure the "crisis of meaning" that he discerns in contemporary culture infected with eclecticism, historicism, scientism, pragmatism, and nihilism (nos. 86-90), John Paul II prescribes a threefold therapy: a recovery of philosophy's "sapiential dimension as a search for the ultimate and overarching meaning of life" (no. 81); a reaffirmation of human reason's "capacity to know the truth, to come to knowledge which can reach objective truth" (no. 82); and the use of "a philosophy of a genuinely metaphysical range, capable, that is, of transcending empirical data in order to attain something absolute, ultimate and foundational in its search for truth" (no. 83). John Paul II points out that by metaphysics he does not mean "a specific school or a particular current of thought" (no. 83), and he has already affirmed that "the church has no philosophy of her own nor does she canonize any one particular philosophy in preference to others" (no. 49).[32]

As to whether metaphysics is necessary for the inculturation of the Christian faith into Confucianist Asia, the answer is straightforward if by metaphysics is meant simply the general affirmation of the human mind's capacity to know reality objectively. No Asian philosophers—indeed, no philosopher of any stripe—can deny this capacity without self-contradiction, since the very act of denying it necessarily affirms it. They would concur with John Paul II's affirmation of the "universality" of "truth," though with the three important qualifications elaborated above.[33] In this context Asian philosophers would no doubt consider unfounded and even offensive *FR*'s accusation that "certain conceptions of life coming from the East" betray a "lack of confidence in truth" because they allegedly assume that "truth reveals itself equally in different doctrines even if they contradict one another" (no. 5).

As to whether metaphysics can serve as an effective tool for inculturating the Christian faith in Confucianist Asia, the answer depends on what is meant by metaphysics beyond the general meaning indicated above. Metaphysics may refer to a style of philosophizing or a way of thinking and a particular school of

---

[32] This stance does not prevent the magisterium from acclaiming the merits of Saint Thomas's thought and making him the guide and model for theological studies. But *FR* argues that "this has not been in order to take a position on properly philosophical questions nor to demand adherence to particular theses" (no. 78). There is no doubt a bit of revisionist history here, in light of Leo XIII's *Aeterni Patris* (1879) and Pius X's imposition of twenty-four "Thomistic" philosophical theses. For a study of the position of Thomas Aquinas in *FR*, see Georges Cottier, "Tommaso d'Aquino, teologo e filosofo nella *Fides et Ratio*," in Mantovani, Thuruthiyil, and Toso, *Fede e ragione*, 187-94.

[33] *FR* itself explicitly acknowledges that "the objective value of many concepts does not exclude that their meaning is often imperfect" (no. 96). As has been pointed out above, Asian philosophers would insist that the meaning of *all* (not "many") is *always* (not "often") imperfect.

thought. The second meaning, though distinct from the first, is unavoidable because it is not possible to speak of metaphysics in the abstract. In spite of the disclaimer that he does not intend to propose "a specific school or a particular current of thought," John Paul II cannot but espouse a specific metaphysics. In fact, the pope's brand of metaphysics may be called "critical realism," since he insists—adamantly and repeatedly—that metaphysics ought to maintain the possibility "to know a universally valid truth" (no. 93). It does not matter much whether this critical realism is of the Thomistic stamp or some other variety such as Lonergan's or Rahner's.

Of course, there has not been anywhere one style of philosophizing and one school of metaphysics. As Kenneth L. Schmitz has shown, in the West metaphysics has been developed both as a style of thinking (metaphysics as "fundamental enquiry") and a philosophical discipline (metaphysics as "ontological discourse"), and in this double form it has undergone radical shifts as a result of the triple revolution in modernity, namely, the empirio-mathematical, historical, and linguistic turns.[34] Therefore, if Western (and even Christian) metaphysics is used as a tool for the inculturation of the Christian faith in Confucianist Asia, both as a style of thinking and an ontological discipline, there must be a deep sensitivity first of all to the distinctive style of philosophizing in Confucianism.

In his masterful description of the Chinese way of thinking, Hajime Nakamura has argued that the Chinese characteristically did not develop "non-religious transcendental metaphysics."[35] This does not mean, of course, that there is no "metaphysics" in China. Indeed, among the ancient Chinese philosophies, Taoism can surely be said to have a metaphysical character. Neo-Confucians were attracted to certain aspects of Buddhist metaphysics and developed their own metaphysics (e.g., Chu-Hsi's Sung-hsüeh philosophy). The Hua-yen sect incorporated some metaphysical doctrines of Mahāyāna Buddhism. However, metaphysical thinking was completely abandoned when Taoism turned into a religious art of achieving immortality; even Chu-Hsi, the founder of Sung-hsüeh philosophy, did not elaborate a metaphysical system; and in the Hua-yen sect, the

---

[34] See Kenneth Schmitz, "Postmodernism and the Catholic Tradition," American Catholic Philosophical Quarterly 73/2 (1999): 242. Schmitz argues that because of the empirio-mathematical turn in modernity, metaphysics as philosophical enquiry was replaced by epistemology as the primary philosophical discipline, and Aristotle's concept of contingency as the result of the unintended conjunction of the causes ("causal contingency") was replaced by Pascal's concept of contingency as probability ("predictive contingency"). Later, because of the historical turn, metaphysics as a mode of discourse was forced to recognize its intrinsic condition of historicity, and the concept of contingency as predictive contingency was replaced by the concept of contingency as unrepeatable event ("non-predictive contingency"). Finally, in the linguistic turn, contingency is understood as the arbitrariness of linguistic signs (as in Saussurean linguistics) or as the conventionality of relations (as in Anglo American language analytic philosophy). See Kenneth Schmitz, "An Addendum to Further Discussion," American Catholic Philosophical Quarterly 73/2 (1999): 277-79. This narrative of the recent career of metaphysics shows how complex the question about the use of metaphysics as a tool for inculturation, especially the inculturation of the Christian faith in Confucianist Asia, is.
[35] Nakamura, Ways of Thinking of Eastern Peoples, 243.

Buddhist all-important distinction between Absolute Reality and the phenomenal world is rejected. This anti-metaphysical trend of Chinese thought was not due to a lack of intellectual sophistication but to a distinct way of thinking, and awareness of this difference will help overcome what Robert Solomon calls the "transcendental pretense" of the Enlightenment.[36]

The style of thinking that accounts for the nondevelopment of metaphysics among the Chinese has been referred to variously as "emphasis on the perception of the concrete," "nondevelopment of abstract thought," "emphasis on the particular," "fondness for complex multiplicity expressed in concrete form," "the tendency toward practicality," and "reconciling and harmonizing tendencies."[37] David Hall and Roger Ames characterize the Chinese way of thinking as *"first problematic*, or alternatively, *analogical* or *correlative* thinking" and the Western way as *"second problematic"* or *"causal"* thinking.[38] The Chinese way of thinking is described as "neither strictly cosmogonical nor cosmological in the sense that there is the presupposition neither of an initial beginning nor of the existence of a single-ordered world. This mode of thinking accepts the priority of change or process over rest and permanence, presumes no ultimate agency responsible for the general order of things, and seeks to account for states of affairs by appeal to correlative procedures rather than by determining agencies and principles."[39]

With this basic difference in modes of thinking in mind, it would be difficult to concur fully with John Paul II's threefold recommendation for the inculturation of the Christian faith in Confucianist Asia. First, he suggests that Christians in Asia should "draw from this [Asian] rich heritage the elements compatible with their faith in order to enrich Christian thought" (no. 72). This procedure seems to envisage inculturation as a straightforward business of adapting elements of one culture to another, without due attention to the different—at times, incommensurable—modes of thinking among cultures.[40]

Second, John Paul II appears to hold that nothing short of metaphysics can give a coherent account of divine revelation: "Metaphysics thus plays an essential

---

[36] See Robert Solomon, *The Bully Culture: Enlightenment, Romanticism, and the Transcendental Pretense 1750-1850* (Lanham, Md.: Rowman and Littlefield, 1993). The transcendental pretense refers to the claim that rational objectivity and universal science, allegedly the fruits of the Enlightenment, should be the norm to judge all non-Western cultures.

[37] See Nakamura, *Ways of Thinking of Eastern Peoples*, 177-294.

[38] Hall and Ames, *Anticipating China*, xvii.

[39] Ibid., xviii. Graphically, the difference between the Western and the Chinese modes of thinking is illustrated by the former's preference for the circle and the latter's for the square as images of perfection.

[40] Apparently John Paul II is operating under the two Greco-Roman models of inculturation, that is, assimilation of non-Christian *philosophy* and incarnation in non-Christian *culture* respectively. Aloysius Pieris has convincingly argued that these two models are not applicable to Asia. See his *An Asian Theology of Liberation* (Maryknoll, N.Y.: Orbis Books, 1988), 51-53. See also Phan, *"Fides et Ratio* and Asian Philosophies," 345-46.

role of mediation in theological research. A theology without a metaphysical horizon could not move beyond an analysis of religious experience nor would it allow the *intellectus fidei* to give a coherent account of the universal and transcendent value of revealed truth" (no. 83). Depending on what is meant by "metaphysics" and "metaphysical horizon," this view belittles the epistemological validity of the narrativistic and aphoristic mode of thinking, knowing, and expressing that is characteristic of Chinese philosophy and no less able to "give a coherent account" of its worldview. It seems to require that an Asian Christian theology must of necessity take the form of systematic exposition, as has been done so far in the West, if it is to achieve self-coherence.[41]

Third, and perhaps of a piece with his second point, John Paul II specifies that "in engaging great cultures for the first time, the church cannot abandon what she has gained from her inculturation in the world of Greco-Latin thought. To reject this heritage would be to deny the providential plan of God, who guides the church down the paths of time and history" (no. 72). What John Paul II intends to say in this excerpt is highly ambiguous: (1) If the church cannot abandon its gains in its inculturation in the world of Greco-Latin thought in engaging great cultures *for the first time*, does it mean that the church is free to do so later, perhaps when the local church has reached sufficient maturity? (2) What is being included in the church's Greco-Latin "heritage"? Theology, liturgy, ethics, canon law, institutions, and so on? In terms of theology, does it mean, for instance, that an Asian Christology must employ categories such as person, nature, hypostatic union, and so on, perhaps in translation? And how far should this Greco-Latin heritage be extended? Until the Middle Ages, but no further? (3) What is meant by saying that denying the church's Greco-Latin heritage is tantamount to denying the "providential plan of God"? Is it being implied that God has sanctioned and canonized the development of Western (even conciliar) theology? (4) If it is now God's providential plan to bring the Christian faith into Confucianist Asia, should the new Asian theologies be incorporated into the heritage of the church? If so, what are the mechanisms whereby this incorporation can be carried out effectively? How can this be done when papal and other official documents are all written in Rome, in Western languages, and then promulgated (and at times enforced) with authority and power to the churches of the non-Western world?

The Rites Controversy Revisited

As a concrete example of the inculturation of the Christian faith in Confucianist Asia, perhaps no doctrine and practice can be as illuminating and challenging,

---

[41] It is unfortunate that the *ratio* in *Fides et Ratio* is successively reduced from rationality to philosophy to metaphysics. This gradual reduction is all the more misleading because *metaphysics* is currently understood not as reflective thinking or fundamental inquiry but mainly as a mode of ontological discourse (e.g., "onto-theology") and even, in popular circles, as astrology.

both historically and theologically, as the cult of ancestors.[42] My interest here is neither to rehearse this painful episode in the history of the Asian churches in which cultural misunderstandings, theological dogmatism, ecclesiastical rivalries, and international politics were all deeply enmeshed with a praiseworthy desire to incarnate the Christian faith into the Chinese culture, nor to examine the theological and liturgical validity of the cult of ancestors in itself.[43] Rather, I would like to show how the inculturation of the Christian faith in Confucianist Asia with regard to the cult of ancestors cannot be adequately carried out on the sole basis of the method proposed by John Paul II in *FR*.

The cult of ancestors posed a difficult challenge to the earliest missionaries to China and other countries influenced by Confucianism.[44] Basically, the question was whether the cult is theologically acceptable. At issue was the nature of this cult, that is, whether it has a "religious" character or is a purely civil or political ceremony. If the former, then it is superstition and must be forbidden; if the latter, then it may be tolerated, and Christians' participation in it would be permissible, due care being exercised to prevent misunderstanding and scandal. The final position of the Catholic church toward the cult of ancestors, after repeated and severe condemnations by several popes, was acceptance, and the ground for this complete about-face is the alleged nonreligious nature of this cult.[45]

The question of interest here is whether the issue of the cult of ancestors would have been more correctly and speedily resolved had the method of inculturation, which is now advanced by John Paul II, been known and applied? No doubt there were many metaphysical and, more generally, philosophical issues at stake. Philosophically, the cult of ancestors obviously implies certain views regarding the human person, the person's survival after death, the nature of this post-mortem life, and the relationship between the dead and the living. Ethically, it concerns the heart of the moral life as Confucianism understands it, namely, as the proper performance of the duties entailed by various relationships, the most important of which is the relationship between children and

---

[42] Systems of ancestor veneration are best known from Africa, China, Taiwan, Japan, Korea, and Vietnam. In Asia, ancestor worship is an amalgamation of folk religion, Confucianism, Taoism, Buddhism, and Shinto. It has been suggested that ancestor worship may have emerged from the worship of guardian spirits. This shift occurred when the family supplanted the clan or tribe as the basic unit of society, so that prayers addressed to tribal spirits were now redirected to the deceased members of the family. In Asian countries ancestor veneration has been connected with other Taoist practices such as magic, divination, witchcraft, geomancy, and so forth.
[43] For a history of the controversy, see George Minamiki, *The Chinese Rites Controversy from Its Beginning to Modern Times* (Chicago: Loyola University Press, 1985).
[44] I prescind here from the special question of the cult of Confucius in the Temple of Literature.
[45] See the instruction of the Propaganda Fide, *Plane compertum est* (1939). See Phan, *Mission and Catechesis*, 28.

their parents.[46] Filial piety is the central virtue for every Confucian. Further-more, the cult of ancestors has implications for marriage and the family, since a man who does not have children by his wife may be morally bound by filial piety to marry another woman and have children by her so as to perpetuate this cult. Politically, the cult of ancestors functions as the glue that binds society together, from the king as the August Son of Heaven to the humblest citizen of the country, and provides continuity across generations. Theologically, the cult of ancestors raises, at least for Christians, the question of the relationship be-tween this cult and the worship of God.

In view of these complex aspects of the cult of ancestors, it is questionable whether a method for the inculturation of the Christian faith in Confucianist Asia that relies principally on philosophy and metaphysics is adequate to the task. Indeed, were one to follow John Paul II's three suggestions discussed in the previous section, one would run into intractable difficulties. First, it is im-practicable, even counterproductive, simply to select from the Chinese cult of ancestors elements that are compatible with the Christian faith and incorporate them into Christian worship since, apart from their immediate context, these rites lose all their meaning. In fact, it is only when it is viewed apart from its context that the cult of ancestors can be regarded as nothing more than a civil and political act. The oft-endorsed practice of "baptizing" non-Christian rituals not infrequently amounted to a cultural cannibalism and colonialism that di-vested these rituals of their own religious meanings and made them serve the Christian purpose.

Furthermore, metaphysics would not be the most effective tool to evaluate the cult of ancestors. The issue here is not whether Chinese philosophy would deny personhood or post-mortem survival or even the immortality of the "soul," all of which are postulated by the cult of ancestors.[47] Nor is it about whether Chinese philosophy is open to the affirmation of "God"; in fact, the existence of a transcendent being may be said to be implied in the Chinese concepts of *t'ien*, *t'ien ming*, *te*, and *tao*.[48] Even after all these metaphysical realities are affirmed,

---

[46] *The Doctrine of the Mean* XX, 8, specifies five relationships and three virtues: "The duties of universal obligation are five, and the virtues wherewith they are practiced are three. The duties are those between sovereign and minister, between father and son, between husband and wife, between elder brother and younger, and those belonging to the intercourse of friends. Those five are the duties of universal obligation. Knowledge, magnanimity, and energy, these three, are the virtues universally binding. And the means by which they carry the duties into practice is singleness." See James Legge, trans., *The Doctrine of the Mean* (Oxford: Clarendon Press, 1893).

[47] *FR* affirms that "it is metaphysics which makes it possible to ground the concept of personal dignity in virtue of their spiritual nature" (no. 83). If this means that it is in virtue of metaphysics alone that personal dignity can be defended, then *FR*'s statement is gratu-itous. Moreover, even if the statement is granted, there is still a further question to be settled, namely, *which* metaphysical argument for the dignity of the person is apodictic. For a study of the notion of person in *FR*, see Sabino Palumbieri, "*Fides et Ratio*: la persona, punto di sintesi," in Mantovani, Thuruthiyil, and Toso, *Fede e ragione*, 331-52.

[48] For a discussion of *t'ien* and transcendence, as well as *t'ien ming*, *te*, and *tao*, see Hall and Ames, *Thinking through Confucius*, 201-37.

it still remains to be determined whether the cult of ancestors with all its manifold rituals is acceptable to Christians ethically, politically, and theologically. And on this question there is little that metaphysics can settle apodictically.

Last, it would be even less helpful to invoke the church's Greco-Latin heritage as the criterion for judging the validity of the cult of ancestors. Indeed, it was the early missionaries' approach to this cult from the vantage point of the Western understanding of worship that prevented them from achieving a full understanding of its meaning. Even the basic terms framing the debate were misleading. Should the term *cult* be translated as "worship" *(latria)* or "veneration" *(dulia)?* Should one use "worship of ancestors" or "veneration of ancestors"? Needless to say, the validity of the cult of ancestors, according to Roman Catholic sensibilities, depends very much on which of these expressions is used. And yet, the cult of ancestors cannot properly be understood in these terms. Nor would it be very helpful to find equivalents for the cult of ancestors in Roman Catholic devotional practices, such as the cult of Mary and the saints, since these practices are undergirded by very different theological worldviews.

As has been said above, to obtain a comprehensive understanding of John Paul II's teaching on inculturation, especially the inculturation of the Christian faith in Asia, one should not limit oneself to *FR.* The pope's fuller and richer insights can be found elsewhere, especially in his apostolic exhortation *Ecclesia in Asia,* which he promulgated in the wake of the Special Assembly for Asia of the Synod of Bishops on 6 November 1999.[49] *FR*'s somewhat narrow views should therefore be supplemented by those the pope proposes in *Ecclesia in Asia,* as well as in another apostolic exhortation, *Ecclesia in Africa* (1995). Only by taking these papal documents together can a relatively adequate method for the inculturation of the Christian faith in Asia be devised.

---

[49] For an analysis and evaluation of this apostolic exhortation, see Peter C. Phan, "*Ecclesia in Asia*: Challenges for Asian Christianity," *EAPR* 37/3 (2000): 215-32, as well as the essays by Michael Amaladoss, Edmund Chia, John Manford Prior, and James Kroeger in the same issue.

PART TWO

Inculturation

Toward an Asian American Theology

4

Kingdom of God

A THEOLOGICAL SYMBOL FOR ASIANS?

A quick glance at the history of recent theology will reveal that the symbol of kingdom/reign of God/heaven has returned to center stage after languishing for centuries in the wings.[1] This dramatic comeback is one of the byproducts of the nineteenth century quest for the historical Jesus.[2] Thanks to Johannes Weiss and Albert Schweitzer,[3] the apocalypticism of early Judaism became the context in which Jesus' life and preaching were interpreted; and as a result, Jesus' central message was now seen to be the kingdom of God. The centrality of this

---

[1] Benedict Viviano expresses his amazement that the theme of the kingdom of God, central in the preaching of Jesus, "played hardly any role in the systematic theology I had been taught in the seminary. Upon further investigation I realized that this theme had in many ways been largely ignored in theology and spirituality and liturgy of the church in the past two thousand years, and when not ignored, often distorted beyond recognition" (*The Kingdom of God in History* [Wilmington, Del.: Glazier, 1988], 9).

[2] The revival of the symbol of the kingdom of God took place within the context of the emergence of eschatology as a central theological theme. For a history of this renascence of eschatology, see Peter C. Phan, *Eternity in Time* (Selinsgrove, Pa.: Susquehanna University Press, 1988), 26-31. For contemporary discussions of the kingdom of God, see Bruce Chilton, ed., *The Kingdom of God in the Teaching of Jesus* (Philadelphia: Fortress Press, 1984); and Wendell Willis, ed., *The Kingdom of God in Twentieth-Century Interpretation* (Peabody, Mass.: Hendrickson, 1987).

[3] See Johannes Weiss, *Jesus' Proclamation of the Kingdom of God* (1892; Philadelphia: Fortress Press, 1971). Weiss defended the thesis that Christ's central mission was to proclaim the immanence of God's kingdom, in which he himself was to be manifested as the Messiah. Albert Schweitzer, in *The Quest of the Historical Jesus* (1910; Minneapolis: Fortress Press, 2001), argued for the "consequent (or thoroughgoing) eschatology" according to which Jesus expected a speedy end of the world and, when this proved a mistake, attempted but failed to bring it about through his own death. Whether one agrees with the theses of Weiss and Schweitzer or not, there is no denying that they brought the symbol of the kingdom of God into the theological limelight. For an evaluation of Weiss and Schweitzer, see Wendell Willis, "The Discovery of the Eschatological Kingdom: Johannes Weiss and Albert Schweitzer," in Willis, *The Kingdom of God in Twentieth-Century Interpretation*, 1-14; and T. Francis Glasson, "Schweitzer's Influence—Blessing or Bane?" in Chilton, *The Kingdom of God in the Teaching of Jesus*, 107-20.

symbol is not restricted to New Testament studies.[4] It has also functioned as an interpretative category for trinitarian theology,[5] Christology,[6] the theology of church and world,[7] ethics and spirituality,[8] and mission.[9]

But more than influencing a particular theological treatise, the symbol of the kingdom of God has shaped a *way* of doing theology and its fundamental *character*. This is true especially in the case of liberation theologies of various provenances and stripes. Jon Sobrino has argued at length and convincingly that whereas for Latin American theology the liberation of the poor is the *primacy of reality*, the kingdom of God rather than the resurrection of Jesus is its *eschaton*. In Sobrino's view there are several convergences between liberation theology and the theme of the kingdom of God. Liberation theology presupposes a "pretheological" option for the poor, who are the addressees of the reign of God. Furthermore, it has certain formal characteristics that correspond to the symbol of the kingdom of God: it is concerned with historicizing the transcendental

---

[4] For a biblical exegesis of the symbol of the kingdom of God, see Dennis C. Duling, "Kingdom of God, Kingdom of Heaven," *The Anchor Bible Dictionary*, vol. 4, ed. David Noel Freedman (New York: Doubleday, 1992), 50-70.

[5] See, for instance, Jürgen Moltmann, *The Trinity and the Kingdom: The Doctrine of God,* trans. Margaret Kohl (San Francisco: Harper & Row, 1981); and Leonardo Boff, *Trinity and Society,* trans. Paul Burns (Maryknoll, N.Y.: Orbis Books, 1988).

[6] See, for instance, Edward Schillebeeckx, *Jesus: An Experiment in Christology*, trans. Hubert Hoskins (New York: Seabury, 1979); Albert Nolan, *Jesus before Christianity* (Maryknoll, N.Y.: Orbis Books, 1992); Dermot Lane, *Christ at the Center* (New York: Paulist Press, 1991); Jürgen Moltmann, *The Way of Jesus Christ: Christology in Messianic Dimensions*, trans. Margaret Kohl (San Francisco: HarperSanFrancisco, 1990); and Jon Sobrino, *Jesus the Liberator: A Historical-Theological View*, trans. Paul Burns and Francis McDonagh (Maryknoll, N.Y.: Orbis Books, 1993), esp. 105-34 ("The Kingdom of God in Present-Day Christologies"); idem, "Jesús el Reino de Dios significado y objectivos ultimos de su vida y misión," *Christus* 45 (1980): 17-25. Methodologically, a Christology that makes the symbol of the reign of God its center starts from the preaching and deeds of the "historical Jesus" rather than from the church's dogmatic teachings about the Christ (see Sobrino, *Jesus the Liberator*, 40-44).

[7] See, for instance, Johannes Metz, *Theology of the World*, trans. William Glen-Doepel (New York: Herder and Herder, 1969; Jürgen Moltmann, *The Church in the Power of the Spirit*, trans. Margaret Kohl (San Francisco: Harper & Row, 1977); Leonardo Boff, *The Base Communities Reinvent the Church*, trans. Robert Barr (Maryknoll, N.Y.: Orbis Books, 1986); idem, *Church: Charism and Power*, trans. John Diercksmeier (New York: Crossroad, 1985); Ignatio Ellacuría, *Conversión de la Iglesia al reino di Dios* (Santander, Spain, 1984); R. Munõs, *La Iglesia en el pueblo* (Lima, 1983); A. Quiroz, *Eclesiología en la teología de la liberación* (Salamanca, 1983); and Jon Sobrino, *The True Church and the Poor* (Maryknoll, N.Y.: Orbis Books, 1984).

[8] See, for instance, H. Merklein, *Die Gottesherrschaft als Handlungsprinzip* (Würzburg, 1978); G. M. Soares-Prabhu, "The Kingdom of God: Jesus' Vision of a New Society," in *The Indian Church in the Struggle for a New Society*, ed. D. S. Amalopavadass (Bangalore, 1981), 579-629; Jon Sobrino, *Spirituality of Liberation: Toward Political Holiness*, trans. Robert Barr (Maryknoll, N.Y.: Orbis Books, 1988); and John Fuellenbach, *The Kingdom of God: The Heart of Jesus' Message for Us Today* (Manila, 1989).

[9] See, for instance, *God's Kingdom and Mission. Studia Missionalia* 46 (Rome: Gregorian University Press, 1997).

realities of faith (as historical theology), with denouncing and unmasking historical sin (as prophetic theology), with transforming reality (as praxic theology), and with making the people the subjects of theology and the agents of faith (as popular theology). Finally, by choosing the kingdom of God as its eschaton, liberation theology avoids the danger of identifying the kingdom with the church and helps retrieve the importance of the historical Jesus for theology.[10]

In the footsteps of liberation theology, this chapter explores whether and how the biblical symbol of the kingdom of God can be meaningful to Asians. It first highlights some of the problems this symbol, as interpreted by contemporary exegetes and theologians, poses for Asians, who do not share the Hebrew and Western cultural assumptions and experiences of kingdom and kingship. Second, it examines some attempts made by Asian theologians to speak of the kingdom of God. The chapter concludes with suggestions for inculturating this central Christian symbol in the Confucian socio-cultural context of Asia.

KINGDOM OF GOD AS A THEOLOGICAL SYMBOL: CHALLENGES FROM ASIA

It has been pointed out by biblical scholars that even though the specific term *kingdom of heaven* (Hebrew *malkût šāmayîm*) is not found in the Hebrew Bible, the *idea* of God as king *(melek)* and reigning *(yimlōk)* over Israel, all peoples, and the cosmos is widespread, especially in post-exilic Judaism.[11] Since Jesus' own understanding of the kingdom of God was deeply rooted in the Hebrew concept, it is useful to give a succinct summary of how the Hebrews understood this symbol. For Israel, Yahweh's kingship was based first of all upon God's saving deeds performed on its behalf throughout its history—the deliverance from its slavery in Egypt, guidance during its wandering in the desert, the establishment of the covenant, the gift of the land, protection from surrounding enemies, the institution of the monarchy, and the return from exile. Furthermore, God has demonstrated God's sovereign power by creating and ruling over the cosmos and by extending God's lordship over all nations. Finally, because of the repeated failures of its political and religious leaders, Israel projected its

---

[10] See Sobrino, *Jesus the Liberator*, 122-25. See also idem, "Central Position of the Reign of God in Liberation Theology," in *Mysterium Liberationis: Fundamental Concepts of Liberation Theology*, ed. Ignacio Ellacuría and Jon Sobrino (Maryknoll, N.Y.: Orbis Books, 1993), 350-88. According to Sobrino, the reason why liberation theology prefers the symbol of the reign of God rather than the resurrection of Jesus as the central category around which to organize the whole content of theology is its ability to hold together transcendence and history and to denounce the presence of the anti-Reign.

[11] "The kingdom of God" literally translates the Greek *hē basileia tou theou*, and "the kingdom of heaven (of the heavens)" *hē basileia tōn ouranōn*. It has been argued that since the kingdom of God/heaven is not primarily territorial, political, and national, *hē basileia* should be translated as "rule," "reign" or "sovereignty" rather than "kingdom." On the other hand, because God's rule has political, economic and social implications, "kingdom" is to be preferred. In this chapter *kingdom* and *reign* are used interchangeably.

hope in the final and decisive coming of God in the eschatological future when God will establish God's eternal kingdom through a Davidic messiah or a priestly ruler or even directly.[12]

The idea of God's rule, affirmed in various ways in the Hebrew Bible, reached its apogee in the New Testament. The expression "reign of God" or "reign of heaven" occurs more than 150 times in the New Testament. Whether one thinks of Jesus as an apocalyptic prophet or a teacher of subversive wisdom,[13] and however one interprets the phrase "kingdom of God," there is no doubt that the reign of God was the central focus of Jesus' preaching (in particular, his parables) and ministry (in particular, his miracles).

Despite Jesus' frequent use of the symbol of the reign of God, he did not give it a clear definition.[14] In summary form, it may be said that for Jesus the kingdom of God meant the active presence of God his Father, inaugurated in his own life and death. This brought about a reign characterized by gratuitous forgiveness and reconciliation, by universal justice and peace, in opposition to the anti-reign of division and hatred, injustice and oppression, a reign that calls for a radical conversion issuing in personal and social transformation.

Leaving aside the question of *when* Jesus thought the kingdom of God would come, with its three possible answers,[15] the symbol of the kingdom of God as used in the New Testament poses a host of questions for a contemporary Asian theology. Without pretension to exhaustiveness, they can be enumerated as follows:

---

[12] See Rudolf Schnackenburg, *God's Rule and Kingdom* (New York: Herder and Herder, 1963).

[13] Scholarly consensus holds that Jesus was the eschatological prophet insofar as his teaching was shaped by his conviction that the kingdom of God was already inaugurated in his life, though still an outstanding reality. Marcus Borg has argued that this eschatological consensus disintegrated in the 1980s. Some scholars hold that Jesus was a Cynic sage (e.g., Burton Mack) or a teacher of subversive wisdom (e.g., Marcus Borg) rather than the eschatological prophet. Obviously, with this alternative view of who Jesus was, the notion of the kingdom of God has also undergone drastic revisions. Jesus' warnings about the destruction of Jerusalem and the Temple are no longer understood to refer to eschatological events but to the historical consequences of not attending to Jesus' subversive teachings. See Marcus Borg, "A Temperate Case for a Non-Eschatological Jesus," *Foundations and Facets Forum* 2/3 (1986): 81-102; and idem, *Meeting Jesus Again for the First Time* (New York: HarperCollins, 1994). Though the more recent view has the merit of highlighting the sapiential tradition of Jesus' teaching, it does not give a satisfactory account of the clear indications in the New Testament about the intrinsic connections between Jesus and the coming of the kingdom of God. In this chapter I hold the view that Jesus' preaching was indeed shaped by the expectation of the imminent end of the world and that he was the apocalyptic prophet.

[14] Norman Perrin has insisted that the kingdom of God is more a rich symbol than a clear concept and resists exhaustive definition. See *Jesus and the Language of the Kingdom: Symbol and Metaphor in New Testament Interpretation* (Philadelphia: Fortress Press, 1976).

[15] The three answers are that the kingdom of God (1) is totally future (A. Schweitzer's "thoroughgoing eschatology"), (2) is already realized in the present (C. H. Dodd's "realized eschatology"), or (3) is already inaugurated in the person of Jesus but not yet fulfilled in history (Oscar Cullmann's "already and not-yet eschatology"). For nine variations of these types of eschatology, see Phan, *Eternity in Time*, 26-31.

1. Regarding the very expression itself, in proclaiming God's *kingdom*, how can one dissociate this symbol from its connotations of absolute power and totalitarianism (perhaps even its patriarchalism), in particular in Communist countries such as Vietnam, China, and North Korea, where one political party retains absolute power? Can a royal symbol encourage the people of these countries to achieve forms of government in which basic human rights are respected? Furthermore, in the recent history of most Asian countries, with the exception of Thailand, experiences with emperors and kings have been by and large negative. Terminologically, should the metaphors of king, kingdom, and monarchical reign continue to be used to speak of God and God's rule? Should they not be replaced by other, more democratic symbols?

2. Christian theology often emphasizes the spiritual and transcendent nature of the reign of God. Asia is the cradle of most world religions; presumably it is not difficult to convince Asians of the transcendent dimension of human existence. Rather, the challenge is to convince them that the reign of God demands not only individual conversion leading to salvation, however conceived, but also that unjust and oppressive structures, both socio-political and economic, be removed and replaced by just and liberating structures. Insisting on the socio-political and economic implications of the reign of God is urgent in Asia, in Communist countries where political and religious freedoms are curtailed as well as in democratic ones (for example, Japan, South Korea, Taiwan, Singapore, Hong Kong) where capitalism and market economy reign supreme and produce their own victims of poverty and dehumanization.

3. It has been argued that the addressees of the kingdom of God in the New Testament are the poor, both economically and sociologically, that is, those who lack the basic necessities of life and those marginalized by the society.[16] In the Asian context, who are the addressees of the reign of God? Are they only the economical and sociological poor or also the religious? Asia is characterized not only by the abject poverty of the teeming masses but also by their profound religiousness. How can the proclamation of the reign of God embrace both the poor and the religious?

4. The New Testament presents the reign of God as purely God's initiative and gratuitous gift. Against nineteenth-century liberal theology Johannes Weiss and Albert Schweitzer argued that Jesus understood the kingdom apocalyptically, not as something humans can "build" but as a reality God alone would bring about as an alternative to human striving. Many contemporary liberation theologians, however, insist that the gratuitousness of God's kingdom is not opposed to human action but requires it as a response to God's free gift. How can this tension between gift and task be conveyed in the Asian context in which salvation is seen to be the outcome of both pure grace from a compassionate being (for example, the Amida Buddha in Pure Land Buddhism) and of personal self-cultivation (for example, according to Zen Buddhism and Confucianism)?

---

[16] See J. Pixley and C. Boff, *The Bible, the Church, and the Poor* (Maryknoll, N.Y.: Orbis Books, 1989); and George M. Soares-Prabhu, "Class in the Bible: The Biblical Poor, a Social Class?," *Vidyajyoti* 49 (1985): 320-46.

5. One of the distinctive features of Jesus' understanding and practice of the kingdom of God is his opposition to the anti-kingdom. As Sobrino puts it:

> The Kingdom of God is a utopia that answers the age-old hope of a people in the midst of historical calamities; it is, then, what is good and wholly good. But it is also something liberating, since it arrives in the midst of and in opposition to the oppression of the anti-Kingdom. It needs and generates a hope that is also liberating, from the understandable despair built up in history from the evidence that what triumphs in history is the anti-Kingdom.[17]

It is in the context of Jesus' struggle against the anti-kingdom that his miracles, in particular his casting out devils, can and should be understood. In proclaiming the kingdom of God to Asians, how can the forces of the anti-kingdom in Asia be identified and named? What liberating actions can and should the Christian church undertake as an "option for the poor" so that the kingdom of God is truly good news for the people of Asia?

6. Finally, the biblical symbol of the kingdom of God stands for a *final* and *absolute* salvation from all evils, both physical and spiritual. Moreover, it connotes an eternal *personal* union between God and God's people. How can the final and absolute character of the kingdom of God be conveyed to Asians, among whom on the one hand there are many who believe only in a limited salvation, that is, from immanent forces (for example, Taoists, Confucianists, shamanists, and animists), while on the other hand there are many who believe in an absolute salvation, that is, as the passing beyond and liberation *(moksa)* from all impediments of existence *(samsara)* and as the passing beyond all attachments into *nirvana* and the realization of emptiness *(śunyatā)*?

Furthermore, how can the personal nature of the union with God in the kingdom be maintained for Asians, some of whom believe that the self is illusion *(māya)* and that salvation is consequently the liberation of the self from the conditions of historical existence and personhood, like the drop of water into the sea, or the light of the candle dissolving into the sun?

THE KINGDOM OF GOD IN ASIAN THEOLOGY

These challenges, and many others that the Christian church faces in speaking of the kingdom of God to Asians are daunting indeed, especially because as a theological symbol, the kingdom of God is not confined to a particular section or treatise of theology but is the foundation upon which to construct the cathedral of Christian theology or, to vary the metaphor, the leitmotif around which to compose the symphony of the Christian message. As Sobrino puts it, the kingdom of God is the *eschaton* of liberation theology. A majority of younger Asian theologians, who develop their own version of liberation theology, also

---

[17] Sobrino, *Jesus the Liberator,* 72.

adopt the kingdom of God as their foundational interpretative category.[18] To speak of the reign of God in Asia is, in a sense, to do theology *simpliciter*.

Recently, a number of theologians from countries such as Sri Lanka, South Korea, Taiwan, the Philippines, Hong Kong, and Vietnam have focused on the symbol of the kingdom of God as a central theological category. In light of the challenges described above, I would like to review these efforts. My purpose is not to present a comprehensive exposition of what may be called Asian *basileia* theology but to discern its major contours and identify its strengths as well as its weaknesses. I will concentrate on the works of C. S. Song, who is arguably the ablest and most prolific exponent of *basileia* theology.

In recent Asian Christian theology there have been two major tendencies, one focusing on inculturation, the other on liberation.[19] Though ultimately these two streams should flow into one single theological river,[20] there is no doubt that the liberationist tendency privileges the symbol of the reign of God.

Planetary Theology

Tissa Balasuriya, a Sri Lankan Oblate, makes the kingdom of God the central symbol of his planetary theology. For him, "the most fundamental fact of Asia for Christianity and theology is human life itself—the struggle for life, which is the basic issue for the vast majority of Asia's massive and growing population."[21] The answer to this challenge is Jesus' proclamation of the kingdom of God, since there is, according to Balasuriya, a similarity between Jesus' society and contemporary Asia:

> Within a context of such deep-seated exploitation Jesus presented a radical new teaching, backed up by the witness of his life. He announced it as the "kingdom of God." In today's terminology we may say that he is speaking of a new person and a new society, of new personal and societal values. This was his good news, his gospel. He dethroned the prevailing values of money, power, prestige, and group selfishness. Instead he proposed sharing, service, selfless love of the human person, and a universal solidarity.[22]

It is clear that Balasuriya intends to translate Jesus' message about the rule of God into economic, political, and social terms ("a new person and a new society") and

---

[18] For recent Asian liberation theologies, see Peter C. Phan, "Experience and Theology: An Asian Liberation Perspective," *Zeitschrift für Missionswissenschaft und Religionswissenschaft* 77 (1993): 99-121.

[19] See Virginia Fabella, ed., *Asia's Struggle for Full Humanity* (Maryknoll, N.Y.: Orbis Books, 1980).

[20] See Aloysius Pieris, *An Asian Theology of Liberation* (Maryknoll, N.Y.: Orbis Books, 1988), 87-88; 93-96.

[21] Tissa Balasuriya, *Planetary Theology* (Maryknoll, N.Y.: Orbis Books, 1984), 134.

[22] Ibid., 167. On the basis of his understanding of the kingdom of God, Balasuriya goes on to unfold its implications for church reforms, catechetics, worship, and spirituality.

promote its implications for a social ethics ("sharing, service, selfless love of the human person, and a universal solidarity").

The Theology of Aloysius Pieris

Another Sri Lankan, Jesuit Aloysius Pieris, argues most forcefully that the addressees of the kingdom of God in Asia are not only the economically and sociologically poor but also the religious, or more exactly, the poor who are religious and the religious who are poor. In Pieris's reading of the history of the Christian mission in Asia, the kingdom of God was not able to penetrate into Asia in the past because Christians failed to keep the two poles of Asian reality together: poverty and religiousness. To remain *in* Asia and to become a part *of* Asia now, the kingdom of God must address together the religiousness of the poor and the poverty of the religious.[23] This task is demanded not only by the peculiar situation of Asia but also by Jesus, the proclaimer of the kingdom, who, in Pieris's words, has undergone the double baptism of the "Jordan of Asian religion" and the "Calvary of Asian poverty."[24]

In identifying the addressees of the reign of God in Asia in this way, Pieris has made a momentous contribution to the Asian *basileia* theology and enriched the Latin American liberation theology to which he is indebted.[25] Thus, the Jesus of the reign of God is "the poor monk" who embodies in himself both poverty and religiousness.[26]

The reign of God, when realized in the world, creates what Pieris calls a "contrast society," by which he means "a society where only Yahweh and no other god would reign, a human community governed by love. This is what the phrase 'Kingdom of God' meant for Jesus."[27] It is a society characterized by *obedience* to God, who calls us to be poor, and by religious *poverty*.[28]

---

[23] Pieris carefully distinguishes between unjustly *forced* poverty and *voluntary* poverty. It is through the latter that the former will be eliminated. "Freedom from need" will bring about "freedom from want" (see *An Asian Theology of Liberation*, 20, 37, 61, 88).

[24] Ibid., 45-50.

[25] Pieris suggests that the tools of an Asian liberation theology must include, in addition to praxis and sociological analysis, "introspection," that is, meditation on and dialogue with the wisdom of Asian religions (see ibid., 80). Elsewhere Pieris speaks of the dynamic polarity and mutual nourishment between the mystical experience of *prajña* and the prophetic demands of *agape*, between the mystical and the prophetic experience, embodied in Buddhism and Christianity respectively (see *Love Meets Wisdom: A Christian Experience of Buddhism* [Maryknoll, N.Y.: Orbis Books, 1988], 110-35).

[26] For an interpretation of Pieris's understanding of Jesus as the poor monk, see chapter 6 herein.

[27] Aloysius Pieris, *Fire and Water: Basic Issues in Asian Buddhism and Christianity* (Maryknoll, N.Y.: Orbis Books, 1996), 173.

[28] Pieris applies this notion of kingdom of God to religious life, which, he argues, must be governed basically by the prophetic vows of obedience and poverty, with the vow of celibacy acquiring its prophetic power from the other two vows. See *Fire and Water*, 172-82.

Minjung Theology

Whereas these two Sri Lankan theologians offer an outline of an Asian *basileia* theology, a full-fledged version was elaborated in the 1970s by a group of Korean theologians under the rubric of *minjung* theology. By *minjung* (the popular mass) is meant "the oppressed, exploited, dominated, discriminated against, alienated and suppressed politically, economically, socially, culturally, and intellectually, like women, ethnic groups, the poor, workers and farmers, including intellectuals themselves."[29] Ahn Byung-mu interprets the *ochlos* (the crowd) of Mark's gospel to mean the people who gathered around Jesus, that is, the condemned and alienated class, such as sinners, tax collectors, and the sick. Though not organized into a political group, these people were feared by the powerful. They were, however, unconditionally accepted by Jesus, who sided with them and announced to them the advent of the kingdom of God.[30]

Minjung theologians identify the *ochlos* of the New Testament with the poor and oppressed Koreans throughout the history of Korea, especially during the colonization by the Chinese and the Japanese and under the regime of Park Chung-hee. In the nineteenth century Christianity was introduced into Korea, not as the faith of the oppressing and exploiting colonizers, as in many other Asian countries, but as a seed for liberation from the Chinese and Japanese domination. Japanese and Chinese languages being imposed as the official languages, the appearance of the Bible in Korean (and in the Hangul script) was a veiled invitation to the *minjung* to rise up for their dignity and independence. Jesus' message of the kingdom of God had a liberative effect on the poor and alienated Korean people.

The *minjung* are thus the people of God or members of the kingdom of God. Because of their prolonged and unjust suffering, the *minjung* are weighed down by *han*, another word left untranslated. *Han*, literally "anger" or "resentment," is a mixture of many things: a sense of resignation to inevitable oppression, indignation at the oppressors' cruelty, anger at oneself for allowing oneself to

---

[29] Chung Hyun Kyung, "'Han-pu-ri': Doing Theology from Korean Women's Perspective," in *We Dare to Dream: Doing Theology as Asian Women*, ed. Virginia Fabella and Sun Ai Lee Park (Hong Kong: Asian Women's Resource Centre for Culture and Theology, 1989), 138-39. A distinction is drawn between *daejung*, the confused masses, and *minjung*, the conscientized people. For a discussion of *minjung* theology, see Jung Young Lee, ed., *An Emerging Theology in World Perspective: Commentary on Korean Minjung Theology* (Mystic, Conn.: Twenty-Third Publications, 1988); The Commission on Theological Concerns of the Christian Conference of Asia, ed., *Minjung Theology: People as Subjects of History*, rev. ed. (Maryknoll, N.Y.: Orbis Books, 1983); David Kwang-sun Suh, *The Korean Minjung in Christ* (Hong Kong: Christian Conference of Asia, 1991); Andrew Sung Park, *The Wounded Heart of God: The Asian Concept of Han and the Christian Doctrine of Sin* (Nashville, Tenn.: Abingdon, 1993); and Phan, "Experience and Theology," 118-20.

[30] See Ahn Byung-Mu, "Jesus and the Minjung in the Gospel of Mark," in *Voices from the Margin: Interpreting the Bible in the Third World*, ed. R. S. Sugirtharajah (Maryknoll, N.Y.: Orbis Books, 1991), 85-103.

be oppressed. These emotions, accumulated and intensified by injustice upon injustice, can be a powerful source of psychological energy and an explosive potential for revolution if released in a socially organized way.

The process of resolving the *han* is called *dan*, literally "cutting off." It takes place on both individual and collective levels. On the individual level, it requires self-denial or renunciation of material wealth and comforts. This self-denial will cut off the *han* in our hearts. On the collective level, *dan* can work toward the transformation of the world by raising humans to a higher level of existence. This process is composed of four steps: realizing God's presence in us, worshiping him and allowing this divine consciousness to grow in us, practicing what we believe, and overcoming injustices by transforming the world.[31] Some *minjung* theologians, especially Hyun Young-hak and Korean feminist theologians, advocate more traditional methods to release the *han*, such as rituals, drama, mask dance, and shamanism.[32]

So far, *minjung* theology of *basileia* moves beyond that of both Balasuriya and Pieris by identifying the kingdom of God with a particular group of people, namely, the Korean *minjung* themselves. The *minjung* are not only the addressees of the message of the kingdom of God but constitute the kingdom of God itself. Jesus is identified with the *minjung*. *Minjung* theologians tend to identify the various struggles for liberation in Korean history as manifestations of the Jesus event. This is perhaps because in Korea, unlike in other Asian countries, Christianity from its inception was a politically engaged faith and played a significant role in the struggle for national liberation. Hence, whereas Pieris looks toward non-Christian religions and their poor adherents as the source for the theology of the kingdom of God (because outside of Korea it was these religions that stirred anticolonialist sentiments), *minjung* theologians welcome the Christian message of the reign of God and draw upon their own national resources rather than Buddhist or Confucianist sources to release the *han* and develop a *basileia* theology.

With regard to the term *kingdom,* however, some *minjung* theologians such as Suh Nam-dong find the symbol of the kingdom of God inappropriate. Suh draws a distinction between the kingdom of God and the millennium, between political messianism and messianic politics. According to Suh, the symbol of the kingdom of God has become abstract and otherworldly; it is the ideology promoted by dictatorial rulers practicing their "political messianism." On the contrary, the idea of millennium is concrete and this-worldly; it is the symbol of hope of the *minjung* in their "messianic politics."[33]

---

[31] See Jung Young Lee, "Minjung Theology: A Critical Introduction," in Lee, *An Emerging Theology in World Perspective*, 10-11.

[32] See Chung Hyun Kyung, "Opium or Seed for Revolution? Shamanism: Women-Centred Popular Religiosity in Korea," in *Theologies of the Third World: Convergences and Differences*, ed. Leonardo Boff and Virgilio Elizondo (Edinburgh: T. & T. Clark, 1988), 96-104.

[33] See Suh Nam-dong, "Historical References for a Theology of *Minjung*," in The Commission on Theological Concerns of the Christian Conference of Asia, *Minjung Theology*, 164-77.

Despite criticisms that have been voiced against it,[34] *minjung* theology has made a significant contribution to the formation of a distinctively Asian theology and in particular to the theology of the reign of God. In such a theology the symbol of the kingdom of God no longer remains a Semitic or Western category but takes on a peculiarly Korean face, drawn with the blood and tears of the *minjung*, and becomes a powerful stimulus for the struggle for liberation.

The Theology of C. S. Song

Of all contemporary Asian theologians, C. S. Song, a Presbyterian Taiwanese, is no doubt the most prolific writer on the theme of the kingdom of God.[35] For several years now Song has been persistently advocating an Asian theology. The means with which to construct such a theology, Song suggests, are "imagination, passion, communion, and vision": the imagination is that in which we were created in God's image; passion enables us to feel the compassion of God in us and in others; communion makes us responsible for one another and for God; and vision perceives God's presence in the world and enables us to envision a new way of doing theology.[36]

Among the immense and varied resources of Asia, Song privileges the personal stories of Asian people and their folktales, old and new. And since the stories of most Asian people are of poor, suffering, and powerless people, an authentic Asian theology must of necessity be a liberation theology. Song believes that the most needed skill for Asian theologians is the ability to listen to the whispers, groaning, and shouts from the depths of the misery of Asian humanity. This ability is the "third eye," that is, a power of perception and insight *(satori)* that enables theologians to grasp the meaning beneath the surface of things and phenomena.[37]

---

[34] For a critique, both negative and positive, of *minjung* theology, see Lee, *An Emerging Theology in World Perspective*. In general, *minjung* theology has been criticized for its syncretism, its subordination of scripture to experience, its romanticizing of the *minjung*, its overemphasis on structural evil, its identification of the *minjung* with the people of God, its identification of Jesus with the *minjung*, and its anthropocentrism.

[35] For Song's theological works, see, in particular, *Third-Eye Theology: Theology in Formation in Asian Settings* (Maryknoll, N.Y.: Orbis Books, 1979; rev. ed. 1990); *The Compassionate God* (Maryknoll, N.Y.: Orbis Books, 1982); *Theology from the Womb of Asia* (Maryknoll, N.Y.: Orbis Books, 1986); his christological trilogy entitled *The Cross in the Lotus World,* comprising *Jesus, the Crucified People* (New York: Crossroad, 1990); *Jesus and the Reign of God* (Minneapolis: Fortress Press, 1994); and *Jesus in the Power of the Holy Spirit* (Minneapolis: Fortress Press, 1994). For a fuller presentation of Song's theology, especially his Christology, see chapter 7.

[36] Song, *Theology from the Womb of Asia*, 3.

[37] Song has proposed ten theses on the nature and method of an Asian liberation story theology in C. S. Song, *Tell Us Our Names: Story Theology from an Asian Perspective* (Maryknoll, N.Y.: Orbis Books, 1984), 3-24. For Song's own liberation theology, see ibid., 163-205, and *The Tears of Lady Meng: A Parable of People's Political Theology* (Geneva: The World Council of Churches, 1981; Maryknoll, N.Y.: Orbis Books, 1982).

Beginning with the concrete socio-political and economic situation of the people in which God's "pain-love"[38] is manifested and actively working for their liberation, Song articulates a *basileia* theology that is both profoundly biblical and distinctively Asian.

Unsurprisingly, Song grounds his theology of the reign of God in the message of the Hebrew prophets and the preaching of Jesus, especially his parables. From these sources he derives the conviction that salvation includes political and economic salvation.[39] That is, the kingdom of God is both a kingdom of grace and a kingdom of justice, peace, freedom, and love. Song categorically states that the God of the Hebrew-Christian faith is a "political God."[40] "God's politics" means two things for Song: first, it is a "politics against the barbarism of power,"[41] that is, a power that deprives people of their political, economic, and spiritual freedom. Second, it means that "the God of the prophets, and for that matter the God of Jesus Christ, is a God who takes sides. . . . God takes the side of the poor against the rich."[42]

Song is quick to point out that God's politics does not mean that Christians should *replace* secular power and government with another, perhaps sacred, power and government of their own to bring about the kingdom of God. Rather, what is called for is what Song calls "the transposition of power": "What it aims at is the transformation of power. God's politics has to do with transformation of human politics. It does not seek to rule and dominate but rather to effect a repentance of power. And in this transformation, or *metanoia* of power, is found the essence of God's politics."[43]

Commenting on the parable of the workers in the vineyard (Mt 20:1-15), which he considers "paradigmatic of the reign of God that has already begun in Jesus Christ,"[44] Song writes: "In this parable Jesus makes it clear that that power is the goodness of God. It is the power of mercy, goodness, and love that becomes evident in the demonstration of God's reign. The reign of God is to be

---

[38] On Song's notion of God's "pain-love," see Song, *Third-Eye Theology*, 83-88. In Chinese, the word for love is *thun-ai*, literally "pain-love." The Vietnamese word *thuong* means both to love and to be wounded. For Song, the love that feels pain for its object becomes a pain-love. The more intense love is, the deeper the pain and the more powerful pain-love is. God's love for us is pain-love. The cross is God's excruciating pain-love. It is rooted in the love of the God who bears pain for the world. Song, however, rejects Kazo Kitamori's and Jürgen Moltmann's attempts to internalize suffering into God's own intra-trinitarian life. As he puts it: "Salvation is not God's solitary act of struggle within God's own self. It is the divine-human drama that actualizes itself in human community" (ibid., 85).

[39] "Salvation experienced as liberation from the land of enslavement is first and foremost a political salvation" (ibid., 219).

[40] "The God who commissioned Moses to lead the people out of Egypt is a political God. Throughout the history of Israel, Yahweh never ceased to be a political God" (ibid., 222).

[41] Ibid.

[42] Ibid., 231.

[43] Ibid., 241.

[44] Ibid., 253.

characterized as the power that does good, manifests mercy, and embodies love."[45]

In a commentary on the parable of the wicked tenants in the vineyard (Mk 12;1-11; see also Mt 21:33-44; Lk 20:9-18), Song reminds us that "justice is one of the most fundamental principles of God's politics" and that "Christians as such do not hold political power. . . . But the power of God's love given them through Jesus Christ becomes their power to judge abuses of power by those in positions of political authority. Herein is the essence of the political mission of the church, namely, the transposition of power."[46]

God's politics, which gives the people the power to challenge, criticize, and judge the abuses of those in power, naturally leads to what Song calls the "politics of the cross."[47] The politics of the cross, Song points out, does not dispense people from getting themselves organized, devising strategies and tactics, becoming informed of the intricate power plays by which dictators seek to oppress and manipulate them, and employing the most effective means to achieve their goal of liberation. In this sense, the "dove ethic" must be reinforced by "serpent politics."[48]

But Song reminds us that "what transpired in the final struggle of Jesus with power politics was the power and wisdom of the cross. . . . Whatever the reasons for not pursuing revolution, the fact is that Jesus opted for the politics of the cross."[49] The politics of the cross, however, does not mean weakness and ineffectiveness. Indeed, "the powerless cross proves so powerful that throughout the centuries it has empowered countless persons to struggle for justice and freedom. . . . The politics of the cross has taken form in resistance, in revolt, in revolution. But above all, it has inspired a great many persons to believe in self-sacrifice as the most powerful weapon against self-serving political power. It has encouraged them to use nonviolence, not just for tactical reasons but out of love, to carry the cause of the people to the court of rulers."[50] Hence, essential to Song's theology of the reign of God is both the "people politics" and the "politics of the cross."

Song brought these scattered reflections on the reign of God[51] together in his christological trilogy, especially in the second volume, *Jesus and the Reign of*

---

[45] Ibid.

[46] Ibid., 255.

[47] Song, *Tell Us Our Names*, 176.

[48] "A 'dove politics' without 'serpent politics' can be a weak ethic, an absurd ethic, even a foolish ethic. Conversely, 'serpent politics' without a 'dove ethics' is a politics of deceptive, venomous, and destructive power" (ibid., 178).

[49] Ibid., 179.

[50] Ibid., 180.

[51] See ibid., 163-80 ("The Rat and the Ox: Rethinking the Christian Power Ethic"); and Song, *Theology from the Womb of Asia,* 177-86 ("Reign of God"). In the former book Song contrasts "power politics" of the anti-God with "people politics" of God, God of the people, God in the people, and God with the people. In the latter Song stresses the smallness and humility yet powerful growth of the reign of God as conveyed by the parables of the mustard seed and the leaven.

God, the most extensive Asian *basileia* theology to date. Here Song states explicitly:

> The heart of Jesus' message is the reign of God *(basileia tou theou)*. In all he said and did he was at pains to make clear that God's reign is primarily concerned with the people victimized by a class-conscious society and a tradition-bound religious establishment. God's reign, in light of what Jesus said and did, inaugurates an era of people. It sets a new stage for their life and history. It marks a fresh beginning of the divine-human drama of salvation.[52]

Moving from a study of the message of Jesus to that of his life and ministry,[53] Song attempts to elaborate a theology of the reign of God that on the one hand offers us clues as to why Jesus said and did certain things, and on the other hand enables us to understand and live out the meaning of Jesus and his message of God's reign in our present-day world. With regard to the relationship between the reign of God and Jesus' words and deeds, Song holds that

> the vision that inspired him [Jesus] to say what he did and compelled him to do what he did was the reign of God. This vision of God's reign is the *hermeneutical* principle of the life and ministry of Jesus. It is the *ethical* standard of his lifeview and worldview. It is the *theological* foundation of his relationship to God and to his fellow human beings. And it is the *eschatological* vantage-point from which he relates the present time and the end of time. In short, the vision of God's reign is like the magnifying lens that gives us an enlarged picture of life and the world as Jesus sees them and of life and the world as we must also see them.[54]

Using the two biblical images of a great banquet (Lk 14:16-24) and the new heaven and new earth (Rv 21:22-24), Song sketches Jesus' vision of the reign of God.[55] Like the banquet to which all are invited, the reign of God is characterized by inclusiveness: "The way of Jesus derived from the way of God's reign

---

[52] Song, *Jesus and the Reign of God*, ix.

[53] Song rejects the biographical and philosophical approaches to a theology of the reign of God, the former constructing a biography or "life" of Jesus, the latter starting with a set of theological principles such as those elaborated by the Western tradition. See ibid., x-xi.

[54] Ibid., 2.

[55] Song prefers the expression *reign of God* to *kingdom of God*. The latter "conveys the notions of national territory, feudal system, and monarchical structure, in a word, a culture of authoritarianism. And linked with God's salvation as most Christians see it, it is given a false notion of a heavenly realm of inestimable joy and happiness reserved solely for them. . . . Though the expression 'the reign of God' is not totally adequate, it at least does not represent the notion of a boundary, be it political or religious. Implied in it is the faith that it is God who exercises the rule and not the ecclesiastical authorities, the confession that God exercises the rule in a very special way, uplifting the dispossessed and empowering the oppressed" (ibid., 39).

tells us many things. First and foremost, it tells us who God is and how God carries out God's saving activity in the world. The God illuminated by Jesus' way with people is the God who does not discriminate against them on account of creed, color, or sex. God is a classless God, too."[56]

And like the new heaven and new earth, the reign of God always and necessarily contains socio-political and economic dimensions. The redemption brought about by the reign of God is "not the redemption of individual souls but the redemption that brings the dead back to life, rights the wrongs committed by those in power, and eradicates injustices inflicted on the powerless by demonic systems and establishments."[57]

This vision of the reign of God as comprehensive inclusiveness and sociopolitical and economic liberation must, Song insists, be rooted in the reality of the present world; it must not be pictured as a purely eschatological event occurring at the end of time and in the beyond. In this way the reign of God promotes what Song terms "a culture of empowerment"; that is, it enables oppressed and dispossessed people to realize the injustice of their condition (conscientization) and to take action against it.[58]

Though the reign of God is God's deed, an event brought about by God, it needs two things, according to Song: First, it needs eyewitnesses, people who sight it, identify it and distinguish it from counterfeits. Second, it needs witnesses in another sense, that is, people who embody it by their personal involvement in it in one way or another. Like Jesus, people of today must bear witness in a situation of conflict and struggle for freedom, justice, love, and life over against slavery, injustice, hate, and death.[59]

Finally, it is important to note that, despite his repeated and emphatic insistence on the sociopolitical and economic dimensions of the reign of God, Song does not forget that God's reign also brings forgiveness of sin and deliverance from demonic powers and that, above all, it reaches its fulfillment only in the eschatological resurrection. However, Song hastens to add that the resurrection is not an event unrelated to what we are doing now for the reign of God:

> The resurrection is not a denial of the past. It is sacrament of tears shed, pain sustained, and death remembered. This sacrament affirms that the tears shed are not in vain, that the pain sustained is the birthpang of hope,

---

[56] Ibid., 8.

[57] Ibid., 57. The idea that the reign of God includes the socio-political and economic dimensions of human existence is well taken. However, at times Song seems to overstate the socio-political and economic dimensions in Jesus' understanding of the reign of God: "Jesus must be at pains to rebuild a culture on the foundation of God's reign as he understood it. The reign of God for him is very much more a social and political vision than a religious concept. It has to be the texture of a society. It must be the foundation of a community. The reign of God is, thus, a cultural happening" (ibid., 105).

[58] "*The reign of God creates a culture of empowerment*. It *is* a culture of empowerment" (ibid., 136).

[59] Ibid., part 3, "Witness."

and that death is remembered not to be feared but to be transformed into life. . . . To believe in life resurrected from the ruins of human conflict comes from God who is the power of transformation. And to work toward change in the human condition is a calling in response to the vision of God's reign.[60]

So far I have shown how deeply biblical Song's *basileia* theology is. But it has also another aspect that demands attention, namely, its distinctive Asianness. Indeed, it is already Asian in the very way Song privileges and emphasizes certain biblical teachings on the reign of God rather than others because of the specific situation of Asian people. Song consistently reads the biblical message through the lens of the poverty and oppression to which a large number of Asians are subjected. Moreover, in developing his *basileia* theology Song makes extensive use of Asian socio-political and economic histories, both ancient and contemporary, from the Chinese folktale of Lady Meng[61] to the current situations in the Philippines, Vietnam, Taiwan, Japan, Korea, Thailand, and Hong Kong, just to mention the places to which Song most frequently refers.

Furthermore, Song derives his theological insights from a great variety of Asian stories, poems, novels, individual biographies, songs, dances, and art works. He also mines the sayings and teachings of religious sages as well as the sacred texts of Asian religions for parallels with the teachings of the Christian Bible on the reign of God.[62] As Song puts it, "The totality of life is the raw material of theology. Theology deals with concrete issues that affect life in its totality and not just with abstract concepts that engage theological brains. No human problem is too humble or too insignificant for theology. Theology has to wrestle with the earth, not with heaven."[63]

True to his methodological precepts, Song offers a *basileia* theology that is rooted in the earth and, more specifically, in the Asian humus, while not ignoring its transcendental character. Nurtured by the message and actions of the Hebrew prophets and Jesus for justice, human dignity, peace, and love, and bathed in the blood and tears of dispossessed and oppressed Asian people, and inspired by their struggle for liberation, Song's theology of the reign of God is by far the most developed and the richest among contemporary Asian theologians.

BASILEIA TOU THEOU, STILL A MEANINGFUL SYMBOL FOR ASIANS?

In this concluding section I address the six issues raised by the symbol of the kingdom of God outlined above in the light of the theologies of the reign of God proposed by the Asian theologians whose works I have discussed. In particular, I carry out my reflections on the reign of God with reference to the Confucian culture, a feature common to many Asian countries.

---

[60] Ibid., 286.
[61] See Song, *The Tears of Lady Meng.*
[62] For Song's use of stories in his theology, see, in particular, Song, *Tell Us Our Names.*
[63] Ibid., 6.

1. To preach and witness to the reign of God is the primary mission of the Christian church, even in Asia. The first challenge to this mission is not only to find an appropriate translation for the expression *basileia tou theou* in various Asian languages.[64] A much more arduous task is to convey accurately the substance of the biblical message about the reign of God as well as to strip away the many distortions that have accrued to its meaning throughout the history of its interpretation. One of the persistent distortions is the patriarchal and authoritarian connotations attached to the symbol of the kingdom of God. As we have seen, Song prefers the expression *reign of God* to that of *kingdom of God* to avoid the latter's patriarchal and authoritarian implications.

For cultures heavily influenced by Confucianism, such as those of China, Taiwan, Vietnam, Korea, and Japan, the dangers of patriarchalism and hierarchical authoritarianism, and correlatively those of blind obedience and preservation of the status quo, are particularly acute. Confucian society is regimented by correct relationships between sovereign and subject, between husband and wife, and between parents and children. Asked about what a government should be, Confucius replied: "Let a prince be a prince, the minister a minister, the father a father, and the son a son."[65]

In this cultural context it is vitally important to affirm the basic equality of all persons in the reign of God and to stress the prophetic character of the reign of God as well as the duty of speaking truth to power. Song has pointed out that Asian Christians tend to identify obedience to God with obedience to political authorities and to regard involvement in political and social affairs as irrelevant to the Christian faith and even harmful to salvation. In light of the biblical teaching on the reign of God, he asserts categorically: "The more Christian political concern takes on an insurrectional, rebellious, and subversive character under a repressive state authority, the more it resembles the politics of God. To state it more clearly, if the church has no message of justice to proclaim to a ruling authority that practices injustice toward its people, the church has opted out of the politics of God."[66]

Of course, filial piety, the Confucian virtue par excellence, remains a fundamental virtue in the kingdom of God. But because God is the Father, "from whom every family in heaven and on earth is named" (Eph 3:15), all piety that is rendered to human kings and fathers must be subordinated to and measured by our filial piety and obedience to God, who alone reigns in the *basileia tou theou*.

---

[64] In general, there is no difficulty in finding an equivalent for *basileia* in Asian languages, since many of the Asian countries had (e.g., China, Korea, Vietnam, and Cambodia) or still have (e.g., Thailand and Japan) emperors or kings. As for *theos*, in the seventeenth century there was in China a lengthy and acrimonious debate as to whether the appropriate Chinese word for God is *t'ien* (heaven) or *t'ien chu* (lord of heaven) or *shang-ti* (lord on high).

[65] *The Analects of Confucius*, translated and annotated by Arthur Waley (New York: Vintage Books, 1939), XII, 11. See also *The Doctrine of the Mean*, trans. James Legge (Oxford: Clarendon Press, 1893), XX, 8; and chapter 6 herein.

[66] Song, *Third-Eye Theology*, 236.

2. These reflections already adumbrate the second issue, namely, how to communicate to Asians the truth that the reign of God includes socio-political and economic dimensions. It is common knowledge that religions such as Hinduism and Buddhism tend to foster, at least among the masses, disregard for and escape from the present world and everyday life *(samsara)*, which is considered as illusion *(māya)* or suffering *(dukkha)*. The goal would be to seek release *(moksa)* or liberation *(nirvana)* from life, whether this individual life is seen as an essential self *(atman* or *jīva)* or as a series of an uncountable number of instants, each caused and conditioned, migrating and inhabiting successive bodies (reincarnation).

Similarly, Taoist ethics of non-contrivance *(wu wei)* and its insistence on the duty of following non-deliberate and non-purposive intuition or spontaneity *(tzu-jan)* in nature, society, and individuals may foster passivity in front of evil and injustice. Furthermore, the Taoist injunction that individuals and the state should keep in close touch with the primitive and undifferentiated source of creativity, which is like an "uncarved block," may discourage initiatives to reform oppressive structures and institute forward-looking plans of action rather than reversion to the origin *(fan)*.

Confucianism, which was criticized by Taoism for its notion of the human person as a rational and moral being with obligations to the society and the state, affirms the goodness of the human person and the correspondence between the ethical orientation of the human person and that of the universe. Confucius, witnessing the social and political chaos of his times, prescribed as remedy a return to the ways of virtue neglected since the sage emperors of antiquity. The virtues, as embodied by the gentleman *(chün-tzu)*, include humaneness *(jen)*, reciprocity *(shu)*, propriety *(li)* through the rectification of names *(cheng-ming)* and rites, and filial piety *(hsiao)*.

Confucian ethics, however, focuses primarily on the self-cultivation of the individual, though individual behavior is acknowledged to have an impact on social units such as the family and the state. Indeed, *The Great Learning* affirms that if one wishes to order the state, one must first practice self-cultivation through the investigation of things, sincerity of thought, and rectification of the heart, and then proceed to regulate one's family.[67] The normative movement is from the individual to the family to the state. In this sense Confucianism can be said to lack a full-fledged social ethics.[68]

To this apparent lack of social concern and ethical individualism a Christian theology of the reign of God brings the message about the God who takes sides, about social justice and liberation, and about the necessity of overcoming oppressive structures, even by means of revolution as the last resort. Furthermore, it can help Asian religions retrieve the potential for social transformation of

---

[67] James Legge, trans., *The Great Learning* (Oxford: Clarendon, 1893), par. 6.

[68] This conclusion is also affirmed by Peter K. H. Lee and Wong Yuk, "Ta-T'ung and the Kingdom of God," *Ching Feng* 41/4 (1988): 239: "Confucianism has yet to develop fully the idea of social justice. Confucianists would have difficulty with the idea of public ownership."

some of their teachings. Pieris has reminded us of the political and economic implications of the Buddhist practice of voluntary poverty. The Buddhist monk embodies in himself both religiousness and poverty. He is quintessentially one who has renounced Mammon for religious reasons so that he may help the socio-economic poor by radically transforming oppressive social structures imposed by Mammon. With the former the monk achieves interior liberation from greed or acquisitiveness (which the Buddha identifies as the cause of all sufferings in his second "Noble Truth"); with the latter he brings about social emancipation from structural poverty imposed upon the masses.[69]

Similarly, in light of the theology of the reign of God, Confucius's teachings regarding the mandate of heaven *(t'ien-ming)* of the king (and by extension, political authorities in general) and the duty of the ruler to practice virtue *(te)* to preserve the mandate of heaven can be retrieved for the common good and social transformation.[70] Already the *Book of Odes (shi ching)* instructs the king: "Cultivate your virtue. Always strive to be in harmony with Heaven's Mandate."[71] Again, the *Book of History (shu ching)* says: "Let the king be serious in what he does. He should not neglect to be serious with virtue."[72]

Following this tradition Confucius repeatedly emphasized the duty of the king to lead the people with virtue and propriety: "Lead the people with governmental measures and regulate them by law and punishment, and they will avoid wrongdoing but will have no sense of honor and shame. Lead them with virtue and regulate them by the rules of propriety *(li)*, and they will have a sense of shame and, moreover, set themselves right."[73] Asked about what is most important for the state, armament, food, or the confidence of the people, Confucius replied that he would give up the first two, because "no state can exist without the confidence of the people."[74] Again: "If a ruler sets himself right, he will be followed without his command. If he does not set himself right, even his commands will not be obeyed."[75] Finally, for Confucius, the fact that a state has a small population is no cause for concern; rather, his concern is for the "unequal distribution of wealth": "For when wealth is equally distributed, there will not be poverty; when there is harmony, there will be no problem of there being too

---

[69] Pieris points out that the Buddhist monastic community *(sangha)* as symbol of poor religiousness and religious poverty fulfills a role not purely religious but political as well. Indeed, by practicing what Pieris calls "religious socialism," Buddhist *sanghas*, especially those in rural areas, have preserved the seeds of liberation that religion and poverty have combined to sow (see Pieris, *An Asian Theology of Liberation*, 43).

[70] In general, Confucianists before the T'ang dynasty (618-907) understood the mandate of heaven to mean the decree of God determining the course of one's life, whereas scholars under the Sung dynasty (960-1279), especially Chu Hsi, took it to mean the nature of things.

[71] *Book of Odes*, ode no. 235. See *A Source Book in Chinese Philosophy*, trans. and comp. Wing-Tsit Chan (Princeton, N.J.: Princeton University Press, 1963), 7.

[72] *Book of History*, "The Announcement of Duke Shao," in Chan, *A Source Book*, 8.

[73] *The Analects*, 2.3, in *A Source Book*, 22.

[74] *The Analects*, 12.7, in *A Source Book*, 39.

[75] *The Analects*, 13.6, in *A Source Book*, 41.

few people; and when there are security and peace, there will be no danger to the state."[76]

From this small sample of Confucius's sayings it is clear that even in the Confucian tradition the power of the ruler is not regarded as absolute and permanent, derived as it were from some divine source, as might be implied by the emperor's title of Son of Heaven. Rather it is based on the mandate of heaven, that is, a self-existent moral law, the heart of which is virtue. The future of a dynasty is not secured by some divine right but by the ruler's good deeds to promote justice, economic equality, and peace.

Even before Confucius, Li Ko had defended the right of the people to remove an unjust ruler who has lost heaven's mandate because of his lack of virtue: "The ruler exists to shepherd his people and rectify their errors. If he, himself, pursues secret debauches and disregards the affairs of the people, the people will not be rectified when they are in error, so that the evil will become greater. If with evilness he supervises the people, he will fall and be unable to get up. . . . When such (a ruler) comes to his doom, there is no one to mourn him, and of what good then is he?"[77]

Together with the Hebrew-Christian symbol of the reign of God, these teachings of Asian religions should be harnessed to formulate a vision of and a plan of action for justice and peace.

3. The symbol of the kingdom of God is addressed as a challenge not only to the powers that be, as a word of truth to power, but also as good news to the masses. Pieris has argued convincingly that the vast majority of Asian people are both religious and poor, and that the message of the kingdom of God, if it is to become a life-giving truth not only *in* but also *of* Asia, must be presented to the religious poor as its primary addressees. This means that Christian mission today must abandon its focus on the Asian elite, for example, the mandarins in the case of Matteo Ricci or the Brahmins in the case of Roberto de Nobili. Rather, Christians should announce the good news of the reign of God first to the common people who are most often poor and oppressed, the *minjung*. To be effective, however, this proclamation must not be simply a matter of words but a praxis, together with the *minjung*, to achieve freedom, justice, and physical well-being for all those who are deprived of basic human rights.

Furthermore, Christians should jettison the notion that they have a well-formulated and universally valid theology to teach Asian religious poor and nothing to learn from them. At most, it is thought, they have to "inculturate" the symbol of God's reign in Asia by adapting Christian theology to indigenous modes of thought and local customs. On the contrary, an Asian theology must be a *common* effort by both Christians and non-Christians to understand what God is saying to Asians today and to construct a theology on the basis of their common experiences, religious as well as socio-political. In addition to Basic

---

[76] *The Analects*, 16:1, in *A Source Book*, 45.

[77] Li Ko, *Lu Yü*, I, 15, in Fung Yu-lan, *A History of Chinese Philosophy*, vol. 1, *The Period of the Philosophers*, trans. Berk Bodde (Princeton, N.J.: Princeton University Press, 1952), 41.

Christian Communities, there must be Basic Human Communities in which Christian theology is incubated and grows. In other words, Christian mission must be both inculturation (including interreligious dialogue) and liberation, which are simply two sides of the same coin. It is in this double context that a theology of the reign of God will be developed that is recognizably faithful to the Christian tradition and distinctly Asian.

4. It is in the experience of liberation, I submit, that the gratuitousness of the kingdom of God can be best understood and lived. History has shown that religious practitioners often run the risk of taking their own ascetical efforts as the cause of their spiritual enlightenment and transformation, and therefore of thinking that they earn their salvation through their work. On the contrary, the poor, who are often crushed and dehumanized by extreme poverty, deprived as they are of the most basic things that give a minimal sense of human dignity, will most often receive a crumb of bread or a bowl of rice as a gift from on high or from the compassion of a passer-by.

Of course, once conscientized of their plight as the result of oppression, the poor will eventually make claim to what is rightfully theirs and will take part in actions that bring about their liberation. It is here that the theology of the kingdom of God will help confirm the poor's sense of the gratuitousness of their liberation by showing them that they can achieve freedom and justice for themselves because God has taken their side first, because, as Song has argued, God is not neutral but has made a preferential option for the poor.

Confucianism has widely been characterized as humanism engaged in moral self-cultivation, with its prescriptions for a good society based on virtue, just government, and harmonious human relations. Confucius's saying that "it is man that can make the Way great, and not the Way that can make man great" is often cited as proof of thoroughgoing humanism.[78] On the other hand, the experience of liberation of the poor in the kingdom of God can convincingly show that human effort and divine grace are not mutually contradictory. On the contrary, as Gustavo Gutiérrez has argued,

> gratuitousness is the atmosphere in which the entire quest for effectiveness is bathed. It is something both subtler and richer than a balance maintained between two important aspects. This alternative perspective does not represent an abandonment of efficacy but rather seeks to locate efficacy in a comprehensive and fully human context that is in accord with the gospel. That context is the space of freely bestowed encounter with the Lord.[79]

In the kingdom of God as experienced by the poor, human effort and divine grace are not in inverse but direct proportion: the more human, the more divine; the more divine, the more human.

---

[78] *The Analects*, 15.28, in *A Source Book*, 44.
[79] Gustavo Gutiérrez, *We Drink from Our Own Wells: The Spiritual Journey of a People*, trans. Matthew O'Connell (Maryknoll, N.Y.: Orbis Books, 1984), 109.

5. The message about the kingdom of God will be ethereal and abstract unless the signs of the anti-kingdom are clearly identified and named. In Asia, in my judgment, the anti-kingdom is not constituted by non-Christian religions with their alleged superstitions and immoralities, as missionaries thought in the past. Nor is it necessarily Communism with its atheist ideology, as opponents of the "Evil Empire" would have us believe. In some cases Communism can be the cauldron in which the Asian Christian churches are purified of their unholy alliance with foreign political and economic powers.

Rather, the demons who must be exorcised from the kingdom of God are, in Asia as well as elsewhere, the men and women who continually seek to oppress God's beloved people for their personal gains, political and economic. This is true not only in the model of capitalism (Japan) and in the "four little dragons of Asia" (Hong Kong, Singapore, Taiwan, and South Korea) but also in countries that are still officially Communist but which have begun to embrace capitalism as the new messiah offering a panacea for all ills (Vietnam and China).

Another demon is the pervasive patriarchal and androcentric social and moral system regnant both in the Christian churches and in many Asian countries.[80] Other demons include sex tourism (in Thailand and the Philippines), cheap labor, and ecological destruction. The kingdom of God cannot be built in Asia unless these demons are given names and exorcised.

6. Finally, the nature of salvation, which is the goal of the kingdom of God, must be broached. Confucianism does not propose belief in a savior or a messiah who would bring supra-temporal or transcendent salvation. Rather, it acknowledges the importance of a good teacher who exemplifies his teachings in his own life and who, ideally, should also be a ruler, a sort of Platonic philosopher-king, in order to put his teachings into practice for the good of the state. The ideal is to be the "Inner Sage and Outer King." The Inner Sage is one who has achieved virtue within self, and the Outer King is one who has done great deeds for the world. Salvation, if such a word could be used in reference to Confucianism, consists solely in realizing the full human potential in oneself through moral self-cultivation and assisting others to become the gentleman or superior man *(chün-tzu).*

Perhaps the best way to explain what Confucianism means by salvation is by way of the concept of *ta-t'ung* (great unity) mentioned in the *Li-yün* chapter of the Confucian classic *Li-chi.*

When the Great Way was practiced, the world was shared by all alike. The worthy and the able were promoted to office and people practiced good faith and lived in affection. Therefore they did not regard as parents

[80] Asian feminist theologians have consistently criticized patriarchalism and androcentrism in their churches and societies. See Virginia Fabella and Sun Ai Lee Park, eds., *We Dare to Dream: Doing Theology as Asian Women* (Hong Kong: Asian Women's Resource Centre for Culture and Theology, 1989); and Chung Hyun Kyung, *Struggle to Be the Sun Again: Introducing Asian Women's Theology* (Maryknoll, N.Y.: Orbis Books, 1990).

only their own parents, or as sons only their own sons. The aged found a fitting close to their lives; the robust their proper employment; the young were provided with an upbringing; the widow and the widower, the orphaned and the sick, with proper care. Men had their tasks and women their hearths. They hated to see goods lying about in waste, yet they did not hoard them for themselves; they disliked the thought that their energies were not fully used, yet they used them not for their private ends. Therefore all evil plotting was prevented and thieves and rebels did not arise, so that people could leave their outer gates unbolted. This was the age of Great Unity.[81]

If Confucianism retrojects this "golden age of Great Unity" into the past, Christianity projects it into the eschatological future under the symbol of the kingdom of God. Despite fundamental differences in their visions of what constitutes the ultimate happiness for humanity, there are many commonalities between the Confucian and Christian construals of the "messianic age": common possession of earthly resources, good faith, universal love, care of the weak in society (the aged, the young, the widows, the widowers, the orphans, the sick), justice, peace, work for the common good, and absence of evil.

It must be mentioned that to this list of inner-worldly blessings the Christian faith adds the personal union of humans with the Triune God in grace as an essential element of the reign of God. But this union with the divine must not be viewed as something antithetical to or transcending the earthly blessings. Rather, the latter must be seen as *sacraments,* that is, instruments and signs of the personal union between humans and the Triune God. In this way, the symbol of God's reign, though not identical with the Confucian utopia of the Great Unity, can find deep resonances or "thick resemblances" with what constitutes for Confucianists the ultimate happiness for humanity.

The symbol of *basileia tou theou* retains a profound meaning and relevance for Asians. It is no accident that the Institute for Interreligious Affairs on the Theology of Dialogue of the Federation of Asian Bishops' Conference met in Pattaya, Thailand, 17-22 November 1985, to reflect on the meaning of the kingdom of God for Asia. The meeting issued a final statement, which concludes with these words: "Thus we persist in the hope that men and women of faith and good will, strengthened by the experience of common humanity, will join in the building of God's Kingdom, whose completion He alone can bring about."[82]

---

[81] See the text (with minor changes) in Peter K. H. Lee and Wong Yuk, "Ta-T'ung and the Kingdom of God," *Ching Feng* 31/4 (1988): 225.

[82] See Gaudencio B. Rosales and C. G. Arévalo, eds., *For All the Peoples of Asia: Federation of Asian Bishops' Conferences. Documents from 1970 to 1991* (Maryknoll, N.Y.: Orbis Books, 1992; Quezon City, Philippines: Claretian Publications, 1992), 255.

5

Jesus the Christ with an Asian Face

Imagine that the first disciples of Jesus had turned to the East rather than to the Greco-Roman world to carry out the Lord's "great commission" (Mt 28:18-20), that East Syrian Christianity, which came to China in the seventh century, had gained wide acceptance, or that the missionary enterprise of such luminaries as Matteo Ricci in China, Roberto de Nobili in India, and Alexandre de Rhodes in Vietnam had transformed the cultures of these lands. Imagine this historical improbability and ask how Jesus' question, "Who do you say that I am?" (Mt 16:15), would have been answered. Would the church have continued to confess Jesus as "the Messiah, the Son of the living God" (Mt 16:17), and would it have proclaimed him, in the words of the Council of Chalcedon, the only-begotten Son of God in one *hypostasis* or *prosopon* in two *physeis*, human and divine? To phrase the question in the words of Raimundo Panikkar, "Does one need to be spiritually a Semite or intellectually a Westerner in order to be a Christian?"[1]

In the past the Asian churches were content with rehashing the creedal formulas and the theological systems devised by the West. In Christology, for instance, not only the dogmatic teaching but also the ontological categories of Chalcedon were accepted as universally normative. In Asian seminaries, courses on Christology consisted mainly in finding appropriate translations for such expressions as *incarnation, hypostatic union, nature, person, homoousios, atonement,* and the like. Furthermore, since Christian mission in Asia was intimately bound with Western imperialism, the imported portrait of Jesus was what has been called the Colonial Christ, that is, Jesus as the white, male, all-powerful lord conquering souls and empires for God and implanting his own church.

Since the nineteenth century, however, a distinctly Asian theology has begun to emerge as Asian theologians attempt to articulate their Christian faith in the context and in terms of their own cultures and socio-political conditions. In this chapter I present some recent efforts of Asian Christians to answer Jesus'

---

[1] Raimundo Panikkar, "The Jordan, the Tiber, and the Ganges: Three Kairological Moments of Christic Self-Consciousness," in *The Myth of Christian Uniqueness: Toward a Pluralistic Theology of Religions*, ed. John Hick and Paul Knitter (Maryknoll, N.Y.: Orbis Books, 1987), 89.

question: "Who do you say that I am?"[2] In the first part I describe the context and the corresponding method that inform Asian theology in general and Christology in particular. In the second part I expound some salient Asian Christologies that hold promise of theological and spiritual fruitfulness for the Asian people. I conclude with critical reflections on the appropriateness of these Christologies to the Christian tradition and their adequacy for the Asian context.

CONTEXT AND METHOD

The Asian continent is composed of several subcontinents with at least seven major linguistic zones, far more than in any other continent.[3] Given such a cultural and linguistic diversity, Asian theology is a *rara avis* defying exact description and neat categorization.[4] Nevertheless, there exist throughout Asia, despite genuine differences, a common religio-cultural heritage and a similar socio-political context. Since all theologies are necessarily context-dependent

---

[2] Recall that Jesus asked two distinct questions: "Who do people say that the Son of Man is?" and "Who do you say that I am?" (Mt 16:14-16). Interestingly, in Asia the first persons to reflect on who Jesus is from the perspective of Asia's religious traditions were not Christians but Indian Hindus such as Ram Mohun Roy (Jesus as Supreme Guide to happiness), Keshub Chunder Sen (Jesus as true *Yogi*), Swami Vivekananda (Jesus as *Jivanmukta*, that is, one who has achieved liberation while alive), Rabindranath Tagore (Jesus as the Son of Man seeking the "poor" of the earth), and Mahatma Gandhi (Jesus as the Supreme *Satyagrahi*, that is, lover and fighter for truth). They are the "people" of Jesus' first question. In this chapter I will prescind from these attempts by non-Christians to find the meaning of Jesus Christ for them. For excellent studies of these "Christologies," see M. M. Thomas, *The Acknowledged Christ of Indian Renaissance* (London: SCM Press, 1969) and Stanley J. Samartha, *The Hindu Response to the Unbound Christ* (Bangalore: Christian Institute for the Study of Religion and Society, 1974).
[3] The seven linguistic zones are the Semitic, the Ural-Altaic, the Indo-Iranian, the Dravidian, the Sino-Tibetan, the Malayo-Polynesian, and the Japanese. As Aloysius Pieris, a Sri Lankan theologian, has pointed out, language represents a way of *experiencing* reality and religion is its *expression*. Language is a *theologia inchoativa*. Given the fact that there is linguistic heterogeneity in Asia and that Asian theologians are not able to communicate with one another except in a language not their own (indeed, they have to use the languages of their colonizers), Asian theology is deprived of one of the most fruitful elements of its methodology. See Aloysius Pieris, *An Asian Theology of Liberation* (Maryknoll, N.Y.: Orbis Books, 1988), 70-71.
[4] For introductions to Asian theology, see Barbara and Leon Howell, *Southeast Asians Speak Out: Hope and Despair in Many Lands* (New York: Friendship Press, 1975); Gerald H. Anderson, ed., *Asian Voices in Christian Theology* (Maryknoll, N.Y.: Orbis Books, 1976); Douglas J. Elwood, ed., *What Asian Christians Are Thinking: A Theological Source Book* (Quezon City, Philippines: Newday Publishers, 1976); idem, *Asian Christian Theology: Emerging Themes* (Philadelphia: The Westminster Press, 1980); Dayanandan T. Francis and F. J. Balsudaram, eds., *Asian Expressions of Christian Commitment* (Madras: The Christian Literature Society, 1992); and R. S. Sugirtharajah, ed., *Frontiers in Asian Christian Theology: Emerging Trends* (Maryknoll, N.Y.: Orbis Books, 1994).

and local,[5] inasmuch as the context determines both the method and the agenda of all theologies, it is helpful to outline briefly the cultural-religious and socio-political contexts of Asia and indicate the challenges they present to Asian theology.[6]

Poverty and Oppression

Aloysius Pieris has repeatedly argued that an authentically Asian theology must take into account two characteristics of the Asian context:

> Any discussion about Asian theology has to move between two poles: the *Third Worldliness* of our continent and its peculiarly *Asian* character. More realistically and precisely, the common denominator linking Asia with the Third World is its overwhelming poverty. The specific character defining Asia within the other poor countries is its multifaceted religiousness. These two inseparable realities constitute in their interpenetration what might be designated as the *Asian context*, the matrix of any theology truly Asian.[7]

The Third Worldliness or the dehumanizing poverty crushing immense masses of Asia is *imposed* or *forced* poverty, the product of oppression and injustice, as distinct from *voluntary* poverty, which is freely assumed as a way of life in solidarity with the poor in their struggle for liberation. Except in Japan, which has a first-world economy, other Asian countries suffer from massive poverty, with destitution for the many and opulence for the few, brought about by colonialism, neocolonialism (with the small elite inheriting the power and wealth of the colonials), economic exploitation by multinational corporations, institutionalized violence, and military dictatorship.

Violence, both political and economic, was perpetrated not only by Westerners to Asians in their wars of conquest (for example, the French in Indochina, the Spaniards in the Philippines, and the British in India) but also by Asians to their fellow Asians (for example, the Japanese to the Koreans, the Chinese to the Vietnamese, and the Vietnamese to the Chams and the Cambodians). And within each country, acts of violence and oppression are committed by one class against another class (for example, the caste system in India), by the racially dominant group against the tribes and ethnic minorities (for example, the Burakumin in Japan, the mountain tribes in Vietnam, and the Tamils in Sri

---

[5] For the contextual character of all theologies, see Peter C. Phan, "Cultural Diversity: A Blessing or a Curse for Theology and Spirituality?" *Louvain Studies* 19 (1994): 195-211; and Robert Schreiter, *Constructing Local Theologies* (Maryknoll, N.Y.: Orbis Books, 1985).

[6] For a discussion of these contexts and their challenges to theology, see Peter C. Phan, "Experience and Theology: An Asian Liberation Perspective," *Zeitschrift für Missionswissenschaft und Religionswissenschaft* 77/2 (1993): 101-11.

[7] Pieris, *An Asian Theology of Liberation*, 69.

Lanka) and by members of one religion against those of another (for example, Hindus and Sikhs, Buddhists and Catholics).

Among the victims of oppression women form a special group. Asian feminist theologians have highlighted the multiple forms of injustice and violence against Asian women. Examples of violence against women include forms of the dowry system, widow burning, forced sterilization and gender determination in China and India, sex tourism in Thailand and the Philippines, discrimination on the basis of religious fundamentalism in Malaysia, the male-oriented emperor system in Japan, and the Confucian family legal system in most Asian countries.

Religiousness: Cosmic and Metacosmic

Besides massive poverty Asia is also characterized by pervasive religiousness. Asia is the birthplace of all the major religions of the world—not only Hinduism, Buddhism, Jainism, Zoroastrianism (southern Asia), Confucianism, Taoism, Shintoism (eastern Asia), but also Judaism, Christianity, and Islam (western Asia). These religious institutions with their sacred texts, rituals, ethical teachings, and mysticism are what Pieris calls the "metacosmic order" embodying the "cosmic religion," that is, the basic subconscious attitude that the *homo religiosus* adopts toward the mysteries of life.[8]

Among the non-Christian religions, Buddhism represents the greatest challenge to Christian theology in Asia because, as Pieris points out, it is the one soteriology that is truly *pan-Asian* in cultural integration, numerical strength, geographical extension, and political maturity; it is not limited to any one language or national group.

Communism and Socialism

In addition to poverty and religiousness in the Asian context, a third characteristic should be mentioned: the presence of Communist regimes. While Communism in Eastern Europe has collapsed, symbolized by the fall of the Berlin Wall, it still survives and will do so for a foreseeable future in China, Vietnam, and North Korea (the only other Communist country is Cuba, but because of its size and economic and military power, it does not pose a threat to the West). While China and Vietnam have embarked upon a limited path of economic liberalization, both politically and ideologically, all three countries have officially maintained a staunchly Communist and areligious stance and brook no opposition.

These Communist countries, to which about half of the Asian population belongs, pose a challenge to Christian theology: Will theology be able to explore the religious and spiritual meaning of the unbelief and atheism that accompany the political realization of the Marxist dream? Or will it continue the

---

[8] Ibid., 71-72.

mindless demonization of Communism and ignore this loudest of questions God is posing to contemporary Christianity?

In sum, the Asian context presents both severe challenges and enormous opportunities to Christianity and Christian theology: What can they do with and say to teeming millions of Asians, most of whom are crushed by abject poverty and live in dehumanizing squalor, and yet are imbued with pervasive religiousness? What can Christian theologians who are not poor say to billions of Asian poor who are not theologians? How can Christianity help these people become "subjects" of their future and destiny and facilitate their struggle for liberation from the aftermath of colonization, political oppression, economic exploitation, Communist regimes, patriarchal domination, and racial discrimination?[9]

Resources and Method

In an *Asian theology* whose form and method are molded by and related to the historical context of Asia, as distinct from a *theology in Asia* whose structure and style are not shaped by such a context,[10] the Asian reality as described above, and not the Bible and/or tradition, is the starting point. Of course, theology, Asian and otherwise, is an intellectual activity, a critical reflection on Christian living. But it is, as Gustavo Gutiérrez has put it, a "second act" following upon the "first act," which is Christian praxis; it "rises only at sundown."[11]

This praxis of love and justice is carried out in a particular context, and theology, in reflecting on the Christian praxis, must first of all be informed by this praxis and familiar with this context in all its dimensions. There are, then, in terms of theological method, two essential steps that must be performed as constitutive parts of an Asian theology: first, personal commitment to and active solidarity with the teeming masses of poor and oppressed Asians in their struggle for justice and liberation; and second, social analysis.[12]

---

[9] For a succinct presentation of the socio-political and religio-cultural challenges of Asia to theology, see K. C. Abraham, ed., *Third World Theologies: Commonalities and Divergences* (Maryknoll, N.Y.: Orbis Books, 1990), 3-27.

[10] For the distinction between "Asian theology" and "theology in Asia," see James A. Veitch, "Is an Asian Theology Possible?" in *The Human and the Holy: Asian Perspectives in Christian Theology*, ed. Emerito P. Nacpil and Douglas J. Elwood (Maryknoll, N.Y.: Orbis Books, 1980), 216.

[11] See Gustavo Gutiérrez, *A Theology of Liberation,* rev. ed., trans. and ed. Caridad Inda and John Eagleson (Maryknoll, N.Y.: Orbis Books, 1988), 9.

[12] There is, therefore, a parallel between the method of Asian theology and that of Latin American liberation theology. As I pointed out in chapter 2, Clodovis Boff describes the method of liberation theology as composed of three mediations: socio-analytic mediation, hermeneutical mediation, and practical mediation. These three mediations are preceded by praxis in favor of justice and liberation. Among Asian theologians, M. M. Thomas uses social analysis consistently throughout his works. See M. M. Thomas, *The Christian Response to the Asian Revolution* (London: SCM Press, 1964); idem, *Salvation and Humanization* (Madras: Christian Literature Society, 1971); and idem, *Towards a Theology of Contemporary Ecumenism* (Madras: Christian Literature Society, 1978).

Concomitant with praxis and social analysis, which are required by Asian poverty, there is a third part of the theological method demanded by the overwhelming presence of non-Christian soteriologies in the Asian reality, namely, what Pieris calls "introspection." Marxism and early Latin American liberation theology were unable to appreciate the religious dimension that Asian cultures attribute to voluntary poverty and therefore fail to understand its revolutionary impact on Asian society. Hence, Pieris argues, "a 'liberation-theopraxis' in Asia that uses only the Marxist tools of *social analysis* will remain un-Asian and ineffective until it integrates the psychological tools of *introspection* which our sages have discovered."[13]

This introspective process will necessitate interreligious dialogue. This dialogue is carried out not only at the level of intellectual discourse and study but also in worship and liturgy, in living together and relating to the society at different levels, and in participating in the people's struggle for life.[14] It is important to note that struggle against poverty and dialogue with Asian religiousness are not two independent activities. Rather they are two sides of the same coin and must be conjoined to achieve their goals. Struggle for justice and freedom without the religious dimension would be no more than social and political activism; more pragmatically, it is destined to dismal failure because it is impossible to transform social structures in Asia without enlisting the collaboration of religions.

On the other hand, interreligious dialogue without the sting of socio-political involvement would run the risk of being an elitist and harmless form of "inculturation" in which, as Pieris has pointed out, non-Christian religious traditions are vandalized and baptized into instruments of apologetics and proselytization.[15] A genuinely Asian theology must be rooted simultaneously in the religiousness of the poor and the poverty of the religious.

An Asian theology must, of course, dig deep into Asian cultures to find the resources for its development. The first resource has to be found in the stories of the billions of Asian people themselves. In recent years, the theme of "people" has assumed a special significance in the discussion of Asian theology. As we

---

[13] Pieris, *An Asian Theology of Liberation*, 80.

[14] Pieris speaks of a *communicatio in sacris* with these religions. The Vatican has spoken of four forms of interreligious dialogue: "dialogue of life," "dialogue of action," "dialogue of religious experience," and "dialogue of theological exchange." See the document *Dialogue and Proclamation,* jointly issued by the Pontifical Council for Interreligious Dialogue and the Congregation for the Evangelization of Peoples (June 20, 1991) in James A. Scherer and Stephen B. Bevans, eds., *New Directions in Mission and Evangelization I: Basic Statements 1974-1991* (Maryknoll, N.Y.: Orbis Books, 1992), 187. For a discussion of the method of interreligious dialogue as theological exchange, see Peter C. Phan, "The Claim of Uniqueness and Universality in Interreligious Dialogue," *Indian Theological Studies* 31/1 (1994): 44-66. Obviously, because there is religious homogeneity in Latin America, this element of interreligious dialogue is absent from Latin American liberation theology; in its place there is an attempt to enter into conversation with *religiosidad popular.*

[15] See Pieris, *An Asian Theology of Liberation*, 80.

discussed in chapter 4, and will return to below, Korean theologians have developed a distinct theology called *minjung* theology as a faith reflection of, by, and for the people in their struggle against oppression.[16]

The second resource is a subset of the first, namely, the stories of Asian women. Given the pervasive patriarchalism of Asian societies, the stories of oppression and poverty of Asian women occupy a special place in theological reflection. Indeed, a growing body of Asian feminist theologians has begun to construct a theology from the perspective of "Asianness" and "womanness."

The third resource is the sacred texts and practices of Asian religions that have nourished the life of Asian people for thousands of years before the coming of Christianity into their lands and since. These religious classics, together with their innumerable commentaries, and religious rituals serve as an inexhaustible fountain of wisdom for Christian theology. Connected with these religious texts and rituals is what is known as philosophy, since in Asia religion and philosophy are inextricably conjoined. Philosophy is a way of life and religion is a worldview, each is both *darsana* (view of life) and *pratipada* (way of life).

The fourth source is Asian monastic traditions with their rituals, ascetic practices, and social commitment. The last point, namely, social commitment needs emphasizing. Pieris has argued that the most appropriate form of inculturation of Christianity in Asia is not the Latin model of incarnation in a non-Christian *culture,* not the Greek model of assimilation of a non-Christian *philosophy,* and not the north European model of accommodation to a non-Christian *religiousness*. What is required of Asian Christians is the monastic model of participation in a non-Christian *spirituality*.[17]

The fifth resource is Asian cultures in general, which are embodied in stories, myths, folklore, symbols, poetry, songs, visual arts, and dance. The use of these cultural artifacts promises to add a very distinctive voice to Christian theology coming from the deepest yearnings of the people of Asia.

ASIAN PORTRAITS OF JESUS

In response to the religio-cultural and socio-political context of their continent and drawing on the resources of their cultures, a number of Asian theologians have recently attempted to formulate their own Christologies. These are presented as alternatives to the Chalcedonian Christology that has dominated Western theology since the fifth century and has been imposed upon Asian

---

[16] For reflections on "theology by the people," see S. Amirtham and John S. Pobee, eds., *Theology by the People* (Geneva: WCC, 1986); F. Castillo, *Theologie aus der Praxis des Folkes* (Munich: Kaiser, 1978); and Ernesto Cardenal, *The Gospel in Solentiname,* 4 vols. (Maryknoll, N.Y.: Orbis Books, 1976).

[17] On the inculturation of Christianity in Asia on the basis of monasticism, see Pieris, *An Asian Theology of Liberation,* 51-58. On Buddhist monasticism, see Aloysius Pieris, *Love Meets Wisdom: A Christian Experience of Buddhism* (Maryknoll, N.Y.: Orbis Books, 1988), 61-72, 89-96.

churches since missionary days.[18] In general, these Christologies are similar to one another inasmuch as they are all *liberation* Christologies. They can, however, be distinguished by the ways in which their proponents attend to the Asian context and make use of Asian resources.[19] These ways, though not mutually exclusive, provide distinctive features to the different portraits of Jesus.

Aloysius Pieris: Jesus as the Poor Monk

Aloysius Pieris[20] has tirelessly argued that an Asian theology must confront the two poles of Asian reality together: poverty and religiousness. The conjunction of these two elements must be practiced in both interreligious dialogue and inculturation.

Religiousness and Poverty

In Pieris's view, Christian churches, and by extension Christian theology, have remained *in* Asia but have not yet become *of* Asia because they fail to conjoin non-Christian religiousness and material poverty. To use his metaphor, they have refused the double baptism of the "Jordan of Asian religion" and of the "Calvary of Asian poverty."[21]

---

[18] For general though by no means comprehensive introductions to Asian Christologies, see Anton Wessels, *Images of Jesus: How Jesus Is Perceived and Portrayed in Non-European Cultures*, trans. John Vriend (Grand Rapids, Mich.: Eerdmans, 1990), 126-57; Priscilla Pope-Levison and John R. Levison, *Jesus in Global Contexts* (Louisville, Ky.: Westminster/John Knox Press, 1992), 55-88; Alfred T. Hennelly, *Liberation Theologies: The Global Pursuit of Justice* (Mystic, Conn.: Twenty-Third Publications, 1995), 195-233; Stanley J. Samartha, *One Christ—Many Religions: Toward a Revised Christology* (Maryknoll, N.Y.: Orbis Books, 1991); Sebastian Kappen, *Jesus and Cultural Revolution: An Asian Perspective* (Bombay: The Bombay Industrial League for Development, 1983); Benigno P. Beltran, *The Christology of the Inarticulate: An Inquiry into the Filipino Understanding of Jesus the Christ* (Manila: Divine Word Publications, 1987); Tissa Balasuriya, "Christ and the World Religions: An Asian Perspective," in *Future of Liberation Theology: Essays in Honor of Gustavo Gutiérrez*, ed. Marc H. Ellis and Otto Maduro (Maryknoll, N.Y.: Orbis Books, 1989), 337-45. For an excellent anthology of essays on Christology by Asian theologians, see R. S. Sugirtharajah, ed., *Asian Faces of Jesus* (Maryknoll, N.Y.: Orbis Books, 1993).

[19] In this chapter I do not discuss the older attempts, especially by Indian theologians, to present Jesus in terms of Hindu theology, e.g., Jesus as *Prajapati* (Lord of Creatures), as *Cit* (consciousness), as *Avatara* (incarnation), as *Isvara* (the cosmic Christ), as *Guru* (teacher), as *Adi Purasha* (the first person), as *Shakti* (power), as eternal *Om* (logos), as *Bodhisattva* (the buddha who postpones enlightenment in order to suffer with human beings).

[20] Aloysius Pieris (b. 1934) is a Sri Lankan Jesuit, the first Catholic to earn a doctorate in Buddhism at the University of Sri Lanka. He is founder and director of the Tulane Research Center in Kelaniya. He has published extensively on liberation theology. His essays have been collected in *An Asian Theology of Liberation*; *Love Meets Wisdom*; and *Basic Issues in Asian Buddhism and Christianity* (Maryknoll, N.Y.: Orbis Books, 1996). For an account of his theological development, see his "Two Encounters in My Theological Journey," in Sugirtharajah, *Frontiers in Asian Christian Theology*, 141-46.

[21] See Pieris, *An Asian Theology of Liberation*, 45-50.

I have already pointed out above that, for Pieris, inculturation of Christianity in Asia should not be undertaken in the models of Latin and Greek Christianity (that is, taking up non-Christian culture and philosophy respectively), simply because in Asia it is impossible to separate non-Christian religions from their cultures and philosophies. Furthermore, the North European model of appropriating the "cosmic" religiousness of tribal societies of the early Middle Ages into Christianity is too late for Asia because in most Asian countries the cosmic religiousness has already been appropriated by the non-Christian "metacosmic" religions.

The only effective way by which the Christian churches *in* Asia can become *of* Asia, Pieris suggests, is to assume the spirituality of non-Christian religions symbolized by the figure of the poor monk.[22] Inculturation is, therefore, not a process to be undertaken apart from the struggle for liberation. Indeed, for Pieris, inculturation and liberation, rightly understood, are but two names for the same process.

Jesus as the Poor Monk

It is in this context of unified Asian religious poverty and poor religiousness that Pieris outlines his liberationist Christology of Jesus as the poor monk. To begin with, he criticizes the two models of Christology that have existed in Asia and that he terms "Christ *against* religions" and "Christ *of* religions."[23]

The "Christ *against* religions" model contains three varieties. First, there is the "colonial Christ" of early-seventeenth-century Western missionaries. This Christ conquers non-Christian religions regarded as responsible for the moral poverty of the pagans, and he does so by means of Western civilization. This colonial Christology, however, ignores the potential of religion to relieve material poverty. Second is the "neocolonial Christ" of the late 1960s. This Christology recognizes the link between religion and material poverty and attempts to conquer non-Christian religions regarded as responsible for material poverty. The means to do so is the Western model of development. This neocolonial Christology, however, fails to perceive the link between religion and structural poverty. Third, there is the "crypto-colonialist Christ" of the late 1970s. This Christology recognizes the link between religion and structural poverty and attempts to conquer non-Christian religions regarded as responsible for structural poverty. The means it uses is political liberation. This crypto-colonialist Christology, however, fails to see the link between religion and liberation.[24]

The "Christ *of* religions" model also contains three types. First is the "gnostic Christ" of nineteenth-century Indian theologians. This Christ is seen to be present

[22] Pieris himself has not used this expression to describe Jesus; it is my own shorthand for his Christology.

[23] For a helpful diagram of these two Christologies, see Pieris, *An Asian Theology of Liberation*, 89.

[24] For Pieris, the negative understanding of the role of religion for liberation is derived from three non-Asian sources: Latin American liberationists' early rejection of religion as contributing to alienation; an unrevised Marxian analysis of religion; and a Western (for example, Barthian) understanding of religion as human work antithetical to faith.

in all religions as the final consummation of all human search for redemption. Unfortunately, this gnostic Christology, which anticipates the fulfillment theology of religions of the 1930 Lambeth Conference and Vatican II, ignores the potential of religion to relieve material poverty. Second is the "ashramic Christ" of late-1960s monks and mystics who voluntarily embraced material poverty. This Christ functions as a protest against forced poverty. This ashramic Christology, however, fails to see the link between religion and structural poverty. Third is the "universal Christ" of the late-1970s inculturationists, who appropriate the language and symbols of non-Christian religions. This universal Christology, however, ignores the link between religion and liberation.

Needless to say, Pieris finds all six versions unsatisfactory on the ground that they all divorce Asian religiousness from Asian poverty. In his view it is precisely this fatal separation between these two realities of the Asian context that accounts for the failure of Jesus, who was no less an Asian than Gautama the Buddha or Muhammad the Prophet, to win large-scale acceptance in Asia. Indeed, Asia has surrendered only less than 3 percent of its population to Christianity! The only way for Christ to return to Asia and strike deep roots there is to don the habit of a poor monk who unites in himself the religiousness of non-Christian religions and the poverty of the Asian masses. In other words, it is only the Jesus who has been baptized in the Jordan of religiousness and on the cross of poverty that can acquire an authentically Asian face. As Pieris puts it succinctly, *"The door once closed to Jesus in Asia is the only door that can take him in today, namely, the soteriological nucleus or the liberative core of various religions that have given shape and stability to our cultures."*[25]

Pieris understands the religiousness that Jesus adopted at the Jordan to be informed by prophetic asceticism, as opposed to what he terms the Zealots' narrow ideology, the Essenes' sectarian puritanism, the Pharisees' spirituality of self-righteousness, and the Sadducees' leisure-class spirituality. This prophetic asceticism is essentially a liberative religiousness.

Jesus' immersion into the religiousness of the poor was followed and completed by his baptism on the cross of poverty on Calvary. To understand the nature of this poverty, Pieris reminds us that in the Bible, as well as in the Asian context, the opposite of poverty is not wealth but acquisitiveness and greed (which the Buddha identifies as the cause of all sufferings in his second "Noble Truth": *tanha, upadana, lobha*). In Pieris's view, Jesus' poverty did not consist merely in being materially poor but much more in his struggle against Mammon, the god opposed to his Abba. It is Jesus' struggle against Mammon that led to his being crucified on Calvary.

The cultural and socio-political figure in Asia today that reproduces Jesus in his immersion into religious poverty and poor religiousness is, Pieris contends, the monk. Speaking specifically of Buddhist monasticism, Pieris shows that it is both the seed from which Buddhism springs and the flower in which it blooms. Buddhist spirituality has an essentially monastic thrust.[26] The monk embodies

---

[25] Pieris, *An Asian Theology of Liberation*, 59.

[26] See Pieris, *Love Meets Wisdom*, 63: "The monastic life is an inherent feature of Buddhist soteriology and almost a constitutive dimension of Buddhist spirituality."

in himself[27] both religiousness and poverty. He is quintessentially one who has renounced Mammon for religious reasons (struggles to be poor through voluntary poverty) so that he may help the poor socio-economically (struggles for the poor by radically transforming oppressive social structures operated by Mammon). With the former the monk achieves interior liberation from acquisitiveness; with the latter he brings about social emancipation from structural poverty imposed upon the masses.

Buddhist monks, of course, do not live alone but in community *(sangha)*, one of three jewels in which Buddhists take refuge (the *triratana*). A quasi-sacramental pointer to the metacosmic goal *(nirvana)* and to a corresponding state of perfection that is the raison d'être of any monastic community, the *sangha* is a visible community of religious poverty and poor religiousness, of a few who assume voluntary poverty to remove the forced poverty of the many. Such a community is therefore not purely spiritual but political as well. Indeed, by practicing what Pieris calls "religious socialism"[28] Buddhist monastic communities, especially those in rural areas, have preserved the seeds of liberation that religion and poverty have combined to produce. Furthermore, by adopting a republican form of government inspired by tribal socialism rather than by monarchical structure, these communities are presented as the ideal society in which there is no room for caste differentiation and in which the ruler is subservient to the will of the people.[29]

The Christology of the poor monk combines what Pieris considers to be the two basic goals of all religions: *wisdom* and *love.* As poverty and religiousness constitute the two fundamental poles of Pieris's Asian liberation Christology, so wisdom and love are the two cornerstones of his liberation theology of interreligious dialogue, which he calls *gnosis* and *agape,* respectively. Although the former is conventionally associated with Asian religions, especially Buddhism, and the latter with Western religions, especially Christianity, *gnosis* (salvific knowledge) and *agape* (redemptive love) are two poles of a tension present in *all* religions, irrespective of geography. Each is incomplete in itself, and therefore they complement and correct each other. An Asian Christology of Jesus as the poor monk must employ both the "agapeic gnosis" of Christians and the "gnostic agape" of Buddhists.[30]

How can the Christology of the poor monk be formulated? True to his liberation method, Pieris maintains that it cannot be constructed in the abstract, apart from praxis. It is born only after the Christian churches in Asia have received the double baptism of the Jordan and of the cross. More concretely, an Asian Christology will emerge only after Asian Christians, by plunging into the waters

---

[27] The masculine form is used intentionally here because the order of nuns (*bhikkuni-sangha*), originally founded by the Buddha himself, has been extinct since the Middle Ages. Pieris explicitly acknowledges the all-male character of Buddhist monasticism as well as of all other Buddhist institutions.

[28] Pieris, *An Asian Theology of Liberation*, 43.

[29] See Pieris, "The Buddhist Political Vision," in *Love Meets Wisdom*, 73-79.

[30] See Pieris, *Love Meets Wisdom*, 114-19.

of religiousness and poverty, succeed in fusing "politics with asceticism, involvement with introspection, class analysis and self-analysis, the Marxist *laborare* with the monastic *orare*, a militant repudiation of Mammon with a mystic relationship with Abba their Father."[31] For Pieris, Christology follows an "ecclesiological revolution"[32] of participation in the twofold reality of Asian religiousness and poverty, of *gnosis* and *agape*. Out of this participation Christology arises as an explication of the many hidden theologies issuing out of the soteriological promises of Asian religions.

This side of Christology must be complemented, Pieris suggests, by the stories that *non-Christian* sages tell of Jesus, that is, not intellectuals and theologians but "those *religious* seekers who have opted to be *poor* in their search for the saving truth and who, during their pilgrimage, encounter Jesus within their own soteriological perspectives."[33]

Jung Young Lee: Jesus-Christ as the Perfect Realization of Change and as the Margin of Marginality

Whereas Pieris makes extensive use of the Asian social context of poverty and of Asian religious traditions, in particular Buddhism, in elaborating his Christology, Jung Young Lee[34] first delves into Taoist philosophy, especially as contained in the *I Ching* (Book of Changes), and later into his experiences as an immigrant in the United States to formulate his answer to Jesus' question: "Who do you say that I am?" (Mt 16:15).

Christ as the Perfect Realization of Change

Drawing on the metaphysics of the *I Ching* crystallized in the concept of the *yin-yang* relationship, which constitute the two primordial components of change,[35] Lee argues for what he terms the "theology of change." It includes both the "theology of the absolute" based on Greek metaphysics, and the "theology of

---

[31] Pieris, *An Asian Theology of Liberation*, 64.

[32] Ibid.

[33] Ibid.

[34] The late Jung Young Lee, born in Korea in 1935, subsequently became a naturalized American and served as a United Methodist minister and professor of systematic theology at Drew University. He authored and edited more than twenty books, among which the most significant for our theme are *God Suffers for Us: A Systematic Inquiry into the Concept of Divine Passibility* (Hague: Martinus Nijhoff, 1974); *The Theology of Change: A Christian Concept of God from an Eastern Perspective* (Maryknoll, N.Y.: Orbis Books, 1979); and *Marginality: The Key to Multicultural Theology* (Minneapolis: Fortress Press, 1995).

[35] For Lee's exposition of the *I Ching*, see Jung Young Lee, *The Principle of Changes: Understanding the I Ching* (New Hyde Park, N.Y.: University Books, 1971); and idem, *The I Ching and Modern Man: Essays on Metaphysical Implications of Change* (Secaucus, N.Y.: University Books, 1975). For a brief summary of the *I Ching* metaphysics of the *yin-yang*, see Lee, *The Theology of Change*, 1-10.

process," based on Alfred North Whitehead's process philosophy. The Greek theology of the absolute emphasizes immovable *being*, whereas the Whiteheadian theology of process privileges *becoming*.

The theology of change based on the *I Ching* includes both being and becoming as the ultimate character of reality. According to Lee, reality is not known in an "either-or" but in a "both-and"; consequently, the theology that claims to know Ultimate Reality must be characterized not by exclusiveness but by inclusiveness:

> "Both-and" philosophy is based on the idea of change, which produces both *yin* and *yang*. *Yin* is rest, *yang* is movement; *yin* is being, *yang* is becoming. *Yin* is responsiveness, *yang* is creativity. If creativity is the character of the ultimate in process theology, responsiveness is the character of the ultimate in substantial or absolute theology. If *yang* is the leitmotif of process theology, *yin* is the leitmotif of absolute theology. Theology of change, however, comprises both *yin* and *yang*, both creativity and responsiveness, both being and becoming, because change is the source of both. Change is, then, the matrix of all that was, is, and shall be. It is the ground of all being and becoming. Thus theology of change, which characterizes the ultimate as being *and* becoming, is that inclusive theology to which we must turn. Process theology represents the turning away from western absolute theology toward the eastern theology of change.[36]

In this theology of change Lee suggests that God must be understood neither as "being itself" nor as "becoming itself" but as "is-ness itself." Being and becoming are mutually exclusive categories, whereas is-ness includes both. Another way of saying that God is is-ness itself is to affirm that God is *change itself*, since change is the source of both being and becoming. Paradoxically, then, change, which changes all things, is itself changeless: "The character of changelessness is a part of the changing reality of God: Changelessness is possible because of change. God is changeless because he is primarily change itself. Changelessness means, then, the changeless pattern of change, or consistent structural change. The changelessness of God does not negate his essential nature as change but affirms the unceasingness of his changing."[37]

It is in this context of the theology of change that Lee develops his Christology. Given the priority of creation over salvation, of God the creator over Christ the savior, Lee argues that the early church's teaching on the equality of Christ with God the creator is mistaken:

> God as the creator is the source of creativity and the source of all that is and will be, while Christ is only what is manifested of God. To identify the creator with the revealer, the Christ, is to deny the inexhaustible nature of the divine creativity. God as creator is more than what is manifested, and

---

[36] Lee, *The Theology of Change*, 20.
[37] Ibid., 43.

his mystery is not and will not be exhausted. He is more than the One revealed in Christ. . . . In other words, Christ is subordinate to the creator, and his work as savior and redeemer is one part of the work of God as creator. . . . Everything that Jesus Christ has done or has been must be understood as an element of divine creativity.[38]

Having asserted this principle of christological subordination to divine creativity, Lee goes on to examine the traditional titles of Jesus. The first is Christ as Word. Lee takes this title to mean that Christ is the "foundation" of the creative process, the "dynamic force that changes and produces new life and new possibilities."[39] Connected with the description of Christ as Word is that of Christ as Wisdom of God. Wisdom, like Word, signifies the creative activity of God.

The title of Christ as the Light implies, for Lee, that Christ also includes darkness, just as life includes death, and good includes evil: "Christ as light cannot be excluded from the darkness, because light cannot exist without darkness nor darkness without light. To exclude Christ from the darkness is in fact to exclude him from light also. Because Christ subjected himself to the condition of existence, the darkness must also be in his light. Conversely, Christ as light enters into our darkness."[40] This view of the correlation between light and darkness is consistent with the *I Ching*'s understanding of the relationship between *yang* and *yin*. Christ as light or *yang* is not entirely exclusive of darkness or *yin*, and the world as darkness or *yin* is not entirely exclusive of Christ as light or *yang*.

Christ as Savior is understood in relation to the notion of sin. For Lee, sin consists in the desire to *be* rather than to *become*, that is, unwillingness to change. By resisting change, we fall into "existential estrangement"; that is, we suffer what the Buddha calls "*dukkha*." To be saved or to accept Christ as Savior, then, means that we must accept change. Again, in terms of *yang* and *yin*, Christ

---

[38] Ibid., 88. Lee seems to have misunderstood the classical teaching on the equality of Christ with God the Father. This equality is based on the *consubstantiality* of the Father and the Son (*homoousios*) and does not entail identity of *functions*. Indeed, as Karl Rahner has convincingly argued, the principle that all *ad extra* actions of the Trinity must be attributed equally to the three divine persons by way of efficient causality (except their intratrinitarian opposed relations) does not mean that their acts of external self-communication (for example, the incarnation of the Logos and the bestowal of the Spirit in grace) can and should be understood by way of the same causality. On the contrary, they should be understood by way of (quasi) formal causality, which implies their distinct modes of subsisting and acting. To put it in Lee's terms, the redemptive act of the Son is not to be "equated" with the creative act of the Father.

[39] Ibid., 89.

[40] Ibid., 92. Lee understands good and evil not as ontic realities but as existential manifestations of the Ultimate Reality, which is the process of change. In this way they are not opposed to one another but mutually correlative and interdependent. In this context the following statement would lose some of its strangeness: "If we believe that God's absoluteness lies in his inclusion of all aspects of the world, and if we admit the existence of evil, then we must grant that God includes the existence of evil. God must be both good and evil. If he were not, we would be forced to posit that evil exists independently of God and in conflict with him" (ibid., 57).

as Savior is *yang,* who initiates and acts, and we who accept his power of change are *yin* by responding to and following him. But by responding, we become active or *yang,* and Christ becomes part of creation or *yin.*

Christ is also called the center of the creative process or the cosmic Christ. For Lee, this title means that Christ is a divine reality. Besides being divine, Christ is also human. For Lee, Christ is both divine and human because he is the primordial origin of the creative process. As such an origin, Christ is "the perfect incarnation of the infinite in the finite world; he is human and divine in the fullest sense. He is fully divine because he is fully human. He is a perfect man because he is a perfect God. . . . In him the power of change is manifested perfectly. He is in perfect harmony with the process of change."[41] In this way he is the perfect mediator between God as creator and humanity as creature.

Finally, in his death and resurrection, Lee points out, Jesus becomes the perfect realization of change, which includes decay and renewal of life. His crucifixion is the perfect symbol of decay, and his resurrection is the perfect symbol of renewal of life: "Thus Jesus as the perfect symbol of the change unites both decay and growth or death and resurrection in the process of constant change and transformation."[42]

Jesus-Christ as the Marginal Person par excellence

In a later work, while still maintaining a Taoist philosophical framework, Jung Young Lee shifts to a more narrative mode of theological reflection and draws upon his experiences as an immigrant and the history of Chinese, Japanese, and Korean immigrants in the United States.[43] He defines immigrants' experiences as being *on the margin* as opposed to being at the center. By their different race and culture, Asian immigrants can never be totally assimilated into American society, even though they may successfully compete with the central people and accommodate their lifestyles and values. They will always remain on the margin.

By marginality Lee means more than being "in-between," that is, the experience of the people-on-the-margin as described by the central people. This in-between experience—with its symptoms of ambivalence, excessive self-consciousness, restlessness, irritability, moodiness, lack of self-confidence, pessimism and the like—has been diagnosed by people at the center as productive of an inferiority complex in the marginalized people.

This classical understanding of marginality is one-sided because, framed by the central group, it focuses only on negative effects. In Lee's view, it needs to

---

[41] Ibid., 98.

[42] Ibid., 100.

[43] Lee describes his immigrant experiences, as well as those of other Asian immigrants, in a beautiful parable of the dandelion with a yellow flower in a green lawn. The dandelion is rooted up every year by the owner of the lawn because its yellow flower is out of place in a green lawn. It tries to survive by not blossoming, hoping to blend in with the green grass. But without its yellow flower the dandelion loses its reason for living and so decides to blossom again. An Asian American, a yellow man, has a dream, and in it he becomes a dandelion (see Lee, *Marginality,* 10-13).

be complemented by the self-understanding of the marginalized people themselves. Lee suggests that from the perspective of the marginalized people, marginality includes also being "in-both." As Asian Americans, Asian immigrants are both Asian and American. To stress in-bothness means first of all affirming one's racial and cultural origins; for an Asian, this means affirming "yellowness," like the dandelion. Being on the margin, however, prevents this affirmation of ethnicity from being exclusive, since the margin is where worlds merge. Thus to stress in-bothness means, secondly, affirming American-ness: "Being in-both Asians and Americans, the affirmation of Asian-ness is also the affirmation of American-ness."[44]

Definitions of marginality as "in-between" and as "in-both" are not mutually exclusive; both have something true to say about the experience of being an immigrant: *"To be in-both is as authentic as to be in-between."*[45] Hence, both definitions need to be brought together in a holistic understanding of marginality. Lee suggests that the category of "in-beyond" would include both "in-between" and "in-both." To be in-between and in-both the Asian and American worlds, one must be in-beyond them. To be in-beyond is to be a hyphenated person: "The hyphenated minority or the minority of 'and' is *extrinsically* in-between because of societal pressure, but *intrinsically* in-both. . . . The condition of in-between and in-both must be harmonized for one to become *a new marginal person who overcomes marginality without ceasing to be a marginal person.*"[46]

What is the impact of marginality upon theology? Lee suggests that as long as third-world theologians continue to validate their work by the criteria of Euro-American theology, which has long dominated racial and ethnic minorities, they will not be able to produce an authentic theology from their own perspective. In epistemological terms, marginal theology rejects the Western exclusivist either-or thinking and adopts the Eastern inclusivist epistemology of neither/nor and both/and. Neither/nor expresses the in-between situation of marginality, whereas both/and expresses its in-both situation. Marginal theology thinks in simultaneous double negations (neither/nor) and double affirmations (both/and): "Being in-between and in-both worlds, total negation (in-between) and total affirmation (in-both) always coexist in new marginal people. Because these ideas coexist, they are not only the most inclusive but also the most relational form of thinking."[47]

It is in this new context of in-beyond marginality of both in-between and in-both with its corresponding epistemology of neither/nor and both/and that Lee develops his Christology. He points out that Jesus' question "Who do you say that I am?" has been consistently wrongly answered in the history of Christianity because Jesus was understood from the perspective of centrality. Traditionally, he was always regarded as the "center of centrality." On the contrary, Lee

---

[44] Ibid., 51.
[45] Ibid., 58.
[46] Ibid., 62.
[47] Ibid., 70.

argues that Jesus is "a new marginal person *par excellence*."[48] To indicate this fact Lee places a hyphen between Jesus and Christ:

> I use a hyphenated "Jesus-Christ" because Jesus is the Christ, while the Christ is also Jesus. In other words, Jesus as the Christ is not enough. He is also the Christ as Jesus. Just as "Asian-American" means an Asian and an American. Whenever I say Jesus, I mean Jesus-Christ; whenever I say Christ, I mean Christ-Jesus. They are inseparable, two facets of one existence.[49]

To show that Jesus was "at the margin of marginality," Lee rereads the story of Jesus' birth, life, death, and resurrection from the perspective of marginality.[50] For him, the birth of Jesus, in a manger, to an unwed mother, is the beginning of his marginalization. John's account of the incarnation of the Logos (1:1-18), in which the Logos is said to be the agent of creation and to be rejected by his own people, indicates divine marginalization. Description of Christ's incarnation as *kenosis* to become a slave is also an indication of divine marginalization. Indeed, "the incarnation can also be compared to divine immigration, in which God emigrated from a heavenly place to this world. As an immigrant in the new world, Christ, like the Asian-American, experienced rejection, harassment, and humiliation."[51]

Jesus' entire life is a story of marginality. In childhood he was exposed to a double marginalization: political (by Roman authority) and cultural and ethnic (by living in the foreign land of Egypt). Furthermore, his hometown of Nazareth was despised (Jn 1:46). In his baptism in the Jordan, Jesus became a new marginal person par excellence, "a person who lives in-beyond by integrating and harmonizing both the total negation (neither/nor) and the total affirmation (both/and) of two different worlds into himself through death and resurrection."[52]

In Jesus' threefold temptation, the devil, in Lee's view, is the personification of self-centering power in the forms of wealth, glory, and dominance.[53] By rejecting these three central forces, Jesus became a person on the margin. Jesus' public ministry was a life of marginality: "He was a homeless man with a group of homeless people around him. He associated with marginal people, although he never closed the door to central-group people. He taught, acted, suffered, and died as a marginal man. He rose from the dead to help us live in-beyond."[54]

For Lee, Jesus' marginality reaches its utmost expression in his death on the cross, which was marked by suffering with humiliation and by the loneliness of

---

[48] Ibid., 71.

[49] Ibid., 78.

[50] Lee does not attempt to reconstruct the historical Jesus. He simply assumes that the stories about Jesus reported in the gospels are historical and reinterprets them from the perspective of marginality. Lee, however, finds very instructive the title of one of the most important current books on the Jesus of history—John P. Meier, *A Marginal Jew: Rethinking the Historical Jesus* (New York: Doubleday, 1991).

[51] Lee, *Marginality,* 83.

[52] Ibid., 85.

[53] Ibid.

[54] Ibid., 86.

rejection. Suffering is a pain expressed in attachment, and loneliness is a suffering expressed in detachment. On the cross Jesus was rejected even by his Father (Mk 15:34). Jesus' death symbolizes tragedy, failure, disappointment, and darkness (total negation), whereas his resurrection symbolizes hope, joy, and life renewal (total affirmation). Again, by combining both death and resurrection, both total negation and total affirmation, Jesus is the new marginal person: "With resurrection, Christ transcended all marginality. He broke the bonds of every cultural, racial, religious, sexual, economic, social, or regional bias that marginalized him and eventually led him to the cross. With resurrection Jesus-Christ is a new humanity, a new marginal person, who lives in-beyond by affirming both worlds."[55]

In sum, in Jesus-Christ and Christ-Jesus, Lee argues that we have both the "margin of marginality" (his ministry and death) and the "creative core" (his resurrection and new life). Like *yin* and *yang*, they are inseparable. In fact, they are identical. By assuming the margin of marginality Jesus becomes the new creative core. By taking up the neither/nor, Jesus also takes up the both/and. But the new core is not another center of centrality; in fact, it marginalizes the old centers of centrality and turns the margins into the new creative core. But the new core will not become another center of centrality, for it remains the margin of marginality. In this way the new creative core can reconcile the center with the margin. Jesus as the new creative core is the perfect new marginal person, "because in him every marginal determinant is nullified, and everyone can overcome his or her marginality. In the creative core of Christ-Jesus, racism is overcome, sexism is no longer in practice, the poor become self-sufficient, the weak find strength."[56]

Chung Hyun Kyung: Jesus as the *Minjung* within the *Minjung*

The use of the stories of suffering people in constructing an Asian Christology brings us to Asian women's Christology. Recently, Asian women have begun to theologize from their own experience as Asian women, and although their number is still small, Asian women's theology has acquired a distinct and important voice.[57]

Asian Women's Theology as God-Praxis

Among Asian women theologians, Chung Hyun Kyung[58] has attempted a comprehensive presentation of Asian women's theology. For her, Asian women's

---

[55] Ibid., 95.

[56] Ibid., 98.

[57] For a history of the development of theology by Asian women, see Chung Hyun Kyung, *Struggle to Be the Sun Again: Introducing Asian Women's Theology* (Maryknoll, N.Y.: Orbis Books, 1990), 1-21. For the social context of Asian women's theology, see ibid., 22-35. See also Virginia Fabella and Sun Ai Lee Park, eds., *We Dare to Dream: Doing Theology as Asian Women* (Hong Kong: Asian Women's Resource Centre for Culture and Theology, 1989).

[58] Chung Hyun Kyung is Korean. She earned her doctorate from Union Theological Seminary in New York. Her major work to date is *Struggle to Be the Sun Again.*

theology is a "cry, plea, and invocation" to God in search of justice and healing. It originates in "God-praxis" and is identical with it, not something that follows it. It is an embodied and critical reflection on Asian women's experiences, and it is aimed at bringing about a community of harmony, peace, and love.[59] Such a theology, in Chung's view, is inductive; that is, it does not begin with the Bible or Christian doctrines but with the stories of women: "The text of God's revelation was, is, will be written in our bodies and our peoples' everyday struggle for survival and liberation."[60] In other words, the first step is "socio-biography," that is, listening with care to the women's stories in order to discern the people's suffering and yearning for freedom.

In addition to women's stories, Asian women's theology should draw from popular religiosity among women (for example, Korean shamanism; folk Chinese Buddhism, which venerates Kwan In; and Filipino worship of Ina). The second step is critical social analysis that includes political, economic, and religio-cultural analysis. The third step is theological reflection in which the Bible and Christian tradition function as the context in which to understand women's experiences.

Christ as the Minjung within the Minjung

On the basis of this methodology, Chung begins her exposition of Asian women's Christology with a critical review of traditional christological titles: Christ as Suffering Servant, as Lord, and as Emmanuel. With regard to the first, Asian women acknowledge that the image of Jesus as the Suffering Servant enables them to see meaning in their own suffering and to accept suffering and service as part of their option for liberation. But, Chung points out, the church's traditional associations of obedience and subservience with this image reinforce the oppression of women by their fathers, husbands, and brothers. Similarly, it is acknowledged that the image of Christ as Lord frees Asian women from the false authority of the world over them so they can claim true authority that springs from their own experiences. Yet, like the image of Christ as Suffering Servant, the image of Christ as Lord has been used to perpetuate Asian women's oppressed status in church and society. The lordship of Christ was transformed into a patriarchal lordship.

Lastly, the image of Jesus as Emmanuel (God-with-us) is cherished by Asian women because it shows that God shares their poor and oppressed condition and is with them in their struggle to reclaim their full humanity. On the other hand, the church's emphasis on the maleness of Jesus rather than on his humanity excludes women from full participation in the church.[61]

Besides these traditional images of Jesus, Asian women theologians have begun to carve their own portraits of Jesus on the basis of their experiences as Asian women. Not surprisingly, given their poverty and oppression by colonialism,

---

[59] See Chung, *Struggle to Be the Sun Again*, 99-101.
[60] Ibid., 111.
[61] See ibid., 53-61.

neocolonialism, military dictatorship, and overarching patriarchy, the most common images of Jesus among Asian women theologians are liberator, revolutionary, and political martyr. These images of Jesus strengthen Asian women in their own struggle for freedom, even to the shedding of their blood for their people.

Naturally, too, Jesus is imaged as mother, woman, and shaman. In the image of Christ as mother, Asian women see Jesus as compassionate, one who feels the suffering of humanity deeply and weeps and suffers with them. Jesus as the female figure is seen as the woman Messiah who liberates the oppressed. As shaman, Jesus is accepted by Korean women as a priestess who helps them release the *han,* that is, the resentment, indignation, and sense of helplessness and total abandonment that have accumulated over years and even centuries of oppression suffered by the *minjung* (people).

Minjung (literally, "the popular mass") is left untranslated. It includes "the oppressed, exploited, dominated, discriminated against, alienated and suppressed politically, economically, socially, culturally, and intellectually, like women, ethnic groups, the poor, workers and farmers, including intellectuals themselves."[62] Since among the *minjung,* women suffer oppression not only as members of the *minjung* in general but specifically as women, and therefore can be categorized as "the *minjung* within the *minjung,*" Christ is said to be "the *minjung* within the *minjung.*"

Finally, because Asian women are often forced to bear an overwhelming share of back-breaking labor, not only in the home but also in factories, Christ is also depicted as a worker enduring the despair and humiliation of unskilled laborers. And because they often suffer hunger as the result of poverty, they also image Christ as the grain of wheat or rice in their meager bowls of gruel.

Chung neatly sums up Asian women's Christologies: "There are *traditional* images of Jesus, which are being interpreted in fresh, creative ways by Asian women, largely based on their experiences of survival in the midst of oppression and on their efforts to liberate themselves. We have also observed *new* images of Jesus that offer a direct challenge to traditional Christologies. These new images of Jesus are also based on Asian women's experiences of survival and liberation."[63]

ADEQUACY AND APPROPRIATENESS

The three Christologies discussed above are but samples of the myriad portraits that Asian theologians have recently drawn of Jesus. Because they are all

---

[62] Chung Hyun Kyung, "'Han-pu-ri: Doing Theology from Korean Women's Perspective," in Fabella and Park, *We Dare to Dream,* 138-39. For a discussion of *minjung* theology, see Jung Young Lee, ed., *An Emerging Theology in World Perspective: Commentary on Korean Minjung Theology* (Mystic, Conn.: Twenty-Third Publications, 1988); David Kwang-sun Suh, *The Korean Minjung in Christ* (Hong Kong: Christian Conference of Asia, 1991); and Peter C. Phan, "Experience and Theology: An Asian Liberation Perspective," *Zeitschrift für Missionswissenschaft und Religionswissenschaft* 77/2 (1993): 118-20.

[63] Chung, *Struggle to Be the Sun Again,* 73.

Christian theology, two broad sets of criteria can be applied to assess their validity: adequacy and appropriatenesss. By the former is meant the power to speak the Christian word in the contemporary idiom in order to understand and transform the condition of the addressee. By the latter is meant the relative coherence of this message with the life and teaching of Jesus as mediated through the Bible and Christian tradition.

The Transformative Power of Asian Christology

As pointed out repeatedly by Aloysius Pieris, both the Christian churches and their theologies are *in* Asia but not *of* Asia. There has been reluctance to break the pot in which Western Christianity has grown and to let the Christian tree strike its roots deep in the Asian soil to become a native plant instead of growing like a stunted bonsai. Even the early attempts by missionaries (such as Matteo Ricci, Roberto de Nobili, and Alexandre de Rhodes, as well as by Asian theologians) to "inculturate" Christianity (the six "Christs" mentioned by Pieris), laudable as they are, amount to no more than trimming rather than transplanting the Christian tree.

In Search of an Adequate Christology

In order for the transplanting process to result in a healthy tree with green foliage and beautiful blooms, knowledge of the local soil and climate is necessary. To obtain this knowledge, Asian theologians have adopted Latin American liberation theology's use of social analysis. Asian women's feminist theology, in particular, has focused on the destructive effects that colonialism, neocolonialism, military dictatorship, and patriarchy have wrought on the *minjung* and especially on women, the *minjung* within the *minjung*. However, as Pieris has warned, social analysis without "introspection" would make theology un-Asian. His insistence on coupling poor religiousness and religious poverty is one of the most important and challenging (even discomforting) insights for an adequate Asian Christology. In this way he offers a positive contribution to the debate among third-world theologians concerning the relative role of liberation (which Latin American theologians favor) and inculturation (which many African and Asian theologians privilege) in the formulation of a third-world theology.

Words, of course, in spite of their performative power, cannot transform sociopolitical conditions by themselves. To do so, a transformative Christology must be preceded and accompanied by christological praxis. The three Christologies examined above insist on the necessity of such a praxis: Pieris speaks of "theopraxis" and, more specifically, monastic practice of voluntary poverty; Chung Hyun Kyung speaks of "God-praxis" as theology itself. This insistence on praxis, together with social and psychological analysis, as part of the theological method assures the adequacy of an Asian Christology for Asia.

Furthermore, to be adequate to the Asian situation, Christology must use the resources of the Asian people, both their philosophies and their stories. Here the works of Jung Young Lee stand out as particularly promising. Lee's consistent use of the Taoist philosophy of the *I Ching* to reinterpret Christian theology in terms of the "theology of change" is an important corrective to recent Asian theologians' tendency to restrict themselves to stories and symbols. It is also an effective example of how an Asian Christology (Jesus as the "perfect realization of change") can and should be "metaphysical" without using the categories of Greek philosophy.

However, a metaphysical Christology runs the risk of being detached from real life, especially the life of the *minjung*. Even Lee himself has shifted to a narrative mode of theologizing. His analysis of marginality as both "in-between" and "in-both" (that is, "in-beyond") and his depiction of Christ as the "new marginal person par excellence" provide useful insights not only into the condition of Asian immigrants in the First World but also the situation of the *minjung*, who are essentially the people on the margin in the Third World. Moreover, this Christology of marginality allows Lee to highlight an important aspect of Jesus' ministry that is left undeveloped by the other two theologians, namely, his ministry of reconciliation. As the new creative core, Jesus reconciles the central people with the people on the margins.

People's real stories as well as folklore, religious mythologies, and symbols make Asian Christology concrete and suffuse it with a transforming power that no metaphysical categories, however intricately chiseled, can provide. People laugh and weep and are transformed by stories and not by concepts. Nevertheless, it must be acknowledged that an adequate Asian Christology must employ both metaphysics and stories, since metaphysical Christology without stories is empty, and story Christology without metaphysics is blind.

Among the three christological proposals, Pieris's is no doubt the most intriguing. For him, an Asian Christology is "the Christic apocalypse of the non-Christian experiences of liberation."[64] This Christology will be the fruit of a genuine interreligious dialogue that fuses wisdom and love. Pieris's proposal is intriguing not only because it has not been written, and therefore its contours and substance remain yet unknown, but also because the common efforts between the Christian non-theologian poor and the poor non-Christian theologians are bound to produce a Christology quite different from the standard Christology of the West.

But how adequate will this Christology of the poor monk be to the Asian situation? Pieris is well aware that monasticism, even in Asia, can be and has been an instrument of oppressive powers, and monastic communities can be and have been oases of wealth and privileges. Hence, his loud and frequent insistence on *poor* religiousness. Moreover, Asian monasticism has been an exclusively male preserve, at least since the abolition of the *bhikkuni-sangha* in the Middle Ages. Finally, it has been vitiated by an anti-sex and anti-marriage

---

[64] Pieris, *An Asian Theology of Liberation*, 86.

stance with a concomitant depreciation of the lay state. Given these historical associations of monasticism with centers of power and wealth, patriarchy, and Manichean spirituality, the portrait of Christ as the poor monk needs the complement and corrective of Asian women's Christology of the *minjung* within the *minjung*.[65]

Further Issues in Asian Christology

There are, in my judgment, three more issues that these three Christologies must develop more explicitly in order to be adequate to the Asian situation. First, as I mentioned in the first part of this chapter, one of the features of the Asian context is the presence of the Communist ideology. An Asian Christology must seek to understand the paradoxical domination of an atheistic ideology in intensely religious countries such as China, Vietnam, and North Korea. It must also find an answer to the challenge of atheism itself, perhaps by reflecting on the desperate cry of Jesus on the cross: "My God, my God, why have you abandoned me?" (Mk 15:34).

The second issue relates to ecology. Recently, capitalism has made a rapid inroad into Communist countries such as Vietnam and China. The market economy is being embraced as the panacea for all ills. Besides the exploitation of cheap labor by multinational corporations and the attendant injustices against the poor, there is also the threat of ecological destruction by technocracy and the development ideology. An adequate Asian Christology must unfold a role of Christ in the cosmos that makes use of the Asian deep sense of harmony with nature. Such a cosmic Christ should not serve the leisure class's occasional retreat into the wilderness to regain mental and physical health after stressful pursuit of a high-power career. Rather, it should serve the interests of the poor who most often are the victims of environmental degradation and the pollution of water and air.[66]

The third issue concerns one of the most common and sacred elements of Asian spirituality, at least in countries heavily influenced by Confucianism, namely, family relationships and, above all, the veneration of ancestors. For most Asians, to be is to be woven into a web of familial relationships, not only with the living but also with the dead. For instance, to enter into marriage is not only to be married to an individual but in a real sense to acquire a new set of

---

[65] Pieris himself is aware of this need and has turned his attention to feminist issues. See his *Basic Issues in Asian Buddhism and Christianity.*

[66] For third-world ecological theology, see Samuel Ryan, "Theological Perspectives on the Environmental Crisis," in Sugirtharajah, *Frontiers in Asian Christian Theology*, 221-35; Eleazar S. Fernandez, "People's Cry, Creation's Cry," *Tugon: An Ecumenical Journal of Discussion and Opinion* 12/2 (1992): 276-94; Jong Sun Noh, "The Effects on Korea of Un-ecological Theology," in *Liberating Life: Contemporary Approaches to Ecological Theology*, ed. Sallie McFague et al. (Maryknoll, N.Y.: Orbis Books, 1990), 125-36.

relationships with the spouse's extended family, including the dead. An essential part of the marriage ceremony includes the introduction of the bride and bridegroom to each other's families and their ritual veneration of their ancestors. Missionaries such as Matteo Ricci, in an effort to make these rituals acceptable to Christianity, have presented them only as civil rituals, not religious rituals, thereby divesting them of their real meaning and power. In the controversy of the so-called Chinese Rites, the Vatican, after bouts of condemnation of these rites as superstition, has finally accepted them as legitimate civil celebrations. To restore their genuine meaning, an Asian Christology must develop the image of Jesus as the *elder brother* of the family, caring for his siblings and responsible for the cult of the ancestors (Jesus as firstborn among the living) and after his death and resurrection, as an *ancestor* mediating the life of God to the community (Jesus as firstborn among the dead).[67]

In sum, because the three Christologies we have discussed focus mainly on Jesus' identification with the *minjung* rather than on his identity, their adequacy to the Asian context is largely assured. The question is whether they are also fully appropriate to the Christian faith.

Dynamic Fidelity to the Christian Tradition

It would be helpful to approach the question of whether these three Asian Christologies are consistent with the Christian faith by examining how they incorporate the biblical witness to Jesus and how they make use of the historical christological traditions.

Asian Christology and the Jesus of the Gospel

With regard to the use of the Bible, Chung Hyun Kyung seems to have joined with Kwok Pui-Lan in rejecting the existence of biblical inspiration, a closed canon, and a biblical theological norm.[68] Furthermore, Chung explicitly calls

---

[67] Obviously, there are close parallels between the Asian veneration of the dead and the African sense of kinship with the ancestors. For a presentation of an African Christology on the basis of this kinship, see Pope-Levison and Levison, *Jesus in Global Contexts*, 101-6. See also Charles Nyamiti, *Christ as Our Ancestor: Christology from an African Perspective* (Gweru, Zimbabwe: Mambo Press, 1984); and Robert Schreiter, ed., *Faces of Jesus in Africa* (Maryknoll, N.Y.: Orbis Books, 1991). For an attempt to construct a Christology within the context of the Vietnamese cult of ancestors, see chapter 6 herein.

[68] Kwok Pui-Lan maintains that the Bible is just one form of human construction among many to speak about God and does not obtain pride of place among the sources of Christian theology; that a closed canon excludes other voices; and that the critical principle norming biblical interpretation (for example, prophetic criticism) is not found in the Bible itself but in the community of men and women who read the Bible and appropriate it for their liberation. See her "Discovering the Bible in the Non-Biblical World," in R. S. Sugirtharajah, *Voices from the Margin: Interpreting the Bible in the Third World* (Maryknoll, N.Y.: Orbis Books, 1991), 299-315.

for the adoption of non-Christian sources (for example, Korean shamanism) to formulate a Christology without worrying too much whether they are in accord with biblical "orthodoxy."[69]

Jung Young Lee pays much attention to New Testament Christology to undergird his portrait of Christ as the perfect realization of change (Christ as Word, Light, and Savior) and as the new marginal person par excellence (his reinterpretation of the life of Jesus from his birth to his resurrection). His use of *I Ching* metaphysics allows him to take seriously biblical texts that affirm both Jesus' humanity and divinity. On the other hand, his reliance on *yin*-and-*yang* metaphysics leads him to invest biblical texts with meanings that are doubtfully there, for example, that Jesus as Light includes also darkness.

Pieris's essays on Christology, programmatic as they are, do not intend to present a complete portrait of New Testament Jesus but so far his liberationist exegesis of certain texts is nothing short of brilliant, for example, his interpretation of the death of Jesus as a baptism in religious poverty (against Mammon). On the other hand, Pieris's concentration on Jesus' double baptism has so far left the resurrection of Jesus virtually unexplored in his Christology.

As a whole, then, Asian theologians practice a liberationist hermeneutics of the New Testament. Such exegesis does not pretend to be objective in the sense of neutral or comprehensive in the sense of inclusive of all the sides of every issue. Rather, it sets out to read the scripture from the perspective of the poor and the oppressed, and in Christology it tends to emphasize Jesus' prophetic message about the reign of God and his mighty deeds in favor of the poor. Such a Christology is liable to the charge of partiality and advocacy by what Lee calls the "central" scholars.

Asian theologians, however, would not regard partiality and advocacy as necessarily negative. They would point out that every interpretation is undergirded by and in turn supports an ideology. The issue is not whether one does or does not have an ideology, but whether one's ideology is conformable to God's universal love for all and preferential option for the people on the margin. For Asian theologians, the two areas in which God has manifested God's self to the Asian people are their religions and their poverty. An Asian biblical hermeneutics must therefore take these two "biases" into account.[70]

---

[69] See Chung, *Struggle to Be the Sun Again*: "My fourth and last hope for the future direction of Asian women's theology is that it move away from the doctrinal purity of Christian theology and *risk the survival-liberation centered syncretism. . . .* We Asian women theologians must move away from our imposed fear of losing Christian identity, in the opinion of the mainline theological circles, and instead risk that we might be transformed by the religious wisdom of our own people. We may find that to the extent that we are willing to lose our old identity, we will be transformed into truly *Asian Christians*" (113).

[70] For reflections on third-world hermeneutics, especially on the need for reading the Bible from the standpoint of the underprivileged, see Sugirtharajah, *Voices from the Margin*, 434-39.

There is one area, however, in which Asian theologians can derive much profit from contemporary first-world biblical research on early Judaism. In his stress on Jesus' denunciations of the religious traditions of his times, for example, Pieris presents a negative portrayal of early Judaism, contrasting Jesus' prophetic spirituality with the "narrow ideology" of the Zealots, the "sectarian puritanism" of the Essenes, the "self-righteousness" of the Pharisees, and the "leisure-class mentality" of the Sadducees. Besides being inaccurate generalizations, these statements may reproduce in Asian theology the anti-Semitism that has been the bane of Western theology. A careful and judicious use of contemporary scholarship on early Judaism, especially on the Pharisees, will correct the age-old Christian bias against Jews and Judaism.[71]

Asian Christology and Western Christological Tradition

The three Asian theologians we have studied are as a whole quite critical of the Western theological tradition in general and of Western Christology in particular. Chung Hyun Kyung points out how traditional christological titles such as Suffering Servant, Lord, and Emmanuel have contributed to the subjugation of Asian women. Pieris offers a trenchant critique of the six early Asian Christologies for their failure to unite religiousness and poverty. Lee rejects the Western Christologies based on Greek metaphysics and process philosophy.

These three theologians do not, however, reject Western theology and Christology *in toto*; besides the hermeneutics of suspicion, they also employ the hermeneutics of retrieval. Chung Hyun Kyung recognizes that the Suffering Servant, Lord, and Emmanuel Christologies have also contributed to the liberation of Asian women. Pieris calls for a union of the Western stress on *agape* with the Eastern emphasis on *gnosis*. Lee acknowledges the usefulness of framing Christology in metaphysical terms, a characteristic of Western Christology, though naturally enough, he prefers Taoist metaphysics.

In general, it must be said, however, that a cavalier dismissal of patristic and medieval Christologies would impoverish an Asian Christology by neglecting their genuine insights and that ignorance of them would severely limit the possibilities of the more than ever necessary dialogue between Western and Eastern theologies. Not least, a thorough knowledge of them will spare Asian Christology the mistakes and deficiencies for which Asian theologians have criticized Western Christologies.

All Christologies are nothing but attempts to answer Jesus' famous question "Who do you say that I am?" (Mt 16:15). Asian theologians have taken up the challenge to answer that question in terms both understandable to their people and faithful to the New Testament witness to Jesus. Their responses join the

---

[71] For helpful and up-to-date introductions to Judaism and to the Pharisees in particular, see "Judaism" and "Pharisees," in *The Anchor Bible Dictionary* (New York: Doubleday, 1992), 3:1037-89 and 5:289-303, respectively.

ever-growing list of Christologies by third-world theologians who paint different faces of Jesus: the liberator, the elder brother, the ancestor, the chief, the
witch doctor, the *christa*, the black Messiah, the guru, and so forth. Whether
these portraitures are authentic representations or fraudulent counterfeits of Jesus,
only time will tell; like all theological hypotheses, their validity is determined
by the *receptio* of the people, either as life-giving *cogitatio fidei* or as ersatz
lucubrations to be dumped in the theological junkyard.

6

Jesus as the Eldest Son
and Ancestor

Recently a number of Asian theologians have bitterly complained that the Christian churches in Asia are only *in* Asia and have not yet become *of* Asia in spite of over three hundred years of missionary activity.[1] As a consequence, theology as taught in Asian churches, largely clones of the Roman ecclesiological model, has been a rehashed version of theological systems developed in the West. In particular, their christological treatises have been nothing more than a translation of Chalcedonian Christology into local tongues.[2] Even the inculturation process, well-intentioned though it is in its attempts to express Christian beliefs in native religious categories, has been no more than cosmetic. Worse, in the name of inculturation or indigenization, at times native religious elements have been vandalized and baptized into instruments of proselytization.[3]

Although the first persons in Asia to reflect on who Jesus is from the perspective of Asian cultural and religious traditions were not Christians but Indian

---

[1] The most vocal critic of this aspect of Asian Christian churches, among Roman Catholics, is no doubt Aloysius Pieris, a Sri Lankan Jesuit. See Aloysius Pieris, *An Asian Theology of Liberation* (Maryknoll, N.Y.: Orbis Books, 1988), 35-50. According to Pieris, "The unholy alliance of the missionary, the military, and the merchant of a previous era now continues with greater subtlety, for the local churches so planted in Asia, being still local churches of former colonizing countries, now continue their alliance with neocolonialism in order to survive" (50). Among non-Roman Catholic theologians, Choan-Seng Song, a Taiwanese Presbyterian, has offered a searing indictment of Protestant Asian churches. See Choan-Seng Song, *Christian Mission in Reconstruction: An Asian Analysis* (Madras: The Christian Literature Society, 1975); and idem, *Third-Eye Theology: Theology in Formation in Asian Settings,* rev. ed. (Maryknoll, N.Y.: Orbis Books, 1990).

[2] Tissa Balasuriya, a Sri Lankan Oblate, rejects an Asian theology modeled on Western theology, which he regards as irrelevant to Asians because it is tribalistic, church-centered, clericalist, patriarchal, capitalistic, devoid of social analysis, and lacking in action-orientation. See Tissa Balasuriya, *Planetary Theology* (Maryknoll, N.Y.: Orbis Books, 1984), 2-10; and idem, "Towards the Liberation of Theology in Asia" in *Asia's Struggle for Full Humanity: Towards a Relevant Theology,* ed. Virginia Fabella (Maryknoll, N.Y.: Orbis Books, 1980), 26.

[3] See Pieris, *An Asian Theology of Liberation,* 38-42, 93-96; and Peter C. Phan, "Christian Mission in Contemporary Theology," *Indian Theological Studies* 31/4 (1994): 297-347, esp. 333-43.

Hindus,[4] there is no dearth of Asian Christian theologians who have attempted to answer Jesus' famous question—"Who do you say that I am?" (Mt 16:15)—on the basis of their own cultures.[5] In the last two decades, younger Asian theologians, mostly under the influence of Latin American liberation theology, have brought new insights to enrich the older, more culture-based Christology.[6]

This chapter intends to make a contribution to these ongoing christological reflections by situating Christ within the context of the Confucian teaching on family relationships, especially on the role of the eldest son, and the Asian practice of veneration of ancestors. It first describes Confucian family ethics and the practice of ancestor veneration as these have been practiced in certain Asian countries, focusing on Vietnam in particular (the author's home country). Second, it explores the possibility of viewing Christ as the eldest son and as an ancestor. Finally, it raises the question of whether this Christology needs to be complemented by liberation Christology, especially as this is presented by Asian feminist theologians.

THE ELDEST SON AND ANCESTOR VENERATION

By Confucianism is meant the social, political, ethical, philosophical, and religious system based on the teachings of Confucius (551-479 B.C.E.) and his successors.[7] Known in Chinese as *ju chia* or School of the Literati—scholars and teachers of the ancient literature, especially of the Five Classics allegedly edited by Confucius *(Book of Poetry, Book of Rites, Book of History, Spring and*

---

[4] For excellent studies of these "Christologies," see M. M. Thomas, *The Acknowledged Christ of Indian Renaissance* (London: SCM Press, 1969); and Stanley J. Samartha, *The Hindu Response to the Unbound Christ* (Bangalore: Christian Institute for the Study of Religion and Society, 1974).

[5] For helpful surveys of Indian Christian theology, see the following chapters in Sergio Torres and Virginia Fabella, eds., *The Emergent Gospel: Theology from the Developing World* (Maryknoll, N.Y.: Orbis Books, 1978): D. S. Amalorpavadass, "The Indian Universe of a New Theology," 137-56; and J. R. Chandran, "Development of Christian Theology in India," 157-72.

[6] These two trends of Asian theology, inculturation and liberation, were brought together, not without controversy, during the Ecumenical Association of Third World Theologians (EATWOT) Asian consultation in 1979. See Fabella, *Asia's Struggle for Full Humanity*, 10-11, 165, 186.

[7] There are many portraits of Confucius or K'ung Ch'iu (his real name); he has been portrayed as a moral teacher, a wise man, an answerer of conundrums, an itinerant tutor, a successful stateman, a diplomat, and even a magician. Some biographers (e.g., Ssu-ma Ch'ien) endow him with supernatural powers. The most authentic sources for the life and teachings of Confucius are *The Analects* and *Mencius*. It is widely acknowledged today that Confucius did not write any books (he is said to have edited the Five Classics) and was not a founder of a religion called Confucianism. Confucius described himself not as an originator of novel ideas but as a transmitter of the ways of the "Ancients." See *The Analects of Confucius*, trans. and annotated by Arthur Waley (New York: Vintage Books, 1939), VII, 1: "The Master said, I have 'transmitted what was taught to me without making up anything of my own.' I have been faithful to and loved the Ancients." Hereafter cited as *Analects*.

Autumn Annals, and *Book of Changes)*—Confucianism is conventionally divided into (1) classical Confucianism, as embodied in the Four Books *(The Analects, The Great Learning, The Doctrine of the Mean,* and *Mencius)*; (2) Han Confucianism, that is, Confucianism that was established as state orthodoxy during the Han dynasty (206 B.C.E.-220 C.E.); it was during this time that the Confucian canon was established and the cult of Confucius emerged as part of the state religion; and (3) Neo-Confucianism, that is, Confucianism as it was revived from the Sung dynasty (960-1279) with the School of Principle (in particular with Cheng I and Chu Hsi) through the Ming dynasty (1368-1644) with the School of Mind, whose main representative is Wang Yang-Ming, until the present day. In 1905 the imperial examination system, whose source was the official Neo-Confucian orthodoxy, was abolished, and in 1928 the cult of Confucius in the Confucian temple was terminated, thus ending the status of Confucianism as a state religion.[8]

The loss of this official status does not mean, of course, that Confucianism has ceased to exercise a profound and indelible influence on the thought and way of life of the Chinese people and of those people who have come under the domination of China, such as the Koreans and the Vietnamese. For our limited purpose here, which is to construct a Christology from the perspective of Vietnamese cultural and religious practices, it is unnecessary to expound the whole Confucian social, political, ethical, philosophical, and religious system of thought. Nor, in our investigation into what Confucianism teaches about family relationships, especially the role of the eldest son, and about ancestor veneration, is it necessary to distinguish sharply the variations these teachings have assumed in their historical development from classical Confucianism to Neo-Confucianism. Nor is it required to distinguish Confucianism from the elements of Buddhism and Taoism that have penetrated it, particularly in the area of metaphysics and forms of mental discipline. Nor, finally, is it necessary to take

---

[8] For general introductions to the life and teachings of Confucius, see *Analects;* David H. Smith, *Confucius* (New York: Scribner, 1973); Herrlee G. Creel, *Confucius and the Chinese Way* (New York: Harper, 1960); and Herbert Fingarette, *Confucius: The Secular as Sacred* (New York: Harper & Row, 1972). For general works on Chinese thought, see Wing-Tsit Chan, *A Source Book in Chinese Philosophy* (Princeton, N.J.: Princeton University Press, 1963); William T. De Bary, ed., *Sources of Chinese Tradition* (New York: Columbia University Press, 1960). On classical Confucianism, see Donald Munro, *The Concept of Man in Early China* (Stanford, Calif.: Stanford University Press, 1969); Tu Wei-Ming, *Centrality and Commonality: An Essay on Chung-yung* (Albany, N.Y.: State University of New York Press, 1976); and E. R. Hughs, *Chinese Philosophy in Classical Times* (London: Dent, 1954). On Neo-Confucianism, see David S. Nivison and Arthur F. Wright, eds., *Confucianism in Action* (Stanford, Calif.: Stanford University Press, 1959); William T. De Bary, ed., *Self and Society in Ming Thought* (New York: Columbia University Press, 1970); idem, *The Unfolding of Neo-Confucianism* (New York: Columbia University Press, 1975); Julia Ching, *To Acquire Wisdom: The Way of Wang Yang-ming* (New York: Columbia University Press, 1976); Tu Wei-Ming, *Neo-Confucian Thought in Action* (Berkeley and Los Angeles: University of California Press, 1976); and Rodney L. Taylor, *The Cultivation of Sagehood as a Religious Goal in Neo-Confucianism* (Missoula, Mont.: Scholars Press, 1978).

into account the many changes that Confucianism has assumed in its migration from China into other countries such as Vietnam.

Family Relationships and the Role of the Eldest Son

Vietnam was under the domination of China for a total of about ten centuries, from 111 B.C.E. to 1427 C.E. (in four periods: 111 B.C.E.-39 C.E.; 43-544; 602-939; 1414-27) with the first occupation by the Han dynasty and the last by the Ming dynasty. From the earliest times of their occupation, Chinese rulers attempted to impose their culture and customs upon the Vietnamese. In 42 C.E. General Ma Vien disseminated, especially among the intelligentsia, Chinese letters, sciences, arts, and ideogrammatic characters. It was, however, only at the beginning of the third century, under the governorship of Si Nhiep, that Confucianism began to exercise a widespread influence on the Vietnamese with the introduction of the Five Classics and the Four Books. Since the eleventh century, with the establishment of schools and especially of the three state examinations *(thi huong, thi hoi,* and *thi dinh),* whose purpose was to select government functionaries (mandarins), Confucianism achieved a prodigious expansion and infiltrated into every level of Vietnamese life from the family to the village to the state, the three basic structures of Vietnamese society. Even after the official abolition of the state examinations in 1915 in Tonkin, in 1919 in Annam, and earlier by desuetude in Cochinchina, Confucianism continues to permeate the Vietnamese way of thinking and living.

Central to Confucian socio-political ethics is no doubt the concept of the cultivation of virtue *(duc).* As antidote to the collapse of the feudal order of his times, an era characterized by the hegemony of various states and almost constant internecine warfare, Confucius recommended a return to the way of virtue taught by the "Ancients" or the Divine Sages, mythological figures historicized as human rulers (for example, Yao, Shun, and Yu the Great), and as exemplified during the Zhou dynasty, especially by Tan, the Duke of Zhou.

The central virtue is *nhan,* variously translated as "humaneness," "humanity," "benevolence," "virtue," "kindness," "and goodness." Perhaps the last word, given its wide connotations, is the best rendering of *nhan.* It is not a single virtue but a complex of virtues. Asked what *nhan* is, Confucius replies that the one who puts into practice the five virtues (courtesy, breadth, good faith, diligence, and clemency) everywhere under heaven deserves to be called good.[9] Elsewhere, Confucius declares that the good person is "in private life, courteous; in public life, diligent; in relationships, loyal."[10] Goodness is so rare that Confucius was willing to ascribe it only to remote mythological figures and seldom discoursed upon it.[11] Humans can approach it by practicing "reciprocity," encapsulated in the famous saying: "Never do to others what you would

---

[9] See *Analects*, XVII, 6.
[10] Ibid., XIII, 19.
[11] See ibid., IX, 1: "The Master seldom spoke of profit or fate or Goodness."

not like them to do to you."[12] However, reciprocity should not be understood as a search for a quid pro quo: indeed, Confucius repeatedly asserts that the good person has no concern for what is profitable or utilitarian; the only reward sought is virtue itself.

In practicing *nhan* one will become what Confucius regards as the ideal person, *quan tu,* best translated as "gentleman." Originally, it designated a member of the aristocracy. Confucius used it to refer to character (Chinese: *te*) rather than birth. The *quan tu* is one who never loses sight of virtue; in everything he does, he does not aim at profit but seeks what is right.[13] The gentleman, says Confucius, "must learn to be faithful to his superiors, to keep promises, to refuse the friendship of those who are not like him. And if he finds he has made a mistake, then he must not be afraid of admitting the fact and amending his ways."[14] In conduct and opinion a gentleman will practice moderation or the "middle conduct" between the two extremes; to exceed is as bad as to fall short. Finally, a gentleman "does not preach what he practices till he has practiced what he preaches."[15]

As a means to discover what is morally right, that is, the way of heaven, Confucius suggests the study of the tradition, literature, rites, and music of the past (especially of the Zhou dynasty), because heaven acted in history.[16] However, for music and rituals to achieve their potentialities, they must be performed with virtue: "A man who is not good, what can he have to do with ritual? A man who is not good, what can he have to do with music?"[17] Confucius condemned the rites and music of his own day, not because they were incorrectly performed, but because, bereft of virtue, they had become an empty shell.[18]

The most important path to virtue, however, is what Confucius calls the "rectification of names" *(chinh danh).* For the purpose of our present reflections,

---

[12] Ibid., XV, 23; see also V, 11; VI, 28. In XII, 2, asked about goodness, Confucius replies: "Behave when away from home as though you were in the presence of an important guest. Deal with the common people as though you were officiating at an important sacrifice. Do not do to others what you would not like yourself."

[13] See ibid., IV, 10: "A gentleman in his dealings with the world has neither enmities nor affections; but wherever he sees Right he ranges himself beside it." In IV, 16: "A gentleman takes as much trouble to discover what is right as lesser men take to discover what will pay."

[14] Ibid., I, 8. In I, 14, Confucius says further: "A gentleman who never goes on eating till he is sated, who does not demand comfort in his home, who is diligent in business and cautious in speech, who associates with those who possess the Way and thereby corrects his own faults—such a one may indeed be said to have a taste for learning."

[15] Ibid., XI, 13. See also IV, 24: "A gentleman covets the reputation of being slow in word but prompt in deed." For further Confucian ideas on the *quan tu,* see *The Doctrine of the Mean,* trans. James Legge (Oxford: Clarendon Press, 1893), chaps. I-XV. Hereafter cited as *Doctrine of the Mean.*

[16] See *Analects,* VIII, 8: "Let a man be first incited by the Songs, then given a firm footing by the study of ritual, and finally perfected by music."

[17] Ibid., III, 3.

[18] See ibid., XVII, 11: "Ritual, ritual! Does it mean no more than presents of jade and silk? Music, music! Does it mean no more than bells and drums?"

this prominent concept in Confucian thought is of major significance. When asked by Tzu-lu what first act he would undertake were he given a state to rule, Confucius replies: "It would certainly be to correct language." To the questioner puzzled by his response, Confucius explains: "If language is incorrect, then what is said does not concord with what was meant; and if what is said does not concord with what was meant, what is to be done cannot be effected. If what is to be done cannot be effected, then rites and music will not flourish. If rites and music do not flourish, then mutilations and lesser punishments will go astray. And if mutilations and lesser punishments go astray, then the people have nowhere to put hand or foot."[19]

The rectification of names, however, goes beyond the correct use of language and the need for words to correspond to reality; more important, it requires that people act according to their proper social standing and relationships to others. More precisely, one's social standing is determined by one's relationships to others, and these in turn dictate certain duties that must be conscientiously carried out in order to achieve justice. In other words, there must be a "rectification" between one's relationships and one's behavior.

For Confucius, there are three basic relationships or bonds *(tam cuong)*: between king and subject, between husband and wife, and between parents and children. Asked about government, he replies: "Let the prince be a prince, the minister a minister, the father a father, and the son a son."[20] Elsewhere, the relationships and the corresponding virtues are listed more fully:

> The duties of universal obligation are five, and the virtues wherewith they are practiced are three. The duties are those between sovereign and minister, between father and son, between husband and wife, between elder brother and younger, and those belonging to the intercourse of friends. Those five are the duties of universal obligation. Knowledge, magnanimity, and energy, these three, are the virtues universally binding. And the means by which they carry the duties into practice is singleness.[21]

Leaving out of consideration the other relationships, we will concentrate on that between parents and children, in particular between the father and the eldest son, since this relationship will be used as a basis for our christological reflections.[22] This relationship on the part of the son is constituted by filial piety

---

[19] Ibid., XIII, 3.

[20] Ibid., XII, 11.

[21] *Doctrine of the Mean*, XX, 8.

[22] It is of utmost importance to recognize that there exists an intimate connection among these three relationships as well as between individual ethics and social ethics. Indeed, this is the whole point of *The Great Learning*, trans. James Legge (Oxford: Clarendon Press, 1893): "The ancients who wished to illustrate illustrious virtue throughout the kingdom, first ordered well their own States. Wishing to order well their States, they first regulated their families. Wishing to regulate their families, they first cultivated their persons. Wishing to cultivate their persons, they first rectify their hearts. Wishing to rectify their hearts, they sought first to be sincere in their thoughts. Wishing to be

(hieu thao). This seems originally to refer to piety toward the spirits of ancestors or dead parents, of which we will speak in greater detail shortly. In the *Analects*, besides this meaning, it also refers to filial conduct toward living parents.

At any rate, for Confucius, filial piety is the foundation and root of all virtues: "The gentleman bends his attention to what is radical. That being established, all practical courses naturally grow up. Filial piety and fraternal submission!—are they not the root of all virtuous actions?"[23] Asked how one should treat one's parents, the Master replies: "Never disobey!" and then adds: "While they are alive, serve them according to ritual. When they die, bury them according to ritual and sacrifice according to ritual."[24]

To have filial piety is not simply to provide for the parents' material needs but to have respect for them.[25] Filial piety takes precedence over public service, or more precisely, piety toward one's parents makes a real contribution to the public welfare. Questioned why he was not in government service, Confucius quoted a text from the *Book of History* as his excuse: "Be filial, only be filial and friendly towards your brothers, and you will be contributing to government."[26] A good son also wants to be near his parents so that at their death he may be able to come back and perform the rites of mourning: "While father and mother are alive, a good son does not wander far afield; or if he does so, goes only where he has said he was going."[27]

A mark of filial piety is to be able to continue the will and transmit the work of the father: "While a man's father is alive, you can only see his intentions; it is when his father dies that you discover whether or not he is capable of carrying them out. If for the whole three years of mourning he manages to carry on the household exactly as in his father's day, then he is a good son indeed."[28] Elsewhere, filial piety is seen in "the skillful carrying out of the wishes of the forefathers, and the skillful carrying forward of their undertakings. . . . Thus they served the dead as they would have served them alive; they served the departed as they would have served them had they been continued among them."[29]

Filial piety does not imply blind obedience or complicity in one's parents' faults. Indeed, it requires gentle correction: "In serving his parents, a son may remonstrate with them, but gently; when he sees that they do not incline to follow

---

sincere in their thoughts, they tended to the utmost their knowledge. Such extension of knowledge lays in the investigation of things" (par. 4). Hence, "from the Son of Heaven to the mass of the people, all must consider the cultivation of the person the root of everything besides" (par. 6).

[23] *Analects*, I, 2. See also I, 6: "A young man's duty is to behave well to his parents at home and to his elders abroad."

[24] Ibid., XI, 5. By "disobey" Confucius meant "not perform the ritual as prescribed."

[25] See ibid., XI, 7. See also XI, 8: "Filial piety does not consist merely in young people undertaking the hard work, when anything has to be done, or serving their elders first with wine and food. It is something much more than that."

[26] Ibid., XI, 21.

[27] Ibid., IV, 19.

[28] Ibid., II, 11.

[29] *Doctrine of the Mean*, XIX, 2-5.

his advice, he shows an increased degree of reverence, but he does not abandon his purpose; and should they punish him, he does not allow himself to murmur."[30]

Before we move on to the discussion of filial piety demonstrated toward deceased parents and ancestors, a brief word should be said about Confucius's attitude toward heaven *(Thien)*.[31] In the *Analects*, besides referring to the sky, heaven has the meaning of providence, nature, God (like the German *Himmel*). Heaven is the dispenser of life and death, wealth and rank.[32] Confucius himself was unwilling to discourse about heaven,[33] though he admitted that heaven produced the virtue that was in him[34] and that he did not know the "decrees of heaven" until the age of fifty.[35] Nevertheless, he believes that "if it is the will of Heaven that the Way shall prevail, then the Way shall prevail. But if it is the will of Heaven that the Way should perish, then it must perish."[36] He even believed that he was known by heaven.[37] As to the will of heaven, the gentleman must learn to know and submit himself to it patiently, because "he who has put himself in the wrong with Heaven has no means of expiation left."[38]

Filial Piety and Veneration of Ancestors

When Confucianism, Taoism, and Buddhism were imported from China into Vietnam (the three religions are called *tam giao*), they did not enter into a religious vacuum; on the contrary, there was already a deep and pervasive body of religious beliefs and practices as ancient as the Vietnamese people. This original religion is often referred to as the cult of spirits. This cult of spirits is, then, the original religion of the Vietnamese into which elements of Confucianism, Taoism, and Buddhism were successfully amalgamated.[39]

---

[30] *Analects*, IV, 18.

[31] I prescind here from the question of whether the term *T'ien* corresponds to the term and concept *God,* an issue that exercised the protagonists in the seventeenth-century Chinese Rites Controversy between the Jesuit missionaries, on the one hand, and the Franciscan, Dominican, and *Missions Étrangères de Paris* missionaries on the other. See George Minamiki, *The Chinese Rites Controversy from Its Beginning to Modern Times* (Chicago: Loyola University Press, 1985).

[32] See *Analects*, XII, 5.

[33] See ibid., V, 12: "Our Master's views concerning culture and the outward insignia of goodness, we are permitted to hear; but about Man's nature and the ways of Heaven, he will not tell us anything."

[34] See ibid., VII, 22.

[35] See ibid., II, 4.

[36] Ibid., XIV, 38. See also IX, 5. This saying reminds one of the statement of Gamaliel (Acts 5:38-39).

[37] See ibid., XIV, 37.

[38] Ibid., III, 13.

[39] See Léopold Cadière, *Croyances et pratiques religieuses des Vietnamiens* (Hanoi: Imprimerie d'Extrême Orient, 1944), 1:6 10. This volume is part of a trilogy by one of the greatest scholars on Vietnamese culture and religions. The second volume was published in 1955, and the third in 1956. Born in 1869, Cadière came to Vietnam as a missionary in 1892 and worked there until his death in 1955. His writings remain a veritable mine of information on Vietnamese culture and religions.

Central to the Vietnamese cult of spirits is the veneration of ancestors, which was performed at three levels, that is, the family *(nha)*, the village *(lang)*, and the state *(nuoc)*, though it is by no means the only religious act of the cult of spirits.[40] There are, for instance, the cult of heaven, of local protector gods, of nature deities, of "patron saints" of professional guilds, and of national heroes, including Confucius, who had his own building called *van mieu*. There is no doubt, however, that when Confucianism was introduced to Vietnam, its teachings on the family as the cornerstone of ethics and of filial piety as the foundation of the virtuous life immeasurably strengthened the ancestor cult that was the hallmark of Vietnamese indigenous religion. The *Analects* report with approval a saying by Master Tseng: "Let there be a careful attention to perform the funeral rites to parents, and let them be followed when long gone with the ceremonies of sacrifice;—then the virtue of the people will resume its proper excellence."[41] Confucius himself argued for a three-year period of mourning as "the universal mourning everywhere under Heaven" and that "when a gentleman is in mourning, if he eats dainties, he does not relish them; if he hears music, it does not please him; if he sits in his ordinary state, he is not comfortable. That is why he abstains from these things."[42] Confucius himself placed emphasis not on the spirits but on the duties of gratitude to and remembrance of ancestral spirits.

As has been mentioned above, ancestor worship in Vietnam was carried out on three levels. At the state level, the emperor, in his capacity as the "August and Holy Sovereign" *(Duc Hoang De)*, as the "Son of Heaven" *(Thien Tu)*, with a "Heavenly Mandate" *(Thien Mang)*, offered, at first every year, then every three years, sacrifices to his royal predecessors who were the ancestors of the country (of course, he also personally owed them worship insofar as they were his own ancestors).[43] On the village level, yearly sacrifices were offered by the village notables in elaborate rituals in a public building called *dinh* to legendary figures and historical personages who were national heroes, or founders or famous benefactors of the village.

Most important, however, ancestor veneration is performed at the family level. To understand this, a brief word must be said about the Vietnamese concept of the soul, funeral rites, and the role of the eldest son.[44]

Popular Vietnamese religion believes that humans have three superior or rational souls *(hon)* and inferior or sensitive souls, seven for men and nine for women *(phach* or *via)*. The latter, deriving from the *yin* principle, enter the

---

[40] In Asia, ancestor worship is an amalgamation of folk religion, Confucianism, Taoism, Buddhism, and Shinto. In Vietnam, as well as in other Asian countries, ancestor veneration has been connected with other Taoist practices.

[41] *Analects*, I, 9.

[42] Ibid., XVII, 21.

[43] The sacrifice is called *Te Nam Giao*, the most solemn act of public worship of Vietnam. We will discuss this worship in greater detail later.

[44] For a comprehensive introduction to Vietnamese culture and religions, see Joseph Nguyen Huy Lai, *La Tradition religieuse spirituelle et sociale au Vietnam* (Paris: Beauchesne, 1981), with ample bibliography, especially of works in Vietnamese.

body at conception and do not survive death; the former, deriving from the *yang* principle, enter the body at birth and survive death. Needless to say, popular Vietnamese religion maintains the immortality of the "soul" and the survival of the "person" after death.

In the past, Vietnamese funerals were given minute regulations in three works: the *Tam Giao Kinh* (Ritual of the Three Religions), the *Tho Mai Gia Le* (Family Funeral Rituals), and the *Gia Long Code* (promulgated by Emperor Gia Long in 1812). Of course, not all the rituals are observed today. Only salient and significant features are mentioned here to help readers grasp the importance of ancestor veneration and the role of the eldest son.

Suppose an old man is dying. During his agony, his eldest son places a three-yard-long piece of white silk on his chest to collect his last breath. Immediately after his death, a member of the family, ordinarily the eldest son, climbs up on the roof of the house, holding a shirt of the deceased, and shouts: "The three *hon* and seven *via* of my father! Come back to be placed with the body in the coffin!" The purpose of this ritual (called *chieu hon*, literally, "recalling the soul") is to prevent the deceased from becoming a wandering soul, without a place in the family's shrine of ancestor worship. Then the white cloth is folded into the form of a human body to represent the soul of the deceased. It is called *hon bach* (white soul) and will be placed near the coffin for veneration. Next, the mourning ritual is established with the eldest son (if he is dead, then his son) being made *tang chu*, that is, the master of mourning. The various acts of washing the corpse, dressing it, placing it in the coffin follow. Then, all the members of the family officially wear mourning clothes, made of coarse material, different in color (mostly white, and never black) and design, according to the relationship they had with the deceased.

Before the corpse is brought to the cemetery for burial, there takes place an important ritual called *chuyen cuu* (moving the coffin) and *yet to* (presentation to the ancestors). The coffin, or at least the *hon bach*, is carried exclusively by members of the family to the ancestral home *(tu duong)*, and there the *truong toc* (the head of the clan), usually the eldest son, announces to the ancestors that the deceased has joined them. After the burial, the *hon bach* is replaced by the wooden tablet that bears on the one side the name of the deceased, family status, and rank in society, and on the other side, the dates of birth and death. It is carried home and placed on the ancestral altar in the house.

A hundred days after the death of the father or mother, the eldest son makes three sacrifices for the peaceful repose of his father or mother *(te ngu)* and recites the following invocation: "May the soul of my father (mother) deign to reside in this tablet."[45] Then the *hon bach*, which has been placed beside the tablet, is withdrawn and buried. The family keeps on the ancestral altar only the tablets of four generations before the father, placed from left to right: the great-great grandparents, the great-grandparents, the grandparents, the father and mother.

---

[45] See E. C. Lesserteur, *Rituel domestique des funérailles en Annam* (Paris: Imprimerie Chaix, 1885), 35-37.

On the first, second, and third anniversaries of the death, solemn sacrifices and celebrations are held in honor of the deceased. Outside of anniversaries, the cult of ancestors is celebrated on the first days of the new lunar year *(Tet)*. With sacrifices and incense, a ceremony is held to invite the ancestors back into the home for the New Year festivities *(ruoc ong ba ong vai)*, and on the third, or seventh, or fifteenth day, another ceremony is held to bid them farewell *(tien ong ba ong vai)*.

Filial piety, and especially filial piety as demonstrated in ancestor worship on the part of the eldest son on the state, village, and family levels, no doubt constitutes the heart and soul of the Vietnamese ethical system and religion.[46] It was the perceived threat posed by Christianity to this ancestor worship that made seventeenth-century Chinese people reluctant to embrace the new religion, and it was also this threat that was the main, though by no means only, reason why more than 100,000 Vietnamese Christians were put to death during half a century of persecution under the three emperors Minh Mang, Thieu Tri, and Tu Duc (1825-83). The question is not simply whether it is possible to remove this perceived threat in Christian mission (which was, at any rate, settled by the 8 December 1939 instruction of the then Propaganda Fide, *Plane compertum est*),[47] but whether it is impossible to conceive Christ in terms of filial piety and ancestor worship.

JESUS AS THE ELDEST SON AND ANCESTOR

Recent trends in Christology have emphasized the need to start with the Jesus of history and to combine what has been called Christology from above or descending Christology (often with an ontological cast and a focus on Jesus' divine nature) with Christology from below or ascending Christology (often with an emphasis on Jesus' Jewishness and his message on the kingdom of God). Furthermore, it is now widely recognized that even in the New Testament there is not a uniform Christology but a pluralism of Christologies that are, though not mutually contradictory, not easily harmonizable with one another.[48] In this section of the chapter I explore the image of Christ as the eldest son and as an ancestor.

---

[46] The best study of this theme remains L. Cadière's essay "La famille et la religion en pays annamite," in Cadière, *Croyances et pratiques religieuses des Vietnamiens*, 1:33-84.

[47] For a discussion of this issue, see Nguyen, *La Tradition religieuse spirituelle et sociale au Vietnam*, 399-442.

[48] See, for instance, Raymond Brown, *An Introduction to New Testament Christology* (New York: Paulist Press, 1994), which speaks of parousia Christology, resurrection Christology, public-ministry Christology, family Christology, conception Christology, and pre-existence Christology. See also John F. Grady, *Models of Jesus Revisited* (New York: Paulist Press, 1994), which presents six contemporary models of Christology. Bernard L. Lee presents three root metaphors of Christology in his *Jesus and the Metaphors of God: The Christs of the New Testament* (New York: Paulist Press, 1993).

Jesus as Eldest Son and Model of Filial Piety

Jesus was born a Jew, socialized as a Jew, and remained Jewish all his life. Hence, he was familiar with all the Jewish traditions regarding family life and with the injunctions of the Torah concerning the duties of children toward their parents.[49] He certainly knew the command to "honor your father and your mother, as the LORD, your God, has commanded you, so that your days may be long and that it may go well with you in the land that the LORD your God is giving you" (Dt 5:16). To the rich young man who asked what he should do to possess eternal life, Jesus answered that he must, among other things, honor his father and his mother (Mt 19:18). A teacher of wisdom, he must have known the teaching of Proverbs:

> My child, keep your father's commandment,
>   and do not forsake your mother's teaching.
> Bind them upon your heart always;
>   tie them around your neck. (Prov 6:20-21)

and:

> A wise child loves discipline,
>   but a scoffer does not listen to rebuke. (Prov 13:1)

After the incident in the Temple at the age of twelve, when he seemed to be causing his parents grief by remaining behind in Jerusalem without their knowledge, the child Jesus was said to return home and there "was obedient to them" and "increased in wisdom and in years, and in divine and human favor" (Lk 2:51-52).

As the "firstborn son" (Lk 2:7; Mt 1:25), Jesus was regarded as "the first fruits of [his father's] vigor " (Gn 49:3; see Dt 21:17) and "the first to open the womb" (Ex 13:2, 12, 15; Nm 18:15), emphasizing both paternal and maternal lines.[50] And as the male firstborn, he was considered to belong to Yahweh and had to be consecrated to Yahweh (Ex 13:2; 12-15; 22:28; 34:1-20; Nm 3:11-13; 8:16-18; and 18:15; Lk 2:22-24). As firstborn son he constituted not only the continuation of the family but also the continuity and permanence of Israel's covenantal relationship with God. As the male firstborn, Jesus enjoyed special privileges that constituted his "birthright": a larger inheritance, a special paternal

---

[49] For studies on Hebrew family, see P. A. H. De Boer, *Fatherhood and Motherhood in Israelite and Judean Piety* (Leiden: Brill, 1974); Norman K. Gottwald, *The Tribes of Yahweh* (Maryknoll, N.Y.: Orbis Books, 1979); Christopher J. H. Wright, *God's People in God's Land* (Grand Rapids, Mich.: Eerdmans, 1983); and J. R. Porter, *The Extended Family in the Old Testament* (London: Edutext, 1967).

[50] I leave aside here the question of what "the brothers and sisters of Jesus" means, whether they were his blood brothers and sisters, or his half-brothers and half-sisters, or his cousins. In general, it cannot be said that the New Testament identifies them without doubt as Jesus' blood brothers and sisters.

blessing, family leadership, and an honored place at mealtimes (Gn 25:5-6; 27:35-36; 42:37; 43:33; Dt 21:15-17).

Like the ancient Vietnamese, the Israelites found the strongest sense of identity, protection, and responsibility in the "Father's house" *(bet-ab)*, which included the head of the household, his wife (or wives), his sons and their wives, his grandsons and their wives, plus any unmarried sons or daughters in the generation below him. But, also like the ancient Vietnamese family *(gia)*, this Israelite family was part of a large clan *(mispaha;* Vietnamese: *bo* or *toc)*. In this context, Jesus was also bound by the obligations of the kinsman-redeemer *(go'el)*: to avenge murder, to raise a male heir for a deceased relative, to redeem the land, and to rescue members from debt slavery.

As the firstborn male and kinsman-redeemer, Jesus can be compared to the Vietnamese *truong toc*, that is, the head of the family-clan.[51] We have already seen the role of the eldest son at the death of his father; in all the funeral rituals, as the *tang chu* (master of mourning) he plays the most important role, from the moment of his father's final agony to that of placing the deceased's wooden tablet on the ancestral altar. As the result of these acts of filial piety, three things follow. First, a new cult is born, that is, the cult of the deceased father; he is the new addition to the list of the family's ancestors. With his tablet installed on the ancestral altar, the father is now due veneration by his descendants, and later on he will be joined by his wife, by all his descendants by line of primogeniture, until the fifth generation. Second, the house in which the deceased lived, which now is inherited by the firstborn son, becomes an ancestral temple in which he alone first, and later, his wife and his descendants by line of primogeniture until the fifth generation, will be offered sacrifices and cult.[52] Third, the firstborn son becomes the minister of the cult of ancestors just begun. It is always the firstborn son, or if he is dead, then his firstborn son, who is the minister of the cult.[53] Younger brothers are given this role only if the eldest son had no children. Because it would be an act of filial impiety to cause this veneration to end for lack of posterity, the eldest son has a most sacred duty to produce a son.[54]

At this point a few objections may be voiced against my proposal to view Christ as the eldest son within the context of Vietnamese ancestor worship. First, there is no ancestor worship among the Jews; the social and religious functions of the Jewish firstborn male, though manifold and important, do not

---

[51] *Truong toc* (chief of the clan), in Tonkin and Annam, is the firstborn son by the principal wife of the oldest branch of the family. In Cochinchina, this title is given to the oldest member of all the branches of the family.

[52] In addition to this home turned ancestral temple, there is a common funerary temple called *nha tho bo* (house of worship of the clan) where all the tablets of the ancestors of all the branches of family up to the fifth generation are placed for worship.

[53] The eldest son receives as part of his inheritance a portion of his father's estate (land or money) called *huong hoa* (literally, "incense fire"), the proceeds of which are to be used to defray the costs of annual sacrifices and that are in principle inalienable.

[54] This duty explains in part the old custom of taking another wife if the first wife fails to produce a male child. On this practice of polygamy, see Cadière, *Croyances et pratiques religieuses des Vietnamiens*, 1:67.

involve offering cult to his ancestors. Second, Jesus' teachings contain statements that seem to go against filial piety. Third, Jesus did not marry and did not have any children; therefore, he failed in his filial piety, at least according to the Vietnamese norms. Fourth, were Jesus to offer ancestor worship, to whom should he have offered it? Apparently not to Joseph, his putative father, but to his eternal father. But does this not imply the death of God the Father?

To answer the first objection: It is true that the Yahwism that became normative in ancient Israel and is reflected in the Deuteronomic and prophetic literature was resolute in its condemnation of ancestor worship. For example, Deuteronomy condemns consulting the dead (18:10-11), making offerings to the dead (26:14), and self-laceration rituals, which were typical of Canaanite death-cult practice (14:1). Jeremiah spoke against those who went to the funeral banquet house and those who lacerated themselves for the dead (16:5-8). The Holiness Code contains prohibitions against conjuring and consulting one's dead ancestors (Lv 19:26-32). Job 14:21 and Qoholeth 9:4-6, 10 affirm the uselessness of necromancy. The dead are said not to be cognizant of the affairs of the living and not able to grant favors to them.[55]

It must be granted that Vietnamese ancestor veneration sometimes contains, especially at the popular level, magical practices assimilated from Taoism. But shorn of these superstitious practices, ancestor veneration as a religious manifestation of deep gratitude and filial piety to one's forbears and of a living communion with them does not seem to be foreign to the Jews. Even the ancient expressions to describe death such as "being gathered to one's kin" and "sleeping with one's fathers" evince a deep belief in unbreakable solidarity with the family and the clan. I do not mean to say that Jesus himself has taught or practiced ancestor veneration in ways similar to the Vietnamese ancestor worship; indeed, historical records about the historical Jesus are completely silent on this theme. But my point is not that ancient Israel or Jesus practiced ancestor worship; rather, it is that it is possible (and theologically fruitful) to portray Jesus as one filled with filial piety who, had he been a Vietnamese firstborn son, would no doubt have taken upon himself with utmost seriousness the responsibilities of ancestor worship.

With regard to the second objection, there are admittedly in Jesus' teaching sayings that at first sight seem to offend filial piety. For example, to one potential disciple who asked to go away first and bury his father, Jesus replied, "Follow me, and let the dead bury their own dead" (Mt 8:22). As one of the conditions to be his disciple Jesus said, "Whoever loves father or mother more than me is not worthy of me" (Mt 10:37). When informed that his mother and brothers wished to speak to him, Jesus said: "Who is my mother, and who are my brothers? . . . Here are my mother and my brothers! For whoever does the will of my Father in heaven is my brother and sister and mother" (Mt 12:48-50). Finally, at the wedding in Cana, his attitude and reply to his mother, who apparently

---

[55] This does not mean that in ancient Israel ancestor worship was not practiced. See Theodore J. Lewis, *Cults of the Dead in Ancient Israel and Ugarit* (Atlanta, Ga.: Scholars Press, 1987).

had asked him to do something about the lack of wine, seems cold and uncaring: "Woman, what concern is that to you and to me? My hour has not yet come" (Jn 2:4). At first reading these statements seem to be offensive to filial piety. However, they should in no way be taken as denying respect and love toward one's parents. Rather, they should probably be understood as emphasizing the radical demands of discipleship or as part of Jesus' teaching of "subversive wisdom."[56]

On the other hand, there are indications that Jesus behaved toward his heavenly Father with tenderest love and affection. Leaving aside the gospel of John, which describes in most intimate terms the relationship between Jesus and the Father (though, of course, Jesus' discourse as reported by John cannot be taken as his *ipsissima verba*), the synoptic gospels tell us that Jesus called God Abba, the expression used by children to address their fathers. In Matthew 11:25-27, we have a rarest testimony to Jesus' total communion with his father. In the garden of Gethsemane, he showed total obedience to his Father (Mt 26:39). And upon dying on the cross, he uttered his complete trust in his Father, "Father into your hands I commend my spirit" (Lk 23:46).

With regard to the third objection, it is commonly acknowledged that Jesus was not married and did not sire any children. But the fact that Jesus did not have children does not by itself make him fall into filial impiety. Even among the Vietnamese those eldest sons who cannot have children to perpetuate ancestor worship are strongly encouraged to adopt children, especially now that polygamy is illegal. These children are truly children of the family, enjoying all the rights of biological children. Of course, in the case of Jesus, he did not adopt us as his children but as his brothers and sisters to assist him and share with him in the worship he rendered to his Father. In this way he truly becomes "the firstborn within a large family" (Rom 8:29), a family of the children of God who are to bear God's image.

It is in this capacity as the eldest son offering worship to God the Father that Jesus can be compared with the Vietnamese emperor in his role of high priest during the *Te Nam Giao* to which we allude briefly below. The Vietnamese believe in the existence of a being they call Ong Troi (Mr. Heaven). This being is the supreme being, personal and transcendent, benevolent and just, who reigns over the universe, above all spirits and deities, and whom the Vietnamese invoke daily, especially in moments of joy and suffering.[57] However, the people themselves do not practice a regular cult of Mr. Heaven; there is no temple in which they offer sacrifices to him. Only the emperor, the Son of Heaven *(Thien Tu)*, is worthy to offer sacrifices to him in the name of his people. Formerly, once every year, and since the nineteenth century once every three years, the emperor, in the most solemn and sublime ceremony of the Vietnamese religion, surrounded by his ministers and mandarins, all clothed in their ceremonial robes,

[56] For Jesus as teacher of subversive wisdom, see Marcus J. Borg, *Meeting Jesus Again for the First Time* (San Francisco: HarperSanFrancisco, 1994).
[57] For an informative discussion of the Vietnamese concept of and belief in heaven, see Cadière, *Croyances et pratiques religieuses des Vietnamiens*, 3:43-50.

offered sacrifices *(te)* to heaven. The sacrifice took place during spring in the open air, on top of a round mound (roundness symbolizing heaven) on a hill south of the imperial capital (the south symbolizing light as opposed to the north representing darkness). Accordingly, the sacrifice is called *Nam Giao* (encounter in the south). In most elaborate rituals with precisely dictated rubrics, the emperor presented offerings of food and drink to heaven, earth, spirits, and imperial ancestors.[58]

If we leave aside the sacrifices to earth, spirits, and imperial ancestors during the *Te Nam Giao* and focus on the sacrifice to heaven, we can see in the role of the emperor that of Christ as the *Thien Tu* (Son of God) and the high priest or "minister of the sanctuary and of the true tent" (Heb 8:2) offering the perfect and eternal sacrifice to God, as magnificently expounded by the letter to the Hebrews. In the name of all of us, whom "he is not ashamed to call . . . brothers and sisters" (Heb 2:11), Jesus, the eldest brother, offers his perfect sacrifice of filial obedience (Heb 1:5; 12:1-11) to God his Father.

Last, with regard to the fourth objection it is evident that from the Christian perspective that there cannot be talk of a physical death of God the Father. There cannot be a literal discourse on Jesus as the eldest son or chief of the clan *(truong toc)* offering sacrifices to his dead heavenly Father. Consequently, our christological proposal, like all theological speech, is no more than a symbol (but not just a symbol), that is, a life-giving metaphor that gives rise to further thought about the meaning of Christ within the Vietnamese culture.

Jesus as the Ancestor Par Excellence

If the metaphor of Jesus as the eldest son offering sacrifices to ancestors may be somewhat novel, that of Jesus as an ancestor or proto-ancestor or ancestor par excellence has been developed in great detail by African theologians.[59] Here I elaborate on some of the distinctive features of the Vietnamese concept of ancestor and explore the ways in which Jesus may be said to be an ancestor in the Vietnamese tradition.

First of all, it is through death that one joins the world of ancestors. As we have seen, during the *chuyen cuu* and *yet to* rituals, the coffin, or at least the *hon bach,* is carried by relatives of the deceased to their ancestral home or common ancestral home, and there the eldest son announces to the ancestors that one of their descendants has joined them, saying, "Upon reaching the dark shores, would

---

[58] For a detailed description of the *Te Nam Giao*, see ibid., 1:85-129.

[59] See, for instance, Charles Nyamiti, *Christ as Our Ancestor: Christology from an African Perspective* (Gwenru, Zimbawe: Mambo Press, 1984); Bénéjet Bujot, *African Theology in Its Social Context* (Maryknoll, N.Y.: Orbis Books, 1992); idem, "Der Afrikanische Ahnenkult und die christologische Verkündigung," *Zeitschrift für Missionswissenschaft und Religionswissenschaft* 64 (1980): 293-306; idem, "Nos ancêtres, ces saints inconnus," *Bulletin de Théologie Africaine* 1 (1979): 165-78; Robert Schreiter, ed., *Faces of Jesus in Africa* (Maryknoll, N.Y.: Orbis Books, 1991); and François Kabasélé, ed., *Chemins de la christologie africaine* (Paris: Desclée, 1986).

you please present yourself to the temple of the ancestors?"[60] However, the deceased does not become an ancestor until his or her tablet is placed upon the ancestral altar. The soul of the deceased is believed truly to reside first in the *hon bach* and then in the wooden tablet when this replaces the former. In popular Vietnamese belief, the deceased has physically left the family house, but his or her soul still lives there, really though mysteriously, in the wooden tablet.

The presence of the ancestors in the family is well described by Cadière:

> This presence of the ancestors in the midst of the family is not a purely passive state. They act. Ordinarily their influence is exercised for the well-being of the living members of the family. When the latter fulfill their obligations of filial piety punctually, then the ancestors, furnished on ritual days with all that they need, happy, tranquil, make their presence felt by distributing all sorts of good things to their descendants. But if they have chosen a defective place for burial, or if they forget to make requisite offerings or if they are cheap, the ancestors will take revenge, or more precisely, they will punish the guilty. Then a geomancer or sorcerer must be consulted, and following their advice, the bones must be relocated, an expiatory sacrifice made in honor of such displeased ancestors.[61]

The presence of the ancestors is particularly felt, of course, on the anniversaries of their deaths. It must be said, however, that there is not a single important event in the life of the Vietnamese family to which the ancestors are not invited, from the celebrations of the New Year to the birth of a child, the death of a member of the family, the celebration of longevity (when a person reaches seventy), the earning of an academic degree, and celebration of an engagement or wedding. In particular, during engagement and wedding ceremonies, the couple is not only introduced to all the members of the two families but also required to perform ritual sacrifices to the ancestors of both families. In this way the couple acquires new relationships with both the living and the dead. Similarly, after candidates earn a degree, especially the doctorate, they are required to return to the native village to pay respect to their ancestors; in Vietnamese this celebration is called *vinh qui bai to* (literally, "triumphant return to venerate the ancestors").

Writing in 1930, Cadière noted:

> It is impossible to hold that the Vietnamese, at this moment in time, do not believe in the survival and real presence of the ancestors in the tablets, that they do not attribute supernatural powers to these ancestors, and that, therefore, the cult they render them is not, properly speaking, a religion. Such a theory is in total contradiction with what can be seen every single

---

[60] See E. C. Lesserteur, *Rituel domestique des funérailles en Annam* (Paris: Imprimerie Chaix, 1885), 10.

[61] Cadière, *Croyances et pratiques religieuses des Vietnamiens*, 1:39.

day in Vietnam. . . . For the immense majority of the Vietnamese, the ancestors continue to be part of the family and the cult rendered them is clearly religious.[62]

In light of this indisputably religious character of Vietnamese ancestor veneration, the opinion of Matteo Ricci and of his fellow Jesuits that it had only civil and social significance, however useful it might have been from the missionary standpoint, missed the mark. But contrary to Dominican and Franciscan missionaries and members of the *Missions Étrangères de Paris*, ancestor worship should not be seen as a threat to Christian orthodoxy but as a rich resource for the reconstruction of an Asian theology and liturgy.

That Jesus' death was his passage to ancestorhood is self-evident. Moreover, as one does not automatically become an ancestor through death but only through being inserted into the company of other ancestors and the veneration by one's descendants, so it seems that Jesus acquired his status as an ancestor through four events: his descent among the dead, his resurrection-exaltation, his becoming the new Adam, and the worship rendered him by his followers.

However 1 Peter 3:18-19 and the creedal formula "he descended into hell" are interpreted, they *can* be taken to mean that Jesus entered the world of his ancestors, through whom he was linked to his clan and tribe. His bringing of salvation to them can be compared with a Vietnamese ritual called *phan huynh*. When a person obtains the rank of superior mandarin, the emperor issues a certificate making the person's deceased parents honorary mandarins. It is the highest honor a son can give his parents. In a most solemn ceremony the certificate is burnt in front of the ancestral altar. It is a most moving manifestation of filial piety and the happiest moment for the entire family gathered around the ancestral altar. The son is now regarded as *qui tu* (the beloved son).[63] Analogously, by bringing salvation to his ancestors Jesus made them share in his own glorification.

Jesus' resurrection-exaltation is his own enthronement as ancestor. He is no longer dead but alive and dwells among his own family of spiritual descendants, his adopted brothers and sisters, just as the ancestors are truly alive and present in the memory of their descendants. Of course, Jesus' resurrection cannot and should not be reduced to this aspect of being made an ancestor alone; indeed, an objective and thorough interpretation of the resurrection event will bring out many other aspects not included in the Vietnamese concept of ancestorhood. Nevertheless, there is no denying that it can be illuminated and enriched by such a concept, especially if the theological hypothesis of immediate resurrection in death is viable.[64]

---

[62] Ibid., 1:41.

[63] See Nguyen Van Huyen, *La civilisation ancienne du Vietnam* (Hanoi: The Gioi, 1994), 49-50.

[64] For a discussion of this notion, see Gisbert Greshake and Gerhard Lohfink, *Naherwartung, Auferstehung, Unsterblichkeit: Untersuchung zur christlichen Eschatologie* (Freiburg: Herder, 1982); and Peter C. Phan, "Contemporary Contexts and Issues in Eschatology," *Theological Studies* 55/3 (1994): 507-36.

The New Testament repeatedly presents Jesus as the new Adam, the ancestor of the new human race. Luke's genealogy of Jesus explicitly links him to Adam. Mark describes how Jesus dwelt among the animals (Mk 1:13). Behind a Pauline hymn (Phil 2:26-11), there is an implied contrast between the old Adam, who sought to make himself equal to God, and Jesus the new Adam, who did not jealously retain his divinity. Besides these hints, there are texts such as 1 Corinthians 15:45-49 and Romans 5:12-21 that explicitly oppose the first Adam and the present Adam, the former marked by filial impiety (disobedience) and the latter by filial piety (obedience), the former a bad ancestor who brings about death and condemnation, and the latter a good ancestor who restores life and justification.

Lastly, just as the ancestors receive the cult of their descendants, so Jesus receives the worship of his spiritual descendants. Ancestor worship is not just a civil and social act of expressing gratitude and solidarity with the forbears; it is rather a religious act. Of course, it is possible and necessary to make a distinction between *latreia* and *dulia*, but such a distinction does not in the least diminish, much less take away, the sacred character of ancestor worship. Through this worship, Christ, just as the ancestors, is made present and is made to share in the lives of his spiritual descendants, just as through this worship the latter are made to participate in the life of Jesus (for example, in the eucharist) and their physical forbears.

Just as we have to speak of Jesus as the model of filial piety in an analogical sense, so also in speaking of him as an ancestor the same rule of analogy must be observed. First of all, there can be no speaking of him as a potentially vindictive ancestor if proper worship is not rendered him, though, of course, one can think of him as the eschatological judge according to the Christian tradition. Second, and more important, ancestorhood must be predicated of him in an eminent sense, that is, he must be regarded as embodying the highest perfection of ancestorhood. He is the ancestor par excellence after God the Father, whose life and goodness he communicates to his spiritual descendants. He can be called the Proto-ancestor.[65] In the light of his life, teaching, death, and resurrection, the Vietnamese concept of ancestorhood must be affirmed and transcended.

ANCESTOR CHRISTOLOGY AND FEMINIST LIBERATION THEOLOGY

The last issue for our consideration here is the ways ancestor worship can and should be corrected and enriched by Asian feminist theology.[66] Scholars

---

[65] See Bénéjet Bujot, *African Theology in Its Social Context* (Maryknoll, N.Y.: Orbis Books, 1992), 79-87. Bujot writes: "The term 'ancestor' can only be applied to Jesus in an analogical sense, or eminent, way, since to treat him otherwise would be to make of him only one founding ancestor among many. That is why the title 'Proto-Ancestor' is reserved for Jesus. This signifies that Jesus did not only realize the authentic ideal of the God-fearing African ancestors, but also infinitely transcended that ideal and brought it to new completion" (80). Obviously, the same thing must be said about Jesus and the Vietnamese ancestors.

[66] For a more detailed discussion of how traditional Christology can be critiqued and enriched by Asian feminist theology, see chapter 5 herein.

of Vietnamese history have argued that until at least the second century B.C.E. Vietnamese culture was matriarchal; it was under the Chinese (Confucian) influence that it became patriarchal and androcentric. This patriarchalism is clear in the system of ancestor worship in which the role of the firstborn male is predominant. The woman ordinarily was not allowed to preside over the cult of ancestors. Moreover, the subordinate position of the woman extended throughout her life. In principle, she was governed by the law of *tam tong* (three obediences): during childhood, she was governed by her father; during marriage by her husband; and during widowhood by her eldest son. Furthermore, the duty of producing a male offspring to perpetuate ancestor worship might lead to her repudiation or to polygamy should she be unable to produce a son. After her husband's death the wife was expected to remain single; the ideal widow was supposed to keep marital fidelity and worship the husband. If she remarried, she was considered unfaithful to her deceased husband *(that tiet)*.

In practice, however, the role of the woman in ancient Vietnam was much more liberated than that which the official ethics prescribed.[67] Generally, it was she who kept the money, administered the family's wealth, and governed the household. Often she was called, perhaps somewhat facetiously, *noi tuong* (interior general or ruler). Polygamy was rare in ancient Vietnam; and even in polygamous marriages, the first wife retained her rights as *chinh that* (the principal one of the house), *nghi that* (the one properly belonging to the house), *nguyen phoi* (the original associate), and *trung that* (the one at the center of the house). Divorce was allowed for at least six reasons (such as disobedience to her husband's parents, not giving birth to a son, dissolute conduct, jealousy, talkativeness, and thieving). But these grounds were overruled by three considerations: first, if the wife had no home to return to; second, if she had done the three years' mourning for her husband's parents; and third, if he had become rich during the marriage. After the death of her husband, the wife still exercised authority over her children, who owed her respect and obedience as to their father. If the children were still minor, she administered the *huong hoa*, that is, the property left aside to pay for the ancestor cult. This administration was also assigned to the eldest daughter should there be no male offspring.[68]

However, there is no gainsaying that women, as Asian feminist theologians have pointed out, were kept in an oppressive condition, and are even today, especially in countries where Confucian family ethics is dominant. This is evident in the common Vietnamese saying that if there is not a man, make use of the woman. Priority is given to the male.

Asian women theologians have attempted to elaborate a Christology that is truly liberative for women. They argue that the church's traditional associations

---

[67] This anomalous fact, namely, that Vietnamese women occupy a much more liberated position in society than that prescribed by official ethics has been well noted by foreigners. See Louis-Eugène Louvet, *La Cochinchine religieuse*, 2 vols. (Paris, 1885). A relevant passage from Louvet is quoted in Nguyen Huu Trong, *Les origines du clergé vietnamien* (Saigon: Tinh Viet, 1959), 50-51.

[68] For an exposition on the position of the woman in ancient Vietnam, see Cadière, *Croyances et pratiques religieuses des Vietnamiens*, 1:65-76.

of obedience and subservience with the image of Christ as the Suffering Servant reinforce the oppression of Asian women by their fathers, husbands, brothers, and sons. Similarly, the image of Christ as Lord has been detrimental to Asian women because it is presented in the context of Confucian patriarchalism. Even the image of Christ as Emmanuel—God with us—has been tainted by its exclusive association with Jesus' maleness.

While preserving the liberating elements in these three traditional images of Jesus as the Suffering Servant, Lord, and Emmanuel, Asian feminist theologians have begun to carve their own portraits of Jesus on the basis of their own experiences as Asian women. Not surprisingly, given their poverty and oppression by colonialism, neocolonialism, military dictatorship, and overarching patriarchalism, Asian women theologians tend to image Jesus as liberator, revolutionary, and political martyr as well as mother, woman, and religious leader.[69]

Such an Asian feminist Christology can legitimately claim to have a foundation in Jesus' teaching on the basic equality of all men, women, and children before God; his attitude of respect for all women, even those the society of his time stigmatized as outcasts and sinners; and his inclusive vision of the kingdom of God, which embraces all human beings.

Such a liberationist Christology need not and does not abolish ancestor veneration; as part of an Asian theology, it will purify the practice of ancestor veneration of elements that privilege the male, both as an ancestor and a minister of the cult of ancestors. Thus purified, ancestor worship remains, I submit, a rich resource for painting a portrait of Christ that would make sense to billions of Asians.

---

[69] See Virginia Fabella and Sun Ai Lee Park, eds., *We Dare to Dream: Doing Theology as Asian Women* (Maryknoll, N.Y.: Orbis Books, 1989); Chung Hyun Kyung, *Struggle to Be the Sun Again: Introducing Asian Women's Theology* (Maryknoll, N.Y.: Orbis Books, 1990); and Nam-Soon Kang, "Creating Dangerous Memories: Challenges for Asian and Korean Feminist Theology," *The Ecumenical Review* 47/1 (1995): 21-31.

7

Jesus with a Chinese Face

CHOAN-SENG SONG'S JESUS-ORIENTED CHRISTOLOGY

A Chinese born in Taiwan in 1929, C. S. Song has spent the greater part of his life in the West, first as a graduate student in Edinburgh, Scotland, and at Union Theological Union in New York, and then as associate director of the Faith and Order Commission of the World Council of Churches in Geneva, Switzerland. He is currently a professor of theology and Asian cultures at the Pacific School of Religion, Berkeley, California. In spite of this lengthy sojourn far from his native country, Song's theological mind and heart are never cut off from the cultural and spiritual sources of the Chinese people. Indeed, in spite of his manifold duties, he continues to function as regional professor of theology at the Southeast Asia Graduate School of Theology in Singapore and to be active in the Programme for Theology and Cultures in Asia.

Song is certainly the most prolific Chinese theologian outside of China and arguably the most influential as well. Among his writings, his christological trilogy, *The Cross in the Lotus World,* is no doubt his magnum opus and certainly a landmark in Asian theology.[1] As implied by its title, the trilogy is Song's sustained effort to construct a Christian theology in the context of Asia.

Reflecting on the first volume of the trilogy, Song writes: "By the expression 'the lotus world' I meant the vast world of Asia into which Christianity entered as a relative latecomer, and the majority of the people of Asia who have remained outside the Christian influence."[2] To plant the cross in the land of the lotus, to bring the alien symbol of the cross and the indigenous symbol of the

---

[1] *The Cross in the Lotus World* comprises *Jesus, The Crucified People* (New York: Crossroad, 1990); *Jesus and the Reign of God* (Minneapolis: Fortress Press, 1993); and *Jesus in the Power of the Spirit* (Minneapolis: Fortress Press, 1994). Song explicitly acknowledges the centrality of Christology in his theology: "Jesus Christ is central in my theological effort. . . . In Jesus Christ, God has to do with law and grace, sin and salvation, goodness and evil" ("Choan-Seng Song Replies," *Occasional Bulletin of Missionary Research* 1/3 [1977]: 13).

[2] Choan-Seng Song, "Five Stages toward Christian Theology in the Multicultural World," in *Journeys at the Margin: Toward an Autobiographical Theology in American-Asian Perspective*, ed. Peter C. Phan and Jung Young Lee (Collegeville, Minn.: The Liturgical Press, 1999), 3.

lotus into mutual interaction, to cross-fertilize the spiritual world of Christianity with the religious traditions of Asia, so that God's reign of justice, peace, and love may be a reality in the world—all these have been Song's longstanding concerns.

This chapter first briefly situates Song's Christology within the context of his method of inculturation and in particular examines his use of Chinese sources to construct a theology for the Chinese. Second, it describes the development as well as the salient features of Song's Christology. The last part evaluates Song's Christology, especially from the perspective of Roman Catholic theology.

FROM APPLICATION OF WESTERN THEOLOGY TO STORY THEOLOGY

Song's 1999 work, *The Believing Heart,* is appropriately subtitled *An Invitation to Story Theology.*[3] Its first part offers Song's most explicit and extended reflections on his theological method to date.[4] According to Song, theological method cannot and should not be defined (and hence, restricted) in advance. Rather "theological method is something of an after-thought. It is a pause you take after you have done the work, an exercise you do to recharge your theological engine, an effort to chart again your theological course."[5] Song compares his doing theology to telling stories. The story comes to be in the telling itself, which often moves in unpredictable directions and even strays into byways, but in this way the story grows in width and depth, with new characters and plots added each time it gets told. Only at the end of the telling can one see how the story has been told. So it is, Song suggests, with doing theology. Theology comes to be in the act of theologizing itself, without a preestablished "recipe" to be followed slavishly. In the course of theologizing, theology expands and changes its shape and direction. Only at the end can one throw a retrospective glance at the result to see if a satisfactory theology has been produced; should the answer be affirmative, then the method can be judged satisfactory and appropriate.

Christological Approaches in Song's Early Writings

From his earliest theological reflections, however, it is clear that Song, notwithstanding his dictum about method as an afterthought, has been concerned from the very beginning of his theological career with the method with which Christology ought to be constructed in and for Asia.[6] Indeed, Song's interest in

---

[3] C. S. Song, *The Believing Heart: An Invitation to Story Theology* (Minneapolis: Fortress Press, 1999).

[4] Ibid., 1-75.

[5] Song, "Five Stages," 2.

[6] Song's earlier reflections on theological method include "The Obedience of Theology in Asia," *SEAJT* 2/2 (1960): 7-15; "An Analysis of Contemporary Culture and Its Implications for the Task of Theology," *SEAJT* 4/4 (1963): 63-73; "Theologia viatorum," *SEAJT* 6/4-7/1 (1965): 115-28; "Confessing the Faith in Asia Today: Prolegomena to

method for Christology was already evinced in his doctoral dissertation. Like most third-world theologians trained in the West, Song was exposed to and influenced by the thought of major Western theologians. In Song's case, it was Karl Barth and Paul Tillich, whose theologies of revelation and their implications for a theology of religion were the themes of his dissertation.[7] As a result of his studies in Edinburgh, New York, and Basel, Song became convinced that "if an Asian engages himself in theological thinking he does so not by setting himself over against Western theology, but by trying to learn from it first."[8] Consequently, Song maintained that the first task of Asian theology is to practice obedience, or more precisely, to carry out a creative *application* of Western theology, in particular the method of neo-orthodox theology, to the Asian context.[9] By this Song did not mean that Asians should repeat what Western theologians have said. Rather, he insisted that "methodology is basic. There is even a universal character in methodology. This is a very important point."[10]

---

the Gospel Incarnate," *Theology and the Church* 6/1-6/2 (1966): 13-34; "Theological Education: A Search for a New Breakthrough," *SEAJT* 9/4 (1968): 5-16; "New China and Salvation History: A Methodological Inquiry," *SEAJT* 15/2 (1974): 52-67; "From Israel to Asia," in *Third World Theologies*, ed. Gerald H. Anderson and Thomas F. Stransky (New York: Paulist Press, 1976), 211-22; "Reflections on Confessing the Faith in Asia," in *Sharing in One Hope*, ed. Commission of Faith and Order (Geneva: World Council of Churches, 1978), 62-77; "New Frontiers in Theology: Ten Theological Theses," *SEAJT* 20/1 (1979): 13-33, republished in *Tell Us Our Names: Story Theology from an Asian Perspective* (Maryknoll, N.Y.: Orbis Books, 1984), 3-24; "Let Us Do Theology with Asian Resources," *East Asia Journal of Theology* 3/2 (1985): 202-8; "Dragon, Garuda, and Christian Theology," in *Doing Theology with Cultures in Asia*, ed. Yeow Choo Lak (Singapore: ATESA, 1988), 26-40; "Freedom of Christian Theology for Asian Cultures," *Asia Journal of Theology* 3/1 (1989): 84-91; "The World of Images and Symbols," in *Doing Theology with People's Symbols and Images*, ed. Yeow Choo Lak and John C. England (Singapore: ATESA, 1989): 1-11; "Doing Theology with Stories of the Spirit's Movement in Asia," *PTCAB* 2/2 (1989): 7-9; "What Is Christian Theology? Raising a Question," *PTCAB* 3/2 (1990): 4-6; and "Rethinking Asian Christian Theology," in *Third-Eye Theology*, rev. ed. (Maryknoll, N.Y.: Orbis Books, 1990), 1-16.

  [7] The title of Song's dissertation is *The Relation of Divine Revelation and Man's Religion in the Theologies of Karl Barth and Paul Tillich*, which he completed under the direction of Daniel Williams at Union Theological Seminary, New York, in 1964. Barth's influence is pronounced in Song's critique of religion, and Tillich's ideas are echoed in Song's earlier understanding of the relation between Christian revelation and non-Christian religions. Of course, in the course of his theological development Song has moved far beyond both Barth and Tillich. One telltale sign is that both theologians, whose works were often referred to in Song's earlier writings, are not discussed at all in his christological trilogy. Barth is mentioned once in the second volume in a footnote but cast in a negative light: "Although Barth did not exempt Christianity as a religion from his theological judgment, his negative view of religion did not contribute to understanding of other religions" (Song, *Jesus in the Power of the Spirit*, 87). For a discussion of Song's dissertation, see Karl H. Federschmidt, *Theologie aus asiatische Quellen: Der theologische Weg* CHOAN-SENG SONGS *vor dem Hintergrund der asiatischen ökumenischen Diskussion* (Münster: LIT, 1994), 91-107.

  [8] Song, "The Obedience of Theology in Asia," 7.

  [9] See ibid., 7-15.

  [10] Ibid., 12.

The importance of method is evident in Song's earlier understanding of the relationship between Christ and non-Christian religions, in which the theology of revelation and the Christocentric method as practiced by Thomas F. Torrance and Karl Barth exercised a powerful influence. In Song's dissertation, as well as in his earliest publications, there was, beside a renewed emphasis on God's transcendence and sovereignty and a *ressourcement* in the Bible as the witness of divine revelation, an emphasis on Christology as the fundamental cornerstone of theological reflection. In his dissertation Song argues that it is precisely Barth's Christocentrism and Tillich's acknowledgment of Christ as God's final and definitive revelation that enabled them, despite their profound differences, to arrive at a constructive view of the phenomenon of religion. Because Jesus Christ is accepted as the decisive criterion of all the manifestations and expressions of humanity's spiritual life, including religions, all religions are ontologically related to divine revelation and hence to Jesus: "Revelation is the ontological ground for the possibility and reality of man's religion. In other words, religion is ontologically related to revelation."[11] Religion has therefore not only a negative but also positive relationship with God's revelation in Jesus.

Methodologically, however, in order to support this positive view of religion, this Christocentrism that is prevalent in neo-orthodox Christology and soteriology, must, according to Song, be extended to the doctrine of creation. Indeed, for Song, this intimate unity of the doctrine of redemption and that of creation is present in both Barth and Tillich: "Jesus Christ is the *Logos* present in the creational act of God and at the same time the *Logos* became incarnate for the redemption of all mankind."[12] At this stage of his Christology, then, Song sought to maintain a balance between redemption and creation, between Christocentrism and the universality of the Christ event, between the normative uniqueness of Jesus and the active presence of God's grace in all human history, between the incarnation of God in the Jew Jesus and the divine indwelling in all creation. Is this delicate balance to be maintained in Song's later Christology?

New Directions in Song's Theological Method and Christology

This fundamentally neo-orthodox methodology underwent a significant shift in the late 1960s. Four factors contributed to Song's methodological innovation, especially in Christology. First, he was appointed professor and principal of Tainan Theological College, the seminary of the Presbyterian Church of Taiwan, in 1965. During his five-year tenure Song sought to implement his predecessor and mentor Hwang Chong-Hui's (Shoki Coe) program of laying the foundation for a theology of the incarnation. This program, contrary to a simple indigenization, aimed at making God's incarnation in Jesus immediately present

---

[11] Song, *The Relation of Divine Revelation and Man's Religion in the Theologies of Karl Barth and Paul Tillich,* 250.

[12] Ibid., 265. Of Barth, Song writes: "Creation is the very basis of Barth's theology and even of his Christology" (see "The Possibility of an Analogical Discourse on God," *SEAJT* 7/2 [1965]: 76).

in the *current* socio-political and economic situation of Taiwan and in the Taiwanese church: "Whatever term one may use, one must remember that the incarnation implies, among other things, an inner transformation of a person, a
family, a community and the world by what is accomplished in and through
Jesus Christ."[13] Obviously this incarnation of the gospel requires that new forms
of thinking and acting be devised, forms that go beyond a mere application of
Western theology to the Taiwanese context and eventually replace the "conventional and foreign modes."[14] How Song developed his concept of the dynamics
of the incarnation and a corresponding Christology to undergird this project of
inculturation and its theological educational program will be examined later.

The second factor is the political activities of the Presbyterian Church of
Taiwan in the 1970s with its three influential declarations: "Public Statement
on Our National Fate" (1971), "Our Appeal—Concerning the Bible, the Church,
and the Nation" (1975), and "A Declaration on Human Rights" (1977). Although Song had already left Taiwan for his post as secretary for Asian ministries of the Presbyterian Church in New York a full year (October 1970) before
the first declaration was issued (30 December 1971), he had exercised a significant influence in forming the social consciousness of the Presbyterian Church
of Taiwan and was working hard to support from abroad the demands of this
church for peace, freedom, justice, human rights, and self-determination through
general election. In 1973, with Hwang Chong-Hui, Song founded Formosan
Christians for Self-Determination to unite all Taiwanese, irrespective of their
faiths, to exercise Christian responsibility toward Taiwan. As a result of this
involvement, Song's theology developed much more explicitly than before the
socio-political implications of the Christian faith.

Song's awareness of the socio-political aspect of the gospel was further deep-
ened by the third factor, namely, his encounter with black theology in the United
States. His official travels to the south of the United States and his collaboration
with Gayraud Wilmore, a prominent exponent of black theology, in the Joseph
Cook Memorial Lectures, brought to Song's consciousness the problem of the
identity of Christianity in Asia. Just as black theology rediscovered the identity
of black Christianity by radically questioning the doctrinal convictions of traditional white theology and by reappropriating the cultural and religious resources
of the Black Church, so Asian Christianity must form its identity vis-à-vis other
religions by questioning the theological presuppositions of the missionary enterprise and by identifying itself with the peoples and their cultures. Once again,
Song was confronted with the task of developing a theological method in which
cultures are not understood as merely passive recipients of the gospel but are
given an independent value and a positive role to play in the inculturation of the
gospel.

The fourth factor influencing Song's theological method was his activity on
behalf of the World Council of Churches. In his capacity as associate director of

---

[13] Song, "The Team Research—The Gospel Incarnate," *Theology and the Church* 8/2-
8/3 (1969): 4.
[14] Ibid., 3.

the Commission on Faith and Order (1973-82), Song came into contact with another aspect of Christian identity, namely, theological pluralism. During his tenure he was involved in a study entitled "Giving Account of the Hope That Is within Us," which was concluded with a declaration called "A Common Account of Hope" (1978). In contrast to earlier studies, this study required that each local church, group, and movement come up with its own answers from its specific context. It was, for Song, an exhilarating experience of the diversity of the expressions of Christian faith. But more important was his discovery that a new theological method and hermeneutical process were required to arrive at a genuinely common ecumenical expression of the faith, a method that takes into account not only the diverse experiences of local Christian churches but also those of the world at large, indeed of the whole of humanity. Song himself has noted the novelty of this method: "In 'A Common Account of Hope' Faith and Order has in fact started a new form of discourse on faith. It has demonstrated that the questions of faith and unity are not merely ecclesiastical matters requiring 'internal settlement.' On the contrary, faith and unity are the concerns of the whole wide world and of the whole of humanity. This shows us clearly that theological exploration of Faith and Order must, from now on, be conducted on a wider horizon."[15]

The World of Stories: An Invitation to Story Theology

This "wider horizon" began to loom larger and larger in the world of Song's theology, and with this widening of the horizon, Song's theological method took on a distinctive characteristic. For inspiration his subsequent writings turned decidedly to the stories of Asian peoples, especially of men, women, and children who are poor, oppressed, and marginalized.[16] These stories are correlated with the master story, namely, the story of Jesus that is revealed in his message about the reign of God. The reign of God becomes, for Song, the hermeneutical key to understand the person and work of Jesus, his relationship to the Hebrew scripture, and his relationship to non-Christians. Looking back on his works Song writes:

> The story of Jesus, it became evident to me, is the story of the reign of God, that is, the reign *of God*. The "reign" and what it stands for in the message and ministry of Jesus is what relates God and Jesus. Through the reign of God the story of Jesus is told as the story of God. Through it the story of God is told in the story of Jesus. The reign of God plays a crucial

---

[15] Song, "Foreword," in *Giving an Account of Hope Together* (Geneva: World Council of Churches, 1979), 8. For a detailed account of the factors influencing Song's method, see Federschmidt, *Theologie aus asiatischen Quellen*, 108-38.

[16] See C. S. Song, *The Tears of Lady Meng: A Parable of People's Political Theology* (Geneva: The World Council of Churches, 1981; Maryknoll, N.Y.: Orbis Books, 1982); idem, *Tell Us Our Names*; idem, *Theology from the Womb of Asia* (Maryknoll, N.Y.: Orbis Books, 1986); Song's christological trilogy, *The Cross in the Lotus World*; and idem, *Believing Heart*.

part in knowing Jesus and experiencing God. It is the key to unlock the mystery surrounding God. It is the key that opens to the nature of Jesus' ministry and even to the secret of what he is and who he is.

Note the word "story" here. From this point on that word takes on an increasingly important place in my theological effort. The reign of God is essentially stories. It consists of stories of God and stories of Jesus. It is not a concept that exists in a theological textbook but not in reality. Nor is it a projection of Christian piety in the world to come, a projection unrelated to the world here and now. The reign of God is a story that unfolds and expands, not a concept that abstracts and defines. It does not set boundaries around itself. In fact it seeks to break the barriers that separate it from the world around it.[17]

From this story of the reign of God in the life and ministry of Jesus, Song moves backward to the stories of the reign of God in the Hebrew scriptures and forward to the stories of the people outside the Christian church. It is important to note that Song does not see the relation between the story of Jesus, on the one hand, and the stories of the Hebrew scriptures and those of the Asian peoples, on the other, in terms of promise and fulfillment but in terms of the presence of God's reign in all three sets of stories: "What, then, relates the Hebrew Scripture and the New Testament? It is not the scheme of promise and fulfillment but the stories of God's reign."[18]

As far as Christology is concerned, what is required is a theological imagination that is able to perceive in human history "a theological feast of stories—the story of Jesus, stories in Asia, stories in Hebrew Scripture, stories from the Christian community, and stories from the rest of the world, told as stories of God's dealing with humanity."[19] Once we perceive that the story of Jesus is reflected in other stories and that other stories are reflected in the story of Jesus, Song claims, "we do not need to construct a theological framework to fit these two sets of stories together. We do not need to work out in advance theological norms and categories that legitimize whatever relationships that may exist between them. Nor do we need to set up criteria that permit us to make a 'correct' selection from both sets of stories in order to theologize about them."[20] How Song theologizes about these stories and in the process constructs his own Christology is taken up in the next part of the chapter.

Chinese Resources for Theology: "From the Pointed-Nosed Christ to the Flat-Nosed Christ"

Before doing so, however, it is useful to examine the kind of resources Song makes use of to construct a theology, in particular a Christology for the Chinese

---

[17] Song, "Five Stages," 10-11.
[18] Ibid., 12.
[19] Song, *Believing Heart*, 69.
[20] Ibid., 67.

people, or as he puts it colorfully, to make a "transposition from the pointed-nosed Christ to the flat-nosed Christ."[21] It is of course impossible to make a complete inventory of all the Asian sources in general and of the Chinese sources in particular mentioned in Song's writings. Here I focus only on the latter, in particular the story of Lady Meng.

Among the Chinese philosophers whose teachings inspire Song's theology, Confucius predominates. But Lao Tzu, Mencius, Chuang Tzu, Mo Tzu and lesser philosophers also appear frequently. It is interesting to note that, for Song, these philosophers appear less as teachers of wisdom and more as genuine prophets deeply concerned about the common good of their societies and as "instruments of God's redeeming love and power in ancient China."[22] Strictly connected with Chinese philosophies are Chinese religions, especially the veneration of ancestors,[23] Taoism, Confucianism, and Buddhism,[24] whose religious and ethical teachings are, for Song, God's revelation for those who live outside of Christianity and with whose followers Christians are urged to enter what Song calls a "dialogical conversion."[25]

Another fertile source for Song's theology is Chinese proverbs and folktales, events of Chinese history, and stories of real people. To do Asian theology, says Song, theologians must "turn to the most indigenous, most authentic and most abundant resource of all Asian resources—folktales, the stories of people—old and new."[26] Folktales such as the story of the ox and the rat of the Chinese zodiac;[27] important historical events such as the Taiping Rebellion,[28] the victory of Communism with Mao Tse-tung, the Cultural Revolution with the Red Guards, the ultra-leftist politics of the Gang of Four, and contemporary movements for freedom;[29] and above all, the stories of poor and oppressed people—all these serve as jumping-off points for Song's reflections on God's active presence among the Chinese people before, after, and apart from Christianity.

Among Chinese folktales there is no doubt that the story of Lady Meng has exercised the most powerful influence on Song's political theology. *The Tears*

---

[21] C. S. Song, *The Compassionate God: An Exercise in the Theology of Transposition* (Maryknoll, N.Y.: Orbis Books, 1982). The expression "flat-nosed" refers to the vision of Sri Ramakrishna in which a figure with beautiful large eyes and a somewhat flat nose appeared. Ramakrishna identified the figure as Master-Yogin Jesus.

[22] Ibid., 159.

[23] On the practice of veneration of ancestors, see *Third-Eye Theology,* 168-75.

[24] On Song's view of Chinese Buddhism as a way of divine providence, see *Compassionate God*, 161-91.

[25] For the seven stages of interreligious dialogue leading to "dialogical conversion," see Song, *Tell Us Our Names*, 121-41. Says Song: "The point is that persons of different religions have the capacity to live each others' dreams and visions—Buddhists in Christians', Hindus in Muslims', or Christians in Confucianists'. I call this 'dialogical conversion'" (140).

[26] Song, *Third-Eye Theology*, 10.

[27] See Song, *Compassionate God*, 163-64.

[28] Ibid., 192-215.

[29] Ibid., 220-34.

of Lady Meng, whose subtitle, *A Parable of People's Political Theology*,[30] expresses well its intent, is Song's theological reflections on a well-known legend
of the conflict between Emperor Ch'in Shih (221-20 B.C.E.), the embodiment of
oppressive power, and Meng Chiang, a simple woman of the people. To carry
out his project of building a wall to protect his country, the emperor ordered that
Wan, the husband of Meng Chiang, be kidnapped during the wedding feast,
murdered, and buried in the wall along with thousands of others to serve as
defenders of the wall. Meng Chiang wandered off in search of her husband and
eventually came to the wall but was unable to retrieve her husband's body to
give it the requisite burial. However, her tears melt the wall, and his bones were
found. The emperor was so touched by Meng Chiang's faithfulness that he offered to marry her. Knowing that she would not be able to refuse his proposal,
Meng Chiang agreed, on the condition that she be allowed to give her husband
a public funeral. Standing on the forty-nine-foot high terrace on the bank of a
river to offer the sacrifice to her husband, Meng Chiang began cursing the emperor for his cruelty and evil deeds. The emperor ordered her body to be chopped
into pieces and her bones crushed to powder and scattered into the river. At
once, so the story goes, the little pieces turned into silver fishes and swam away,
carrying with them the soul of the faithful Lady Meng.

By a masterful combination of this legend with biblical stories, Asian religious traditions, and actual political problems and events in Asia, Song transformed Lady Meng with her faithfulness, her tears, and her denunciation of
oppression into a symbol of the people's power—the "power of people's tears."[31]
In Song's interpretation, the people's helpless tears derive their subversive power
from their language of love, of suffering and compassion, of hope for life, which
is the language of God, against the oppressive power of dictators. This subversive power is also the byproduct of the truth that Song claims people have in
their denunciations of political and economic oppression.

But how should theologians make use of all these resources to construct a
Christology for the Chinese people? How is this Christology to be different
from the one constructed on the basis of the Chalcedonian definition, which the
church has been teaching since the fifth century? Is the central focus of this
Christology to be the church, the Christ, or Jesus himself?

A JESUS-ORIENTED CHRISTOLOGY

Song describes his Christology as "Jesus-oriented,"[32] an expression coined
by Song both to critique Christologies he regards as inadequate and to indicate

---

[30] *The Tears of Lady Meng* is an expanded version of the D. T. Niles Memorial Lecture
entitled "Political Theology of Living in Christ with People," given at the General Assembly of the Christian Conference of Asia held in Bangalore, India, 18-28 May 1981.

[31] See C. S. Song, "Political Theology of Living in Christ with People," in *A Call to
Vulnerable Discipleship* (Singapore: Christian Conference of Asia, 1982): "People have
no weapons except the weapons of tears. People have no power but the power of tears.
We must save our tears and have them in plenty" (13).

[32] Song, *Believing Heart*, 63.

the contour of a Christology he considers appropriate to the Asian context. We first examine the types of Christology Song rejects and then present Song's own Jesus-oriented Christology.

Inadequate Christologies

Not a Church-Centered Christology

We have shown above how Song shifted his theological method from an application of neo-orthodox theology to the Asian context to a narrative approach. In this evolution Song became acutely aware of how church-centered Western Christology has been. By "church-centered Christology" he means the theology of Christ devised to serve the church's interests, especially its economic and political power, often in alliance with secular power. According to Song, this church-centered Christology inspired much of the church's past missionary enterprise, which was often carried out in collaboration with colonial powers.[33] It is this Christology that lies at the root of the church's many errors: "There are many reasons for such errors, but the most fundamental reason is that the church has made itself the center of all things. It has replaced Jesus as the center. Church-centered faith and theology is wrong faith and bad theology. When the church makes itself the center, it preaches and teaches itself, its own survival and ambitions—not Jesus."[34]

Theologically, according to Song, this Christology is undergirded by the *heilsgeschichtlich* interpretation of history, which operates according to the promise-fulfillment scheme and draws a straight line from Israel to Jesus to church.[35] Such a historical interpretation relies on the concept of the divine election of a particular people (Israel, now replaced by the Christian church) to the exclusion of other peoples.[36] Over against this interpretation Song developed his univer-

---

[33] See C. S. Song, *Christian Mission in Reconstruction: An Asian Attempt* (Madras: Christian Literature Society, 1975; Maryknoll, N.Y.: Orbis Books, 1977 [with the subtitle *An Asian Analysis*]).

[34] Song, *Believing Heart*, 61-62.

[35] For Song's synthetic account of this *heilsgeschichtlich* theology of history, see *Believing Heart*, 52-57. Of this theology of history Song says: "This divine scheme of salvation, when tested in Asia and Africa, becomes questionable. It makes one wonder whether God has intended to deal with people outside the Christian church with displeasure. According to the scheme neatly developed by the Christian church, the great majority of people of the world have no place. They have no part in God's salvation reserved for Christians. But is this not precisely the urgency of the Christian mission? Do not Christians have to make all efforts to evangelize them? . . . . Is not our 'great commission' to christianize the world? But as we know, Christianity has failed to christianize the world. There is no evidence that it can do so in the foreseeable future" (53-54).

[36] Song sees Oscar Cullmann as the foremost exponent of this *heilsgeschichtlich* interpretation of history. See his criticism of Cullmann in "New China and Salvation History: A Methodological Inquiry," *SEAJT* 15/2 (1974): 52-67. For Song's criticism of the promise-fulfillment schema, see *Jesus, the Crucified People*, 160-64; *Believing Heart*, 52-57. In *Compassionate God* Song terms the exclusive tendency that this *heilsgeschichtlich* theology of history gives rise to "centrism." For how Song's rejection

salist theology, based on the unified doctrines of creation and incarnation/re-
demption and on the concept of the dynamics of the incarnation, to which we
will return below.

Not a Christ-Centered Christology

If a church-centered Christology is bad theology, a Christ-centered Christology, according to Song, is not an acceptable replacement either. By "Christ-
centered Christology" Song means the images of Christ that various Christian
theological traditions have presented to serve the interests of the church: "Christ-
centered faith and theology often is the church-centered faith and theology in
disguise."[37] The decisive christological question for Song is this: "Is this Christ
actually the Jesus who lived, toiled, suffered, and died on the cross, or the Christ
of Jesus-cult, which sees Jesus as a cultic object that inspires our piety but not
our discipleship? Does the church worship the Jesus who walked the earth and
endured all sorts of pain, even the pain of dying on the cross, or the Christ that
is treated as an object of endless theological debates?"[38]

The Christ as a "cultic object that inspires our piety but not our discipleship"
and the Christ of "endless theological debates" refer first of all to the images of
Christ produced by various Christian theological traditions to defend the church's
exclusion of people of other religions from God's salvation and to justify the
church's discriminatory policies based on race and gender. This Christ, which
is advocated by "Christocentric" Christians and rejected by "theocentric" theologians, is, in Song's view, nothing more than the "Jesus *of the Christian church*
with an exclusive claim to God's salvation."[39] But this Christ also refers to the
Christ produced by the Christian tradition by means of Greek metaphysics, which
defines Jesus in terms of two natures, divine and human, and one hypostasis,
that is, the Logos.[40]

---

of this church-centered Christology affects his understanding of Christian mission, see
his *Christian Mission in Reconstruction* and *Jesus in the Power of the Spirit*, 256-91.
Song summarizes his vision of Christian mission that is not church centered but reign-
of-God centered: "Christian mission becomes part of God's mission of creation and
redemption insofar as it gives witness not to its own growth and to its own strength, but
to the growth and strength of God's reign. It consists in being catalytic for the reign of
God. Christian evangelism can be said to proclaim the gospel, the good news, only
when it does not fancy it alone possesses all the good news of God's salvation and
others possess all the bad news of God's condemnation. Christian mission participates
in what God has been doing in the whole world and in all of creation" (*Jesus in the
Power of the Spirit*, 275).
[37] Song, *Believing Heart*, 62.
[38] Ibid., 62.
[39] Ibid., 63.
[40] Of this metaphysical Christology, Song says: "It ends mostly in the victory of his
[Jesus'] divine nature over his human nature. This has been considered 'orthodox' from
the early centuries of the history of Christianity to the present time. But 'orthodox' in
relation to what? To the traditions of the church? To the prevailing doctrines? To official teachings? Or to the Bible?" (*Jesus and the Reign of God*, xi). With these questions

Song rejects both Christs, because they have, he claims, nothing or little to do with the Jesus who proclaimed the reign of God and was killed for it:

> My proposal is, then, that our faith and theology must be *Jesus-oriented.* Is there any difference, one may ask, between being 'Christ-centered' and 'Jesus-oriented'? A world of difference. First of all, Jesus, who lived, engaged in the ministry of God's reign, and who was executed on account of it, may not be the same as the Christ that Christians from early times to the present have come to know and worship. Even though there is one Jesus of Nazareth, are there not many 'Christs' in the history of Christianity? Should not Jesus of Nazareth be the focus of our theological attention and not a variety of Christs that have come and gone?[41]

Not Jesus-Centered but Jesus-Oriented Christology

Song makes a further important distinction between Jesus-centered and Jesus-oriented. His Christology is the latter, not the former. The word *center,* in Christian usage, connotes exclusivism. Jesus-centered Christology excludes other centers: "The word develops into *centrism,* a worldview that takes itself to include all truth. That is why 'Christocentrism' has given Christians a sense of superiority to women and men of other religions, and endowed them with militant urgency in mission."[42]

In contrast, *orientation* connotes, according to Song, relation and inclusivism:

> Orientation is shaped by relations. . . . An entity interested in orientation is not bent on consolidating itself at the expense of others. Rather it establishes relations with others, and, together with them, develops and expands the sphere of activity and the sphere of meanings. In this way *orientation* refers to actions that are reciprocal rather than single-minded, expansive instead of constrictive, open instead of closed.[43]

Consequently, a Jesus-oriented Christology does not need to choose between Christocentrism and theocentrism. In order to fight against Christian exclusivism some theologians have proposed replacing Christocentrism with theocentrism.[44] Song rejects this proposal. As a Christian, he says, "I do not know God apart from Jesus and Jesus apart from God. I cannot replace God with Jesus, nor can I replace Jesus with God. To be theocentric rather than christocentric is to me a

---

Song implies that metaphysical Christology may be "orthodox" but irrelevant to our contemporary situation: "Theology that ceases to be contemporary becomes historically irrelevant. It neither speaks out of the situations of Jesus' day nor speaks into our situations today. Its primary concern is timeless doctrine" (ibid.).

[41] Song, *Believing Heart,* 63-64.
[42] Ibid., 64.
[43] Ibid.
[44] Though Song has not mentioned the names of these theologians, two readily come to mind: John Hick and Paul Knitter.

false alternative. As a Christian I cannot set Jesus against God, nor can I set God against Jesus."[45]

A Story Christology

How can such a Jesus-oriented Christology be constructed? What are its resources? Are there resources outside of the Bible and the Christian tradition? Can and should these be used? How should these non-Christian stories be correlated to the Jesus story? As we have seen above, in his later theological works Song turns to the world of stories. "In the beginning . . . were stories," Song paraphrases the first verse of the Fourth Gospel.[46] These stories cannot be confined to the world of the Bible and of Christianity: "There are stories outside the Christian church as well as inside it—stories of people around us, stories of the human community to which the Christian community is closely related, and stories of Asia, for example, to which Christians in Asia also belong. The world these stories represent is infinitely larger than the 'Christian world.'"[47] In these stories we encounter God in the light of the story called Jesus. Song interprets John 1:14—"The Word became flesh and lived among us"—to mean that "the story of God became the story of Jesus that lives in our stories."[48]

Jesus and the Reign of God

Jesus and the Reign of God is the title of the second volume of Song's christological trilogy. It represents in a nutshell, according to Song, what is most central about Jesus.[49] Indeed, the stories about the reign of God constitute the key to understanding who Jesus was and is: "We may be able to know Jesus more deeply as we grapple with how he practiced the reign of God in his life and ministry."[50] Song's christological method, then, consists in moving from the message and deeds of Jesus about the reign of God to his life and ministry, or to his person and work. There is a dynamic relationship between the message and the messenger, so that "the deeper we go into the message of Jesus, the closer a glimpse we should be able to gain of Jesus."[51]

---

[45] Song, *Believing Heart*, 63.

[46] Ibid., 65.

[47] Ibid., 66.

[48] Ibid.

[49] Song, *Jesus and the Reign of God*, xii: "The heart of Jesus' message . . . is the reign of God." Again, more specifically: "The vision that inspired him [Jesus] to say what he said and compelled him to do what he did was the reign of God. This vision of God's reign is the *hermeneutical* principle of the life and ministry of Jesus. It is the *ethical* standard of his lifeview and worldview. It is the *theological* foundation of his relation to God and to his fellow human beings. And it is the *eschatological* vantage-point from which he relates the present time to the end of time. In short, the vision of God's reign is like a magnifying lens that gives us an enlarged picture of life and the world as Jesus sees them and of life and the world as we must also see them" (ibid., 2).

[50] Ibid., x.

[51] Ibid., xii.

What is, according to Song, Jesus' message about the reign of God? Song summarizes it as follows:

> The heart of Jesus' message is the reign of God *(basileia tou theou)*. In all he said and did he was at pains to make clear that God's reign is primarily concerned with the people victimized by a class-conscious society and a tradition-bound religious establishment. God's reign, in the light of what Jesus said and did, inaugurates an era of people. It sets a new stage for their life and history. It marks a fresh beginning of the human-divine drama of salvation.[52]

Central to Song's understanding of the reign of God are "people" and their salvation as economic and socio-political and religious liberation.[53] Song states forthrightly who the "people" are and what their role is: *"People are now clues to who the real Jesus is*—people who are poor, outcast, and socially and politically oppressed. What Jesus has said and done is not comprehensible apart from men, women, and children who suffer in body and spirit."[54]

In light of Song's theology of the reign of God, Jesus— both during his ministry for his contemporaries and for the "people" of today—was and is "the enabler of God's reign. He is the facilitator of it. He makes real to people, friends and foes alike, that 'God is active decisively' within their lives and within their society, that they are all involved in God's reign as signs of it or countersigns of it, that they all have to do with 'God active decisively' in the world as collaborators or as opponents."[55]

Jesus Is the Crucified People

How can the Jesus of two thousand years ago speak to the "people" of today. Put differently, how does Song account for the possibility of the story of Jesus

---

[52] Ibid., ix. For Song's succinct reconstruction of what Jesus proclaimed about the reign of God, see *Believing Heart*, 41-44, and *Theology from the Womb of Asia*, 177-86. For a detailed study of Song's theology of the reign of God, see chapter 4 herein.

[53] Song repeatedly privileges the socio-political and economic aspects of salvation present in the reign of God: "Salvation experienced as liberation from the land of enslavement is first and foremost a political salvation" *(Third-Eye Theology*, 219). Again: "The reign of God for him [Jesus] is very much more a social and political vision than a religious concept. It has to be the texture of a society. It must be the foundation of a community. The reign of God is, thus, a cultural happening" *(Jesus and the Reign of God*, 57).

[54] Song, *Jesus, the Crucified People*, 12. Song's concept of "people" is akin to the *minjung* of *minjung* theology. On *minjung* theology, see chapter 4 herein.

[55] Song, *Jesus and the Reign of God*, 163. Song is careful to say that "strictly speaking, Jesus did not bring God's reign into the world, for it is already there. What he did was to engage people in the manifestation of it, to enable them to know it is there, to open their minds' eye to see it. . . . He bears witness to the reign of God and is the reign of God at one and the same time" (162). This is in accord with Song's universalist theology which affirms the presence of the reign of God not only among the Jews but also among non-Christians.

becoming the story of "human beings who are oppressed, exploited, disadvantaged, and marginalized, socially, politically, economically, culturally, and also religiously"[56] and of their stories becoming his story? Or again, how is it possible for the stories of the Jews (for example, the Exodus) to become the story of Jesus (for example, the cross) and vice versa?

Song explains that there is a pattern in which the world of meanings organizes and reorganizes itself. This pattern is composed of a few stages "not necessarily in chronological order but interweaving one with the other":

> In the first place, there is a historical happening experienced by a particular group of people at the intersection of a particular time and space. Second, in due time—it may be decades or centuries—the importance attached to the historical framework of a particular happening is gradually replaced by the importance of the meaning derived from that happening. Third, when the meaning originally generated by that happening is applied to a new group of people in their different circumstances, it undergoes change and acquires new meanings. And last, it is on this level of meanings pressed into symbols and expressed in images that the historical experiences of a particular group of people can interact with the other groups of people from different backgrounds and traditions.[57]

It is important for Song, then, to show that at least one story of Jesus' life, beside his message about the reign of God, can be "identified" with the stories of the people. Given his definition of "people," it is only natural that Song would highlight Jesus' death on the cross. Indeed, for Song, Jesus' death on the cross, with his cry "My God, my God, why have you forsaken me?" (Mt 27:46) must be the starting point of Christology.[58] Song dismisses classical interpretations of Jesus' death as God's deception of the devil to redeem humanity (Gregory of Nyssa's "hook" and Augustine's "mousetrap and bait") as "a theological imagination run wild,"[59] as well as Gustaf Aulén's "Christus victor" theology as "a theology of victory" that "becomes a theology of the victory of Christianity over pagan religions."[60] Furthermore, Jürgen Moltmann's speculation on the cross as an intra-trinitarian event of the Father abandoning his Son appears to Song as a fanciful imagining of "a mutiny within God."[61] Over against these interpretations Song holds that the Cross is a historical crime of violence and injustice perpetrated by political and religious authorities against Jesus because in his message about the reign of God he preached the God of *karuna* (mercy)

---

[56] Song, *Jesus, the Crucified People*, 210.

[57] Ibid., 213-24.

[58] Ibid., 96: "Theological reflection on Jesus, what is called christology, ought to begin with these words of Jesus, and not with the story of his conception and birth. Nor should it begin with Jesus' resurrection."

[59] Ibid., 95.

[60] Ibid., 96-97.

[61] Ibid., 98. For Song's critique of Moltmann's and Kazo Kitamori's understanding of God's suffering, see *Third-Eye Theology*, 75-79.

instead of the God of retribution.[62] And because today people—"those men, women, children, in Jesus' day, today, and in the days to come, economically exploited, politically oppressed, culturally and religiously alienated, sexually, racially, or class-wise discriminated against"[63]—continue to suffer at the hands of political and religious authorities, Song argues that the cross of Jesus is their cross, and their cross is Jesus', and that the cross of Jesus and the cross of the people are the cross of God: "The cross of Jesus is the cross of God. The cross people have to bear is the cross of God too. The cross of Jesus and the cross of suffering men, women, and children are linked in God and disclose the heart of the suffering God."[64]

Hence, Song makes a startling identification between Jesus and the suffering people and makes the people the key to knowing Jesus and God:

> *Jesus, in short, is the crucified people! Jesus means crucified people.* To say Jesus is to say suffering people. To know Jesus is to know crucified people. A critical christological conversion takes place here. Traditional Christian theology tells us that to know Jesus we must know God first. But we stress that to know God we must know Jesus, because Jesus makes God real to us. Now we must go even farther: to know Jesus we must know people. We cannot know Jesus without knowing people at the same time. We cannot talk about Jesus if we do not talk about people simultaneously.[65]

Creation, Incarnation, and Redemption

If Jesus' message about the reign of God and his death on the cross are the thread that binds the stories of the Jews, Jesus, and the people together and identifies these stories with the story of God, what is the power that enables them to do so? What is the basis of the total inclusiveness and universality of Jesus' story? How can a *particular* story have an impact upon *universal* history? To frame the questions in terms of theological categories, are creation, incarnation, and redemption three distinct acts of God, externally and accidentally related to one another, or are the three acts intrinsically united phases of the one and unique action of God in the world? If the incarnation and redemption are carried out by a particular individual such as Jesus, are his actions so circumscribed by time and space that they are devoid of universal significance? Can his particularity in the incarnation and redemption be overcome by the universality of creation so that his story can be found in other stories? Can it be said that a single dynamic runs through these three realities so that there is a single history from its beginning to its eschatological fulfillment?

---

[62] On Song's reflections on Jesus' affirmation of the God of compassion as opposed to the God of retribution, of "Abba" instead of "God," see *Jesus, the Crucified People*, 33-79, 101-23.

[63] Ibid., 215-16.

[64] Ibid., 122.

[65] Ibid., 215.

One way to explain the universality of Jesus' incarnation and redemption is the *heilsgeschichtlich* theology of history with its concept of divine election, which, as we have seen, Song strenuously rejects as guilty of exclusivism: "Jesus should be released from the captivity of the so-called *Heilsgeschichte* and set in the process of history as the continuation of the work of creation."[66] To overcome this exclusivism Song looks back at the history of Israel, especially its demise as an independent nation and exile. Just as the end of Israel as an independent state brought about a radically new understanding of God, who was no longer seen as exclusively concerned with the salvation of God's people, and consequently freed Israel from its religious isolationism and spiritual provincialism, so now, Song argues, the church in Asia, after the end of the missionary era, should break away from its exclusivistic outlook and recognize the *universal* presence of God in the histories of all peoples and at the same time remain connected with the *particular* story of Jesus.

Song's way to achieve this double goal is to develop a theology of creation ("the divine mission of creation") in strict unity with the theology of incarnation and redemption ("the mission of enfleshment"). In other words, the theology of creation, which guarantees universality, must be connected with Christology, which vouchsafes particularity, and vice versa.

In elaborating such a unified and holistic theology, Song proposes two paradigms that he terms the "creation-redemption paradigm" and the "death-resurrection paradigm."[67] In explicating the first paradigm Song so emphasizes the inner relation among creation, incarnation, and redemption that they appear simply as "equiprimordial" aspects or moments of the same action of God in the world: "Creation and incarnation are not to be regarded as two separate entities divided by a chronological gulf. Instead, they are intertwined . . . . Creation and incarnation are thus two moments of one and the same act of God."[68] Later, commenting on the story of creation in Genesis and the description of the new creation in Revelation, Song says that "God's work of redemption leads to the emergence of a new creation" and that "creation and redemption are in reality two sides of the same coin. Where there is creation, there is redemption. Conversely, where there is redemption, there is creation."[69] When creation, by which all humans are linked together in "their common kinship and blood relationship," is intrinsically linked to redemption, it prevents redemption from setting up "a barrier between the Christian community from other communities."[70] In this way the creation-redemption complex "should enable Christians to appreciate the cultures and histories outside the Christian church in a more positive way."[71]

At the heart of the creation-redemption complex, however, is the incarnation. Indeed, for Song, creation is already God's act of incarnation insofar as it

[66] Song, *Christian Mission in Reconstruction*, 35.
[67] See Choan-Seng Song, "Choan-Seng Song Replies," *Occasional Bulletin of Missionary Research* 1/3 (1997): 13-15.
[68] Song, *Christian Mission in Reconstruction*, 52.
[69] Song, *Third-Eye Theology*, 56.
[70] Ibid., 158.
[71] Ibid.

is an act of God's self-emptying and self-giving to a reality other than God. Creation is understood not as an act of God's omnipotence and freedom but as a consequence of the creativity of God's love and compassion, or to use Song's memorable phrase, of God's "heartache."[72] Furthermore, God's creation was from the very beginning geared toward the concrete, historical event of God becoming flesh: "In this flesh, in this particular human being called Jesus Christ, creation and incarnation become one concrete historical event embodying the love of God for the whole world."[73] Again, "Creation detached from incarnation is equivalent to words unspoken. Words remain in the mind of the speaker and thus uncommunicated. But at the creation, words spoken by God were heard and transformed into deeds, events and concrete objects."[74]

Just as creation confers universality, so is the incarnation, which is intrinsically connected with creation, directed toward universality. Whereas in traditional theology the concept of incarnation functions to affirm the preexistence and hence the divinity of Jesus, for Song, it guarantees the connection between God and the world, and hence the "worldliness" and "humanity" of God: "Incarnation . . . is nothing other than God's oneness with man."[75]

Thus, the concept of incarnation functions in Song's theology less as a christological category than as a description of the creative act of God. Running through the creation-incarnation-redemption complex there is an incarnating dynamic that ensures the universalizing tendency of God's self-giving to the world. In virtue of this incarnating dynamic, the mission of the church is seen as the continuation of God's *missio* in God's sending of the Son into the world (the incarnation). The redemptive incarnation is but an event in the process of God's loving self-emptying into the *whole* world. Consequently, the church's mission, which is the continuation of the incarnation, is not to form an identity apart from and over against the non-Christian world but to realize the incarnating movement and dynamic and break down all the barriers dividing the church from the rest of humanity.

Whereas the "creation-redemption paradigm" guarantees the universal thrust of God's one action toward the world, the "death-resurrection paradigm" assures the connection of this action with the concrete history of Jesus of Nazareth and hence its particularity. In this history of Jesus, especially in his death on the cross, God reveals himself as both judge and savior, both condemnation and grace, so that the new creation will not be any kind of transformation but one that passes through the dialectic of death and resurrection, just like Jesus himself.

However, even this death-resurrection paradigm is enveloped in God's incarnating movement or the incarnating dynamic: "The event of the resurrection is already contained in the event of the incarnation."[76] Ultimately, for Song, the

---

[72] Ibid., 53.
[73] Song, *Christian Mission in Reconstruction*, 52.
[74] Ibid.
[75] Ibid., 272. Song prefers the expression "humanization of God" to "incarnation" (217).
[76] Ibid., 254.

creation-redemption paradigm is primary, because it expresses God's self-emptying movement in the incarnation and penetration into the whole of human history in order to transform it. Where God changes Godself through *kenosis* and creatively penetrates the world, there God also changes and transfigures the world. Where God's creative and incarnating acts merge together into *one* movement of self-emptying, there the transformation of the world into God takes place. God's enfleshing or incarnating movement "results in the creation of the God-man Jesus Christ."[77] A new God-man relationship emerges, a "new humanity" that is neither purely divine nor purely human. It is clear, therefore, that of the two paradigms Song leans more heavily toward the creation-redemption one. The precarious and delicate balance between the historical incarnation of God in the particular Jew Jesus and God's universal indwelling in all creation through the divine dynamics of creation and self-emptying is tipped in favor of the latter, just as in his dissertation Song leans more in the direction of Tillich than Barth.

A CHRISTOLOGY FOR ASIANS?

A reader trained in Western theology and its linear logic will no doubt find not only Song's theology but also his exposition rather disconcerting.[78] This is so not only because almost all of his books (except *Christian Mission in Reconstruction*) lack a clear thematic unity, being collections of previously published and generally unrelated essays, but also because Song intentionally adopts a mode of discourse and a style of theologizing that he calls "perceptual and intuitive."[79] As a result, Song often does not *argue* for or against positions, even highly intricate and complex ones, with sustained logical analysis but contents himself with piling up a series of rhetorical questions for or against them. Furthermore, it is not rare to encounter in his works not only stories of the most diverse kinds but also poems, songs, *haiku*s, and even cartoons, which may at best illustrate a theological position but do not marshal convincing evidence for or against it.[80] Most often, when reading chapters of his books, one has the impression of listening to homilies or sermons, passionately and eloquently

---

[77] Ibid., 60.

[78] Song says that "in the long tradition of *logos* theology, that is, theology dominated by reason or rationality, the structure of divine-human relationships is grasped conceptually and analytically. This results in the imposition of a severe limitation on our experience of God—the God who is not an analytical concept to begin with. In other words, scientific and philosophical frameworks that Western theologians employ to get at the essence and nature of the Reality behind all realities are not conducive to penetrating the darkness surrounding the heart of being" (ibid., 61-62).

[79] "In contrast to the conceptual and rationalistic approach to the Reality behind all realities, there is an intuitive approach that some Asians, especially the Chinese and Japanese, tend to stress in their grasp of the reality that transcends their immediate apprehension" (ibid., 62). Song suggests that this intuitive approach is intrinsic to the phenomenon of *satori* in Zen Buddhism.

[80] This is true in particular of *Tell Us Our Names, Theology from the Womb of Asia,* and *The Tears of Lady Meng.*

delivered, but not of being treated to sustained, nuanced, and carefully reasoned theological argumentation.[81]

With regard to Christology, Song's trilogy, in spite of its combined 879 pages, is not a comprehensive presentation of all the themes traditionally associated with this theological treatise. For instance, there is no discussion of the possibility of retrieving the "historical Jesus" from the pages of the New Testament, a much-debated issue in contemporary theology and an indispensable presupposition of Song's christological project. Nor is there an extensive discussion of the nature of Jesus' resurrection. Nor is there a presentation of the historical development of Christology, especially in its patristic and medieval periods. Nor is there an examination of the issue of the divinity and humanity of Jesus and their mutual relation.

That Song has not discussed these and other staple christological themes is no careless oversight on his part. On the contrary, it is highly probable that Song has deliberately omitted them out of his concern to construct a Christology adequate to the Asian context, for which he believes purely historical and metaphysical approaches are not relevant.[82] By the same token, it is necessary to examine whether Song's story Christology does justice to the person and work of Jesus and to the central insights that have become the foundation of the Christian faith. Here, from the perspective of Roman Catholic theology, I bring up for discussion only two issues, one methodological, the other substantive. The first regards the way Song understands the relationship between the so-called Jesus of history and the Christ of faith, and the second regards Jesus' divinity.

The Jesus of Nazareth, the Jesus of History, and the Christ of Faith

As has been shown above, Song is extremely critical of what he calls church-centered and Christ-centered Christologies for their alleged exclusivism. While I am in full agreement with his stance against exclusivism and the subordination of Christology to ecclesiastical interests,[83] it must be pointed out that his use of the term *Christ* is ambiguous and misleading. It is customary to distinguish among the "Jesus of Nazareth" (the "real Jesus" who lived in Palestine in the first century), the "Jesus of history" (the historical reconstruction of the message, work, and person of Jesus of Nazareth by scholars on the basis of the New Testament), and the "Christ of faith" (the Jesus of Nazareth who is now

---

[81] This is true especially of *Jesus and the Reign of God* and *Jesus in the Power of the Spirit*.

[82] See Song's discussion of these two approaches in *Jesus and the Reign of God*, x-xii.

[83] To Roman Catholic theologians, Song's fulminations against exclusivism, while fully justified, sound rather passé, especially after Vatican II. Furthermore, Song's categories of exclusivism and pluralism oversimplify the issue since they do not recognize the possibility of other positions that seek to maintain *both* universality and fidelity to the claim of the uniqueness and normativeness of Jesus as the Christ. For a magisterial study on this question, see Jacques Dupuis, *Toward a Christian Theology of Religious Pluralism* (Maryknoll, N.Y.: Orbis Books, 1997).

risen and glorified as Lord).[84] Of course, we do not have access to and have knowledge of the Jesus of Nazareth except through the testimony of the New Testament, but there is no guarantee that any one Jesus of history fully captures the Jesus of Nazareth (indeed, it is a priori impossible that it does so).

While Song simply assumes that his reconstruction of the Jesus of history, especially his message about the reign of God, corresponds without remainder to the Jesus of Nazareth, contemporary debates about the validity of many such reconstructions, from the "Old Quest" to the "New Quest" to the "Third Quest" to the "Jesus Seminar," have shown that the issue is far more complex than Song takes it to be.[85] For instance, Song's statement that "the reign of God for him [Jesus] is very much more a social and political vision than a religious concept"[86] will be challenged by a majority of New Testament scholars, and rightly so. Furthermore, it is generally recognized that there is a real continuity between the Jesus of Nazareth (not the Jesus of history) and the Christ of faith. It is the same Jesus of Nazareth that is now the risen and glorified Christ, despite the fact that the disciples' understanding of who Jesus was (that is, New Testament Christologies—note the plural here) underwent a radical shift after his resurrection. Song seems to have collapsed the Christ of faith, that is, the identity of the risen Jesus, with the various, more or less adequate or wrong-headed interpretations that the church and theologians have given to the Christ of faith in the course of history. Song is well within his rights to combat any one of these interpretations (Christologies), but for him not even to raise the question of the identity of the Jesus of Nazareth beyond "the Jesus who lived, toiled, suffered, and died on the cross"[87] is surely to fall short of the New Testament witness to the Jesus of Nazareth. To his rhetorical question "Does the church worship the Jesus who walked the earth and endured all sorts of pain, even the pain of dying on the cross, or the Christ that is treated as an object of endless theological debates?"[88] the correct answer cannot be the first alternative, which Song favors, but neither. The church does not worship "the Jesus who walked the earth" *except as he is now the Christ;* and much less does the church worship the Christ as "an object of endless theological debates" who is nothing but more or less adequate historical and theological reconstructions of the Jesus of Nazareth who is the Christ.

These reflections and distinctions, far from being of concern only to scholars, lie, I contend, at the very heart of Song's repeated and passionate defense of

---

[84] For these distinctions, see John Meier, "The Historical Jesus: Rethinking Some Concepts," *Theological Studies* 51 (1990): 3-24.

[85] For a brief and lucid presentation on these quests, see William P. Loewe, "A Misguided Quest? Historical Jesus Research Today," *The Living Light* 33/1 (1996): 6-17. It is amazing how often Song uses the expression "must have been" in his trilogy when he attempts to reconstruct the historical probability of a saying or deed of Jesus. I am not suggesting that Song is unfamiliar with the historical-critical method (he taught Old Testament at Tainan Theological College), but the frequent use of "must have been" to preface his interpretations render them suspect of eisegesis.

[86] Song, *Jesus and the Reign of God*, 57.

[87] Song, *Believing Heart*, 62.

[88] Ibid.

the universality of the Jesus story. As we have seen, Song attempts to ground this universality in the creation-redemption paradigm and the dynamics of God's incarnating and self-emptying act with regard to the world. But this universality will be much more strengthened when it is seen that the particular, historical Jesus of Nazareth is now the living Lord, the universal Christ (and not only the story of Jesus), the Son of God in glory whose power and presence are made active everywhere by the Holy Spirit.[89]

Jesus—God-Man

We are thus brought to the issue traditionally discussed under the nomenclature of the two natures—divine and human—of Jesus. We have mentioned Song's aversion to Greek metaphysical categories. The question here is not whether Song should make use of these categories—of course he need not—but rather whether Song's Christology has fully preserved, through whatever categories he judges most appropriate for the Asian context, the truth that lies at the foundation of the Christian faith and that has been articulated by ecumenical councils from Nicaea to Chalcedon. That Song has fully shown that Jesus is truly and really human remains beyond doubt. Whether he has explicitly affirmed that Jesus is divine in his real identity (ontologically, one may say) is not entirely unambiguous.

Federschmidt has shown that Song prefers to speak of Jesus as the "prototype" or "archetype" of God's love and as "concentration" of God's incarnating dynamics.[90] Such dynamic categories certainly have their advantages in describing what God has accomplished in and through Jesus, but Song has not developed them fully and what Song says by means of them is ambiguous:

> If Jesus (or the story of Jesus) is for Song the "archetype" in the strict sense, and hence the permanent original, which in one way or another gives a push to other, derived divine histories—where can these histories actually happen and where can people discover them, even outside the currents of the Christian Tradition? Or are Jesus and his story to be understood rather as a "prototype," hence as a typical realization of a very common divine action, a realization perhaps highly original and worthy of honor but still not unsurpassable? Song's typological formulations remain ambiguous. However, the burden of his reflections tends rather in the direction of the latter.[91]

The same may be said of Song's notion of Jesus as the "supreme concentration" of God's creative-redemptive power. It is not clear whether Song is speaking of Jesus as "supreme concentration" in the sense that he embodies in himself a greater quantity or intensity of God's power than all others or in the sense that

---

[89] It is curious that in spite of the title of the third volume of his trilogy, there is little in Song's theology that amounts to a full-fledged theology of the Holy Spirit.

[90] Federschmidt, *Theologie aus asiatischen Quellen*, 250-52.

[91] Ibid., 251.

he is God himself so that his embodiment of God's power cannot *in principle* be surpassed by any other. Here again Song's statements are, Federschmidt argues, ambiguous.[92]

Most recently, however, Song has explicitly spoken of Jesus as "not God." Describing the unconditional and all-inclusive nature of God's love, Song says:

> Jesus lived with this kind of love. He dedicated his entire life to it and shared it with others . . . . He practiced, lived, and died for it. He personified it. In this love which is Jesus we Christians come to know that God is love.
>
> Jesus is not God. He is flesh and blood just as we are. But he reflects God as he reflects this kind of love. He shows what God is as he lives this love and seeks to fill others with it. He is God in the world in that he is this love in the world. He is God to us as he is this love. . . . What relates Jesus to God and God to Jesus is not some abstruse trinitarian formula of Father, Son, and Spirit; but the love that has power to save others. What binds Jesus to God and God to Jesus, in spite of the infinite and qualitative difference between Jesus as a human being and God as a divine being, is not the nature of Jesus theologically defined as "human and divine," or as "more divine than human," but the love that helps others live but cannot prevent suffering and death on its behalf.[93]

The above quotation, stylistically, is vintage Song: passionate and powerful but ambiguous and confusing. If the sentence: "Jesus is not God" is taken out of its context, it would be tantamount to an explicit denial of Jesus' divinity. But if it is taken in connection with what Song says about the "trinitarian formula," then, of course, Jesus is not God on the basis of "some abstruse trinitarian formula of Father, Son, and Spirit." No theologian worth his or her salt would say that Jesus' divinity derives from a formula, abstruse or not. Nor would any theologian cognizant with the historical development of the doctrine of the Trinity say that "what binds Jesus to God and God to Jesus" is "the nature of Jesus theologically defined as 'human and divine,' or as 'more divine than human.'" In spite of these statements, then, Song cannot be construed to have denied the divinity of Jesus, since the grounds for his alleged denial are spurious. On the contrary, what Song intends to do is to offer a dynamic explanation of the truth of the divinity of Jesus by describing him as the embodiment of God's unconditional and all-inclusive love, as is clear in his statement: "He [Jesus] is God to us as he is this love to us."

---

[92] Ibid., 252: "Hat der kosmologische Rahmen, den Song hier verwendet, eine Hilfsfunktion, um die soteriologische Bedeutung Jesu auch über die Grenzen des christlichen Traditionskreises hinaus verständlich zu machen, oder wird er nicht doch zu einer selbständigen Spekulation, für die die Geschichte Jesu im Rückblick nur noch den Wert eines (notfalls auch verzichtbaren) Beispiels unter anderen besitzt? Eine ganz eindeutige Antwort fällt auch hier schwer."

[93] Song, *Believing Heart*, 294.

The same ambiguity is found in another statement Song makes when he rejects both Christocentrism and theocentrism:

> Over against these two opposing views, it has to be said that Christian faith is faith in "Jesus-God" and in "God-Jesus." Note the hyphen in both expressions. The hyphen is not an equal sign. While the hyphen does not identify Jesus with God, it does not separate Jesus from God either. It neither equates God with Jesus nor alienates God from Jesus. It is in what Jesus said and did that a Christian comes to know God, leading to an important point: the God that comes to be known through Jesus is the God who is active not only inside the church but outside it, not only among Christians but among people not related to Christianity.
>
> At this point the hyphen that related Jesus to God and God to Jesus develops into the proposition *in*. What we encounter, then, is "Jesus *in* God" and "God *in* Jesus." Jesus was able to say what he said and to do what he did because he was "in" God and God was "in" him. Perhaps it would be more accurate to say that Jesus was in God *through the power of the Holy Spirit* and that God was in Jesus, also *through the power of the Spirit*.[94]

Once again it is clear that Song, though carefully avoiding to say *who* Jesus is in relation to God the Father and *what* he is by "nature," is striving strenuously to affirm an intimate connection between God and Jesus (through the hyphen and the preposition *in*). Traditional theologians would have no problem with what Song *affirms*; they would argue however that Song's functional Christology is not fully appropriate to the affirmations of the Christian faith about who Jesus is, as mediated through the New Testament and the Christian tradition.[95] Song is certainly attempting to express the Christian faith about the identity of Jesus by a dynamic and relational language, but it is questionable whether the hyphen in "Jesus-God" and "God-Jesus" and the preposition *in* in "God in Jesus" and "Jesus in God" can fully express what Christians mean when they profess that Jesus *is* God.

Despite these misgivings I am ready to affirm of Song's Christology what I have written about his theology of the kingdom of God, since these two theologies are inextricably intertwined:

---

[94] Ibid., 63.

[95] There are strong resemblances between Song's functional Christology and that of John Hick. For a concise presentation of the latter's Christology, see John Hick, *The Metaphor of God Incarnate: Christology in a Pluralistic Age* (Louisville. Ky.: Westminster, 1993): "The idea of divine incarnation is better understood as metaphorical than as literal—Jesus embodied, or incarnated, the ideal of human life lived in faithful response to God, so that God was able to act through him, and he accordingly embodied a love which is a human reflection of the divine love" (ix). The similarities between Hick's text and Song's, which is quoted above, are striking. In this connection, it would be interesting to see how Song would develop a pneumatology in which God and Jesus are said to act "through the power of the Holy Spirit."

True to his methodological precepts, Song offers a *basileia* theology that is rooted in the earth and, more specifically, in the Asian humus, while not ignoring its transcendental character. Nurtured by the message and actions of the Hebrew prophets and Jesus for justice, human dignity, peace, and love, and bathed in the blood and tears of dispossessed and oppressed Asian people, and inspired by their struggle for liberation, Song's theology of the reign of God is by far the most developed and the richest among contemporary Asian theologians.[96]

---

[96] See chap. 4, p. 90 herein.

8

Ecclesia in Asia

CHALLENGES FOR ASIAN CHRISTIANITY

With the official promulgation of the apostolic exhortation *Ecclesia in Asia* by Pope John Paul II in New Delhi, India, on 6 November 1999, the Special Assembly for Asia of the Synod of Bishops (hereafter the Asian Synod), which had met in Rome from 19 April to 14 May 1998, in a certain sense came to an end.[1] Proclaimed as "a moment of special grace" (*EA*, 3), the synod had drawn, both during its preparatory stage and in its aftermath, both favorable and unfavorable comments, especially with regard to its *lineamenta* and its *modus operandi*.[2] Similarly, the immediate reception of the exhortation was, as expected, mixed; it was received in some quarters with unfeigned enthusiasm, in others with muted applause, and in still others with unalloyed disappointment.[3]

---

[1] For an English translation of *Ecclesia in Asia,* see *Origins* 29/23 (18 November 1999): 358-84; and Peter C. Phan, comp. and ed., *The Asian Synod: Text and Commentaries* (Maryknoll, N.Y.: Orbis Books, 2002). The document is cited hereafter as *EA*, followed by the number of the paragraph, in parentheses.

[2] Criticisms of the *lineamenta* were sharp; some came from episcopal conferences, in particular the Japanese bishops. For other evaluations, see, for instance, Chrys McVey, "The Asian Synod: What Is at Stake," *EAPR* 35/1 (1998): 143-46; Michael Amaladoss, "Expectations from the Synod for Asia," *VJTR* 62 (1998): 144-151; G. Gisbert-Sauch, "The *Lineamenta* for the Asian Synod: Presentation and Comment," *VJTR* 61 (1997): 8-17; Paul Puthanangady, "*Lineamenta* for the Asian Synod," *Jeevadhara* 27/160 (1998): 231-48: Kuncheria Pathil, "*Lineamenta* for the Asian Synod: Some Observations and Comments," *Jeedvadhara* 27/160 (1997): 249-59; J. Constantine Manalel, "The Jesus Movement and the Asian Renaissance: Some Random Reflections for the Asian Synod," *Jeevadhara* 27 (1998): 133-53; Francisco Claver, "Personal Thoughts on the Asian Synod," *EAPR* 35/2 (1998): 241-48; S. Arokiasamy, "Synod for Asia: An Ecclesial Event of Communion and Shared Witness of Faith," *VJTR* 62/9 (1998): 666-75; Gali Bali, "Asian Synod and Concerns of the Local Church," *Jeevadhara* 27 (1998): 297-330; John Mansford Prior, "A Tale of Two Synods: Observations on the Special Assembly for Asia," *VJTR* 62 (1998): 654-65; and Luis Antonio Tagle, "The Synod for Asia as Event," *EAPR* 35/3-4 (1998): 366-78.

[3] See, for instance, James H. Kroeger, "Asian Synod—Asian Pentecost: Introducing *Ecclesia in Asia*," *SEDOS* 32/1 (2000): 8-11.

THE ASIAN SYNOD IN CONTEXT

As is often the case, how one reacts to the bishops' synods and the ensuing apostolic exhortations largely depends on the expectations one entertains of them. The International Bishops' Synod was established by Pope Paul VI in September 1965, shortly before the close of the Second Vatican Council, as an instrument of episcopal collegiality. The synod, which the pope reserves the right to convoke, is intended to foster a close collaboration between the bishops and the pope. It is, however, advisory and not deliberative. Since its foundation there have been eleven international synods (both ordinary and extraordinary)[4] and eight national or regional synods, including the five continental synods called by John Paul II's *Tertio Millennio Adveniente* to celebrate the new millennium.

Unfortunately, as Michael Fahey, S.J., a highly respected American ecclesiologist, has put it: "Despite high hopes for their success, results of synods have been negligible. Each new synod attracts less and less attention; the structure of their sessions has become unwieldy, they have become rituals with little practical impact on the life of the church. In the last 30 years the institution has not been notable as a wellspring of new ideas or strategies."[5] Furthermore, since the apostolic exhortations that follow these continental synods (so far three have been issued) are not the work of the synodal participants themselves (though the exhortations are supposed to incorporate the synods' "propositions") but are composed by the pope with the assistance of a post-synodal committee, they are often suspected of having filtered the results of the synods to an officially acceptable level. Moreover, being usually quite lengthy and turgid in style, they have aroused little interest, even among the clergy and theologians; it is totally unrealistic to expect that they will be read by the laity, at least in their entirety.

These remarks are not intended to cast a cynical eye on the Asian Synod and *Ecclesia in Asia*. On the contrary, they serve as a warning that unless concrete steps are taken to put into practice at the level of the local churches the synod's fifty-nine "propositions," which have been more or less incorporated into *Ecclesia in Asia*, the Asian Synod will not be unlike one of the many firework displays celebrating the coming of the third millennium, spectacular festivals of sounds and colors but, in the end, nothing more than blurred memories of the extravaganzas. What steps can and should be taken by the Asian churches to prevent their synod from joining the rank of its predecessors, illustrious indeed, but reduced to being a convenient quarry for doctoral dissertations, bereft of real and lasting influence on the life of the churches of Asia?[6]

---

[4] Complete documentation of these eleven general synods has been published by Civiltà Cattolica, Rome, under the supervision of Giovanni Caprile.

[5] Michael Fahey, "The Synod of America: Reflections of a Nonparticipant," *Theological Studies* 59 (1998): 489.

[6] This is not to say that careful studies of these continental synods are of no value; on the contrary, there is a great need of objective and detailed assessments of the apostolic exhortations that resulted from these synods, especially by comparing them with their preceding *instrumentum laboris* and the "propositions" made by the synodal partici-

What is offered here is neither an evaluation of the Asian Synod nor a commentary on *Ecclesia in Asia*. Rather, as an expatriate Vietnamese who has for a quarter of a century been engaged in the study and teaching of theology in the United States of America, and whose academic interest has focused on the Christianity of Asia,[7] I will advance, very selectively, some reflections and proposals as to how certain teachings of the Asian Synod, as embodied in *Ecclesia in Asia*, can be implemented in Asia.[8]

THE CHURCH NOT *IN* BUT *OF* ASIA: THE ASIANNESS OF CHRISTIANITY

By any standard *Ecclesia in Asia* is John Paul II's typical theological product, with its rather forbidding length, its frequent insistence on complete orthodoxy, its abundant citation of the pope's own writings, and its emotional peroration with a prayer to Mary. Besides an introduction and a conclusion, the exhortation is composed of seven parts, dealing with the following themes: the Asian context, Jesus as savior, the Holy Spirit as lord and giver of life, proclamation of Jesus in Asia (with a focus on inculturation), communion and dialogue for mission (with a focus on ecumenical and interreligious dialogue), the service of human promotion, and Christians as witnesses to the gospel.

For an Asian reader, the inevitable question arises: Has the exhortation said anything new and important for the churches of Asia that either has not been said before by these churches themselves or could not have been said without the work of the synod? To both parts of the question the answer is frankly no. Except for the first section on the Asian context, most of the exhortation could have been written prior to and apart from the synod, and what the exhortation says on the other six themes has already been said, powerfully and in great detail, by the various documents of the FABC.[9]

pants. There are indeed already some helpful studies of these synods. For the African Synod (1994), see Africa Faith and Justice Network under Maura Browne, comp. and ed., *The African Synod: Documents, Reflections, Perspectives* (Maryknoll, N.Y.: Orbis Books, 1996); for the Synod of America (1997), see, besides the essay by Michael Fahey cited above, Paul D. Minnihan, "Encountering the American Synod," *Theological Studies* 60 (1999): 597-624. For the Asian Synod (1998), see Phan, *The Asian Synod*. It is to be hoped that there will be similar studies for the Oceania Synod (1998) and the European Synod (1999).

[7] For a brief explanation of the perspective from which I formulate these reflections, see Peter C. Phan, "Betwixt and Between: Doing Theology with Memory and Imagination," in *Journeys at the Margin: Toward an Autobiographical Theology in American-Asian Perspective*, ed. Peter C. Phan and Jung Young Lee (Collegeville, Minn.: Liturgical Press, 1999), 113-33.

[8] The Asian Synod comprises the episcopal conferences of all the churches located in Asia, including East Asia (represented by the Federation of Asian Bishops' Conferences), Western Asia or the Middle East (represented by the Council of Catholic Patriarchs of the Middle East), and Central Asia (Kazakhstan, Uzbekistan, Kyrgyzstan, Tajikistan, and Turkmenistan). In this chapter I limit my reflections to the churches that are members of the FABC.

[9] Sadly, of the exhortation's 240 notes, none refers to the documents of the FABC (except John Paul II's addresses to the FABC). Is this omission intentional? Are not the

This does not mean however that the synod and the exhortation have not rendered a valuable service. After listing the fifteen points of agreement out of the fifty-nine propositions the synod submitted, Luis Tagle acknowledges that there is nothing new in them in comparison with the teachings of the FABC, but he correctly insists that there is something genuinely new in the fact that these issues and concerns have been voiced in a synodal forum and recognized by the church of Rome, and through it, have been brought to the consciousness of the universal church.[10] What was new is not what the Asian bishops said but *that* they said it and *how* they said it at the synod. What they said had been said, at length and with power and depth, for almost thirty years, ever since the founding of the FABC in 1972, in its numerous plenary assemblies and in the documents of its several institutes.[11] But at the synod, they said it again, *to the whole church*, and with surprising *boldness* and refreshing *candor*, with what the New Testament calls *parrhēsia*.

The synod was the first official recognition that the churches of Asia have come of age, or as a synodal participant put it, that they are not branch offices of the Roman Curia. To the universal church the Asian bishops proclaimed, humbly but forcefully, that the churches of Asia not only learn from but also have something to teach the church of Rome as well as the church universal, precisely from their experiences as churches not simply *in* but *of* Asia. The fact that the exhortation has incorporated several elements of the Asian Synod and made them part of the papal magisterium is an eloquent witness to the value of the experiences and wisdom of the Asian churches.

What is new, in a word, is the public recognition of the necessity and validity of the *Asianness* of the churches of Asia. Of course, Asianness is a notoriously slippery concept, and the *Lineamenta* and the exhortation attempt to circumscribe it by listing several cultural and religious values that purportedly constitute the "Asian soul" or "being Asian": "love of silence and contemplation, simplicity, harmony, detachment, non-violence, discipline, frugal living, the thirst for learning and philosophical inquiry . . . , respect for life, compassion for all beings, closeness to nature, filial piety toward parents, elders and ancestors, and a highly developed sense of community" (*EA*, 6). The exhortation also attends to the economic, social, and political contexts in which Christianity exists in Asia (*EA*, 7-8). Unfortunately, when it speaks of the fact that "despite her centuries-long presence and her many apostolic endeavors, the church in many

teachings of the FABC authentic magisterium? There are two references to the work of the FABC (together with the Council of Catholic Patriarchs of the Middle East) for ecclesial communion and collaboration (nos. 3, 26) but not to their *teachings*.

[10] See Tagle, "The Synod for Asia as Event," 370-71.

[11] For a collection of these statements, see Gaudencio Rosales and C. G. Arévalo, eds., *For All the Peoples of Asia: Federation of Asian Bishops' Conferences. Documents from 1970 to 1991* (Maryknoll, N.Y.: Orbis Books, 1992; Quezon City, Philippines: Claretian Publications, 1992); and Franz-Josef Eilers, ed., *For All the Peoples of Asia: Federation of Asian Bishops' Conferences. Documents from 1992 to 1996* (Quezon City, Philippines: Claretian Publications, 1997). These two statements will be cited hereafter as *For All Peoples*, vol. 1 and vol. 2 respectively.

places was still considered as foreign to Asia and indeed was often associated in people's minds with the colonial powers" (*EA*, 9), it uses the past tense and fails to recognize that the foreignness of Christianity in Asia and the perception of its association with colonialism are *present* realities, and this not simply "in many places" but in *all* parts of Asia.

If the Asian Synod is to have a lasting transformative effect on the churches of Asia, so that they may become truly *of* Asia and their association with colonialism may be removed, the most important thing, in my judgment, is that Asian Catholics take their Asianness seriously as the context of their being Christian. In practice, this means that the first and last concern for the leaders of the Asian churches must be not how a particular policy is conformable with canonical requirements and directives coming from Rome or elsewhere but rather how it will respond to the challenges of the Asian social, political, economic, and religious contexts and whether and how it will effectively help Christians live their faith in fidelity to the gospel and the living Christian tradition, here and now, in Asia. Determining this Asianness and making it the perspective through which the Christian faith is consistently expressed and lived should be the top priority for Asian Christianity in the post-synodal era.[12]

Those of us who live close to the ecclesiastical centers of the churches of the so-called Third World sometimes experience the sad irony of these churches trying to be "more Roman than Rome." Perhaps such a phenomenon is understandable when churches lack the necessary resources to be on their own, especially in countries with governments hostile to Christianity, and are still, as it were, in their minority. Now that the Asian churches have come of age, however, they should be able to move to the stage of self-government, self-support, self-propagation, and self-theologizing. As the Asian Colloquium on Ministries in the Church put it in 1977: "The basic fact is that today in our Asian context we are in the process of re-discovering that the individual Christian can best survive, grow and develop as a Christian person in the midst of a self-nourishing, self-governing, self-ministering and self-propagating Christian community."[13]

To assume responsibilities in these areas, while remaining in full communion with the church universal, demands courage, imagination, creativity, collaboration at all levels of church life, and above all trust in the Holy Spirit. This is much more challenging (and uncomfortable) than simply "applying" existing church laws and traditions to the different situations of Asia. But it is only in this way that the churches *in* Asia become truly *of* Asia. As Christian churches they must, of course, proclaim and live the Christian faith, the same *faith* handed down the ages, but not in the theological categories and with the church structures imported from without. Rather, they should do so in the modalities conceived and born from within the Asian contexts. These Asian categories and structures need not be totally different from those of the churches elsewhere; however, whether they are identical with or different cannot and should not be

---

[12] This determination of the Asian context has become the first step in the theological method adopted by the FABC.

[13] *For All Peoples*, 1:77 (no. 9).

determined beforehand and a priori but must be shaped by real experimentations in the concrete situations of each Asian country. The churches of Asia must claim and exercise the God-given right, based on the mystery of divine incarnation (and not a concession granted by a some higher ecclesiastical authority), to find out and determine for themselves how best to proclaim and live the Christian faith in Asia. Such a task is a matter of life and death for the church, since if the church in Asia is not Asian, it is no church at all.

This task of becoming *Asian* churches is all the more urgent in light of the astounding acceptance by *Ecclesia in Asia* of a point made by the Asian Synod that "Jesus is often perceived as foreign to Asia. It is paradoxical that most Asians tend to regard Jesus—born on Asian soil—as a Western rather than an Asian figure" (*EA*, 20). While ways must be found, as the exhortation urges Asian theologians to do,[14] "to present the mystery of Christ to their peoples according to their cultural patterns and ways of thinking" (*EA* 20),[15] the most effective way to present Jesus as an Asian figure is to make the churches authentically Asian.

A NEW WAY OF BEING CHURCH

Another way of making the point I have argued for so far is to say that, for the Asian Synod to have a lasting impact, the Asian churches must, with courage and creativity, find new ways of being church, and hence construct an alternative ecclesiology. This is a theme repeatedly emphasized by the FABC, especially in its third and fifth plenary assemblies in Bangkok, 1982, and Bandung, Indonesia, 1990, respectively. This ecclesiology, in a sort of Copernican revolution, de-centers the church in the sense that it makes the center of the Christian life not the church but the reign of God. Christians must be not ecclesiocentric but regnocentric. Their mission is not to expand the church and its structures *(plantatio ecclesiae)* in order to enlarge the sphere of influence for the church, but rather, to be a transparent sign and effective instrument of the saving presence of the reign of God—the reign of justice, peace, and love—of which the church is a seed. As the exhortation puts it well: "Empowered by the Spirit to accomplish Christ's salvation on earth, the church is the seed of the kingdom of God, and she looks eagerly for its final coming. Her identity and mission are

---

[14] The exhortation lists a series of images of Jesus that may be understandable to Asians: the teacher of wisdom, the healer, the liberator, the spiritual guide, the enlightened one, the compassionate friend of the poor, the good Samaritan, the good shepherd, the obedient one (*EA*, 20). See my discussion on Asian Christologies in chapters 5 and 6 herein.

[15] It is difficult to see how to reconcile this text with another text of the exhortation, which quotes Paul John Paul II's encyclical *Fides et Ratio* (no. 72) insisting on the necessity of appropriating and sharing the linguistic, philosophical, and cultural categories used by ecumenical councils "in the encounter with the various cultures" (*EA*, 20). Are these categories (not doctrines) essential parts of divine revelation and how are they to be made into Asian "cultural patterns and ways of thinking"? For an evaluation of *Fides et Ratio*, see Peter C. Phan, "*Fides et Ratio* and Asian Philosophies: Sharing the Banquet of Truth," *Science et Esprit* 51 (1999): 333-49; and chapter 3 herein.

inseparable from the kingdom of God. . . . The Spirit reminds the church that she is not an end unto herself: In all that she is and all that she does, she exists to serve Christ and the salvation of the world" (*EA*, 17). The new way of being church in Asia and the ecclesiology undergirding it are characterized by the following features.[16]

1. First, the church, both at the local and universal levels, is seen primarily as "a *communion of communities*, where laity, Religious, and clergy recognize and accept each other as sisters and brothers."[17] At the heart of the mystery of the church is the bond of communion uniting God with humanity and humans with one another, of which the eucharist is the sign and instrument par excellence.[18]

Moreover, in this ecclesiology there is an explicit and effective recognition of the fundamental equality among all the members of the local church as disciples of Jesus and among all the local churches insofar as they are communities of Jesus' disciples and whose communion constitutes the universal church. The communion *(koinonia)* that constitutes the church, both at the local and universal levels, and from which flows the fundamental equality of all Christians, is rooted at its deepest level in the life of the Trinity, in whom there is a perfect communion of equals.[19] Unless this fundamental equality of all Christians is acknowledged and put into practice through concrete policies and actions, the church will not become a communion of communities in Asia. Living out this fundamental equality is particularly difficult in Asia, not only because the

---

[16] In elaborating this ecclesiology I make use of some of the FABC's statements, but the reflections on their consequences for church life in Asia are mine and should not be attributed to the FABC.

[17] *For All Peoples*, 1:287 (no. 8.1.1). The exhortation unduly narrows this vision of the church as a communion of churches by saying that in the view of the synod fathers, it applies primarily to the diocese: "The synod fathers chose to describe the diocese as a communion of communities gathered around the shepherd, where clergy, consecrated persons and the laity are engaged in a 'dialogue of life and heart' sustained by the grace of the Holy Spirit" (*EA*, 25). In fact, the FABC's vision applies to the church both at the local and universal levels: "It [the church] is a community not closed in on itself and its particular concerns, but *linked* with many bonds *to other communities of faith* (concretely, the parishes and dioceses around them) and to the one and universal communion, *catholica unitas*, of the holy church of the Lord" (*For All Peoples*, 1:56 [no. 7.8]). In other words, not only the diocese but also the church universal is a communion of communities. The universal church is not a church above the other dioceses and of which the local churches are constitutive "parts" with the pope as its universal bishop. Rather, it is a communion in faith, hope, and love of all the local churches (among which there is the church of Rome of which the pope is the bishop), a communion in which the pope functions as the instrument of unity in collegiality and co-responsibility with other bishops. Furthermore, *EA* emphasizes the gathering of the local church around the bishop, making him the center of unity, whereas the FABC emphasizes the basic equality of all the members of the local church ("as brothers and sisters").

[18] For an extended discussion of communion ecclesiology, see J.-M. R. Tillard, *Church of Churches: The Ecclesiology of Communion*, trans. R. C. De Peaux (Collegeville, Minn.: The Liturgical Press, 1992).

[19] For a theology of the Trinity as a communion and *perichoresis* of persons, see Leonardo Boff, *Trinity and Society*, trans. Paul Burns (Maryknoll, N.Y.: Orbis Books, 1986).

insistence on the hierarchical structure of the church tends to obscure and minimize it, but also because it goes against the class consciousness of many Asian societies.

Furthermore, this vision of church as a communion of communities and its corollary of fundamental equality are the sine qua non conditions for the fulfillment of the church's mission. Without being a communion, the church cannot fulfill its mission, since the church is, as intimated above, nothing more than the bond of communion between God and humanity and among humans themselves. As the exhortation puts it tersely, "Communion and mission go hand in hand" (*EA*, 24).

2. This pastoral "discipleship of equals" leads to the second characteristic of the new way of being church in Asia, that is, the participatory and collaborative nature of all the ministries in the church: "It is a *participatory* Church where the gifts that the Holy Spirit gives to all the faithful—lay, Religious, and cleric alike—are recognized and activated, so that the Church may be built up and its mission realized."[20] This participatory nature of the church must be lived out not only in the local church but also among all the local churches, including the church of Rome, of course, with due recognition of the papal primacy. In this context it is encouraging to read in the exhortation the following affirmation: "It is in fact within the perspective of ecclesial communion that the universal authority of the successor of Peter shines forth more clearly, not primarily as juridical power over the local churches, but above all as a pastoral primacy at the service of the unity of faith and life of the whole people of God" (*EA*, 25). A "pastoral primacy" must do everything possible to foster co-responsibility and participation of all the local churches in the triple ministry of teaching, sanctification, and service in the church and must be held accountable to this task so that these words do not remain at the level of pious rhetoric but are productive of concrete structures and actions.

If the Asian Synod proved that the Asian churches do have something vital to teach the church of Rome and the church universal, then the magisterium in the church can no longer be conceived as a one-way street from Rome to the other local churches. Instead, there must be *mutual* learning and teaching, *mutual* encouragement and correction between the church of Rome and the other churches, indeed among all the local churches. Only in this way can correction be made of the widespread perception, especially in countries with so-called

---

[20] *For All Peoples*, 1:287 (no. 8.1.2). See also ibid., 56 (no. 7.6): "It [the church] is a community of authentic *participation and co-responsibility*, where genuine sharing of gifts and responsibilities obtains, where the talents and charisms of each one are accepted and exercised in diverse ministries, and where all are schooled to the attitudes and practices of mutual listening and dialogue, common discernment of the Spirit, common witness and collaborative action." The exhortation also recognizes this participatory character of the church but emphasizes the fact that each person must live his or her "proper vocation" and perform his or her "proper role" (*EA*, 25). There is here a concern to maintain a clear distinction of roles in ministry, whereas the FABC is concerned that all people with their varied gifts have the opportunity to participate in the ministry of the church.

national or patriotic churches, that the Christian church in Asia is a foreign (indeed, international) organization, comparable to a multinational corporation, that must take orders from a foreign power.

In this context it may be useful to point out that a certain language to describe the relationship between the local bishop and the bishop of Rome, traditional though it is in some ecclesiastical circles, should be avoided to obviate misunderstanding. I refer to words such as *loyalty* and *obedience* to characterize the attitude of bishops to the pope; to Asian ears these terms inevitably suggest oaths of submission of vassals to their lords in a feudal system. In the church loyalty is owed to no one but Christ, and the bishop is not beholden to the pope for his episcopal office nor is he the pope's vicar. It is theologically much more appropriate to describe and live the relationship between the local church and the pope in terms of collegiality and solidarity. Only in this way can the church's teaching office and the pope's ministry of promoting unity be effectively exercised, learning from the varied and rich experiences of being church from all corners of the globe and welcoming respectful but frank warning and correction when errors of intellectual narrowness, moral arrogance, and spiritual blindness have been committed.

3. The third characteristic of a new way of being church in Asia is the *dialogical* spirit: "Built in the hearts of people, it is a church that faithfully and lovingly witnesses to the Risen Lord and reaches out to people of other faiths and persuasions in a dialogue of life towards the integral liberation of all."[21] Ever since its first plenary assembly in Taipei, Taiwan (1974), the FABC has repeatedly insisted that the primary task of the Asian churches is the proclamation of the gospel. But it has also maintained no less frequently that the way to fulfill this task in Asia is by way of dialogue, indeed a triple dialogue, with Asian cultures, Asian religions, and Asians themselves, especially the poor.[22] The exhortation reiterates the necessity of this triple dialogue. In the dialogue with the Asian cultures (inculturation), the exhortation highlights the areas of theology, liturgy, and the Bible (*EA*, 22). In the dialogue with other religious traditions, the document emphasizes ecumenical and interreligious dialogue. It quotes approvingly proposition 41 of the synod: "Interreligious relations are best developed in a context of openness to other believers, a willingness to listen and the desire to respect and understand others in their differences. For all this, love of others is indispensable. This should result in collaboration, harmony and mutual enrichment" (*EA*, 31). In the dialogue with the poor, the exhortation affirms the necessity of the preferential love of the poor (in particular, migrants, indigenous and tribal people, and women and children), defense of human life, health care, education, peacemaking, cancellation of foreign debts, and protection of the environment (*EA*, 32-41). There is no doubt that if the Christian church is to become truly *of* Asia, Asian Christians must be engaged, relentlessly and wholeheartedly, in this triple "dialogue of life and heart" and in

---

[21] *For All Peoples*, 1:287-88 (no. 8.1.3).

[22] For the intrinsic connection between the proclamation of the gospel and dialogue in its triple form, see ibid., 1:13-16.

this way fulfill their inalienable right and duty of proclaiming Jesus to their fellow Asians.[23]

In this context of the proclamation of the gospel and the triple dialogue with Asian cultures, religions, and the poor, it may be appropriate to raise the issue of how to proclaim Christ as the savior and as the only savior in Asia. The exhortation affirms that "there can be no true evangelization without the explicit proclamation of Jesus as Lord" (*EA*, 19) and that this proclamation "is prompted not by sectarian impulse nor the spirit of proselytism nor any sense of superiority" but "in obedience to Christ's command" (*EA*, 20). Therefore, the proclamation must be done with a twofold respect: "respect for man in his quest for answers to the deepest questions of his life and respect for the action of the Spirit in man" (*EA*, 20).

As to how to proclaim that Jesus is the *only* savior, the document frankly recognizes that this proclamation is "fraught with philosophical, cultural and theological difficulties, especially in light of the beliefs of Asia's great religions, deeply intertwined with cultural values and specific world views" (*EA*, 20). This difficulty is compounded by the fact that, as has been mentioned above, Christ is perceived as foreign to Asia, as a Western rather than an Asian figure. Here the exhortation deserves praise for recommending (1) a *gradual* pedagogy in the proclamation that Christ is the only savior,[24] (2) the use of narratives to complement ontological categories in this proclamation,[25] and (3) the legitimate variety of approaches to the proclamation of Jesus.[26]

This is not the place to enter the theological debate regarding exclusivism, inclusivism and pluralism,[27] but in my judgment, the issue of Jesus as the only

---

[23] For a discussion of mission in the form of this triple dialogue, see Peter C. Phan, "Christian Mission in Contemporary Theology," *Indian Theological Studies* 31/4 (1994): 297-347.

[24] *EA*, 20.

[25] *EA*, 20: "In general, narrative methods akin to Asian cultural forms are to be preferred. In fact, the proclamation of Jesus Christ can most effectively be made by narrating his story as the Gospels do. The ontological notions involved, which must always be presupposed and expressed in presenting Jesus, can be complemented by more relational, historical and even cosmic perspectives." The question can be raised as to how "the ontological notions" can be "expressed in presenting Jesus" when Jesus is presented to billions of Asians whose world is as removed from the Hellenistic philosophical categories in which classical Christology is couched as heaven from earth. Furthermore, why should the ontological notions be those of Greek metaphysics and not those of Asian philosophies?

[26] While accepting pluralism in Christology, *EA* insists that "in all evangelizing work, however, it is the complete truth of Jesus Christ that must be proclaimed. Emphasizing certain aspects of the inexhaustible mystery of Jesus is both legitimate and necessary in gradually introducing Christ to a person, but this cannot be allowed to compromise the integrity of the faith" (*EA*, 23). The vexing question is how this "complete truth of Jesus Christ" is to be presented to Asians.

[27] For a magisterial study of religious pluralism and the role of Christ, see Jacques Dupuis, *Toward a Christian Theology of Religious Pluralism* (Maryknoll, N.Y.: Orbis Books, 1997). See also Peter C. Phan, ed., *Christianity and the Wider Ecumenism* (New York: Paragon House, 1990).

savior, interesting though it may be in *theology*, is a red herring in preaching and catechesis. The immediate goal of the proclamation of the gospel is to enable a person to accept Jesus as his or her "personal savior," to use a favorite phrase of Pentecostal Christians, and not as the "only savior." It is this personal and total commitment of the catechumen to Jesus that is being promoted, not the rejection of *possible* ways in which God can reach *other* people, a possibility that can no longer be denied after Vatican II. The vital question is not whether and how *other* people can be saved, but rather, how *I* can fully enter a personal relationship with God. Once a person has found that Jesus is the way to reach God, then out of this personal experience he or she can bear witness to this fact to others. The strength and fervor of this witness are born not out of the theological conviction that Jesus is the *only* savior but out of the deep experience that he is the savior *for me*. Were I to be asked questions about other religions and savior figures, I would have to recognize, joyfully and gratefully, their various good elements and the saving presence of God's Spirit in them. But I will testify to Jesus as *my* way to God and invite others to try out this way for themselves. If they accept Jesus as their personal way to God, then I will have shown that Jesus is the universal and only savior, that is, savior for me as well as for others.[28]

4. The fourth and last feature of the new way of being church in Asia is *prophecy*. The church is "a leaven of transformation in this world and serves as a *prophetic sign* daring to point beyond this world to the ineffable Kingdom that is yet fully to come."[29] As far as Asia is concerned, in being "a leaven of transformation in this world," Christianity must give up its ambition, so enthusiastically endorsed in many missionary quarters at the beginning of the twentieth century, to convert the majority of Asians to Christ.[30] The report of the demise of Asian religions was premature and vastly exaggerated. In Asia, where Christians still form but a minuscule part of the population after four hundred years of mission, and where non-Christian religions have recently staged a vigorous revival, the prospect of a massive conversion of Asians to the Christian faith is utterly unlikely. Christians in Asia must come to terms with the fact that they are destined to remain for the foreseeable future a "small remnant" who must journey with adherents of other religions toward the eschatological kingdom of God.

The objective of the church's mission of "making disciples of all nations" (Mt 28:19) in Asia cannot be adding as many members to the church as possible, even though baptism "in the name of the Father, and of the Son, and of the Holy Spirit" (Mt 28:19) remains the desirable outcome of the church's mission.

---

[28] For a discussion of the uniqueness and universality of Jesus, see Peter C. Phan, "The Claim of Uniqueness and Universality in Interreligious Dialogue," *Indian Theological Studies* 31/1 (1994): 44-66.

[29] *For All Peoples*, 1:288 (no. 8.1.4).

[30] Recall the optimism of the World Mission Conference at Edinburgh in 1910, as expressed by its leader, John R. Mott, and the motto of the Student Volunteer Fellowship: "The evangelization of the world in our own generation." For considerations of the factors making such a goal no longer possible, see Thomas Thangaraj, *The Common Task: A Theology of Christian Mission* (Nashville, Tenn.: Abingdon, 1999), 16-30.

Rather, the primary task of the church is to become a credible "prophetic sign" of the coming reign of God. This new focus of the church's mission must be the light guiding the ordering of its priorities and the choice of its policies, which must not aim at serving the internal interests of the church but the proclamation of the gospel through the triple dialogue mentioned above.

One helpful way to describe this mission of the church is, as Thomas Thangaraj has proposed, to see it as part and fulfillment of the mission of humanity itself, which is composed of three basic tasks: responsibility, solidarity, and mutuality. By *responsibility* Thangaraj means that humans are beings that go forth from themselves and come back to themselves in their reflexive consciousness, interpret themselves, and with a sense of accountability take responsibility for themselves and their actions. They must perform this task in solidarity with one another and mutuality for one another.[31] What the Christian mission adds to the mission of humanity from its faith perspective is to inform these three tasks with a new modality: *crucified* responsibility, *liberative* solidarity, and *eschatological* mutuality.[32]

As a consequence of this view of mission, the churches of Asia must form not only Basic Christian Communities, which the exhortation highly recommends,[33] but also Basic Human Communities. Given the urgent need of Asian Christians to collaborate with their fellow Asians in the task of human promotion, the second kind of community is no less necessary than the first for the church to become a credible prophetic sign of the reign of God.[34] This kind of community broadens the concerns of Christians beyond the narrow walls of their churches and puts them in constant dialogue of life and heart with followers of other religions and even nonbelievers.

DISCOVERING THEIR OWN IDENTITY

"If the Asian churches do not discover their own identity, they will have no future."[35] These prophetic words of the Asian Colloquium on Ministries in the church held in Hong Kong on 5 March 1977 were true then and will be even truer during the post-synodal era. Since then, the FABC has been trying to

---

[31] See Thangaraj, *The Common Task*, 49-58. For Thangaraj, the *missio humanitatis* is "*an act of taking responsibility, in the mode of solidarity, shot through with a spirit of mutuality*" (58).

[32] See ibid., 64-76.

[33] *EA* accepts the synod fathers' emphasis on "the value of basic ecclesial communities as an effective way of promoting communion and participation in parishes and dioceses and as a genuine force for evangelization . . . a solid starting point for building a new society, the expression of a civilization of love" (*EA*, 25).

[34] On Basic Human Communities, see Aloysius Pieris, *Fire and Water: Basic Issues in Asian Buddhism and Christianity* (Maryknoll, N.Y.: Orbis Books, 1996): "What happens in the BHCs is a veritable *symbiosis* of religions. Each religion, challenged by the other religion's unique approach to the liberationist aspiration of the poor . . . discovers and renames itself in its specificity in response to the other approaches" (161).

[35] *For All Peoples*, 1:70 (no. 14.ii).

develop a pastoral approach designed to implement this Asian way of being church called "Asian Integral Pastoral Approach towards a New Way of Being Church in Asia (ASIPA)."[36] The goal is to develop "genuine Christian communities in Asia—Asian in their way of thinking, praying, living, communicating their own Christ-experience to others."[37]

The significance of the Asian Synod and *Ecclesia in Asia* lies, I have argued, not so much in what they say as in the recognition that the churches of Asia have come of age and must continue to pursue the task of becoming *Asian*, relentlessly, courageously, creatively. Only in this way can the Christian church fulfill its missionary vocation, which is the task of the entire church.[38] It is only by living out a new way of being church that Asian Christians will make true what the exhortation states as a fact: "Contemplating Jesus in his human nature, the peoples of Asia find their deepest questions answered, their hopes fulfilled, their dignity uplifted and their despair conquered" (*EA*, 14).

---

[36] See ibid., 2:107-11, 137-39.

[37] Ibid., 1:70 (no. 14.ii).

[38] It is interesting to note that in describing the missionary task of the church, *EA* begins with the pastors—bishops and priests—then proceeds to religious and the laity, in the descending order of importance, whereas the FABC has consistently focused on the primary role of the laity, especially women. Clearly, this variance is not merely rhetorical but indicates an important difference in ecclesiology.

9

Human Development and Evangelization

THE FIRST TO THE SIXTH PLENARY ASSEMBLY
OF THE FEDERATION OF ASIAN BISHOPS' CONFERENCES

This chapter examines the relationship between human development and the church's evangelizing mission as understood in recent Asian theology. One way to carry out this task is to review and evaluate the statements and declarations of the Federation of Asian Bishops' Conferences (FABC) and their various committees and institutes.[1]

The FABC was founded in the wake of the 1970 Asian Bishops' meeting in Manila, Philippines.[2] Its influence on the Asian churches has been deemed to be positive.[3] From its inception to 1985 the FABC held six plenary assemblies,

---

[1] For an assessment of the FABC's theology of inculturation, see Stephen Bevans, "Inculturation of Theology in Asia: The Federation of Asian Bishops' Conferences, 1970-1995," *Studia Missionalia* 45 (1996): 1-23.

[2] For a brief history of the FABC, see C. G. Arévalo, "The Time of the Heirs," in *For All the Peoples of Asia: Federation of Asian Bishops' Conferences. Documents from 1970 to 1991*, ed. Gaudencio Rosales and C. G. Arévalo (Maryknoll, N.Y.: Orbis Books, 1992; Quezon City, Philippines: Claretian Publications, 1992), xv-xxii. For Arévalo, the founding of the FABC represented "an increasing communion among the local Asian churches"and marked "the decisive 'turning to history,' a movement toward realizing a Church in Asia" (xvi).

For later statements, see Franz-Josef Eilers, ed., *For All the Peoples of Asia: Federation of Asian Bishops' Conferences. Documents from 1992 to 1996* (Quezon City, Philippines: Claretian Publications, 1997). These two statements will be cited hereafter as *For All Peoples*, vol. 1 and vol. 2 respectively.

[3] For an overview and assessment of the impact of the FABC on the Asian churches, see Felix Wilfred, "The Federation of Asian Bishops' Conferences (FABC): Orientations, Challenges and Impact," in *For All Peoples*, 1:xxiii-xxx. Wilfred notes that "the FABC has created horizontal communication between the bishops and the bishops' conferences; it has fostered a spirit of collegiality, community and cooperation among them" (xxix). However, he also points out that because the Asian churches, despite real similarities among themselves, are not homogeneous "the FABC can speak only in general terms and cannot address itself specifically to concrete situations" and that because the resources at the disposal of Asian bishops are so limited, "they feel helpless in implementing the grand vision of the FABC" (xxx).

which issued final statements.[4] Besides these plenary assemblies the FABC also had standing institutes, which published statements of their meetings,[5] as well as occasional colloquia, congresses, and consultations.[6] The Bishops' Institute for Social Action (BISA) held seven meetings from 1974 to 1986 and issued statements at the end of each meeting.

Though the present chapter focuses on the FABC's six plenary assemblies and the BISA's seven meetings, it is of great importance to note that for the Asian bishops it would be a serious theological error to separate social action for human development from the other two areas of the Asian churches' mission, namely, interreligious dialogue and inculturation.[7] Indeed, documents on interreligious dialogue and inculturation very often discuss at length the role of the church in promoting human development. Hence, due attention must be given to these two fields of the church's ministry as well.

Furthermore, since collective and official declarations are often the work of compromise to achieve a common viewpoint, I will highlight some of their diversities by drawing on the writings of contemporary, especially Asian, theologians.

HUMAN DEVELOPMENT AND EVANGELIZATION

It is very significant that the FABC's first plenary assembly chose as its theme "evangelization in modern-day Asia." It affirmed that "the preaching of Jesus Christ and His Gospel to our peoples in Asia becomes a task which today assumes an urgency, a necessity and magnitude unmatched in the history of our Faith in this part of the world."[8]

However, in the "new age of mission," says the FABC, evangelization can no longer be understood as a "one-way movement from the 'older churches' to the 'younger churches,' from the churches of the old Christendom to the churches of the colonial lands."[9] Rather, "every local church *is* and cannot be but missionary. Every local church is 'sent' by Christ and the Father to bring the Gospel to its surrounding milieux, and to bear it also into all the world. For every local church this is a *primary task*."[10] Furthermore, evangelization cannot be

---

[4] The locations and dates of the six plenary assemblies are Taipei (April 1974), Calcutta (November 1978), Bangkok (October 1982), Tokyo (September 1986), Bandung (July 1990), and Manila (January 1995).

[5] The bishops' institutes include those for Missionary Apostolate (BIMA), for Interreligious Affairs on the Theology of Dialogue (BIRA), for Lay Apostolate (BILA), and most significantly for our discussion, for Social Action (BISA).

[6] There have been a consultation on Christian presence among Muslims in Asia (1983), an international congress on mission (1979), and two colloquia, one on ministries in the church (1977) and the other on the church in Asia and global transformation (1997).

[7] There were twelve meetings of the BIRA from 1984 to 1991. For the FABC's theology of inculturation, see Bevans, "Inculturation of Theology in Asia."

[8] *For All Peoples*, 1:13 (no. 8). The BIMA III also affirms that the proclamation of Jesus Christ to those who do not yet believe in him remains a priority: "*The necessity of first proclamation has lost none of its urgency in Asia,* where Christians constitute a very small minority" (ibid., 1:104 [no. 9]).

[9] Ibid., 1:130 (no. 14).

[10] Ibid.

conceived as simply a unidirectional proclamation of the good news to a particular culture, a sort of monologue in which only the church speaks and the people simply listen. Rather, according to the FABC, the "essential mode" in which evangelization is carried out in Asia today must be "dialogue," more precisely, "through a more resolute, more creative and yet truly discerning and responsible inculturation; through inter-religious dialogue undertaken in all seriousness; through solidarity and sharing with the poor and the advocacy of human rights."[11]

With regard to the third form of dialogue, namely, dialogue with the people, especially the poor, its goal is "total human development" or "integral human development."[12] The BISA III affirms: "We need to strive for a new society, so that all men may reach full human development. Our work has to be for the development of the whole man and every man. This wholeness of man includes not only individual personal fulfillment, but the growth and blossoming of the whole reality on earth."[13]

It is clear, then, that for the FABC, human development (1) is an *essential* dimension of the evangelizing mission of the church and (2) must aim at the *total* person.

Human Development as a Constitutive Dimension of Evangelization

One point repeatedly stressed by the FABC is that human development and progress in all its aspects—political, social, economic, technological, and cultural—is an intrinsic and constitutive dimension of the church's evangelizing mission. One text frequently invoked by the Asian bishops is the 1971 Synod of Bishops' *Justice in the World,* which affirms that "action in behalf of justice and participation in the transformation of the world fully appear to us as a constitutive dimension of the preaching of the Gospel, that is, of the mission of the Church for the redemption of the human race and its liberation from every oppressive situation."[14] "Human Development," says the BISA V, "is the profound concept that translates sharply for our time the simple and fundamental command of the Gospel that we love one another."[15]

If the link between evangelization and work for human development is not adventitious but essential, it is made more crucial and urgent for the Asian churches, the FABC consistently argues, by the situation of massive poverty and pervasive oppression in all Asian countries. In its first plenary assembly, the FABC declares: "It is our belief that it is from the material deprivation of our poor people, as well as their tremendous human potential, and from their aspirations for a more fully human and brotherly world, that Christ is calling the

---

[11] Ibid., 1:131 (no. 19).
[12] These two expressions are often used by the FABC to characterize the kind of human progress that the church seeks to promote.
[13] *For All Peoples,* 1:208 (no. 5).
[14] Ibid., 1:15-16 (no. 22); 1:20 (no. 5); 1:21 (no. 9); 1:23 (no. 18); 1:208 (no. 4).
[15] Ibid., 1:218 (no. 6).

churches of Asia."[16] Again: "Since millions in Asia are poor, the Church in Asia must be the Church of the poor. One element in holiness, here, is the practice of justice. Evangelization and development are not opposed. In Asia today they are integral parts of preaching the Gospel."[17]

Integral, Total Development

Another idea consistently developed by the FABC is that the human development which the church seeks to promote must be total or integral. This was forcefully expressed at the 1970 historic meeting of 180 Asian bishops in Manila

---

[16] Ibid., 1:16 (no. 22). The second plenary assembly, whose theme is prayer as the life of the church of Asia, affirms: "Far from alienating us from sharing in man's responsibility for the world and for the establishment of just and loving relationships among men and groups in society, prayer commits us to the true liberation of persons. It binds us to solidarity with the poor and the powerless, the marginalized and oppressed in our societies" (ibid., 1:33 [no. 23]). The third plenary assembly, whose theme is the church as a community of faith in Asia, again stresses this urgency: "Our theological vision must be turned ever more resolutely to the Church's responsibility in the world, in the public spheres, in the construction of a more fully human future for Asian peoples. We must go beyond merely seconding Pope John Paul's words, that 'the preference for the poor is a Christian preference,' and that 'it expresses the concern of Christ who came to proclaim a message of salvation to the poor, . . . the poor who are indeed loved by (the) God . . . who guarantees their rights.' We must now make them the real pattern of our daily praxis" (ibid., 1:60 [no. 17.1]). The fourth plenary assembly, whose theme is the vocation and mission of the laity in the church and in the world of Asia, asserts: "Deep in the heart of Asia, the Paschal Mystery of Jesus is being remembered, becomes present and is relived. The immersion into the darkness of suffering, pain, death and despair brings the light of the Resurrection—its hope, justice, love and peace, integral liberation. This we believe is the promise of the Father" (ibid., 1:178 [no. 1.4]). The fifth plenary assembly, whose theme is journeying together toward the third millennium, recognizes the challenge of continuing injustice for the church's evangelizing mission: "We evangelize because the Gospel is *leaven* for liberation and for the transformation of society. Our Asian world needs the values of the Kingdom and of Christ in order to bring about the human development, justice, peace and harmony with God, among peoples and with all creation that the peoples of Asia long for" (ibid., 1:281 [no. 3.2.5]). Finally, the sixth assembly, whose theme is Christian discipleship in Asia today in service to life, asserts: "Like Jesus, we have to 'pitch our tents' in the midst of all humanity building a better world, but especially among the suffering and the poor, the marginalized and the downtrodden of Asia. In profound 'solidarity with suffering humanity' and led by the Spirit of life, we need to immerse ourselves in Asia's cultures of poverty and deprivation, from whose depths the aspirations for love and life are most poignant and compelling. Serving life demands communion with every woman and man seeking and struggling for life, in the way of Jesus' solidarity with humanity" (*Christian Discipleship in Asia Today: Service to Life*, no. 14.2, in *For All Peoples*, 2:8; hereafter cited as *Christian Discipleship*).

[17] *For All Peoples*, 1:23 (no. 18). The BIMA II in 1980 noted: "Among the forms of evangelization called for in our South Asian context our attention was first drawn to the need to promote integral human development and to witness to justice in our societies. . . . We stressed the need for our Churches to stand in protest wherever human rights are denied, irrespective of creed and caste, and to denounce structures of society which perpetuate an unjust social order" (1:100 [no. 12]).

on the occasion of Paul VI's visit to the Philippines. Their message, which has served as the theological manifesto for the FABC's subsequent plenary assemblies, states: "Resolutely we commit ourselves to the concern for the *total development* of our peoples. We believe that man's humanity is God's gift and making, and its promotion a task and duty laid on all of us by Him."[18] The sixth plenary assembly expresses this integral development in terms of "holistic life": "Ours is a vision of *holistic life*, life that is achieved and entrusted to every person and every community of persons, regardless of gender, creed or culture, class or color. It is the fruit of integral development, the authentic development of the whole person and of every person."[19]

This total or integral nature of human development is understood in four senses. First, human development must embrace all the dimensions of the human person as a unity of body-psyche-spirit. The FABC explicitly rejects the reduction of human development to economic and technological progress. As will be seen below, it is precisely this reductionism that, according to the FABC, is causing havoc among the Asian peoples. In particular, with regard to the process of modernization, the FABC, while recognizing its benefits for the future of Asia, is aware that

> modernization often leads to social and cultural dislocation. Traditional values and attitudes are called into question. Traditional symbols lose their power. The beneficiaries of modernization are too often infected with secularism, materialism and consumerism. In some countries there has arisen a new middle class which is highly consumeristic and competitive, and in general insensitive and indifferent to the overwhelming majority of poor and marginalized people.[20]

Second, total human development means that all resources and means, not only technological and material ones, should be pressed into service. In particular, the FABC singles out prayer as an effective means to achieve "integral human development": "Christian prayer is necessary for genuine human liberation and development, and to bring man to his full stature as a son of God."[21]

Third, in order to be total and integral, the church's efforts for human development must go hand in hand with the other two components of its mission, namely, inculturation and interreligious dialogue. Indeed, it is part of the originality and depth of the FABC's theology of human development that it is not conceived as an activity the church undertakes in parallel to dialogue with other religions and inculturation but as intimately intertwined with these two activities,

---

[18] Ibid., 1:6 (no. 21). Emphasis added.

[19] *Christian Discipleship*, no. 10.

[20] *For All Peoples*, 1:276 (no. 2.1.6).

[21] Ibid., 1:41 (no. 16). Note that the two terms *development* and *liberation* are often used together, given the fact that in Asia lack of full human development is the result of oppressive structures. The FABC notes that these two terms are to be understood in the sense given them by *Populorum Progressio* and *Evangelii Nuntiandi*. See ibid., 1:58n.

whose success conditions the full development of the human person in Asia. The FABC repeatedly links the three ministries together:

These are the elements of crucial importance in the task of preaching the Gospel in Asia today:
— *Inculturation*, which renders the local church truly present within the life of our people.
— *Dialogue* with the great Asian religions, which brings them into contact with the Gospel, so that the Word in them may come to full flower.
— *Service of the poor*, uniting with them in the struggle for a more human world.[22]

Fourth, human development, to be total and integral, must go beyond the human family and be extended to the cosmos as such. The BISA VII underlines the ecological motif of the FABC's understanding of human development:

A new spirituality that will suffuse evangelization and embrace the plan of God for the whole creation is imperative. Mere individual salvation is not enough; salvation must be for the whole person, all people and even for the cosmos. This spirituality must not be inward looking but must place the Church at the service of the whole human race.[23]

In sum, for the FABC, human development is not merely an ethical injunction but a strict imperative and a constitutive dimension of the church's evangelizing mission. Furthermore, it must aim at the total and integral perfection of the human person as a unity of body, soul, and spirit; of the human community; and of the cosmos. It must avail itself of all the means and resources available and must be carried out in tandem with inculturation and interreligious dialogue.

THE METHOD OF SOCIAL ACTION FOR HUMAN DEVELOPMENT

The FABC is deeply aware that though human development is an essential part of the proclamation of the gospel, the gospel itself does not provide ready-made solutions for the social, political, economic, and cultural problems of contemporary Asia: "The need has been felt to analyse critically and technically the problems we are faced with. We cannot jump from our faith experience to the

---

[22] Ibid., 1:23 (no. 20).
[23] Ibid., 1:230 (no. 5). The BISA VII is here echoing and expanding a statement of the BISA VI: "The task of evangelization in the field of human development is not worthy of the name unless it is suffused with spirituality. This spirituality embraces the plan of God for the whole creation. It is a spirituality that cannot be reduced to merely individual salvation but embraces the whole man and all men and the rest of creation" (1:226 [no. 18]).

concrete decisions of social action without due technical investigations and due account of the ideologies under whose influence we are living."[24]

To help persons engaged in programs of human development arrive at appropriate policies and effective courses of action, the BISA VII has outlined a methodology called the *pastoral cycle*. It is composed of four steps. The first *(exposure-immersion)* exposes the agents of human development to and immerses them in the concrete situation of the poor with whom and for whom they work: "Exposure is like a doctor's visit for diagnosis; immersion is like the visit of a genuine friend entering into the dialogue-of-life. Exposure-Immersion . . . follows the basic principle of the Incarnation."[25]

The second step is *social analysis*. The objects to be investigated include the social, economic, political, cultural, and religious systems in society, as well as the signs of the times, the events of history, and the needs and aspirations of the people. Indeed, without this technical analysis, the International Congress on Mission points out, "the naivete of all too many Christians regarding the structural causes of poverty and injustice often leads them to the adoption of ineffective measures in their attempts to promote justice and human rights."[26] The FABC does not specify which method of social analysis is to be employed. However, it warns of the danger of "deception either by ideology or self-interest" and of incompleteness.[27]

This brings us to the third step, namely, "integration of social analysis with the religio-cultural reality, discerning not only its negative and enslaving aspects but also its positive, prophetic aspects that can inspire genuine spirituality."[28] This step requires *contemplation* in order to discover God's active presence in the society and preferential love for the poor. This contemplative dimension of human development brings the agents of social development into a sympathetic and respectful dialogue with Asia's great religions and the religiosity of the poor. Through this double dialogue, the authentic values of the

---

[24] Ibid., 1:204 (no. 9).

[25] Ibid., 1:131 (no. 8). This exposure-immersion should not be seen merely as a temporary phase, though often it takes place in a short period of time. The FABC repeatedly insists that the church must share the lives and the poverty of the people to whom it proclaims the good news: "Quite clearly, then, there is a definite path along which the Spirit has been leading the discernment of the Asian Church: the Church of Asia must become the Church of the poor" (ibid., 1:145 [no. 6]). This phase corresponds to *praxis*, which Latin American liberation theology insists is the methodological presupposition for doing theology.

[26] Ibid., 1:145 (no. 9). Indeed, almost all documents issued by the FABC and its various institutes begin with a careful analysis of the social, political, economic, cultural, and religious condition of Asia or parts of Asia as appropriate.

[27] Ibid., 1:231 (no. 9). Implicitly, the FABC considers Marxist social analysis, which was favored by early Latin American liberation theology, insufficient for the Asian situation.

[28] Ibid., 1:231 (no. 10). The FACB's sixth plenary assembly suggests that "social analysis be integrated with cultural analysis, and both subjected to faith-discernment" (ibid., 1:285 [no. 7.3.2.1.1]).

Gospel are discovered and appreciated such as "simplicity of life, genuine openness and generous sharing, community consciousness and family loyalty."[29]

The fourth step is *pastoral planning,* which seeks to complete the first three steps by formulating practical and realistic policies, strategies, and plans of action in favor of integral human development. As these policies, strategies, and plans of action are implemented, they are continuously submitted to evaluation by a review of the first three steps of the pastoral cycle.[30]

HUMAN DEVELOPMENT IN ASIA: CHALLENGES AND RESPONSES

On the basis of this pastoral cycle, what does the FABC propose for human development and progress in contemporary Asia? In other words, corresponding to the four steps of the pastoral cycle, it may be asked: (1) How does the FABC understand exposure to and immersion in the world of Asia as a part of evangelization? (2) Which problems and challenges facing the peoples of Asia and the church does it discern? (3) Which cultural and religious resources does it appeal to in formulating the church's responses to these problems and challenges? And (4) What policies, strategies, and concrete plans of action does it recommend for the church's ministry? It is impossible to answer these questions in full, given their complexity and extensive scope. I single out only the most significant elements of the FABC's documents in answering these questions, keeping in mind the chronological progression of these documents, since their focus shifted according to the events and issues that arose during the FABC's quarter-century existence.

The Asian Church's Preferential Option for the Poor

With humility and courage the Asian bishops have made the preferential option for the poor the fundamental direction of the church of Asia. At the 1970 historic meeting in Manila, they declared

> It is our resolve, first of all, to be more truly "the Church of the poor." If we are to place ourselves at the side of the multitudes in our continent, we

---

[29] Ibid., 1:232 (no. 11). Aloysius Pieris calls this step "introspection": He argues that "a 'liberation-theopraxis' in Asia that uses only the Marxist tools of *social analysis* will remain un-Asian and ineffective until it integrates the psychological tools of *introspection* which our sages have discovered" (Aloysius Pieris, *An Asian Theology of Liberation* [Maryknoll, New York: Orbis Books, 1988], 80).

[30] See *For All Peoples,* 1:232 (no. 12). There is a parallel between the FABC's "pastoral cycle" and the method of Latin American liberation theology. Clodovis Boff describes the method of liberation theology as composed of three mediations: socio-analytic mediation (=social analysis), hermeneutic mediation (=contemplation), and practical mediation (=pastoral planning). These three mediations are preceded and accompanied by praxis in favor of justice and liberation (=exposure-immersion). See Clodovis Boff, *Theology and Praxis: Epistemological Foundations,* trans. Robert R. Barr (Maryknoll, New York: Orbis Books, 1987).

must in our way of life share something of their poverty. The Church cannot set up islands of affluence in a sea of want and misery; our own personal lives must give witness to evangelical simplicity, and no man, no matter how lowly or poor, should find it hard to come to us and find in us their brothers.[31]

The church of Asia as the "church of the poor" has become the *cantus firmus* of all the documents of the FABC and its various institutes. This option for the poor, according to the FABC, is mandated not only by Jesus and his message but also by the situation in Asia, where the teeming masses labor under crushing poverty.

In the midst of this dehumanizing poverty and oppression, however, there exists a gap, as the 1979 International Congress in Mission honestly confessed, between the words the Asian church preaches and its witness: "The Church in Asia is not known by the multitudes of the poor to be passionately concerned for their rights and dignity as human beings nor selflessly committed to their total liberation from social injustice and oppression."[32]

Given the persistence of this situation, in its latest plenary assembly, in 1995, the FABC felt compelled to urge once again:

Like Jesus, we have to "pitch our tents" in the midst of all humanity building a better world, but especially among the suffering and the poor, the marginalized and the downtrodden of Asia. In profound "solidarity with suffering humanity" and led by the Spirit of life, we need to immerse ourselves in Asia's cultures of poverty and deprivation, from whose depths the aspirations of love and life are most poignant and compelling. Serving life demands communion with every woman and man seeking and struggling for life, in the way of Jesus' solidarity with humanity.[33]

The Changing Faces and Challenges of Asia

The FABC is aware that Asia is an extremely vast and varied continent, containing two-thirds of the world's population; therefore, it is impossible to provide

[31] *For All Peoples*, 1:5 (no. 19).

[32] Ibid., 1:145 (no. 8). In its third plenary assembly in 1982, the FABC is even harsher in its evaluation of the Asian churches: "How often too, our communities, especially among those more favored in life, have failed to grow in awareness of situations of social injustice, of the violation of human dignity and human rights massively present around them. . . . How indifferent and hesitant, only too often, has been our involvement in the concerns of human development and liberation; in issues where the rights of women, the poor and the powerless, are crushed; where the relationships and structures which perpetuate injustice and exploitation in society are extended and reinforced. . . . How little, in Asia, have we spoken or taken action against the oppression and degradation of women, especially among the poor and less educated, for the purposes and profits of various exploitative industries, tourism, the sex-trades, and the like" (ibid., 1:58 [9.7-9.8]). One can hardly accuse the FABC of covering up its inadequacies and failings, a practice allegedly typical of Asians to "save face."

[33] *Christian Discipleship*, no. 3.

a common description of the social, political, economic, cultural, and religious situation of Asia. Nevertheless, in order to gauge the scope of the task of human development in Asian countries, it is important to examine how the FABC, in the light of its social analysis, envisions the challenges facing Asia and the church today. Given space constraints, it is only possible to list these challenges with the help of the successive summaries given by the FABC and its institutes.

In 1983 the BISA VI asked if there were "new or old and increasing obstacles and challenges to human development in Asia in the 1980s" and answered its own question as follows:

> The new challenges that aggravate the old challenges to human development are the increasing militarization of the continent, the militant resurgence of traditional non-Christian religions like Islam, Buddhism and Hinduism and Asia's increased dependence on global economies . . . unjust trade and aid conditions, export-oriented industries and capital intensive technology, transnational corporations, agribusiness enterprises and tourism. . . , The global centers of economic power manipulate the mass media in Asian countries to create artificial needs that promote the production of luxury goods. This results in a consumerism which subtly undermines the deeply religious values of Asian cultures and erodes the moral fiber of the Asian peoples.[34]

Three years later, in 1986, the FABC's fourth plenary assembly enumerated the following problems affecting the workers:

> We likewise recognize that these dreams and efforts for integral liberation are being shattered by complex, mutually reinforcing powers that are often beyond the control of workers: the dominance of transnational corporations and large local companies in traditional industries and their incursion in agribusiness, taking advantage of cheap labor or appropriating the land of small landowners; the banning of strikes and trade unions and so repressing legitimate protests; the exodus of rural workers into already overcrowded urban slums as the cities' cheap labor; the lack of supportive organizations among the vast majority of urban workers, small landowners and landless peasants; long hours of work, harassment, job insecurity and accident hazards; deterioration of health; unemployment and underemployment. Clearly, political, economic and agricultural structures have made both urban and rural workers cogs of an anonymous productive machine, their work a dispensable commodity depending only on the law of supply and demand.[35]

In particular, the fourth plenary assembly singled out the plight of Asian women:

---

[34] *For All Peoples*, 1:224 (no. 5).
[35] Ibid., 1:187-88 (no. 3.7.2).

International media have highlighted how tourism and the entertainment industries have exploited, degraded and dehumanized Asian women. . . . Many are the injustices heaped upon them because of the traditional societies which discriminate against them and because of the new economic and industrial situations. Dowry, forced marriages, wife-beating and destruction of female fetuses weigh heavily on them, driving many to desperation and even suicide. Modern industry exploits their work. . . . There is discrimination against them in the employment policies, and as domestic workers they are also abused. In general, Asian society views women as inferior.[36]

Finally, in 1995 the sixth plenary assembly listed grave threats to human development:

We were alarmed at how the global economy is ruled by market forces to the detriment of peoples' real needs. We considered the insecurity and vulnerability of migrants, refugees, the displaced ethnic and indigenous peoples, and the pain and agonies of exploited workers, especially the child laborers in our countries. . . . We recognized the growing violence, terrorism, conflicts and nuclear proliferation fueled by the arms race and greed for profit. . . . In the area of religious pluralism, we reflected on the growing fundamentalist extremism and fanaticism discriminating and excluding people who belong to other religious traditions. . . . As we reflected on these negative areas, we could not ignore the immense damage to the ecosystem of our planet which offends justice and the rights of people.[37]

These lists, though by no means exhaustive, of the challenges to human development in Asia seem endless and overwhelming. What is significant is that in analyzing these challenges the Asian bishops look for their structural causes:

We bishops and our experts came to see the causes of this distressing situation. Because of colonialism and feudalism and the introduction of Western classical capitalism, the traditional texture of Asian society with its inbuilt balances has been disrupted. Often the economies of these countries are not geared primarily to satisfying the requirements of the nation but rather to responding to external markets, and within the nation, not to the basic needs of people (food, housing, education, jobs) but to the demands of a consumer society. The principal beneficiaries of this system are the foreign markets and investors and the local elites. The victims are the poor who are the majority of the people.[38]

---

[36] Ibid., 1:182-83 (no. 3.3.1).

[37] *Christian Discipleship*, no. 7.

[38] *For All Peoples*, 1:212 (nos. 4 and 5). In terms of the social mediation of the method of Latin American liberation theology, the Asian bishops go beyond the *empirical* explanation (e.g., poverty as vice) and the *functional* explanation (poverty as backwardness) to the *dialectical* explanation (poverty as a collective and conflictive phenomenon, as the

As mentioned above, the Asian bishops are deeply ambivalent about modernity and the process of modernization in Asia. In particular, they strongly criticize the economic system associated with modernization, namely, capitalism or free enterprise. While recognizing that capitalism "proved its ability to organize labor for higher productivity and to unleash the modern technological imagination" and that it "has considerably liberated the entrepreneurial and managerial classes," the bishops note that "it has also degraded the working class to being a dispensable commodity."[39] On the other hand, the FABC is also highly critical of centrally planned economies or socialism. While recognizing that socialist economies "have rightly stressed that it is the workers who create the economy," the bishops point out that "they have mediated workers' control and solidarity exclusively through a centralized state. The workers are left with a new form of social domination, viz. the state."[40]

Cultural and Religious Resources

Despite the overwhelming challenges facing human development in Asia, the Asian bishops profess courage and hope. The basis for their optimistic attitude is rooted, of course, in the Christian faith, but it also springs from their conviction that Asia possesses rich resources to respond to these challenges. As the BISA I wrote with justifiable pride:

---

result of exploitation and oppression). As the first plenary assembly in 1974 said about the Asian poor: "Poor, in that they are deprived of access to material goods and resources. . . . Deprived, because they live under oppression, that is, under social, economic, and political structures which have injustice built into them" (ibid., 1:15 [no. 19]). Again, the BISA I affirmed: "Our people are deprived of the goods and opportunities to which they have a right because they are *oppressed*. They live under economic, social, and political structures which have injustice built into them" (ibid., 1:199 [no. 2]). For the three ways of understanding the cause of poverty, see Leonardo Boff and Clodovis Boff, *Introducing Liberation Theology*, trans. Paul Burns (Maryknoll, N.Y.: Orbis Books, 1987), 25-27.

[39] *For All Peoples*, 1:189 (no. 3.8.2). In 1978 the BISA IV drew an interesting parallel between contemporary Asia and nineteenth-century Europe: "The Asian nations are now living through a cycle comparable to that of 19th century Europe in which human beings and human values are sacrificed ruthlessly to maximum profits. The application of *laissez faire* economy to the already unbalanced systems of Asia, with little of the checks and balances that evolved in developed economies, demonstrates that it can be as pernicious now as it was then" (ibid., 1:212 [no. 6]).

[40] Ibid., 1:189 (no. 3.8.3). In 1978 the BISA IV rejected both Communism and classical capitalism: "Communism plays a very important role in Asia by the very fact that some 46% of all Asians live in communist states. We are aware that communism presents different faces throughout the world. But its Asian face makes us apprehensive, although we cannot deny that they also present some positive aspects. We have criticized classical capitalism because while professedly promoting economic growth, it has deprived man of the just fruits of his labor. We now criticize communism because, while professedly promoting liberation, it has deprived man of his just human rights. In their historical realization both have hindered true human development, the one creating poverty in the midst of affluence, the other destroying freedom in the pursuit of equality" (ibid., 1:213 [no. 13]).

The overwhelming majority of our people are poor, but let it be clearly understood what we mean by "poor." Our people are *not* poor as far as cultural tradition, human values, and religious insights are concerned. In these things of the spirit, they are immensely rich. . . . If, then, the Church in Southeast Asia is to be a Church of the people, it must be a Church that recognizes in what our people are rich: our Asian traditions, cultures, values.[41]

What are the resources at the disposal of the church in its efforts for human development? Again, it is only possible to list them here without much commentary. They are the teeming masses of the poor themselves, who are not only the object of evangelization but also its primary agents;[42] the Asian youth who form some 60 percent of the population with their idealism, energy, zeal, determination, and commitment;[43] Asian religions with their scriptures, rituals, spiritual and monastic traditions, their techniques of contemplation, and their commitment to social justice;[44] prayer;[45] and Asian philosophies of ontological complementarity *(yin-yang)* and cosmic harmony.[46] The bishops repeatedly recommended that these abundant resources be harnessed to meet the challenges facing human development in Asia today.

Responses and Plans of Action for Integral Human Development

The issue under consideration here is not the Asian church's specific plans for the social, political, and economic progress of Asia. Indeed, as a community

---

[41] Ibid., 1:199 (nos. 2-3).

[42] The International Congress on Mission affirms: "The poor are ultimately the privileged community and agents of salvation (as has always been the case in the history of salvation)" (ibid., 1:144 [no. 4]).

[43] On Asian youth and their role in evangelization and human development, see ibid., 1:181-82. The fourth plenary assembly says: "The youth of Asia are the Asia of today. The compulsive struggles for liberation in Asia are reflected in the pains of growth among the youth and in their deepest longings for a new world and a meaning for life. The People of God in Asia must become in a certain sense a 'Church of the young'" (ibid., 1:182 [no. 3.2.5]).

[44] The second plenary assembly says: "The spirituality characteristic of the religions of our continent stresses a deeper awareness of God and the whole self in recollection, silence and prayer, flowering in openness to others, in compassion, non-violence, generosity" (ibid., 1:35 [no. 35]).

[45] On prayer as a means for social transformation, see the entire document of the second plenary assembly in ibid., 1:29-44. One statement bears quoting: "Christian prayer is necessary for genuine human liberation and development, and to bring man to his full stature as a son of God" (ibid., 1:41 [no. 16]).

[46] The BIRA IV/11 says: "When we look into our traditional cultures and heritages, we note that they are inspired by a vision of unity. The universe is perceived as an organic whole with a web of relations knitting together each and every part of it. The nature and the human are not viewed as antagonistic to each other, but as chords in a universal symphony. The whole reality is maintained in unity through a universal rhyme *(Rta; Tao).*" See ibid., 1:319 (no. 6). Obviously, this concept of harmony and balance is vital for developing an ecological theology.

of faith, the church can only say with certainty which policies and concrete plans of action, from the moral standpoint, are acceptable insofar as they agree or conflict with the values of the gospel. But the church is unable to judge apodictically which policy and course of action will lead to a greater degree of total human development in a particular location and at a specific time. In general, as pointed out above, the church insists that any concrete plan for human development must aim at the integral, total development and liberation of the whole person, each and every person, the human community, and the cosmos itself, and ought to make use of all the resources available, not only technological and material ones.[47]

Within these parameters it is possible to enumerate some of the key recommendations put forward by the FABC for human development. First and foremost, the FABC again and again insists that the church of (and not only in) Asia must be "the church of the poor," with a conscious and effective preferential option for the poor.

Second, it also repeatedly insists that action for social, political, and economic development must be carried out in tandem with interreligious dialogue and inculturation. Without inculturation, social action is cut off from the deepest roots of the people for and with whom it is done; without interreligious dialogue, it is bereft of the transforming power of religious symbols and rituals.

Third, in connection with interreligious dialogue, the FABC recommends that in order to be effective, action for human progress be performed in cooperation with the followers of other religions. This is demanded not only because of the minuscule number of Christians in Asia and their extremely limited resources, but also because certain social evils—for example, discriminations based on the caste system and injustices caused by religious fundamentalism—cannot be eradicated without necessary changes in religious understanding and structures.[48]

Fourth, since division among Christians is a scandal to Asians and constitutes a serious obstacle for evangelization, the FABC urges that "all Christian Churches should make a joint effort at evangelizing in the measure which the imperfect union already existing among them allows."[49] It goes without saying

---

[47] See ibid., 1:213 (no. 12): "Our task, therefore, is not to propose specific blueprints for social, economic and political measure on existing situations and proposals against the values of the Gospel in order to point up directions which genuine humanization must take."

[48] Thus, with regard to the dialogue between Christianity and Hinduism, the BIRA III says: "Christianity can stress the social and structural dimensions of religious commtment and encourage every value and attitude that would give a positive role to man and his creative effort in history to build up a new humanity of justice and brotherhood, while questioning in itself the tendency to privatize and ritualize religion and its easy acceptance of the evils of the caste system" (ibid., 1:121 [no. 11]). With regard to religious revivalism and fundamentalism, the fourth plenary assembly says: "The negative aspect of the phenomenon, tending to religious dogmatism, fundamentalism and intolerance in precept and practice, has even led to violence and serious conflicts" (ibid., 1:181 [no. 3.1.9]).

[49] Ibid., 1:98 (no. 6).

that this joint effort should be extended to projects for human development as part of evangelization.

Fifth, the church cannot carry out its task of promotion of social transformation without enlarging significantly the role of the laity, especially women and youth.[50]

Sixth, in connection with the role of the laity, the FABC recommends the establishment of more Basic Christian Communities: "The basic fact is that today in our Asian context we are in the process of re-discovering that the individual Christian can best survive, grow and develop as a Christian person in the midst of a self-nourishing, self-governing, self-ministering and self-propagating Christian community."[51]

Seventh, the FABC urges that the various institutions of the church, such as high schools, colleges and universities, health-care facilities, and other social service agencies, direct their activities primarily in the service of the poor.[52]

Eighth, the use of mass media is strongly encouraged for evangelization and human development.[53]

Ninth, with regard to economic models themselves, after criticizing both classical capitalism and socialism, the FABC argues that

the future, it would seem to us, lies in pioneering new forms of worker participation in industry—ranging from the renewal of the cooperative movement to worker cooperation in mixed or privately held enterprises. This also means shaping an appropriate technology that prevents the concentration of power in the hands of a few, and supporting the use of technology in the service of labor and not the reverse. Such a model means developing small-scale technology that workers can own and control, at least as a cooperative.[54]

---

[50] On the role of the laity, see the entire document of the fourth plenary assembly on the vocation and mission of the laity in ibid., 1:178-98.

[51] Ibid., 1:77 (no. 49). Though the language here is reminiscent of the Chinese Patriotic Church with its three "selfs," the intention is not to encourage division and schism but co-responsibility and collegiality of the laity in forming truly local churches.

[52] On education for justice and human development, see ibid., 1:33-34, 156-59, 185-86, 214-15. In particular, regarding the role of Catholic universities, the FABC says: "The Catholic university is urgently asked to play a leading role in development education. Hence, the Catholic university should search for and formulate a model of human development, based on the social teachings of the Church" (158 [no. 16]). On health services, see ibid., 1:190-91: "But even greater than the concern for the renewal of our traditional health institutions should be our concern for the great masses of the poor in rural areas who are very often deprived of the basic benefits of modern medicine due to their poverty and the lack of adequate medical services" (191 [no. 3.9.6]).

[53] See ibid., 1:162-63, 186-87, 291-92. The use of media in favor of the poor is incumbent especially on the laity, especially because the mass media in Asia are predominantly controlled by authoritarian governments or by a handful of economically and politically powerful persons: "This vision will require of the People of God, especially of its leadership, a supportive stance toward the systematic formation and training of the laity to assume even greater responsibilities in the media" (187 [no. 3.6.6]).

[54] Ibid., 1:189 [no. 3.8.4]).

This is as far as the FABC has gone to recommend a particular economic system for human development appropriate for Asia, one which seems to negotiate a middle path between laissez-faire economy and centrally controlled economic development.

Tenth, the FABC is aware that the church's social action often encounters the reality of conflict. But it takes care to stress two points: First, "conflict is not necessarily violence (which needs another process of discernment), nor is it necessarily opposed to Christian charity. Secondly, conflict is often a necessary means to attain true dialogue with people in authority. The poor do not achieve this until they have shown they are no longer servile and afraid."[55]

A NEW WAY OF BEING CHURCH

By way of evaluation, it may be said, on the one hand, that the FABC's theology of human development represents no significant departure from the current social teaching of the church, especially as this has been articulated by Popes Paul VI and John Paul II. Its insistence on human development and liberation as an intrinsic dimension of evangelization and on the necessity of aiming at total and integral development echoes the teaching of Paul VI. Its criticism of capitalism and socialism reflects much of John Paul's. And, of course, even if it has not cited the works of Latin American liberation theologians, it is heavily indebted to them for its insights on the preferential option for the poor; Christ as the liberator; the church as the "church of the poor"; salvation as including social, economic, and political liberation; basic Christian communities; and social analysis as an intrinsic element of the theological method.

On the other hand, the FABC has also modified and significantly enriched the contributions of papal social teaching and Latin American liberation theology. Methodologically, in addition to social analysis, it has included "contemplation" or "introspection" in the way of doing theology.[56] Most important, it has made interreligious dialogue and inculturation necessary phases of the church's work for liberation to avoid possible distortions of a one-sided emphasis on the material and political aspects of salvation.[57] In so doing, it can avail itself of richer and vaster resources for human development that are deeply rooted in the histories and lives of the peoples of Asia.[58] As a consequence, it has expanded and enriched basic Christian communities with "basic human

---

[55] Ibid., 1:213 (no. 9).

[56] As mentioned above, the necessity of using contemplation has been repeatedly urged by Aloysius Pieris (see *An Asian Theology of Liberation*, 79-81).

[57] It may be argued that by combining these three aspects of the church's ministry, the FABC has improved upon papal teachings on human development and most Western theologies of inculturation and interreligious dialogue.

[58] For a discussion of Asian resources for doing theology, see Choan-Seng Song, *Third-Eye Theology*, rev. ed. (Maryknoll, N.Y.: Orbis Books, 1990), 1-16; idem, *Theology from the Womb of Asia* (Maryknoll, N.Y.: Orbis Books, 1986); and John C. England and Archie C. C. Lee, eds., *Doing Theology with Asian Resources* (Auckland, New Zealand: Pace Publishing, 1993).

communities."[59] Furthermore, while adopting the dialectical analysis of poverty as the result of oppression and exploitation, the FABC is much less critical
of the development model than Latin American theologians and has welcomed
the assistance of various international organizations such as the United Nations,
the World Council of Churches, Caritas Internationalis, Misereor, Sodepax, and
so on.[60]

A complete evaluation of the FABC's theology of human progress, however,
cannot limit itself to its theoretical aspects. Indeed, in all its declarations on
human development in Asia, what the FABC has been doing is proposing a new
way of being church, not in the sense of a novel abstract ecclesiology, but a new
concrete praxis for all Christians. The FABC's sixth plenary assembly, review-
ing its achievements during its twenty-five year existence, admitted as much:
"The overall thrust of activities in recent years has been to motivate the Churches
of Asia towards 'a new way of being Church,' a Church that is committed to
becoming 'a community of communities' and a credible sign of salvation and
liberation."[61]

Despite the remarkable progress of the Asian churches in the last quarter of
the century, as recently as 1991 the FABC Office of Evangelization admitted
with candor:

> The Church remains foreign in its lifestyle, in its institutional structures,
> in its worship, in its western-trained leadership and in its theology. Chris-
> tian rituals often remain formal, neither spontaneous nor particularly Asian.
> There is a gap between leaders and ordinary believers in the Church, *a
> fortiori* with members of other faiths. The Church has created a powerful
> priestly class with little lay participation. Seminary formation often alien-
> ates the seminarian from the people. Biblical, systematic and historical
> theology as taught are often unpastoral and unAsian.[62]

Again:

> The Church is often giving a counter-witness to its evangelizing mission.
> This is most notable in its lack of practical identification with the poor, its
> lack of concrete involvement in interfaith dialogue and its lack of real
> interest in interculturation. . . . The Church is an institution planted in
> Asia rather than an evangelizing community of Asia.[63]

---

[59] On "basic human community," see Aloysius Pieris, *Fire and Water: Basic Issues in
Asian Buddhism and Christianity* (Maryknoll, N.Y.: Orbis Books, 1996): "What happens in the BHCs is a veritable *symbiosis* of religions. Each religion, challenged by the
other religion's unique approach to the liberationist aspiration of the poor . . . discovers
and renames itself in its specificity in response to the other approaches" (161).

[60] For a critique of the development model, see Gustavo Gutiérrez, *A Theology of
Liberation*, trans. Sister Caridad and John Eagleson (Maryknoll, N.Y.: Orbis Books,
1991), 13-25.

[61] *Christian Discipleship*, no. 3.

[62] *For All Peoples*, 1:337 (no. 13).

[63] Ibid., 1:338 (no. 15).

Words such as these would have sounded as an anti-Christian diatribe had they not come from an official organ of the FABC itself.

This FABC's harsh criticism of the Asian churches was not prompted by self-hatred but by a deep and lively sense of the church's critical role in the present situation of Asia, indeed of the possibility of its very survival. The 1977 colloquium on ecclesial ministries expressed this self-understanding of the church in dramatic terms:

> We are fast approaching one of the most decisive turning points of world history and church history in Asia. Asia, with 60% of the planet's population, will at the turn of the century be the most populous, and probably the least Christian continent in terms of numbers. If Asian Christianity is not by then the leaven in the dough of the new Asia that is taking shape, it runs the risk of being wiped out in the dramatic events which might take place within the next few decades.[64]

Again:

> The decisive new phenomenon for Christianity in Asia will be the emergence of genuine Christian communities in Asia—Asian in their way of thinking, praying, living, communicating their own Christ-experience to others. . . . If the Asian Churches do not discover their own identity, they will have no future.[65]

With the hindsight of more than twenty years, arguments pro and con the fulfillment of this prediction may be mounted from any quarter. One thing remains indisputable, however, and that is, if the Christian church does not become "a servant Church: servant of God, servant of Christ, servant of his plan of salvation; servant of the Asian peoples, of their deep hopes, longings and aspirations; servant of the followers of other religions, of all men and women, simply and totally for others,"[66] it will cease to be the church of the gospel of Jesus Christ. And one way to become a "servant church" is for Christians fully to engage in efforts for the integral, total development and liberation of the Asian peoples.

---

[64] Ibid., 1:69 (no. 13).
[65] Ibid., 1:70 (no. 14, ii).
[66] Ibid., 1:340 (no. 23).

10

Catechesis and Catechism as Inculturation of the Christian Faith

LESSONS FROM ASIA

There are four terms in the title of this chapter—*faith, catechesis, catechism,* and *inculturation*—and it is their mutual relationships that will be the focus of my reflection. While the first three possess a distinguished pedigree in the theological lexicon, the last is a neologism, though the process to which it refers is arguably as old as salvation history and Christianity itself. In this essay I attempt to show how catechesis and in particular one of its instruments, namely, the catechism, have contributed to the inculturation of the Christian faith. To make the discussion concrete I invoke two historical examples, both from Asia, the one in the seventeenth century, the other in the twentieth, the former from Vietnam, the latter from the Philippines. I argue that the ways these two catechetical manuals attempt to make the Christian message understandable to their respective audiences provide illuminating lessons for our own catechetical task of inculturating the Christian faith in the United States today.

FAITH, CATECHESIS, INCULTURATION

One of the fundamental theses of this chapter is that there exists an intrinsic connection among faith, catechesis, and inculturation such that any one of them would be seriously defective without the other two. In the history of Christianity this trinity of ecclesial activities, like the three divine persons, has always functioned in *perichoresis*, embracing and drawing life from one another like three partners in a dance. The degree to which they have intertwined has varied, of course, according to time and place, but that they have always functioned in tandem can hardly be gainsaid.

In our times, with a deeper sense of historical conditioning, contextual dependence, and cultural pluralism, on the one hand, and with the church's becoming increasingly a worldwide church in its planetary unity as well as its profound diversity and the relative autonomy of the local churches being more fully recognized, on the other, the consciousness of the reciprocal relationship among faith, catechesis, and inculturation has emerged in greater clarity and forcefulness, not only in theological reflection but also in catechetical praxis. As a result, the *General Directory for Catechesis* has made inculturation one of the basic elements of the catechetical method.[1] Given the complexity of the three realities under consideration and their mutual relationship, a brief word on each is called for.

A Faith That Is Necessarily Inculturated

Faith as Trust and Assent

In reaction to the pre–Vatican II's one-sided emphasis on faith as the intellectual assent to a body of doctrines and the external acceptance of the symbolic, ritualistic, and disciplinary elements of the church, there has been in the aftermath of Vatican II an emphasis on faith as an interpersonal relationship with God, that is, on *fides* as *fiducia* (trust and commitment). While the retrieval of the existential dimension of faith is a theological gain with beneficial implications for ecumenical and interreligious dialogue, one must nevertheless guard against the danger of conceiving faith as a wholly inner experience, a private encounter between the individual and God, apart from the believer's socio-political, cultural, and religious contexts.[2] As far as the Christian faith is concerned, faith, as Saint Paul reminds us, comes from hearing (Rom 10:17), and what is heard includes, besides the "inner word" *(verbum internum)* of the Spirit, an external word *(verbum externum)* proclaimed by the church.[3]

Inculturated Faith

There is, then, no naked faith, unclothed in cultural forms. Christian faith, and any religious faith for that matter, is necessarily expressed in a particular culture. Faith as a personal act of total and absolute commitment to God (the *fides qua*) is always embodied in an act of adherence to a set of beliefs (the *fides quae*), celebrated in particular forms of community worship and lived according

---

[1] Congregation for the Clergy, *General Directory for Catechesis* (Vatican City: Libreria Editrice Vaticana, 1997). Hereafter cited as *GDC*.

[2] Corresponding to the different conceptions of faith are the various models of revelation. In his *Models of Revelation* (Garden City, N.Y.: Doubleday, 1983), Avery Dulles presents five models of revelation: doctrine, history, inner experience, dialectical presence, and new awareness. The conception of faith under criticism corresponds to the model of revelation as inner experience (see *Models of Revelation*, 68-83).

[3] In *The Nature of Doctrine: Religion and Theology in a Postliberal Age* (Philadelphia: Westminster, 1984) George Lindbeck notes the important role of the "external word" for the origination of faith in his critique of what he calls the "experiential-expressive model" (34), but he goes overboard in placing the priority on the external word, contradicting what he wrote elsewhere: "Turning now in more detail to the relation of religion and experience, it may be noted that this is not unilateral but dialectical. It is simplistic to say (as I earlier did) merely that religions produce experiences, for the causality is reciprocal. Patterns of experience alien to a given religion can profoundly influence it" (33).

to concrete moral norms. In fact, this unavoidable inculturation occurs on two related levels or moments. On the one hand, God's act of self-communication, to which faith is a response, did not fall straight from heaven to earth, as it were, but has taken flesh in a particular history, place, language, and culture, namely, those of the Jewish people and supremely in the life of the Jew Jesus. On the other hand, in line with this divine incarnation, our faithful response to God's self-gift in the forms of doctrines, liturgical celebrations, and moral practices necessarily takes on the contours of a particular location in time and space.

Thus, when faith and the gospel message are said to be transcultural, what is meant is not that they exist apart from a specific culture, floating above time and space, like a Platonic form. Faith and the gospel message are always and everywhere incarnated in specific cultures. Nor does it mean that there is some inner "core" in faith and the gospel message that can be detached from its historical embodiment and subsequently transplanted from culture to culture, as the seed-and-husk metaphor suggests. Indeed, just as the successive layers of the onion, which, when peeled off to reach the inner core, reveal nothing, so when the Christian faith is removed from its context-dependent doctrines, ways of worship, and moral teachings, there is no Christian core to be found. It does not follow that the celebrated distinction between faith and belief or between the gospel message and its cultural forms is invalid; indeed, such a distinction is necessary if inculturation is to be possible at all. But this distinction does not negate the fact that though faith is not identical with beliefs, and though the gospel message is not identical with its cultural expressions, faith can never exist apart from its articulation in beliefs. Similarly, the gospel message cannot exist apart from its cultural enfleshments. When Christian faith and the gospel message are said to be transcultural, what is meant is that no culture is to be regarded as incapable of and unqualified to embody such a faith and message, and therefore no culture may be absolutized as the only adequate or the privileged vehicle of the transmission of the Christian faith.[4]

Catechesis as Inculturation of the Christian Faith

Catechesis according to Recent Magisterial Documents

A glance at the Roman magisterium of the last thirty years will reveal that catechesis has occupied the lion's share of its attention. Between the *General Catechetical Directory* in 1971 and the *General Directory for Catechesis* in 1997,

---

[4] Another way to express this transcultural character of Christian faith is to say that it is a *translatable* phenomenon. Andrew Walls speaks of the "translation principle" of Christianity and argues that translation into the vernacular is the linguistic consequence of the Incarnation. See Andrew Walls, *Missionary Movement in Christian History* (Maryknoll, N.Y.: Orbis Books, 1996). Lamin Sanneh suggests that behind the translation of the Bible into the vernacular lies the theological principle that all cultures, and all the languages in which they are embodied, are equally worthy in God's eyes and therefore equally capable of bearing the divine message. See Lamin Sanneh, *Translating the Message* (Maryknoll, N.Y.: Orbis Books, 1989).

veritable *magna cartas* for catechesis have been issued: *Evangelii Nuntiandi* (1975), *Catechesi Tradendae* (1979), *Redemptoris Missio* (1990), and the *Catechism of the Catholic Church* (1992), not to mention John Paul II's many other encyclicals.[5] There is no room here to analyze in detail the teaching of the Roman magisterium on catechesis of the last three decades, but it is helpful to summarize it in the following six statements.[6]

1. Catechesis is an essential component of the church's evangelizing mission and must be understood and carried out within that perspective, not in opposition or separation from evangelization.

2. The concept of evangelization or mission itself has been vastly broadened to include not only verbal proclamation of the good news but also all other activities of the church, such as personal witness of life, preaching, liturgy of the word, sacramental celebrations, popular piety, ecumenical dialogue, fostering social justice, inculturation, and interreligious dialogue.

3. Carried out in intimate connection with these church activities, catechesis is still understood as the *teaching* of Christian doctrine directed toward the *maturation* of the faith.

4. Catechesis is also an important part of the mission *ad gentes,* the necessity of which is strongly reaffirmed.

5. Local catechisms are not made redundant by the existence of a universal catechism; on the contrary, their necessity and usefulness are strongly and repeatedly affirmed.

6. However, local catechisms should not be simply abbreviations or simplifications of the *CCC* but should be composed as part of the process of the church's evangelizing mission, namely, ecumenical dialogue, inculturation, and interreligious dialogue.

Catechesis according to the GDC

These ideas are taken over and further developed by the *GDC*. An explanation of how the *GDC* views the connection between catechesis and inculturation is in order.[7]

1. The *General Directory for Catechesis*. The *GDC* proposes to achieve a balance between the principal requirements for catechesis posited by two decades of catechetical reflections: "—on the one hand the contextualization of catechesis in evangelization as envisaged by *Evangelii Nuntiandi*;—on the other hand the appropriation of the content of the faith as presented in the *Catechism of the Catholic Church*" (*GDC*, 7). Clearly then, according to the new directory, the two issues that should guide contemporary catechesis are inculturation and

---

[5] These Roman documents will be abbreviated respectively as *GDC, EN, CT, RM,* and *CCC.*

[6] For a brief analysis of the recent teaching of the Roman magisterium on catechesis, see Peter C. Phan, "Catechesis as an Instrument of Evangelization: Reflections from the Perspective of Asia," *Studia Missionalia* 48 (1999): 290-96.

[7] See Phan, "Catechesis as an Instrument of Evangelization," 297-303.

the appropriation of the teachings contained in the *CCC*, or, to join the two issues together, the challenge for contemporary catechesis is how to inculturate the teachings of the *CCC*.[8]

2. *Evangelization*. Compared with its 1971 predecessor, the *GDC* stands out in its resolute and consistent placing of catechesis within the church's mission of evangelization. Indeed, its entire first part (one-third of its total of three hundred pages) focuses on catechesis as an intrinsic and integral task of evangelization. Here lies the relative novelty as well as the significance of the new directory. Repeating the teachings of Paul VI and John Paul II, the *GDC* sees evangelization as a complex process of transmitting divine revelation composed of "stages" or "essential moments" (*GDC*, 47-49), among which the "ministry of the word" is "a fundamental element" (*GDC*, 50). The functions of the ministry of the word in evangelization are fivefold: (1) "the primary proclamation," directed to nonbelievers, those who have chosen unbelief, those Christians who live on the margins of Christian life, and those who follow other religions; (2) pre- and post-baptismal catechesis: the catechesis of unbaptized adults in the catechumenate, the catechesis of baptized adults who wish to return to the faith or of those who need to complete their initiation, and the catechesis of children and the young; (3) "permanent catechesis" for those Christians who have been initiated into the basic elements of the Christian faith but who need constantly to nourish and deepen their faith throughout their lives; (4) the homily in the celebration of all the sacraments; and (5) theology, which is "the systematic treatment and the scientific investigation of the truths of the Faith" (*GDC*, 51).

Within the process of evangelization, catechesis is intimately related to the "primary or first proclamation." Between these two forms of the ministry of the word there is a "complementary distinction": "Catechesis, 'distinct from the primary proclamation of the Gospel,' promotes and matures initial conversion, educates the convert in the faith and incorporates him into the Christian community" (*GDC*, 61). Nevertheless, the *GDC* acknowledges that "in pastoral practice it is not always easy to define the boundaries of these activities" (*GDC*, 62), and not rarely these two forms of evangelization do need to take place simultaneously.

This first proclamation is followed by the "catechesis at the service of Christian initiation," which is "an essential 'moment' in the process of evangelization" (*GDC*, 63). This "initiatory catechesis" must be comprehensive and systematic, including not only instruction but also an "apprenticeship of the entire Christian life," and preparing to incorporate the catechized person into the community.

---

[8] For studies on the *GDC*, see Catherine Dooley, "The *General Directory for Catechesis* and the Catechism: Focus on Evangelizing," *Origins* 28/3 (1998): 33, 35-39; idem, "Baptismal Catechumenate: Model for All Catechesis," *Louvain Studies* 23 (1998): 114-23; Michael Horan and Jane Regan, *Good News in New Forms: A Companion to the* General Directory for Catechesis (Washington, D.C.: National Conference of Catechetical Leadership, 1998); Cesare Bissoli, "*Il Direttorio generale per la Catechesi:* Origine, contenuiti, confronto," *Salesianum* 60 (1998): 521-47; Maria Piera Manello, "Un nuovo *Direttorio Generale per la Catechesi*," *Rivista di scienze dell'educazione* 35/3 (1997): 425-39; and the journal *The Living Light* 34/2 and 34/4 (1997-98).

In addition to this initiatory catechesis, there is catechesis at the service of ongoing formation in the faith. This "continuing catechesis" can take different forms: study of the Bible, study of the social teaching of the church, liturgical catechesis, occasional lecture, spiritual formation, and theological instruction (*GDC*, 71).

Lastly, there is catechesis and religious instruction in schools. This instruction too is evangelization insofar as "it is called to penetrate a particular area of culture and to relate with other areas of knowledge. As an original form of the ministry of the word, it makes present the Gospel in a personal process of cultural, systematic and critical assimilation" (*GDC*, 73).

Whatever form catechesis takes, however, its fundamental tasks are promoting knowledge of the faith, liturgical education for a full, conscious and active participation in the liturgy, moral formation, and initiation to prayer (*GDC*, 85).[9] Besides these fundamental tasks, catechesis must also perform two additional tasks: educating the catechized "to live in community and to participate actively in the life and mission of the church," including its ecumenical dimension, and initiating them into the missionary work of the church, including interreligious dialogue (*GDC*, 86). All these tasks, the *GDC* insists, are necessary and mutually interdependent, each realizing in its own way the object of catechesis (*GDC*, 87).

3. *Inculturated Catechesis*. Compared with the old directory, the *GDC* has a new part in which, instead of listing the basic Christian doctrines to be communicated in catechesis, it discusses how the contents of the *CCC* should be inculturated into local churches. Obviously, this part is of great interest to our discussion here because it speaks at great length about how catechesis should be carried out and especially about how the catechism should be composed at the local level. The *GDC* insists that the gospel message is "christocentric" (*GDC*, 98) and "trinitarian" (*GDC*, 99), and that it is this "trinitarian christocentricity" that determines the internal structure, the pedagogy, and the practical implications of catechesis (*GDC*, 100). In light of this trinitarian christocentricity, the message of the gospel must be presented as a message of both salvation (*GDC*, 101) and liberation (*GDC*, 103).

The inculturation of this message of salvation and liberation is a "profound and global process and a slow journey." The *GDC* continues, "It is not simply an external adaptation designed to make the Christian message more attractive or superficially decorative. On the contrary, it means the penetration of the deepest strata of persons and peoples by the Gospel which touches them deeply, 'going to the very center and roots' of their cultures" (*GDC*, 109).

There are two basic principles governing this process: "compatibility with the Gospel and communion with the universal Church" (*GDC*, 109). With regard to catechesis, there are four concrete tasks: (1) relying on the local church, especially the catechist, as the principal factor of inculturation; (2) writing local catechisms that respond to the demands of different cultures; (3) making use of the catechumenate and catechetical institutes, incorporating, with discernment,

---

[9] These four tasks correspond to the four "pillars" of the *CCC*.

the language, symbols, and values of the cultures; and (4) offering an effective apologetics to assist the faith-culture dialogue (*GDC*, 110).

Compatibility with the gospel, which is one of the two principles governing inculturation, is further explained in terms of *integrity* or *authenticity,* comprehensiveness, and hierarchialism. By integrity or authenticity two things are meant: first, "intensive integrity," that is, a presentation of the gospel message "without ignoring certain fundamental elements, or without operating a selectivity with regard to the deposit of faith"; and second, "extensive integrity," that is, a presentation that "gradually and increasingly proposes the Christian message more amply and with greater explicitness, in accordance with the capacity of those being catechized and with the proper character of catechesis" (*GDC*, 112). By comprehensiveness is meant a coherence that is achieved by organizing the contents of the faith "around the mystery of the Most Holy Trinity, in a christocentric perspective" (*GDC*, 114). By *hierarchialism* is meant harmony that is achieved by observing the "hierarchy of truths," that is, by adhering to the fact that "some truths are based on others as of a higher priority and are illumined by them" (*GDC*, 114).[10]

4. *Contexts of Inculturation.* This inculturation of catechesis is both a need and a right of every Christian individual and Christian community, and it involves the community as community (*GDC*, 167-68). There is the need to adapt catechesis first according to age, that is, adults, infants and young children, young people, and the aged (*GDC*, 171-88), and then according to special conditions, such as the disabled and the handicapped, the marginalized (for example, immigrants, refugees, nomads, traveling people, the chronically ill, drug addicts, prisoners), professionals (for example, workers, artists, scientists, university students), and rural and urban people (*GDC*, 189-92).

The remaining two categories to which catechesis should be adapted are of special importance for catechesis in places such as Asia but also in the United States, which is becoming religiously pluralistic. The first refers to the religiously plural context, and here the *GDC* speaks of catechesis, on the one hand, and popular devotions, non-Catholic Christians, Jews, followers of other religions, and new religious movements, on the other. The *GDC* acknowledges that "Christians today live in multi-religious contexts; many, indeed, in a minority position" (*GDC*, 200). It stresses that in this context catechesis has three tasks: deepening and strengthening the identity of believers; helping Christians not only to discern the elements in those religions that are contrary to the Christian message but also to accept the seeds of the gospel that are found in them and that can sometimes constitute an authentic preparation for the gospel; and promoting a lively missionary sense among believers (*GDC*, 200).

[10] The *GDC* argues that this "hierarchy of truths" is present in the way the history of salvation is told (with Jesus Christ as the unifying center), the Apostles' Creed is formulated (with the doctrine of the Trinity as its structure), the sacraments are understood (with the eucharist occupying a unique place), moral theology is organized (with the double commandment of love of God and neighbor as its summary), and prayer is taught (with the Our Father as its heart) (115).

The last category is the socio-cultural context, and here the *GDC* discusses inculturation proper. In this context catechesis is charged with six tasks: knowing in depth the culture of persons and the extent of its penetration into their lives; recognizing the cultural dimension in the gospel itself; proclaiming the conversion demanded of cultures by the gospel; witnessing to the transcendence of the gospel over cultures; promoting a new expression of the gospel in accord with the culture being evangelized; and maintaining the content of the faith integrally (*GDC*, 203).

Catechetical inculturation follows a series of methodological steps:

> a listening in the culture of the people to discern an echo . . . of the word of God; a discernment of what has an authentic Gospel value or is at least open to the Gospel; a purification of what bears the mark of sin (passions, structures of evil) or of human frailty; an impact on people through stimulating an attitude of radical conversion to God, of dialogue, and of patient interior maturation. (*GDC*, 204)

The *GDC* also points out that catechetical inculturation must not be restricted to a few experts but must involve the whole people of God; that it must be guided and encouraged, and not forced; that it must be an expression of and mature in the community, and not exclusively the result of erudite research; and that it requires the cooperation of all the agents of catechesis (*GDC*, 206).

One important element of inculturation is language. The *GDC* states that though catechesis must make use of the forms and terms proper to the culture, nevertheless it must

> respect and value the language proper to the message, especially biblical language, as well as the historical-traditional language of the Church *(creed, liturgy)* and doctrinal language *(dogmatic formulations)*. . . . In the process of inculturating the Gospel, catechesis should not be afraid to use traditional formulae and the technical language of the faith, but it must express its meaning and demonstrate its existential importance. (*GDC*, 208)

5. *Local Catechisms*. Lastly, the *GDC*, following its predecessor, suggests three concrete steps toward catechetical inculturation: a socio-cultural and religious analysis of the state of the diocese, developing a plan of action, and elaboration of instruments and didactic aids for catechetical activity (*GDC*, 279-83). Among these, "catechisms excel all others. Their importance derives from the fact that the message transmitted by them is recognized as authentic by the Pastors of the Church" (*GDC*, 284). These local catechisms are declared to be "invaluable instruments for catechesis," because it is through them that "the Church actualizes the 'divine pedagogy' used by God himself in Revelation, adapting his language to our nature with thoughtful concern" (*GDC*, 131).

Every catechism adopted by the local church must have three characteristics. First, it is to be official, and as such qualitatively different from other catechetical aids, such as didactic texts, nonofficial catechisms, and guides. Second, it is to be "a synthetic and basic text in which the events and fundamental truths of the Christian mystery are presented in an organic way and with regard to the "hierarchy of truth." Third, it is "a reference point to inform catechesis" (*GDC*, 132).

The *GDC* insists that in elaborating this kind of catechism the local church should exercise a "mature creativity" (*GDC*, 134). It makes it clear that an inculturated local catechism is not "a mere summary of the *Catechism of the Catholic Church*" (*GDC*, 134) because the latter lacks genuine adaptations to the local conditions. Local catechisms can be diocesan, regional or national in character. Furthermore, they can be structured in different ways; for example, they can be organized according to a trinitarian structure, or the stages of salvation, or a biblical theme, or an aspect of the faith, or the liturgical year (*GDC*, 134).

In summary, the *GDC* represents a comprehensive and organic synthesis of the teachings of Paul VI and John Paul II on evangelization and catechesis. Its long-term influence and significance do not lie in any new doctrine but in its fundamental approach to catechesis as an intrinsic moment of the evangelizing mission of the church and in its strong insistence on the necessity of local catechisms that both creatively and faithfully inculturate the contents of the faith as presented by the *CCC*.

Inculturation as a Catechetical Process

Semiotics of Culture

Inculturation as a catechetical process presupposes the concept of culture. By *culture* is meant, in the words of Louis Luzbetak, "(1) a plan (2) consisting of a set of *norms*, *standards*, and associated *notions* and *beliefs* (3) for *coping* with the various demands of life, (4) shared by a *social group*, (5) *learned* by the individual from the society, and (6) organized into a *dynamic* (7) *system* of control."[11]

Semiotically, culture is composed of three dimensions.[12] First of all, as ideational, culture is a system of beliefs, values, attitudes, and rules for behavior; it provides a framework for interpreting the world and living and acting in the world. Second, as performance, culture is constituted of rituals by which the members participate in their culture in an embodied way. Third, as material, culture provides the artifacts and symbols, such as language, food, clothing, music, the plastic arts, and the creation of space, with which the members build

---

[11] Louis Luzbetak, *The Church and Cultures: New Perspectives in Missiological Anthropology* (Maryknoll, N.Y.: Orbis Books, 1988), 156.

[12] For a semiotic interpretation of culture, see Robert Schreiter, *The New Catholicity: Theology between the Global and the Local* (Maryknoll, N.Y.: Orbis Books, 1997), 29. Schreiter depends on the work of Jens Loenhoff, *Interkulturelle Verständigung. Zum Problem grenzüberschreitender Kommunikation* (Oplade: Leske und Budrich, 1992).

up their identity. All three dimensions must be taken into account in order to understand any particular culture fully.

Within the perspective of the semiotics of culture, the focus is on culture as a communication structure and process.[13] Three elements make up this communication structure and process. First, there are the *signs* or *symbols*, that is, the constituent parts of the culture. They are the *"who, what, when, where, how,* and *what kind"* forming the "surface" or "first level" of culture.[14] These signs correspond to culture as material mentioned above.

Second, there is the *message* carried by the signs. This message is constituted by the linkages among the signs revealing their "functions" (their "structural integration") and forms the *"immediate whys,"* or the "second" or "intermediate level" of culture.[15] This message may be manifest or latent to the members sharing the same culture. In addition to this intermediate meaning, there is the third level of culture, its deeper meaning, its ultimate *whys,* often referred to as the "mentality" of a people deriving from the underlying premises and assumptions of their thought processes, the values and interests of their basic attitudes, the goals and ideals of their fundamental motivating forces. This mentality (the group's "psychological integration" of culture) is revealed in the people's worldview, myths, rituals, philosophy, and religion.[16] These meanings, both intermediate and ultimate, correspond to culture as ideational.

Third, there are the codes along which the message of the signs is carried. Like the grammar of a language, codes are the basic rules according to which cultural signs function. They "encompass the rules of action of a culture, of what is done and what is not to be done. In so doing, they not only define the range of activity of the sign, but can also tell us something of basic messages."[17] They govern culture as performance.

Theological Foundation of Inculturation

By *inculturation* is meant "the penetration of the deepest strata of persons and peoples by the Gospel which touches them deeply, 'going to the very center and roots' of their cultures" (*GDC,* 109). There is, as Pope John Paul II has pointed out, a double movement in this process: penetration of the gospel into a particular socio-cultural milieu; and introduction of the people of this milieu, together with their culture, into the church (*RM,* 52). As a result, there is a *mutual* enrichment and transformation between the local culture and the Christian faith. Clearly, then, inculturation is not just a passing fad but rather a permanent and crucial task of evangelization and catechesis. As John Paul II has

---

[13] For a helpful presentation of the semiotics of culture, see Robert Schreiter, *Constructing Local Theologies* (Maryknoll, N.Y.: Orbis Books, 1985), 49-73.

[14] Luzbetak, *The Church and Cultures,* 238.

[15] Ibid.

[16] See ibid., 249-79.

[17] Schreiter, *Constructing Local Theologies,* 67.

said: "A faith that does not become culture is not fully accepted, not entirely thought out, not faithfully lived."[18]

Theologically, inculturation is deeply rooted in and governed by four fundamental doctrines of the Christian faith: creation, incarnation, the death and resurrection of Jesus, and Pentecost. The biblical stories of *creation* represent God as not only bringing all things into existence but also ordering humans to "be fruitful and multiply, and fill the earth and subdue it" (Gn 1:28). By carrying out this mandate, humans create their cultures and in this way share in God's creative power. Christians have the added task of imbuing this culture-making process with gospel values so that their faith may be inculturated into their cultures and their cultures transformed by faith. This inculturation is therefore an essential part of the mission of "cultivating" the earth that God entrusted to humanity at the dawn of history.

The goodness of God's creation has been marred by human sin, however, and as a consequence humanity and its cultures need healing and restoration. God's redemptive plan reached its climax in the incarnation, death and resurrection of Jesus. The *incarnation* of the Word has been regarded as *the* theological foundation and model of inculturation, insofar as it took place in a particular history, in a clearly circumscribed time and place. The Word of God did not assume a human "nature" abstractly conceived, but became a first-century Jew, living out with his people all the things that made up their Jewish culture. As the *GDC* says, "This is the original 'inculturation' of the Word of God and is the model of all evangelization by the Church 'called to bring the power of the Gospel into the very heart of culture and cultures'" (109). Like the incarnated Word, catechists must empty themselves of their own cultural assumptions and customs in order to enter fully into the cultures of the people they evangelize,

---

[18] John Paul II, "Address to the Italian National Congress of the Ecclesial Movement for Cultural Commitment," *Insegnamenti* V/1 (1982), 131. For helpful overviews of inculturation as a theological problem, see Marcello de C. Azevedo, "Inculturation," in *Dictionary of Fundamental Theology*, ed. René Latourelle and Rino Fisichella (New York: Crossroad, 1995), 500-510; and Hervé Carrier, "Inculturation of the Gospel," in Latourelle and Fisichella, *Dictionary of Fundamental Theology,* 510-14. General works on inculturation have recently grown by leaps and bounds. Among the most helpful, from Catholic perspectives, are Schreiter, *Constructing Local Theologies;* idem, *The New Catholicity*; Aylward Shorter, *Toward a Theology of Inculturation* (Maryknoll, N.Y.: Orbis Books, 1988); Stephen B. Bevans, *Models of Contextual Theology* (Maryknoll, N.Y.: Orbis Books, 1992); Gerald Arbuckle, *Earthing the Gospel: An Inculturation Handbook for the Pastoral Worker* (Maryknoll, N.Y.: Orbis Books, 1990); and Michael Gallagher, *Clashing Symbols: An Introduction to Faith and Culture* (New York: Paulist Press, 1998). My own works include "Contemporary Theology and Inculturation in the United States," in *The Multicultural Church: A New Landscape in U.S. Theologies*, ed. William Cenkner (New York: Paulist Press, 1996), 109-30, 176-92, "Cultural Diversity: A Blessing or a Curse for Theology and Spirituality?" *Louvain Studies* 19 (1994): 195-211; "The Christ of Asia: An Essay on Jesus as the Eldest Son and Ancestor," *Studia Missionalia* 45 (1996): 25-55; "Jesus as the Eldest Brother and Ancestor? A Vietnamese Portrait," *The Living Light* 33/1 (1996): 35-44; and "How Much Uniformity Can We Stand? How Much Unity Do We Want? Church and Worship in the Next Millennium," *Worship* 72/3 (1998): 194-210.

live like them as far as possible, and announce to them the gospel in terms taken from their cultures.

But God's redemptive acts include not only the Word's incarnation but also his *death* on the cross and *resurrection*. The Son of God did not simply assume human culture. In his death he also saved it from its sins by vanquishing the enslaving power of evil and liberated it for a new life in his resurrection. So, in inculturating the gospel catechists must not uncritically take on each and every element of a particular culture but must also purify it of its dehumanizing aspects and transform it according to the values of the gospel. Catechists "must discern, on the one hand, which riches to 'take' up as compatible with the faith; on the other, . . . must seek to 'purify' and 'transform' those criteria, modes of thought and lifestyles which are contrary to the Kingdom of God" (*GDC*, 109).

Finally, the paschal mystery also includes *Pentecost*. At his visible descent upon the world, with his diverse gifts and by the power of his unifying love, the Holy Spirit created one church out of different peoples. Guided and sustained by the Spirit, catechists will be able to recognize the presence of divine grace already at work in all cultures, even before the preaching of the gospel, and to gather up all the elements of truth and goodness and beauty present in them and integrate them into the Christian faith, so that all the peoples of the earth can profess in their own tongues the one faith in Jesus.

From the preceding reflections on how inculturation is rooted in the mysteries of creation, incarnation, death and resurrection, and Pentecost it is clear that the process of inculturating the Christian faith into local cultures is governed by two basic principles: "compatibility with the Gospel, and communion with the universal Church" (*GDC*, 109). Without the first criterion inculturation will lead to the loss of Christian identity and syncretism; without the second, it will destroy the unity of the universal church.

ALEXANDRE DE RHODES'S *CATHECHISMUS* (1651)

Inculturation through catechesis is not a one-way act from the active catechist to the passive catechized, from the culturally unmediated gospel message to the receiving culture; rather, it is an active process of interaction between the gospel *as embodied in the culture* of the catechist and the culture of the catechized. In this process of reciprocal communication there must be mutual acceptance and dialogue, critical awareness and discernment, transformation and growth on the part of both the catechist and the catechized. Both the catechist and the catechized, indeed the whole church, are active agents of inculturation.

Of course, this process of inculturation is rendered somewhat easier when the catechist and the catechized share the same culture and can be presumed to be able to understand each other, at least on the linguistic and cultural levels. It is, however, fraught with difficulties and possibilities of misunderstanding when the catechist and the catechized come from different cultures and do not even speak the same language. The history of Christian mission in China provides painful lessons in this regard, especially in connection with finding Chinese equivalents for the term *God* and the cult of ancestors and Confucius.[19]

Fortunately, mission in Asia was not only frustrated by failures in inculturation but also studded with successes, especially in catechesis. These were due not only to the oft-mentioned works of Matteo Ricci in China[20] and Roberto de Nobili in India,[21] but also to the lesser known but arguably more successful work of Alexandre de Rhodes in Vietnam. Of the three, de Rhodes wrote a catechism proper and offered explicit reflections on how to adapt catechesis to local conditions.[22]

De Rhodes's Catechetical Strategies in Vietnam

Born in Avignon, then a papal state, on 15 March 1593, de Rhodes joined the Jesuit novitiate in Rome to pursue his missionary vocation. Shortly after his ordination in 1618 de Rhodes was granted permission to go to the mission in Japan. He arrived in Macao in 1623, but because of the persecutions in Japan, he was sent to Cochinchina (now Central Vietnam) in 1624. In 1627 he was sent to Tonkin (now North Vietnam) where he worked until 1630. Exiled from Tonkin in 1630, he returned to Macao, where he remained until 1640. In 1640 he was sent for the second time to Cochinchina, where he worked off and on until 1645. Again exiled from Cochinchina in 1645, he went back to Macao and was sent to Rome to fetch temporal and spiritual help. After his arrival in Rome in 1649, he began lobbying for the establishment of the hierarchy in Vietnam. Because his plan infringed the *padroado* agreements between Portugal and the Holy See, he was dispatched to Paris in 1652 to look for missionaries to Vietnam. In 1654 he was made superior of the Jesuit mission in Persia where he died on 5 November 1660.

---

[19] For a history of the positions of Rome vis-à-vis the cult of ancestors, see George Minamiki, *The Chinese Rites Controversy from Its Beginnings to Modern Times* (Chicago: Loyola University Press, 1985).

[20] Ricci's "catechism," *T'ien-chu Shih-i*, proved enormously influential among the Chinese. For an English translation, see *The True Meaning of the Lord of Heaven*, trans. Douglas Lancashire and Peter Hu Kuo-chen (St. Louis: Institute of Jesuit Sources, 1985).

[21] Of Roberto de Nobili's voluminous writings the most important, from the catechetical perspective, is his *Kandam* or *Gnanopadesam*. For a helpful collection of de Nobili's writings in English, see Roberto de Nobili, S.J., *Preaching Wisdom to the Wise*, trans. and intro. Anand Amaladass and Francis X. Clooney (St. Louis: The Institute of Jesuit Sources, 2000).

[22] For an extensive discussion of de Rhodes's missionary work in Vietnam and his catechism, see Peter C. Phan, *Mission and Catechesis: Alexandre de Rhodes and Inculturation in Seventeenth-Century Vietnam* (Maryknoll, N.Y.: Orbis Books, 1998). For helpful histories of the catechism as a theological genre, see Pietro Braido, *Lineamenti di storia della catechesi e dei catechismi: Dal "tempo delle riforme" all' età degli imperialismi (1450-1870)* (Turin: Editrice Elle Di Ci, 1991); Berard Marthaler, *The Catechism Yesterday and Today: The Evolution of a Genre* (Collegeville, Minn.: The Liturgical Press, 1995); and Phan, *Mission and Catechesis*, 107-21.

Given the enormous success of de Rhodes's mission in Vietnam,[23] it is instructive to examine briefly how de Rhodes attempted to make the Christian message understandable to the Vietnamese, especially in his *Cathechismus*.[24] There are three important texts in which de Rhodes explains his own catechetical method, and they deserve to be quoted in full and pondered carefully.

The first text occurs in the context of de Rhodes's arrival in Tonkin in March 1627. After telling the curious crowd that had gathered around the newly arrived Portuguese merchants that he had a precious pearl to sell so cheap that everybody could afford to buy, that is, the true *way*, de Rhodes added:

Text A

Having heard of the law that they call *dao* in scholarly language and *dang* in popular language, which means the *way*, they became all the more curious to know from me what was the true law, the true way that I wanted to show them. Thereupon I talked to them about the sovereign Principle of all created beings. I decided to announce it to them under the name of the Lord of heaven and earth, finding no proper word in their language to refer to God.

Indeed, what they commonly call *Phat* or *But* designates nothing but an idol. And knowing that the cult of idols was held in high esteem by the leaders and doctors of the kingdom, I did not deem it proper to designate God with these words. Rather, I decided to employ the name used by the apostle Saint Paul when he preached to the Athenians who had set up an altar to an unknown God. This God, he said, whom they adored without knowing him, is the Lord of heaven and earth (*duc Chua troi dat*).

It was therefore under this name full of majesty even in the hearts of the pagans that I first announced to them that the true way consisted first

---

[23] According to de Rhodes, when he left Tonkin in 1630, there were 5,602 Christians after barely three years of missionary work. During his second mission in Cochinchina between 1640 and 1645, de Rhodes baptized some 3,400 people. These numbers do not tell the whole story of the success of de Rhodes's work; to be added to these statistics are his establishment of the society of catechists who carried out a highly effective work of evangelization during the Jesuits' absence from Vietnam, his contribution to the alphabetization of the Vietnamese language, and his catechetical writing.

[24] The full title of de Rhodes's catechism in Vietnamese is *Phep giang tam ngay cho ke muan chiu phep rua toi ma beao dao thanh duc Chua bloi*. Its Latin title is *Cathechismus Pro ijs, qui volunt suscipere Baptismum in octo dies divisus*. It was published in Rome in 1651 by the Propaganda Fide, with the Vietnamese and Latin texts facing each other. (Hereafter cited as *Cathechismus*.) For a discussion of the history, structure, and method of this catechism, see Phan, *Mission and Catechesis*, 107-54. Besides this catechism, de Rhodes also wrote two extremely important works on early Vietnamese Christianity: *Histoire du Royaume de Tunquin, et des grands progrez que la prédication de l'Evangile y a faits en la conversion des infidèles. Depuis l'année 1627 jusques a l'année 1646* (Lyon, 1651), hereafter cited as *Histoire du Royaume*, and *Divers voyages et missions du P. Alexandre de Rhodes en la Chine et autres Royaumes de l'Orient. Avec son retour en Europe par la Perse and l'Arménie* (Paris, 1652), hereafter cited as *Divers voyages*.

and foremost in fulfilling our legitimate duties to the Lord of heaven and earth by the means God has revealed to us.[25]

The second and most important text constitutes de Rhodes's *magna carta* of the catechetical method that he developed explicitly for the Vietnamese people:

Text B

Among those who announce the doctrine of the gospel to other kingdoms of pagans there are many who are of the opinion that it is necessary first to destroy the errors of paganism and disabuse their minds of these errone-ous views before establishing and teaching the doctrines and principles of the Christian religion. This method, they claim, follows the order God has given to a prophet, saying: I have commanded you to destroy and pull up, to build and plant. Others, as far as the most august mystery of the holy Trinity is concerned, maintain that it should be expounded to catechu-mens only after they have been disposed to receive baptism in order to avoid troubling their minds with doubts, which this most sublime and ineffable mystery might induce.

From my own experience, however, I believe that between these two options there is another method of teaching more appropriate for the people of this kingdom. This method requires that one not attack the errors of the Tonkinese sects before establishing the truths knowable by the light of natural reason, such as the truths concerning the creation of the world, the end for which the sovereign Principle of created things has ordered the rational creatures, and the obligations incumbent upon them to know and serve God. The goal is to build in the hearers' minds a sort of firm founda-tion on which the rest of their faith can be supported and not to turn them away, which often happens, by our rebutting and ridiculing their devo-tions, false though they are, and their superstitious observances.

I have often been more successful, as far as I can tell, in impressing upon them feelings of piety and natural love toward the Creator and the First Principle of their being. Then, by means of a narrative of the history of the universal flood and of the confusion of languages, I inspire in them a sense of fear of God, whom they must fear and adore. Then follows a refutation of the idolatry that, incidentally, the devil himself had not in-troduced into the world until after the flood.

I am in perfect agreement with others that we must not expound to the pagans whom we wish to convert the mysteries of the holy Trinity, the incarnation, and the passion of the Son of God, attempting to sow the holy seed of these great truths in their hearts before we have uprooted the er-rors and superstition of idolatry.

Nevertheless, I do not believe that we should wait until the time of bap-tism to propose to the catechumens the faith in the Trinity of the divine

---

[25] *Histoire du Royaume*, 129-30. All translations of de Rhodes's works are mine.

persons. On the contrary, we must begin with an exposition of this mystery, and then it will be easier to go from there to the incarnation of the Son of God, who is the Second Person, and to what he has suffered to save the world lost by sin, and to his resurrection and other mysteries of our religion. After all, this is the order and method followed by the apostles in the symbol of the faith that they have left us.

For myself, during the many years I have been engaged in teaching the pagans, I have not found anyone objecting to our faith with regard to the exposition of the incomprehensible mystery of the Trinity. On the contrary, I have always found that they have more difficulty in believing in the incarnation. The reason for this is that they do not find it strange that God, whose nature they recognize by the light of natural reason to be incomprehensible and exceeding the scope of our knowledge, is not amenable to explanation with regard to what we propose to their belief concerning God's attributes and three persons.

On the other hand, we have the greatest trouble in convincing them that the one who is pure spirit, eternal, and immortal, and who reigns in heaven crowned with glory, was clothed in the flesh, born in time, subject to death, and exposed to all sorts of shame and misery.

That is why, when it is time to propose to the catechumens the mysteries of the passion, we must do it with skill and a little differently from when we present them to Christians by observing three things. First, we must throw in much sharper relief the miraculous events happening in the death of Jesus Christ, such as nature recoiling from the crime committed against his person, the sun withdrawing its rays and refusing to shine upon the earth guilty of such an execrable sacrilege, the tombs opening up, the rocks bursting asunder, the earth shaking, and all the creatures experiencing pains at the death of their creator. From all this the conclusion is drawn that if he died, he chose to do so of his own free will and that he granted his murderers the power to kill him in order to redeem and save the human race.

Second, after explaining the great love and the wonderful virtues that Jesus Christ has shown in his suffering and death, it is appropriate to expose to them for the first time the image of the cross for their adoration, with lighted candles and other similar ceremonies of devotion.

Third, we must never explain the passion and death of the Redeemer without adding immediately the narrative of his glorious resurrection, how he rose by his own power on the third day, and how he went out in triumph from the tomb where he had been placed. In this way it is made clear that if he could give himself life by overcoming death, he was the Lord of life and death, and that as such he could have prevented his own death and could have been delivered from the hands of the Jews had he so wanted.

These things should be repeated often and impressed upon their minds so that they may conceive more love and respect for the Savior. Experience has taught me that the deeper love and devotion they have for the

Savior's passion, the firmer they become in their Christian faith and the more constant in their practice of virtues.[26]

The third text contains de Rhodes's reflections on the ease with which he succeeded in converting the "idolatrous priests [Buddhists monks], who are usually the most obstinate." This success de Rhodes attributes to the particular method he uses in catechizing Vietnamese pagans:

Text C

I found them marvelously open to reason. I baptized two hundred of them who will be of unbelievable help to us in converting others. One of them brought me five hundred of those he had disabused of error by teaching them the truths of faith, and they have since become our most fervent catechists. They were all delighted when I pointed out to them how our religion conforms to right reason, and they admired above all God's Ten Commandments, finding that nothing more reasonable or more worthy of being laid down by the Supreme Ruler of the world could be uttered. My favorite method was to propose to them the immortality of the soul and the afterlife. From there I went on to prove God's existence and providence. Advancing thus from one degree to the next, we gradually came to the more difficult mysteries. Experience has shown us that this way of instructing the pagans is very useful. I have explained it at length in my catechism, which I divide over the course of eight days, wherein I try to propound all the main truths the idolaters should be taught.[27]

De Rhodes's Catechetical Method

These three fundamental texts give us in a nutshell the method de Rhodes adopted in his catechesis in Vietnam. It would be useful to lay it out in systematic form:

1. No catechetical method is universally applicable. A method that is apt for "other kingdoms of pagans" (Text B) may not be effective in Vietnam. One has to discover through "experience" (this word is used repeatedly in Texts B and C) which method is most appropriate and effective for the people one is catechizing.

2. Experience taught de Rhodes that two approaches were counterproductive in Vietnam. The first was to *begin* with an attack on Vietnamese religious beliefs and practices. A critique of these traditions is, de Rhodes concedes, *necessary* because they do contain doctrinal errors and superstitious practices, but it should not be undertaken as the *preliminary* step before one teaches the truths of Christianity. The Vietnamese people are deeply religious; preliminary "rebutting and ridiculing" (Text B) of their religions would, as is often the case,

---

[26] Ibid., 175-78.
[27] *Divers voyages*, 96.

offend their religious sensibility and close their ears and hearts to the gospel. This "refutation of idolatry" was to be done only *after* one spoke of the existence of God, creation, the fall, the flood, and the Tower of Babel (Text B). De Rhodes notes that this order is not only logically and psychologically sound but also *historically* correct, because, according to him, it was only *after* the flood that the devil brought idolatry into the world (Text B).

3. The second approach to be rejected for the Vietnamese people concerned the *ordering* of Christian doctrines. Some missionaries maintained that the doctrine of the Trinity should not be presented to catechumens at the beginning of catechesis but should be postponed toward its end, right before baptism. The reason for this order was to "avoid troubling their minds with doubts" (Text B). De Rhodes rejects this proposal for three reasons. Theologically, the doctrine of the Trinity is presupposed by the doctrine of "the incarnation of the Son of God, who is the Second Person" (Text B). Experientially, in the many years of teaching pagans de Rhodes had not found anyone objecting to the doctrine of the Trinity. Traditionally, the proposed order was not the one followed by the creed. Hence, de Rhodes recommended that the exposition of the trinitarian mystery be done at the *beginning* of catechesis (Text B).

4. This does not mean that one *starts* with the doctrine of the Trinity. Rather, one must commence with truths "knowable by the light of natural reason," such as the creation of the world, the aim of human life, and the obligations of knowing and serving God (Text B). Other "natural" truths with which one should begin catechesis for the Vietnamese include "the immortality of the soul and the afterlife" (Text C). The goal is to establish in the hearers' minds "a sort of firm foundation on which the rest of their faith can be supported" (Text B) so that Christianity is shown "to conform to right reason" (Text C). This is one of the reasons why Vietnamese Buddhist monks admired and accepted the Christian doctrines and ethics (Text C).

5. The most difficult Christian doctrine to teach the Vietnamese, in de Rhodes's experience, was that of the incarnation, passion, and death of the Son of God. To the Vietnamese mind these seem to contradict God's spirituality, eternity, immortality, and omnipotence. Interestingly, de Rhodes noted that presenting christological doctrines to pagans requires a *different* method from the one used to explain them to believers (Text B). To make them credible, de Rhodes suggested a triple strategy: highlighting the cosmic wonders associated with Christ's death, fostering devotion to the suffering Christ, and connecting Christ's passion with his resurrection. The point was to affirm as strongly as possible the freedom of Jesus in accepting his passion and hence his lordship over all his enemies and all things, including humankind's most powerful adversary, death (Text B).

6. As one attempts to tailor one's catechetical method to the local situation, its religious language must be pressed into service. In so doing, two guidelines should be observed. First, words that at first sight seem equivalent to Christian concepts may not be appropriate; attention must be paid to their different philosophical and religious contexts. Second, biblical usage provides a useful guide in coining new theological terms (for example, *duc Chua troi dat* [Lord of heaven

and earth] for God, on the basis of Acts 17:23-25). This second rule makes it clear that de Rhodes's method was patterned by divine revelation and not by natural reason, that is, "by the means God has revealed to us" (Text A).

7. Finally, in catechesis it is necessary to link doctrine with praxis, instruction with worship. Christian truths are shown to have practical implications both for worship, for example, devotion to the passion of Christ (Text B), and ethics, for example, "our legitimate duties to the Lord of heaven and earth" (Text A) and "the practice of virtues" (Text B).

Over three centuries separate de Rhodes and his Vietnamese audience from our cultural context and catechetical practice. Indeed, the gap dividing his world and ours is in many places unbridgeable. We would betray de Rhodes's own methodological insights were we to apply his approach to our contemporary situation as if it were a recipe. For example, our theology of non-Christian religions is no longer as negative as de Rhodes's and the use of miracles as proofs of Jesus' divinity is no longer thought justifiable, as it was in his day. Nevertheless, de Rhodes's attempts at making the Christian faith understandable to his Vietnamese audience by means of an appropriate translation of Christian vocabularies (especially the term *God*), frequent recourse to Vietnamese proverbs to validate Christian teachings, liturgical adaptation, and institution of new church organizations command nothing but respect and admiration. Similarly, his genuine respect for what is true and good in the Vietnamese religions, in particular Confucianism, anticipated Vatican II's position on non-Christian religions.

With regard to Vietnamese cultural practices in particular, de Rhodes's attitude was in the main subtle and complex. (1) Generally, those practices he considered morally unacceptable (such as polygamy and worship of ancestors), he firmly rejected, appealing to the law of the gospel and the teaching of Christ, his twin criteria for acceptability, and when possible, invoking Vietnamese wisdom embodied in proverbs and sayings to support his position. (2) Practices that were apparently good (for example, various marks of respect toward the parents and the ancestors during the Vietnamese New Year [*Tet*]), he preserved and gave a Christian meaning. (3) Practices that were in his judgment liable to superstition but possessed a strong potential for pastoral and spiritual enrichment (for example, swearing the oath of allegiance to the prince) he purified by omitting objectionable elements or by transforming them with a Christian interpretation. (4) Finally, he was in principle opposed to introducing into the Vietnamese culture Christian practices (such as wearing crucifixes and holy medals), which, though laudable in themselves, would set the Vietnamese Christians culturally apart from their compatriots.

In sum, despite limitations and weaknesses, de Rhodes's *Cathechismus* is a landmark in the history of the inculturation of the gospel by means of catechisms. However, though still containing useful lessons for our contemporary task of catechetical inculturation, de Rhodes's catechism is dated. To see how the Christian faith should be inculturated today, we would do well to examine a recent national catechism, *Catechism for Filipino Catholics*.

CATECHISM FOR FILIPINO CATHOLICS (1997)

One of the functions of the *CCC* is to encourage and assist in "the writing of new local catechisms, which take into account various situations and cultures, while carefully preserving the unity of faith and fidelity to Catholic doctrine."[28] While most countries have contented themselves with translating the *CCC*, in whole or in part, the Philippines has published a national catechism whose aim is to "'inculturate' the saving message of Christ in our concrete Filipino context" and which is intended therefore to be "authentically Filipino."[29] The *Catechism for Filipino Catholics* is intended not as a textbook but as a proximate source book for the preparation of catechetical materials, religion textbooks, and other guides.[30]

A National Source Book for Catechesis

The *CFC* was the end product of a long process of preparation begun in 1984, completed in 1994, and approved by the Congregation for the Clergy in 1997, indeed the first to receive this honor since the publication of the *CCC*. It was prepared by the *National Catechetical Directory for the Philippines* (1984) and the Second Plenary Council of the Philippines (1991). As to be expected, the *CFC* made extensive use of the *CCC* (1992) in its drafts as well as its revisions.

The *CFC* claims to be "truly Christ-centered and Trinitarian, and grounded solidly in the Bible, Church teaching, and human experience."[31] Furthermore, it claims to be "truly 'inculturated' in the context of our Filipino cultural and religious values and traditions."[32] The concern for a truly "inculturated catechesis" was uppermost in the composition of the *CFC*: "There is an urgent demand, *first* of all, for a catechism that addresses itself to our Philippine context, with its particular needs, characteristics and crises . . . a truly *inculturated catechesis* which responds to the concrete stiuation and culture of Filipino Catholics and families today, in terms of our own Filipino culture and values" (*CFC*, 6).

Structurally, the catechism is divided into three parts, flanked by the introduction called "Foundations"—which discusses the identity of the Filipino Catholic and the themes of revelation, faith and unbelief—and the epilogue, which is a commentary on the Our Father. The three parts, which are designed to reflect the Trinity, are entitled "Christ, Our Truth," "Christ, Our Way," and "Christ,

---

[28] John Paul II, apostolic constitution *Fidei Depositum* (11 October 1992), no. 3.

[29] Catholic Bishops' Conference of the Philippines, *A Primer* (Manila: ECCCE and Word and Life Publications, 1997), 3.

[30] See *Catechism for Filipino Catholics* (Manila: ECCCE and Word and Life Publications, 1997). Hereafter cited as *CFC*, followed by the number of the paragraph, not of the page.

[31] Catholic Bishops' Conference of the Philippines, *A Primer*, 6.

[32] Ibid.

Our Life" in order to emphasize the Christ-centeredness of the Christian faith. The first part deals with doctrines, speaking of believing in God the Father (head and faith); the second with the moral life, speaking of following Christ (hands and love); and the third with worship and sacraments, speaking of trusting in the Holy Spirit (heart and hope). Each chapter seeks to achieve three goals: integration, inculturation, and community formation, and is composed of five sections: opening, context, exposition, integration, and questions and answers.

An Inculturated Catechesis

As far as inculturation is concerned, the *CFC* attempts to achieve it in several ways. First, it opens with an elaboration of what constitutes a Filipino and a Filipino Catholic (chapter 1). It describes five predominant Filipino characteristics, which constitute the *Filipino identity* (family-oriented, meal-oriented, suffering-oriented, hero-oriented, and spirit-oriented) and relates them to Jesus, showing how Jesus responds fully to each of them (*CFC*, 34-16). Furthermore, according to the *CFC*, there is a *Filipino way* of accepting Jesus as the fulfillment of the Filipino self-identity, that is, with and through Mary, Filipinos being *"pueblo amante de Maria"*(*CFC*, 45). Being a Catholic Filipino, then, is to experience that the "Filipino *identity, meaning, suffering, commitment* and *worldview* are all *tied to Jesus Christ*" (*CFC*, 52), so much so that "growing more mature in the following of Christ has meant becoming more truly and authentically *Filipino*" (*CFC*, 28). Being *Christian* and being *Filipino*, then, are not mutually contradictory but define and reinforce each other.

Second, in every chapter the *CFC* prefaces the exposition of each element of Catholic doctrine, morality, and worship with an explanation of the Filipino *context* in which details of Filipino national history, church history, language, and culture are mentioned, "all the most diversified situations, challenges, failures and hopes that constitute the 'given' in the midst of which a certain aspect of our Catholic faith is understood and lived out in both its richness and limitations."[33]

Third, in expounding the Christian faith the *CFC* cites not only the magisterium of the universal church but also the magisterium of the Philippines, particularly as spelled out in the documents and decrees of the Second Plenary Council of the Philippines: "These two sources are *complementary* and *constantly integrated* in the catechism. They are what makes the *CFC* unique, i.e., a '*Catholic Catechism*' for '*Filipinos.* '"[34]

Fourth, in the section called "Integration," the *CFC* always relates its three parts—doctrine, morality, and worship—by considering how a doctrine affects the way Christians live and worship, how a Christian way of living affects what Christians believe and how they worship, and how a liturgical celebration reflects what Christians believe and influences how they live.

---

[33] Ibid., 12.
[34] Ibid.

Fifth, in the final section, entitled "Questions and Answers," the *CFC* does not simply offer "brief summary formulae that could be memorized," as the *CCC* (22) envisages, but also asks questions about the ways to live the Christian doctrines in the Filipino context. In sum, the *CFC* tries to bring about inculturation

— by stressing the Filipino dimension in the *Opening* and the *Context;*
— *exposing the strengths and weaknesses* of the Filipino understanding and practice of the topic;
— stressing concrete Filipino experiences in the *Integration*'s examples;
— with *Questions and Answers* formulated not for rote memory but to incite thinking of what's really real.[35]

STANDING ON THE SHOULDERS OF GIANTS: LEARNING FROM THE PAST

By any measure, the *CFC* is an impressive catechetical achievement and a persuasive proof that theology in Asia has come of age. Like de Rhodes's *Cathechismus,* it deliberately seeks to incarnate Christian doctrine, morality, and worship in the cultural context of its audience. Though separated from each other by more than three centuries, both de Rhodes and the authors of the *CFC* were deeply convinced that the Christian faith and the local culture do not destroy each other and that, to the contrary, by means of an inculturated catechesis and with the help of an appropriate catechism, these two realities can be made to enrich each other, the Christian faith taking root in the culture of the people to be catechized, and the culture transformed through purification, enlightenment, and elevation by the truths and values of the Christian faith.

But do these two catechisms and their methods have anything to teach us in our task of catechetical inculturation in the United States? Of course, it would be anachronistic to turn de Rhodes into a contextual theologian, but there is no denying that his sensitivity to cultural differences was deep, his impulse for adaptation as a missionary strategy overarching, and his catechetical achievements by no means negligible. Compared to de Rhodes's *Cathechismus,* the *CFC* has the distinct advantage of being able to draw on the best fruits of contemporary biblical and theological scholarship as well as on the most tried and true catechetical methods. In spite of all their remarkable achievements, however, neither of these catechisms can serve as a foolproof recipe for our work of inculturation in the United States. The cultural gulf separating seventeenth-century Vietnam and the contemporary Philippines, on the one hand, and the United States, on the other, is too vast to permit a simple duplication of the methods of the *Cathechismus* and the *CFC,* even though, admittedly, the commonalities between the Philippines and the United States are extensive and significant, not least in the common use of English. Nevertheless, with these caveats, it is helpful to spell out some of the important lessons that can be derived from these two catechisms for our task of inculturation.

---

[35] Ibid., 9.

1. Inculturated catechesis presupposes an important shift in the understanding of the evangelizing mission of the church, of which catechesis is an essential part. This new concept is embodied in the phrase "evangelizing cultures."[36] What *Cathechismus* did in a rudimentary way, and the *CFC* in a systematic and comprehensive way, was to promote not only the conversion of individuals, which remains an important goal of evangelization and catechesis, but also to shape the Vietnamese and Filipino cultures according to the gospel.

Culture here is understood not in the classic sense of the intellectual and artistic development of the individual (a "cultured person"), but in the anthropological sense of the characteristic traits of a human group (usually, an ethnic or national group) or subgroup (for example, youth), its typical ways of feeling, thinking, acting, and constructing its social, political, economic, and religious organizations. Paul VI and John Paul II have made culture into a field of evangelization. Paul VI charged evangelizers and catechists to "affect" and "upset" through the power of the gospel "mankind's criteria of judgment, determining values, points of interest, lines of thought, sources of inspiration and models of life" (*EN*, 19). John Paul II established the Pontifical Council of Culture and asked the council to help the church answer these questions: "How is the message of the church to be made accessible to new cultures, to contemporary modes of understanding and feeling? How can the church of Christ make itself understood to the modern mind?"[37]

2. While not ignoring the conversion and formation of individual consciences, inculturated catechesis in the United States must take up the challenge of evangelizing the American culture, as *Cathechismus* and the *CFC* did. This task demands, first of all, a careful analysis of the American culture, or more correctly, cultures in the plural, since the United States is becoming culturally pluralistic. There should be something analogous to de Rhodes's description of the political, social, and religious conditions of seventeenth-century Vietnam and chapter 1 of the *CFC*, in which the cultural identity of the Filipino is outlined. What are the characteristics of being an American and an American Catholic? Obviously, such a task cannot be performed by the catechists alone but must be carried out with the collaboration of sociologists and cultural critics.[38]

3. What will emerge from this cultural analysis is the necessity in the United States for what has been termed new evangelization or second evangelization,

---

[36] For an exposition of this concept, see Hervé Carrier, *Evangelizing the Culture of Modernity* (Maryknoll, N.Y.: Orbis Books, 1993); idem, *The Gospel and Cultures: From Leo XIII to John Paul II* (Vatican City, 1987); idem, "Evangelization of Culture," in Latourelle and Fisichella, *Dictionary of Fundamental Theology*, 282-87; Leonardo Boff, *New Evangelization: Good News to the Poor*, trans. Robert Barr (Maryknoll, N.Y.: Orbis Books, 1991); and Kenneth Boyack, ed., *The New Catholic Evangelization* (New York: Paulist Press, 1992).

[37] John Paul II, to the Pontifical Council for Culture, 16 January 1984.

[38] A helpful book in this regard is Richard G. Cote, *Re-Visioning Mission: The Catholic Church and Culture in Postmodern America* (New York: Paulist Press, 1996). See also Peter C. Phan, "Multiculturalism, Church, and the University," *Religious Education* 90/1 (1994): 8-29; and idem, "To Be Catholic or Not to Be: Is It Still the Question? Catholic Identity and Religious Education Today," *Horizons* 25/2 (1998): 159-80.

re-evangelization, or new stage of evangelization.[39] Whereas "first evangelization" is directed to non-Christian cultures, "new evangelization" is directed to populations that were christianized in the past but are now living in a secularized world. Secularized cultures, such as the American culture, generally adopt an indifferent and even hostile attitude toward Christianity, or relegate it to the private sphere. Carrier has described the challenges presented by such cultures: material prosperity but "spiritual poverty," faith inadequate and superficial and lacking the support of a vibrant Christian community, faith once received but now rejected and repressed, faith inactive and dormant, widespread distrust of organized religion.[40]

In this type of secularized culture, the challenge to the "new evangelization" and catechesis is twofold. On the one hand, there is the task of inculturating Christian doctrine, morality, and worship into the American culture, for example, by relating the eucharist to Thanksgiving. On the other hand, there is the urgent necessity of cultural critique. Ironically, one of the characteristics of Western secularization is the *culturalization* of Christianity. Many Christian symbols have become so enmeshed in the American culture that they have become parts of the "civil religion." Consequently, they have lost their subversive power and have become purveyors of "cheap grace." Even words such as *church, grace, salvation, redemption, sin,* and *virtue* have become hackneyed and trite, or worse, slogans to attract votes in campaign seasons. Major Christian feasts such as Christmas and Easter have become for many Americans little more than occasions, much exploited commercially, for gift-giving and showing goodwill to all. Hence, it may be necessary to retrieve the critique of religions and culture as practiced by *Cathechismus* and the *CFC*. Inculturated catechesis must point out and reject, in an act of countercultural witness, elements of the culture that are contrary to the gospel.

One of the areas where this countercultural catechesis is required is mass culture, especially the media, not only because it is currently devoid of Christian values but also because it is the arena where Christian faith can act most effectively upon culture.[41] Connected with mass culture is youth culture, since the young are the most numerous and voracious consumers of mass culture and the media. It goes without saying that catechesis must address this youth culture since the young are the future of the church.[42]

4. Another dimension that will become more pressing for catechesis in the United States in the twenty-first century is the increasing cultural and ethnic pluralism in the American population. In the next few decades there will be a significant emergence of minority groups, mainly blacks, Hispanics, and Asians, both among the laity at large and among candidates to the priesthood and religious life. The immigrants of this "second wave," to use an expression

---

[39] See John Paul II, *RM*, 33.
[40] See Hervé Carrier, "New Evangelization," in Latourelle and Fisichella, *Dictionary of Fundamental Theology*, 288-89.
[41] On catechesis and the means of social communication, see *GDC*, 160-62, 209.
[42] For catechesis to youth, see *GDC*, 181-84.

of Hispanic Jesuit theologian Alan Figueroa Deck, like those of the "first wave," such as the Irish, Italians, Germans, and Eastern Europeans, have to cross the economic and socio-political divide separating them from the mainstream of American society. But, unlike them, those of the second wave, mostly poor and ecclesiastically powerless, also have to overcome the gap marginalizing them from the power centers now occupied predominantly by the Catholics of the first wave.

But this demographic shift presents the American Catholic church not only with challenges but with opportunities as well. The newcomers—Cubans, Mexicans, Nicaraguans and other Central and South Americans, Haitians, Vietnamese, Chinese, Japanese, Koreans, Thai, Hmong, Filipinos, and others—bring with them rich cultural as well as religious traditions and increase substantially the number of church members (and last but not least, vocations) with which the American Catholic church can be renewed and strengthened. But their presence requires an inculturated catechesis, of a very complicated sort, that *Cathechismus* and the *CFC* could not even envisage, since both of them dealt with largely homogeneous ethnic groups.[43] This catechesis must help them establish a satisfactory dwelling place not only between the two often conflicting cultures—their own and the American—but also beyond them, creating a new culture that is a synthesis of both.[44]

5. Finally, *Cathechismus* and especially the *CFC* have established an intrinsic link between catechesis and the work for social liberation (the "preferential option for the poor"). Pope Paul VI forcefully affirms that the good news of the kingdom of God is a "message of liberation" (*EN*, 30). The *GDC*, following Paul VI (*EN*, 33), cautions that this work of liberation "cannot be confined to any restricted sphere whether it be economic, political, social or doctrinal" but "must embrace the whole man in all his aspects and components, extending to his relation to the absolute, even to the Absolute which is God" (*GDC*, 104). The document further insists that Christian morality be presented in catechesis as a demand and consequence of the "radical liberation" wrought by Christ (*GDC*, 104). Catechesis in the United States must foster this consciousness and practice of social justice as an intrinsic part of evangelization, not only because there still exist subtle forms of discrimination (for example, racism and sexism) in American society but also because as the only surviving superpower, the United States can and must, through its military and economic power, bring about justice and peace in the world.

Catechesis in the United States is facing a daunting task and is undertaking a new voyage fraught with dangers and opportunities. Cultural and ethnic pluralism; fewer priestly and ethnically more diverse vocations; rapid increase of

---

[43] For a catechesis that takes into account ethnic differences, see *GDC*, 207: "Catechesis also places special emphasis on multi-ethnic and multi-cultural situations in that it leads to a greater discovery and appreciation of the resources of diverse groups to receive and express the faith."

[44] For reflections on the challenges and opportunities Asian Catholics present to the American Catholic church, see Peter C. Phan, "Asian Catholics in the United States: Challenges and Opportunities for the Church," *Mission Studies* 16/2, 32 (1999): 151-74.

ethnic church members; ideological polarities and bitter division among various groups; unrelenting debates about the role of women in the church; uncertainties about certain moral problems; culturalization of the Christian faith; epistemological relativism associated with postmodernity—all these factors and others conspire to make catechesis in the United States an extremely difficult task. Fortunately, giants have preceded us in the task of evangelization and catechesis. Though of another time and place, they, along with magisterial documents, can provide us with helpful insights on how to inculturate the Christian faith in our own country.

11

The Dragon and the Eagle

TOWARD A VIETNAMESE AMERICAN THEOLOGY

Like the American population, the ranks of the Christian churches in the United States are constantly swelled by a steady stream of refugees and immigrants. This is particularly true of the Roman Catholic Church, whose membership has dramatically increased in recent years by the coming of Asian and Spanish-speaking people. Among Asians, there is no doubt that the Vietnamese and Vietnamese Catholics form a most significant group.[1]

In this chapter I first give a brief report on the Vietnamese Catholics in the United States. Next I delineate the social, cultural, and ecclesial condition of immigrants as the context in which a Vietnamese American theology is to be constructed. The last part offers suggestions as to how a Vietnamese American theology can be formulated. In this way it is hoped that the dragon *(Lac Long)*, which, according to Vietnamese mythology, is the god from whom the Vietnamese descend, can live in harmony with the eagle, the symbol of the United States. Metaphors aside, these reflections are intended to contribute to the process of healing and reconciliation between the two peoples who for various reasons were caught for decades in a disastrous war against each other.[2]

VIETNAMESE AMERICAN CATHOLICS

The victory of Communist North Vietnam over South Vietnam in April 1975 provoked the largest ever exodus of Vietnamese, and in particular Vietnamese

---

[1] The first two parts of this chapter are adapted from my earlier essay "Vietnamese Catholics in the United States: Christian Identity between the Old and the New," *U.S. Catholic Historian* 18/1 (2000): 19-35. See also Peter C. Phan, "Asian Catholics in the United States: Challenges and Opportunities for the Church," *Mission Studies* 16/2, 32 (1999): 151-74. For a general history of Asian Americans, see Ronald Takaki, *Strangers from a Different Shore: A History of Asian Americans* (New York: Penguin Books, 1989).

[2] For reflections on the meaning of the so-called American War in Vietnam and its aftermaths, see Peter C. Phan, "Escape to Freedom: Twenty-five Years after the Fall of South Vietnam," *America* 182/15 (29 April 2000): 12-14.

Catholics, to the United States of America. Vietnamese refugees settled in various parts of the world, in particular Canada and Australia, but the country of choice was and is the United States, partly because it has the best organized resettlement programs (in particular, the agencies of the United States Catholic Conference) and partly because it is perceived as offering the greatest opportunities for educational and economic advancement.

Vietnamese in America

To date, there are no exact statistics on the Vietnamese population in general or on Vietnamese Catholics in the United States; however, the number of Vietnamese in the United States is estimated at slightly over one million. Before 1975 there were eighteen thousand Vietnamese living in America.[3] Their number increased dramatically after the fall of South Vietnam by refugees from Communism. Their flight from Vietnam occurred in five waves: the first consisted of about 130,000 people who arrived in the immediate aftermath of the collapse of South Vietnam in April 1975; the second wave was ethnic Chinese who left in 1978-79; the third wave was 300,000 "boat people" who came between 1978 and 1982 after being temporarily sheltered in various refugee camps, mainly in Thailand, the Philippines, and Hong Kong; the fourth wave was of a much smaller number of people who were reunited with their families through various official programs such as Orderly Departure Program and Humanitarian Operations between 1983 and 1989; and the fifth wave includes those who have come after 14 March 1989.[4]

In terms of education and professional training, Vietnamese of the first wave were noticeably superior to those of the four later groups, which consisted mostly of students, small-business owners, farmers, fishermen, craftsmen, unskilled laborers, young men fleeing the military draft for the war against Cambodia, and children sent by their parents to have a better life. These people had much lower levels of education, fewer job skills, and practically no knowledge of English; therefore, they experienced much difficulty in adjusting to the new environment.[5]

In terms of religious affiliation, Vietnamese refugees and immigrants represent the whole spectrum of religious traditions in Vietnam, from the indigenous religion often called animism to the three ancient imported religions, that is,

---

[3] See Ruben Rumbaut, "Vietnamese, Laotian, and Cambodian Americans," in *Asian Americans: Contemporary Issues and Trends*, ed. Pyong Gap Min (Thousand Oaks, Calif.: Sage Publications, 1995), 232-70.

[4] See James M. Freeman, *Changing Identities: Vietnamese Americans 1975-1995* (Boston: Allyn and Bacon, 1995), 29-41.

[5] See Darrel Montero, *Vietnamese Americans: Patterns of Resettlement in the United States* (Boulder, Colo.: Westview Press, 1979); Nathan Caplan, John K. Whitmore, and Marcella H. Choy, *The Boat People and Achievement in America: A Study of Family Life, Hard Work, and Cultural Values* (Ann Arbor, Mich.: University of Michigan Press, 1989); and Paul James Rutledge, *The Vietnamese Experience in America* (Bloomington, Ind.: University of Indiana Press, 1992).

Buddhism, Confucianism, and Taoism, to the native religion of Caodaism, and, of course, Christianity (Catholic and Protestant).[6] Though Catholic Christianity constitutes only 8 percent of the total population in Vietnam, in the United States 30 percent of Vietnamese Americans are Catholic. The reason for this high proportion is that many Vietnamese Americans are Catholics who fled North Vietnam to the South in 1954 to escape Communism. Having had firsthand experiences of the evils of Communism, they had much greater incentives to emigrate in 1975.

Like most other recently arrived ethnic groups, the Vietnamese tend to settle close to one another. California has the largest number of Vietnamese and Vietnamese Catholics (Orange County, which has a city named Little Saigon, and San Jose), followed by Texas (Houston, Dallas/Fort Worth, and Port Arthur), Louisiana (New Orleans), and Virginia-Washington, D.C. As a whole, the Vietnamese have done well in their new country, as testified by the high educational achievements of their young and their economic successes.[7]

Vietnamese American Catholics

In general, Vietnamese Catholics are deeply attached to their Vietnamese churches and hold their pastors in high esteem. They spare no resources to have their own churches and their own priests so as to be able to worship in their mother tongue and to preserve their religious and cultural customs. Most dioceses where there is a sizeable number of Vietnamese Catholics have at least one, and in many cases, several Vietnamese parishes (for example, San Jose, California; Atlanta, Georgia; New Orleans, Louisiana; Dallas and Fort Worth, Texas; Arlington, Virginia; and Washington, D.C.). Even where there are no Vietnamese parishes, Vietnamese Catholics often worship together, using the facilities of American parishes.

By and large, the relation between Vietnamese American Catholics and the hierarchy of the American Catholic church has been marked by mutual respect and friendly collaboration. Only rarely has the relationship between the Vietnamese Catholic community and the local bishop been marred by controversies (for example, in San Jose, California, and Port Arthur, Texas). Fortunately, these conflicts have been peacefully resolved.

There are currently approximately five hundred Vietnamese priests (diocesan and religious), twenty permanent deacons, and several hundred sisters.

---

[6] For information about these religions, see Peter C. Phan, *Mission and Catechesis: Alexandre de Rhodes and Inculturation in Seventeenth-Century Vietnam* (Maryknoll, N.Y.: Orbis Books, 1998), 13-28.

[7] On the educational achievements of Vietnamese Americans, see Nathan Caplan, Marcella H. Choy, and John K. Whitmore, *Children of the Boat People: A Study of Educational Success* (Ann Arbor, Mich.: Michigan University Press, 1991); and James Freeman, *Changing Identities*, 69-86. Freeman writes: "The academic achievements of Vietnamese schoolchildren in America are almost legendary: valedictorians of high schools and colleges, a Rhodes scholar, winners of science competitions, high grade point averages, high scores on the Scholastic Aptitude (now Assessment) Test" (69).

Even among the clergy there are "success stories": a good number of Vietnamese priests are pastors, responsible for not only Vietnamese but also American parishes; a few of them hold the office of vicar general; and some have even been made monsignors. Vietnamese vocations to the priesthood and religious life have been numerous. In some dioceses (for example, Orange, California, and New Orleans, Louisiana), Vietnamese priests constitute a significant percentage of the clergy; and in some religious societies, such as the Society of the Divine Word, a high number of members are Vietnamese.

Among the dozen Vietnamese male religious orders the most numerous are the Congregation of Mary Co-redemptrix *(Dong Dong Cong)*, which was founded by a Vietnamese priest and is headquartered in Carthage, Missouri. Every August the society organizes a celebration in honor of Mary, regularly attracting forty thousand participants. There are about twenty female religious societies, the largest of which is the Congregation of the Lovers of the Cross *(Dong Men Thanh Gia)*, also an indigenous congregation, founded by Bishop Lambert de La Motte in the seventeenth century and divided into groups according to the dioceses to which the members belonged in Vietnam (for example, Ha Noi, Hue, Thanh Hoa, Vinh, Cho Quan, Qui Nhon, and Phat Diem).

Two of the several official organizations for Vietnamese Catholics in the United States deserve mention: the Vietnamese Catholic Federation in the United States of America, whose general assembly meets every four years; and the Community of Vietnamese Clergy and Religious in the United States of America, whose general assembly meets every two years. Within the National Conference of Catholic Bishops there is the Committee on Migration, with responsibility for refugees and immigrants.

Like many other ethnic groups, Vietnamese Catholics are deeply concerned with preserving their language, culture, and religious traditions. To achieve this goal they publish numerous newspapers, magazines, and journals, among which the most important are *Dan Chua* (People of God), *Duc Me Hang Cuu Giup* (Our Lady of Perpetual Help), *Thoi Diem Cong Giao* (Catholic Periodical), and *Hop Tuyen Than Hoc* (Theological Selections). Other activities include Vietnamese language classes and catechetical instruction in Vietnamese (there is a well-attended biannual national catechetical conference). Occasions on which Vietnamese cultural traditions are solemnly celebrated are weddings and funerals. Other more public occasions include the lunar New Year *(Tet)*, the commemoration of the fall of South Vietnam (30 April), and the feast of the martyrs of Vietnam (24 November). Vietnamese American Catholics also contribute generously to the church in Vietnam, especially for the restoration of old churches or the building of new ones and for assistance to victims of natural disasters.

A Different Way of Being a Christian

When Vietnamese Catholics came to the United States, they brought with them their own ways of living the Christian faith. To understand Vietnamese Catholicism it is important to remember that it developed in dependence on the growth of missionary activity since the sixteenth century. The type of church organization and Christian life that were brought to Vietnam by missionaries unavoidably mirrored those of contemporary Europe, today often referred to as post-Tridentine Catholicism, that is, shaped by the Council of Trent (1545-63). It has, of course, been renewed in various degrees by the reforms mandated by Vatican II. Vietnamese American Catholics stand, then, between a more conservative post-Tridentine Catholicism and a more progressive Vatican II Catholicism. Which side they favor largely depends on their particular regions of origin, generally more open in the south and more traditional in the north. In spite of regional differences, the following traits seem to be common to Vietnamese Catholicism.

1. In terms of ecclesiological model, Vietnamese American Catholics tend to see the church primarily as a social institution. This model exaggerates the role of visible and canonical structures and the importance of the hierarchy. It has often led to the error known as *institutionalism,* characterized by clericalism, juridicism, and triumphalism. This ecclesiological model is strongly buttressed by the Confucian culture with its emphasis on deference for authority and tradition. It also responds well to the Vietnamese church's need to strengthen its corporate identity and social cohesiveness, given its minority status in Asia.

2. Connected with this emphasis on the institutional aspects of the church is the relatively passive role of the laity. Despite the fact that Vietnamese American Catholic lay members, especially the younger ones, are highly educated and successful in various professions, they have as yet no effective voice in the day-to-day operation of parish life. The local priest most often wields absolute power. Besides excessive reliance on the clergy, the laity's lack of competence in theological matters may account for the minimal role of the laity in church organization, since training in fields other than secular is generally regarded as inappropriate for the laity.

3. Another consequence of institutionalism is an excessive concern with the internal problems of the church and neglect of dialogue with other believers. Vietnamese American Catholics still look on the followers of other religions with suspicion, despite Vatican II's insistence on the necessity of interreligious dialogue. Furthermore, they have barely begun to reflect upon, much less enact, the task of inculturating the faith into their own cultures, in spite of ample resources available in their adopted country for this purpose.

4. Vietnamese American Catholics are also reluctant to take upon themselves the challenges of social justice, even though most of them are vigorously opposed to Communism, and understandably so, since many of them have been victims of Communist oppression. In general, Vietnamese American Catholicism is still heavily shaped by individualistic pietism, with insufficient knowledge of the social teaching of the church, and consequently with little engagement in the socio-political and economic realms in the spirit of the gospel.

The above four observations are not intended to convey a negative evaluation of Vietnamese American Catholicism. On the contrary, Vietnamese American Catholics form a vibrant and vigorous community that has already made invaluable contributions to both the American church and society, not only from their cultural traditions but also from their Catholic heritage.

5. One area in which Vietnamese American Catholics have already visibly transformed the American church is the number of priestly and religious vocations they have produced. Beside hundreds of Vietnamese priests who came in and after 1975, many dioceses (for example, Orange, California, and New Orleans, Louisiana) and religious societies (especially the Divine Word Society) have been enormously enriched by new Vietnamese vocations. Also to be mentioned are hundreds of sisters of various orders, some of which are of Vietnamese origin (such as the Lovers of the Cross), who are serving generously in many dioceses and who can easily raise vocations in the hundreds if they have the resources. This large number of vocations could be attributed to the high respect in which priests and religious are held among Vietnamese (which has, of course, its own negative side), but certainly it has roots in the devout faith of Vietnamese American Catholic families.

6. This fervent faith is nourished no doubt not only by the sacraments but also by popular devotions. Indeed, the cultivation of popular devotions is a distinguishing characteristic of many Vietnamese American communities and constitutes an important contribution that Vietnamese American Catholics make to the American church. While post–Vatican II Catholics tend to downplay popular devotions for their alleged superstitious character and their tendency to alienate people from this-worldly concerns, Vietnamese Catholics have continued to foster practices of popular devotion (for example, Marian devotions, pilgrimages, novenas, Benediction, prayers to the saints) and derive much spiritual nourishment from them. These popular devotions will play a much more significant role if their tendency toward excessive sentimentalism and individualism can be minimized and their potential for community-building, liberation, and social justice can be retrieved.

7. Intimately connected with popular devotions is another major characteristic of Vietnamese American Catholic communities and parishes, that is, the flourishing of communal activities, often in tandem with sacramental celebrations (especially baptism, marriage, and funerals), certain calendrical feasts (for example, the New Year), and cultural customs (such as death anniversaries). In addition, there are a large number of pious associations (such as confraternities, sodalities, youth groups) that provide the laity with the opportunity to exercise leadership and be actively involved with the community, especially in its liturgical and spiritual life. Recently, more modern associations have been added, such as Bible study groups, charismatic prayers group, RENEW, Cursillo, and so on. These associations with their manifold activities are reliable indices of the vibrancy of Vietnamese American Catholic communities.

8. In addition to being nourished by sacraments and devotions, the faith of Vietnamese churches has been tested in the crucible of suffering and even persecution. The memory of martyrdom is still fresh in the minds of Vietnamese American Catholics, especially that of 117 martyrs (of whom twenty-one were foreign missionaries) canonized in 1988. More recently, many Vietnamese Catholics have suffered for their faith under the Communist regime and as a result have chosen exile in the United States and elsewhere. While this experience might have rigidified their conservative political views, it has no doubt enriched

and fortified their faith in a way not available to those enjoying religious freedom.

9. Asia is the birthplace of almost all world religions (including Christianity). In Vietnam the three main religious traditions are Confucian, Taoist, and Buddhist. Scratch the surface of every Vietnamese Catholic, and you will find a Confucian, a Taoist, and a Buddhist, or, more often than not, an indistinguishable mixture of the three. Vietnamese Catholics live within a cultural framework undergirded by Taoist, Confucian, and Buddhist values and moral norms. They are socialized into these values and norms not only through formal teachings but also, and primarily, through thousands of proverbs, folk sayings, songs, family rituals, and cultural festivals. Many Vietnamese Catholics do not find it strange or difficult to inhabit different religious universes. It is this rich and varied religious heritage, latent but pervasive, that Asian American Catholics bring with them to the United States. It will be one of their most significant contributions to the American church.

10. Lastly, most if not all first-generation Vietnamese immigrants in the United States have experienced socio-economic deprivation, extreme in some cases, before they came here. This experience of poverty makes Vietnamese American Catholics sensitive to the sufferings and needs of their fellow nationals and generous in their financial support for the church as well as their relatives in Vietnam. This sense of solidarity with victims of poverty and of natural disasters is also a characteristic of many Vietnamese American Catholic communities and should be fostered with care, since the struggle against poverty and oppression is an essential part of the inculturation of the gospel, especially in a society whose economic and military policies have caused sufferings in many parts of the world, and in Asia in particular.

Vietnamese American Catholics live between two cultures and two churches. Neither fully American nor fully Vietnamese, they are *both* Vietnamese *and* American. Being both, they have the opportunity and the challenge to fuse both worlds, their own cultural values and Catholicism and the American culture and the American Catholic church into something new, so that they stand not only *between* these two cultures and churches, but also *beyond* them.

DWELLING IN THE INTERSTICE BETWEEN TWO CULTURES AND TWO CHURCHES

As refugees forced to flee their country or as immigrants voluntarily seeking a better life in the United States, Vietnamese American Catholics face a double challenge: how to maintain their cultural heritage in a new land and how to forge a new Christian identity in a new ecclesial environment. In a very short time they have made a disconcerting journey from their predominantly premodern society to the modern and postmodern culture of America. As Catholics the Vietnamese have brought their ecclesial experiences to a church that bears a resemblance to their Catholicism but most of the times baffles them. The remaining issue is how to envision the space Vietnamese American Catholics occupy both as citizens of American society and as members of the American

Catholic church. From this space flow the tasks that are incumbent upon them as citizens and church members as well as the responsibilities of American society and the American church toward them.

Betwixt and Between

Despite profound personal and spiritual differences, Vietnamese American Catholics share one common trait and fundamental predicament: They all are immigrants. And being immigrant means being at the margin, or being in-between, or being betwixt and between.[8] American Vietnamese will never be "American enough", because of their race and culture *American* will function only as a qualifier for the noun *Vietnamese*. On the other hand, Vietnamese Americans are no longer regarded by their compatriots in Vietnam as authentically Vietnamese; they have "left" Vietnam and become Americans; *Vietnamese* functions only as a qualifier for *American*. In fact, Vietnamese Americans have been given a special name by the Vietnamese government—*Viet kieu* (Vietnamese foreigners).

However, to be betwixt and between is not totally negative and need not cause cultural schizophrenia. Paradoxically, being neither this nor that allows one to be *both* this *and* that. The process of rapid and extensive globalization and internationalization has compressed the geographical and cultural boundaries and made them exceedingly porous, so that there is today little connection between the passport one holds and the languages one speaks, the clothes one wears, the foods one eats, the music one listens to, the views one professes, and the religion one practices. The constant flow of persons, technologies, finance, information, and ideology across continents and countries has brought about de-territorialization and multiple belongings and loyalties. While this is true of almost everyone in the modern world, only the immigrant experiences this "both-and" situation of multiple identities and loyalties as a permanent, day-to-day, existential condition which he or she must constantly negotiate, often without the benefit of clear guidelines and helpful models. Furthermore, the believing immigrant must consciously accept this predicament as his or her providentially given mission and task and must devise ways to create a space in which to live a fruitful life and not to fall between the two at times conflicting and competing cultures. Belonging to both worlds and cultures, immigrants have the opportunity to fuse them together and, out of their respective resources, fashion a new and different world, so that they stand not only *between* these two worlds and cultures but also *beyond* them. Thus, being betwixt and between can bring about personal and societal transformation and enrichment.

---

[8] On this understanding of being an immigrant, see Jung Young Lee, *Marginality: The Key to Multicultural Theology* (Minneapolis: Fortress Press, 1995); and Peter C. Phan, "Betwixt and Between: Doing Theology with Memory and Imagination," in *Journeys at the Margin: Toward an Autobiographical Theology in American-Asian Perspective*, ed. Peter C. Phan and Jung Young Lee (Collegeville, Minn.: The Liturgical Press, 1999), 113-33.

Between Two Churches

What has been said of the destiny of immigrants between the two cultures applies equally to their ecclesial situation. Here too they stand between two churches, at the boundary between the American Catholic church and the churches of their native countries. Belonging fully to neither, they feel estranged in both and do not occupy positions of power in either church. For most American Catholics, Vietnamese American Catholics' religious practices seem to be a throwback to their own Catholicism of the 1950s, with clerical dominance and lay submissiveness, with colorful processions and pious devotions. On the other hand, Vietnamese American Catholics, both clerical and lay, do not fare much better when they return home for a visit. While welcoming them, the local hierarchy often looks upon them (especially the clerics) with suspicion, fearing that they have been contaminated by the liberal and even heretical ideas and lax morality of the American church.

Nevertheless, while belonging fully neither to the American church nor the Vietnamese church, Vietnamese American Catholics belong to both. Vietnamese American Catholics live a Catholic life in a way no "pure" American Catholic can because of their indelible Asian religious traditions, and they live a Catholic life in a way no "pure" Asian Catholic can because of the distinctly American Catholic ethos that they have absorbed through sheer contiguity and symbiosis with the American society and Catholic church. Here again their betwixt-and-between position should not be viewed only as a negative, producing marginalization, but also as an opportunity and a task to create a new way of being Catholic. Here lies their unique contribution to the church.

In the Interstice between Two Worlds

But in order to accomplish this mission, where should Vietnamese American Catholics stand? What is their social location, the specific space they occupy within the American society and church? How should they be part of the societal and ecclesial realities? In speaking of the inculturation of an immigrant into the modern and postmodern culture, scholars have outlined three possible strategies that Robert Schreiter, following Jonathan Friedman, terms antiglobalism, ethnification, and primitivism.[9] The first is a total retreat from the ideals and values of globalization to defend and preserve one's cultural identity, either through a complete rejection of modernity as found in fundamentalism or through strategies of hierarchical control as in revanchism.[10] The second is the attempt to rediscover a forgotten cultural identity through retrieval of real or imagined cultural traits with the result that often a hybridized culture is constructed through

---

[9] See Robert Schreiter, *The New Catholicity: Theology between the Global and the Local* (Maryknoll, N.Y.: Orbis Books, 1997), 21-25. The work of Jonathan Friedman referred to is *Cultural Identity and Global Process* (London: Sage, 1994).

[10] Fundamentalism is found in all religions, from Judaism to Islam to some Catholic and Protestant conservative groups. Revanchism is present in the restorationist policies of the post–Vatican II era in the Catholic church.

the process of ethnogenesis.[11] The third is the attempt to select a period or an aspect of one's previous, premodern culture and use it as a framework for dealing with globalization.[12]

None of the these three strategies, I submit, is a satisfactory solution for Vietnamese Americans. In light of what has been said about the existential condition of the immigrant, I argue that the reason they are unsatisfactory lies in their common presupposition that an immigrant must be either completely inside or completely outside the American culture. Anything less than complete opposition to or total absorption into the American culture conceived as an integrative system is unacceptable. Antiglobalism is in favor of the first option, whereas ethnification and primitivism are implicitly in favor of the second. Whereas antiglobalism rejects inculturation altogether, acknowledging no common space whatsoever between the American culture and Vietnamese cultures, ethnification and primitivism accept absorption into the American culture as an ideal by means of a retrieval either of an allegedly lost culture or a forgotten normative cultural dimension or period.

In contrast to these three strategies I propose that we view the predicament of Vietnamese Americans as neither completely inside nor completely outside the American society but as belonging to both, but not entirely, because they are *beyond* both.[13] The same thing should be said about Vietnamese American Catholics. They are neither completely outside the American Catholic church and their native Asian churches nor completely inside them; they belong to both but not completely, because they are also *beyond* both. In other words, they live and move and have their being in the interstice between the American culture and their own, between the American church and their Asian churches. Because of this inalienable interstice, there should be no attempt to incorporate Vietnamese Americans into American society and Vietnamese American Catholics into the Catholic church in such a way that they would lose their distinct identity both as Vietnamese and as Vietnamese Catholics. Nor should there be an attempt to keep them apart from the American society and the American church in a kind of ghetto in such a way that they would be marginalized from church and society.

Furthermore, given the present reality of culture in the United States as globalized, conflictual, fragmented, and multiple, this space is not some preexisting no man's land, peacefully and definitively agreed upon in advance by the powers that be of the two cultures and the two churches. Rather, the interstice is to be carved out by the Vietnamese American Catholics themselves, in everyday living, by trial and error, in creative freedom, over the course of a lifetime.

---

[11] This strategy is proposed, for example, by some African American or Native American groups who attempt to recover their lost or suppressed cultural or tribal traditions to construct their cultural identity by means of some celebration, e.g., Kwanzaa.

[12] This practice is found, for example, among Catholics who choose the patristic or medieval period as a benchmark for the renewal of the church and theology. Some Asians have made certain practices such as veneration of ancestors the defining trait of their cultures.

[13] On the concept of the immigrant as being "in-beyond," see Lee, *Marginality*, 55-70.

Its boundaries, quite porous to be sure, are ever shifting and are subject to being redrawn and renegotiated as new circumstances and needs arise. What remains indisputable is that Vietnamese American Catholics have a right to this cultural and ecclesial interstitial space where they can fulfill their God-given mission of being the bridge between East and West, between the church of Asia and the church of North America.

Interculturation

This does not mean that inculturation or interculturation is an arbitrary and haphazard process, bereft of guiding principles, theological and canonical, or without a supervising authority. Indeed, in the process of interculturation between the Vietnamese culture and the American culture, all three dimensions (signs, message, and codes)[14] and three levels of culture (the surface, the intermediate level, and the mentality)[15] must be brought into play. Interculturation is the process whereby the American culture and the Vietnamese culture are brought into a reciprocal engagement in such a way that both of them are transformed from within. Essential to interculturation is *mutual* criticism and enrichment between cultures. The expressions of both cultures are transformed as the result of this process.

Strictly, interculturation is a three-step trajectory. In the first place, what Louis Luzbetak calls "individual building-blocks of culture"—the signs and symbols—of one culture are assigned functional equivalents in another culture. Here, obviously, *translation* plays a predominant role.

Then comes the stage of *acculturation,* in which the two cultures borrow elements from each other. However, often such mutual borrowing still operates at best at the intermediate level. Furthermore, because of the unequal power relations between the American culture and the immigrants' cultures, there is danger that the latter will be dominated and absorbed by the former. Also, in this cultural exchange there are plenty of opportunities for mutual misunderstanding because the codes through which the meaning of the signs of culture are carried may be hidden and different. Acculturation may lead to either juxtaposition (elements of both cultures are unassimilated and are allowed to operate side by side) or syncretism (the basic identities of both cultures are lost or diluted).

The third stage, the level of *inculturation* proper, engages the deepest level of the two cultures together, their worldview, their basic "message," as expressed in their philosophies and religions. Obviously, this task requires that immigrants achieve a measure of intellectual sophistication and institutional autonomy that enables them to confront the American culture as equals in a truly multi-ethnic and pluralistic society.

---

[14] On the semiotic interpretation of culture as composed of sign, message, and code, see Robert Schreiter, *Constructing Local Theologies* (Maryknoll, N.Y.: Orbis Books, 1985), 49-73.

[15] On the three levels of culture, see Louis Luzbetak, *The Church and Cultures: New Perspectives in Missiological Anthropology* (Maryknoll, N.Y.: Orbis Books, 1988).

What has been said about the encounter between the American culture and the Vietnamese culture applies as well to the encounter between the American church and Vietnamese American Catholics. A similar three-stage process of interculturation takes place. There is the first and essential phase of translating significant religious texts from English into Vietnamese and vice versa, a work largely still to be done for and by Vietnamese American Catholics.[16] Whereas many classics of Asian philosophy are available in English, very few Christian classics have been translated into Vietnamese. I am thinking not only of the Bible but also of patristic and medieval classics as well as works on spirituality. As a result, many Vietnamese American Catholics are deprived of the theological and spiritual heritage of Western Christianity and therefore do not possess the necessary resources to enter into a fruitful dialogue with the Western church.

Next is the phase of finding the ways by which both the American church and Vietnamese American Catholic communities can critique and enrich each other on the ten (and other) characteristics listed above. For example, from the perspective of the American church, Vietnamese American Catholics will be challenged to correct their predominantly institutional model of ecclesiology by means of other models in which the role of the laity is duly recognized and its active participation fostered, dialogue with followers of other religions undertaken, and social justice seriously pursued. On the other hand, through the experiences of Vietnamese American Catholics the American church may rediscover the importance of priestly and religious vocations, popular devotions, pious associations, martyrdom, and solidarity with the poor and the oppressed. No less important, in a religiously pluralistic country, such as the United States has become, the manifold non-Christian heritage of Vietnamese American Catholics can serve as a springboard for the church to learn from the spiritual riches of other religions.

The mention of non-Christian religions brings us to the third and deepest level of interculturation, which is also the most difficult and challenging. Connected with this level are some of the most controversial themes in contemporary theology, such as religious pluralism, the salvific values of non-Christian religions, the uniqueness of Christ, the necessity of the church, praxis for liberation, and interfaith dialogue.[17] This is not the place to broach these theological issues, but there is no doubt that the presence of Vietnamese American Catholics will bring them to the fore. Furthermore, Vietnamese American Catholics are in a privileged position to help their fellow Catholics in Vietnam deal with these thorny issues, since they have at their disposal, and hence are duty bound to take advantage of, opportunities for theological education that have been denied to their fellow Catholics for more than fifty years in Vietnam.

---

[16] For an account of how profoundly translation affects the work of inculturation, see Lamin Sanneh, *Translating the Message: The Missionary Impact on Culture* (Maryknoll, N.Y.: Orbis Books, 1989).

[17] For an excellent presentation of these issues, see Jacques Dupuis, *Toward a Christian Theology of Religious Pluralism* (Maryknoll, N.Y.: Orbis Books, 1997).

Three Theological Tasks

Theologically, Vietnamese American Catholics have to perform the three tasks that Anselm Kyongsuk Min prescribes for Korean American theology.[18] The first is to retrieve both the Western and the Asian traditions for the needs of Asian communities in America, whose needs and circumstances as immigrants are different from those of their fellow Asians in Asia.

The second task is to reflect on the theological significance of the Asian American experience itself. Such an experience, Min points out, has at least four dimensions: separation, ambiguity, diversity, and love of the stranger (xenophilia). The Asian American experience is, first of all, that of separation from the old, familiar, ancestral ways of doing things: "For a people so devoted to the tradition, living in America brings with it pain of radical separation, the repression of nostalgia for the old culture and old identities, dying to old self and being born again, born to the truth of human life as pilgrimage of the *homo viator*, the wayfaring human being."[19] Second, the experience of separation is also that of ambiguity. "It means no longer having the certainties of the home tradition available for every moment of decision and crisis, but rather meeting such a moment in a creative, inventive way, improvising, compromising, agonizing, and in any event learning to live with a large dose of ambiguity, the very ambiguity of life itself."[20] The third experience is the pain of diversity. Coming from a relatively homogeneous culture, Asian Americans must learn to live with those who are different in ethnicity, language, religion, and culture. They must learn to overcome ethnic prejudices and narrow nationalism. From this comes the fourth experience, that of learning to love the stranger. Min suggests that the event of 29 April 1992 in Los Angeles, in which Korean businesses were systematically looted and burned by African Americans and Hispanic Americans, should teach Korean Americans that they cannot live just for themselves but must learn to live with others with some solidarity of interests.[21]

The third and last task is to elaborate a political theology appropriate to Asian Americans as citizens of the United States who have both domestic responsibilities toward the common good and international responsibilities as citizens of the sole surviving superpower in an increasingly globalizing world. Min warns against the danger of focusing on only ethnic and cultural issues and forgetting the duty of prophetic criticism: "As citizens of a country with the historic bur-

---

[18] See Anselm Kyongsuk Min, "From Autobiography to Fellowship of Others: Reflections on Doing Ethnic Theology Today," in Phan and Lee, *Journeys at the Margin*, 148-51.

[19] Ibid., 149.

[20] Ibid., 150.

[21] The need for racial reconciliation and solidarity is impressively developed by Andrew Sung Park in *Racial Conflict and Healing: An Asian-American Theological Perspective* (Maryknoll, N.Y.: Orbis Books, 1996).

dens of colonialism, slavery, and imperialism," Asian Americans "too need particular sensitization to this international dimension of U.S. power. They cannot simply disallow all political responsibility for what their political, military, and economic representatives do overseas in their names."[22]

TOWARD A VIETNAMESE AMERICAN THEOLOGY

In line with Min's three suggestions I would like to sketch the contours of a Vietnamese American theology. Such a theology has barely begun, and what follows is nothing more than a series of unsystematic reflections on how Vietnamese Christians must make full use of *both* American and Vietnamese cultural and religious resources to understand and express the Christian faith. In their *both-and* and *beyond* social and religious situation, they cannot do otherwise.

Resources and Methodology

With regard to cultural resources, there are in the Vietnamese philosophical tradition no writings by Vietnamese thinkers that have achieved the canonical status of the Chinese Five Classics and Four Books with which a Vietnamese Christian theology could enter into dialogue or that it could use as its resource. This does not mean that there is no Vietnamese philosophy or no philosophical writings in Vietnamese. On the contrary, there is a substantial body of these writings.[23] Unfortunately, however, they still remain mostly unknown and are not readily accessible since they are not yet transcribed into the national script.

While recourse to these writings remains necessary, a Vietnamese American theology should not be limited to a dialogue with these ancient philosophical texts. It must bring into play other resources of Vietnamese culture. Among these, pride of place must be assigned to literally thousands of proverbs, sayings, and traditional songs. This body of Vietnamese popular or oral literature, which has been carefully collected and studied, is rightly regarded as the most

---

[22] Min, "From Autobiography to Fellowship of Others," 151. In this context Min develops his concept of "solidarity *of* others": "The model I propose, solidarity of others, is an inherently dialectical model and must be grasped in all its dialectic. Opposed to all particularism and tribalism, it is not opposed to particularity as such. It advocates solidarity of others, not unity of the same. This is crucial, especially in view of the fact that global interdependence and universalization have historically been purchased by making victims of individuals, but most often of groups, based on gender, ethnicity, status, culture, and religion, by excluding and marginalizing them as others whose otherness must be either repressed or reduced to the same" (155-56).

[23] For a list of writings belonging to the Vietnamese *ju chia* (School of the Literati) tradition (in Vietnamese, *nho*), see Vu Dinh Trac, *Viet Nam trong Quy Dao The Gioi* (Orange, Calif.: Lien Doan CGVN tai Hoa Ky, n.d.), 51-60. See also his two dissertations, *Triet Ly Chap Sinh Nguyen Cong Tru* (Orange, Calif.: Hoi Huu Publishers, 1988) and *Triet Ly Nhan Ban Nguyen Du* (Orange, Calif.: Hoi Huu Publishers, 1993).

authentic treasure of Vietnamese wisdom and worldview.²⁴ Among contemporary philosophers, the numerous writings of Kim Dinh present a rich source of
insights into the Vietnamese cultural heritage and can serve as a valuable basis
for a Vietnamese American theology.²⁵ Vietnamese literature, past as well as
contemporary, is also a fertile source for theological reflection. Among literary
works, Nguyen Du's epic *Doan Truong Tan Thanh,* more popularly known as
Truyen Kieu, remains an indispensable source of Vietnamese worldview.²⁶ But
this chef-d'oeuvre should not be allowed to eclipse other literary works, especially contemporary poetry and novels, which embody a different but no less
important understanding of the Vietnamese ethos. In addition, life stories of
ordinary Vietnamese, especially those who suffer from poverty and all forms of
oppression, provide a rich vein for Vietnamese American theology. Finally,
Vietnamese American theology must enter into dialogue with the sacred texts
and ritual practices of Vietnamese Buddhism, Confucianism, Taoism, and indigenous religion.²⁷

---

²⁴ See the monumental, four-volume study (a total of 2,360 pages) by Nguyen Tan
Long and Phan Canh, *Thi Ca Binh Dan Viet Nam* (Los Alamitos, Calif.: Xuan Thu,
1969-1970). Other useful works include Nguyen Van Ngoc, *Tuc Ngu Phong Dao,* 2
vols. (Hanoi: Vinh Hung Long Thu Quan; reprinted Xuan Thu, 1989); Vu Ngoc Phan,
Tuc Ngu Ca Dao Dan Ca Viet Nam, 11ᵗʰ ed. (Hanoi: Nha Xuat Ban Khoa Hoc Xa Hoi,
1998); and Nguyen Nghia Dan, *Dao lam nguoi trong tuc ngu ca dao Viet Nam* (Hanoi:
Nha Xuat Ban Thanh Nien, 2000). There is a slim volume of 95 pages by Huynh Dinh
Te, *Selected Vietnamese Proverbs* (Oakland, Calif.: Center for International Communication and Development, 1990).
²⁵ Kim Dinh (1914-97) has published more than thirty books on Vietnamese *ju chia*
and Vietnamese philosophy. More than anyone else, Kim Dinh was responsible for
retrieving the sources of the Vietnamese *ju chia* (which he terms "original" *ju chia*) and
constructing a Vietnamese philosophy. Another important contributor to the retrieval
and elaboration of Vietnamese philosophy is Tran Van Doan, professor of philosophy at
National Taiwan University. See his "Tu Viet triet toi Viet than," *Dinh Huong* 11 (1996):
16-22; "Tong hop ve Triet hoc va Viet Triet," *Dinh Huong* 12 (1997): 41-90; "Viet Triet
di ve dau," *Dinh Huong* 13 (1997): 4-43; and "Viet Triet kha khu kha tung," in *Viet
Nam: De Ngu Thien Ky,* ed. Vuong Ky Son (New Orleans: Trung Tam Van Hoa Viet
Nam, USA, 1994), 69-116. For Tran Van Doan, Vietnamese philosophy is humanistic
(vi nhan) but not anthropocentric *(duy nhan)* insofar as humans are conceived as the
center or the Archimedian point of reality and as self-realizing (though not self-cre-
ative); it champions the "human way" *(dao nhan).* In addition, Vietnamese philosophy
advocates balance and harmony *(trung dung)* as well as self-transcendence *(sieu viet).*
In other words, the nature of Vietnamese philosophy is characterized by humanism *(nhan),*
balanced harmony *(trung),* and self-transcendence *(viet).* Finally, according Tran Van
Doan, the Vietnamese mode of thinking is relational *(tuong quan),* dialectical *(vien
viet),* dynamic *(dong tinh),* holistic *(toan the tinh),* pragmatic *(thuc tien),* and symbolic
(bieu tuong).
²⁶ Nguyen Du (1765-1820) is universally regarded as the greatest Vietnamese poet.
For an English translation of this epic, see *The Tale of Kieu,* trans. Huynh Sanh Thong
(New Haven, Conn.: Yale University Press, 1983).
²⁷ One of the most important studies on Vietnamese Zen is by Cuong Tu Nguyen, *Zen
in Medieval Vietnam: A Study and Translation of the Thien Uyen Tap Anh* (Honolulu:
University of Hawaii Press, 1997).

A Vietnamese American theology, however, must not confine itself to reiterating the past wisdom of the Vietnamese culture. Rather, it must bring this wisdom into a fruitful confrontation with the experiences of Vietnamese immigrants in the United States. These experiences are unique to Vietnamese expatriates struggling to survive in the interstices between two cultures and churches. They are unavailable to those living in the native country, even though Western and American ideas and values have been exported to all corners of the world through the process of globalization. In this way, what is true, good, and beautiful in the Vietnamese culture can be enriched further by the truths and values found in the American culture, just as what is defective in it can be corrected. For example, the communitarian ethos, characteristic of the Vietnamese worldview, by which the individual is subordinated to the collective welfare of the family and society, can sometimes lead to the suppression of the individual's autonomy and dignity. Here, it should be corrected by the typically American respect for and promotion of the individual's inalienable rights. Thus, a Vietnamese American anthropology will be a dialectical fusion of communitarianism and individualism that is a genuinely new *tertium quid* emerging from the encounter between two different cultures.

Theological Themes

In the remaining pages I would like to highlight a list of themes, by no means exhaustive, that I consider essential to a Vietnamese American theology.

1. Basic to the Vietnamese worldview is what is called "three-element philosophy" *(triet ly tam tai).*[28] The three elements are heaven, earth, and humanity *(thien, dia, nhan* or *troi, dat, nguoi),* forming the three ultimates constituting the whole reality. "Heaven" refers to the firmament above humans (as opposed to the earth), to the law of nature, and to the Creator, endowed with intellect and will. The firmament is the place where the Creator dwells; the law of nature is the Creator's will and dispositions; and the Creator is the supreme being who is transcendent, omnipotent, and eternal. "Earth" refers to the material reality lying beneath humans (as opposed to heaven above); it gives rise to entities composed of the five constituents *(ngu hanh)* of metal, wood, water, fire, and earth, and to matter in general, which is essentially directed upward to heaven. "Humanity" refers to human beings "whose heads carry heaven and whose feet trample upon earth" *(dau doi troi, chan dap dat),* that is, humans as the link or union between heaven and earth. Humans express the power of heaven and earth by being "the sage inside and the king outside" *(noi thanh ngoai vuong),* that is, by orienting upward to heaven *(tri tri)* through knowing heaven, trusting in heaven, and acting out the will of heaven, on the one hand, and by orienting downward to earth *(cach vat)* through the use of material things for the benefit

---

[28] For an elaboration of this *tam tai* philosophy, see in particular Vu Dinh Trac, *Triet Ly Chap Sinh Nguyen Cong Tru,* 203-13; and idem, *Triet Ly Nhan Ban Nguyen Du,* 91-144.

of all. As the center connecting heaven and earth, humans as the microcosm unite the male and the female, the positive and negative, light and darkness, spirit and matter *(yin* and *yang)*, and the characteristics of the five constituents: subtlety (water), strength (fire), vitality (wood), constancy (metal), and generosity (earth). In this way humans practice the "human heart" *(nhan tam)* and the "human way" *(nhan dao)*.

The most important principle of the *tam tai* philosophy is that all three constitutive elements of reality are intrinsically connected with one another and mutually dependent. Heaven without earth and humanity cannot produce or express anything. Earth without heaven and humanity would be an empty desert. Humanity without heaven would be directionless, and without earth it would have nowhere to exist and to act. Each of the three elements has a function of its own to perform: heaven gives birth; earth nurtures; and humanity harmonizes *(Thien sinh, dia duong, nhan hoa)*. Consequently, human action must be governed by three principles: it must be carried out in accord with heaven *(thien thoi)*, with the propitious favor of earth *(dia loi)*, and for the harmony of humanity *(nhan hoa)*.[29]

It is clear that a Vietnamese American theology can and should make use of this *tam tai* philosophy not only to construct a theology of the Trinity but also an integral anthropology. First, with regard to the Trinity, it is possible to correlate God the Father with heaven, God the Son to humanity, and God the Spirit to earth and to elaborate their roles in the history of salvation in the light of those of heaven, earth, and humanity.[30] The Father's role is to "give birth" through "creation"; the Son's is to "harmonize" through redemption; and the Spirit's is to "nurture" through sanctifying grace. These roles are truly distinct from one another (hence trinitarian and not modalistic) but intimately linked with one another (hence one and not subordinationist or tritheistic). Like heaven, earth, and humanity, the three divine Persons are united in a *perichoresis* or *koinonia* of life and activities. In this trinitarian theology God's transcendence and immanence are intrinsically related. God, though transcendent, is conceived as internally connected with and dependent on humanity and earth to carry God's activities in history. Indeed, the Trinity is conceived as inscribed in the structure of reality itself.[31]

---

[29] This philosophy is claimed to be represented on the upper surface of the bronze drum, especially the one discovered at Ngoc Lu in 1901 and now preserved at the Center for Far-Eastern Antiquities *(Vien Dong Bac Co)* in Hanoi. This philosophy has been elaborated by Kim Dinh in his *Su Diep Trong Dong* (San Jose, Calif.: Thanh Nien Quoc Gia, 1984). See also Vu Dinh Trac, "Triet ly truyen thong Viet Nam don duong cho Than Hoc Viet Nam," *Dinh Huong* 11 (1966): 23-47. Vu Dinh Trac believes that traditional Vietnamese philosophy is constituted by *tam tai* philosophy, *yin-yang* metaphysics, and agricultural philosophy. These three strands are illustrated by the various symbols on the upper surface of the Ngoc Lu bronze drum.

[30] For an attempt to construct a trinitarian theology on the basis of *yin-yang* metaphysics, see Jung Young Lee, *The Trinity in Asian Perspective* (Nashville, Tenn.: Abingdon, 1996).

[31] For an attempt at conceiving reality in trinitarian terms, see Raimon Panikkar, *The Cosmotheandric Experience: Emerging Religious Consciousness* (Maryknoll, N.Y.: Orbis Books, 1993).

Second, a Christian anthropology constructed in light of the *tam tai* philosophy will offer an integral understanding of human existence. In this anthropology there is no opposition between theocentrism and anthropocentrism, nor between theocentrism and geocentrism, nor between geocentrism and anthropocentrism. Indeed, *tam tai* philosophy is opposed to any *ism* that is exclusive of any other perspective. The human is understood neither as subject nor object but as intrinsically *related* to the divine and the ecological, just as the divine is intrinsically related to the ecological and the human, and the ecological is intrinsically related to the divine and the human. This anthropology will be an important corrective to the American culture, which tends to view, under the influence of modernity, God and humanity as competitors and humans as unrelated to their ecology.

2. Any Christian philosophy must of course reflect on Christ as both divine and human. In Vietnamese American theology I would highlight two aspects of Christ. First, Jesus can be regarded as the immigrant par excellence, the marginalized one living in the *both-and* and *beyond* situation.[32] This in-between, on-the-margin status is foundational to the incarnation as well as to Jesus' entire ministry, including his death and resurrection. But Jesus' being on the margin creates a new circle with a new center, not of power but of love, joining and reconciling the two worlds, human and divine. Vietnamese Americans can readily relate to this figure of Christ the immigrant from their experiences, sometimes painful, of living as marginalized immigrants in the United States. But, like Jesus, they are called to create a new circle, made up of both Americans and Vietnamese, with a new center, not in order to exclude anyone but to help both Americans and Vietnamese to move *beyond* their ethnic identities and create a new reality *both* Vietnamese *and* American.

Second, from the Vietnamese religious perspective Jesus can be regarded as the elder brother and the paradigmatic ancestor. The veneration of ancestors is one of the most sacred duties for Vietnamese. This religious practice constituted one of the serious problems for missionary work in Asia.[33] A Christology that presents Jesus as the elder brother and the ancestor has much to recommend it, not only for missionary purposes but also for fostering Vietnamese ethics, especially familial, at the center of which lies filial piety. This latter aspect is all the more urgent for Vietnamese Americans who are encountering tremendous difficulties in preserving the rite of ancestor veneration, especially at weddings and funerals.[34]

3. The theology of the church in Asia, especially in the Roman Catholic Church, has long been characterized by an excessive focus on the church's institutional

[32] For an elaboration of Jesus as the immigrant par excellence, see Lee, *Marginality*; see also chapter 5 herein.

[33] For an account of the so-called Rites Controversy, see George Minamiki, *The Chinese Rites Controversy: From Its Beginnings to Modern Times* (Chicago: Loyola University Press, 1985).

[34] For a Christology of Jesus as the elder brother and the ancestor, see chapter 6 herein; see also Peter C. Phan, "Jesus as the Eldest Brother and Ancestor? A Vietnamese Portrait," *The Living Light* 33/1 (1996): 35-43.

aspects, in particular the hierarchy and its power. Asian ecclesiology, in other words, has been ecclesiocentric. In recent years, thanks to the work of the Federation of the Asian Bishops' Conferences, theological attention has been turned away from intra-ecclesial issues to the mission of the church toward the world, especially the world of Asian peoples.[35] Ecclesiology is now focused on the reign of God as its goal; the church exists for the sake of the kingdom of God. The church's evangelizing mission is now understood in terms of the threefold task of inculturation, interreligious dialogue, and liberation.[36]

Such a kingdom-centered ecclesiology is called for in Vietnamese American theology. As Min has correctly pointed out, Asian immigrants cannot be oblivious to the fact that politically and economically they, immigrants though they are, now belong to a country that exercises enormous influence and not infrequently an unjust and oppressive control over the rest of the world through the process of globalization. The task of socio-political and economic liberation, which is a constitutive dimension of evangelization, becomes all the more urgent for Vietnamese Americans. Furthermore, because Vietnamese Americans are religiously diverse, the need for interreligious dialogue is no less pressing in the United States than in Asia. Finally, for Vietnamese Americans the inculturation of the Christian faith is no doubt a much more challenging and complex task in America because they are confronted with not only one but at least two very diverse cultures. Of course, these tasks of inculturation, interreligious dialogue, and liberation cannot be separated from the other aspects of evangelization such as proclamation, personal witness, and worship.[37]

4. Another area that Vietnamese American theology must attend to is liturgy and sacramental worship. In most Asian Roman Catholic churches liturgical and sacramental celebrations are largely determined by officially approved books composed in Latin by the experts in Rome and then translated into the vernaculars. These translations in turn have to be approved—again by Rome—before they can be used. Little input by the local churches has been made, though liturgical "adaptation" within prescribed limits is allowed. Recently some liturgical inculturation has been carried out in Vietnam. Noteworthy is that the prayers for the dead in the Eucharistic Prayers of the Mass have been expanded to mention explicitly the ancestors; also important are the liturgies in celebration of the lunar New Year *(Tet)* and for burial. Nevertheless, these adaptations remain timid and pallid attempts to make worship culturally and religiously meaningful to the Vietnamese. A major task of liturgical inculturation is still to be carried out

[35] See the documents of the Federation of Asian Bishops' Conferences and its various offices in Gaudencio Rosales and C. G. Arévalo, eds., *For All the Peoples of Asia: Federation of Asian Bishops' Conferences. Documents from 1970 to 1991* (Maryknoll, N.Y.: Orbis Books, 1992; Quezon City, Philippines: Claretian Publications, 1992); and Franz-Josef Eilers, ed., *For All the Peoples of Asia: Federation of Asian Bishops' Conferences. Documents from 1992 to 1996* (Quezon City, Philippines: Claretian Publications, 1997).

[36] See chapters 9 and 10 herein.

[37] See chapter 4 herein.

by Vietnamese American theology by taking into account, among other things, what has been described as Vietnamese popular religiosity.[38]

5. The last aspect of Vietnamese American theology concerns ethics and spirituality. Asians are often viewed as embodying such values as love of silence and contemplation, closeness to nature, simplicity, detachment, frugality, harmony, nonviolence, love for learning, respect for the elders, filial piety, compassion, and attachment to the family. While these characteristics may be exaggerated and even caricatured, there is no doubt that there is a core of truth in this description of what has been called the Asian soul. Vietnamese cultural critics have often pointed out how Vietnamese philosophy and literature, especially Vietnamese proverbs and popular songs, have prescribed as moral ideals total harmony with heaven, earth, and humanity, equilibrium and balance in mind and body, psychological wholeness and integrity, interior peace and calm, solidarity and sharing.

Obviously, these ideals are hard to practice in the United States, which prizes professional competition, material success, individual autonomy, democratic egalitarianism, and self-fulfillment. However, there is little doubt that these ideals can correct the excesses of the American way of life. On the other hand, challenged and enriched by American moral ideals, Vietnamese Americans can avoid the risk of yielding to leisurely quietism, political and social withdrawal, avoidance of public responsibilities, and spiritual escapism. Vietnamese American moral and spiritual theology is called to develop a way of uniting the best of the two cultural and moral traditions while avoiding the excesses of both.

The Vietnamese have chosen the bamboo tree as their national symbol. Vietnamese villages are typically surrounded by high rows of bamboo bonding the villagers with one another and shielding them from natural disasters and human invaders. Bamboo shoots provide poor people with nourishing food. Bamboo canes are used to build houses and bamboo leaves are used for roofing. Bamboo wood is woven into the most common utensils. Above all, bamboo is extremely resilient; it bends but cannot be easily broken, like the Vietnamese spirit during centuries of oppression and colonialism. For Christians, the cross is the symbol of God's unconditional love for humanity and final victory over evil. Vietnamese Americans, as Vietnamese and as Catholics, live in the shadow of the bamboo and the cross in a new country, now gratefully adopted as their own. If they are faithful to both their cultural heritage and their Christian faith, their cruciform bamboo will grow and prosper in the soil of the New World. A Vietnamese American theology is an indispensable fertilizer to bring about the flourishing of this cruciform bamboo.

---

[38] See Peter C. Phan, "How Much Uniformity Can We Stand? How Much Unity Do We Want? Church and Worship in the Next Millennium," *Worship* 72/3 (1998): 194-210; and idem, "The Liturgy of Life as 'Summit and Source' of the Eucharistic Liturgy: Church Worship as Symbolization of the Liturgy of Life?," in *Incongruities: Who We Are and How We Pray*, ed. Timothy Fitzgerald and David A. Lysik (Chicago: Liturgy Training Publications, 2000), 5-33.

Index

249